Matthias Heinrich Nagel

Anonymous Point Collection – Improved Models and Security Definitions

Anonymous Point Collection – Improved Models and Security Definitions

by
Matthias Heinrich Nagel

KIT Scientific Publishing

Karlsruher Institut für Technologie
Institut für Theoretische Informatik

Anonymous Point Collection – Improved Models and Security Definitions

Zur Erlangung des akademischen Grades eines Doktors der Naturwissenschaften von der KIT-Fakultät für Informatik des Karlsruher Instituts für Technologie (KIT) genehmigte Dissertation

von Matthias Heinrich Nagel

Tag der mündlichen Prüfung: 29. Januar 2020
1. Referent: Prof. Dr. Jörn Müller-Quade
2. Referent: Prof. Dr. Ralf Reussner

Impressum

KIT Scientific Publishing

Karlsruher Institut für Technologie (KIT)
KIT Scientific Publishing
Straße am Forum 2
D-76131 Karlsruhe

KIT Scientific Publishing is a registered trademark
of Karlsruhe Institute of Technology.
Reprint using the book cover is not allowed.

www.ksp.kit.edu

Print on Demand 2020 – Gedruckt auf FSC-zertifiziertem Papier

ISBN 978-3-7315-1023-9
DOI 10.5445/KSP/1000117751

Karlsruhe Institute of Technology

KASTEL

Anonymous Point Collection—Improved Models and Security Definitions

Zur Erlangung des akademischen Grades eines

Doktors der Naturwissenschaften

von der KIT-Fakultät für Informatik
des Karlsruher Instituts für Techologie (KIT)

genehmigte

DISSERTATION

von

Matthias Heinrich Nagel

Tag der mündlichen Prüfung: 29. Januar 2020

1. Referent: Prof. Dr. Jörn Müller-Quade
2. Referent: Prof. Dr. Ralf Reussner

Acknowledgments

First and foremost, I would like to thank my advisor Jörn Müller-Quade for granting me the opportunity to write this thesis, for his frankness and his kindness. He not only shared his love-hate relationship with Universal Composability with me, but inspired me that provable security matters. Moreover, I am grateful for a lot of good moments we had. I wish to thank Ralf Reussner for taking interest into my work and accepting to be my co-referee.

This thesis would not have been possible without Andy Rupp. He had the initial idea for the topic and also co-authored two publications. I have to thank for all the knowledge and insights on recent cryptographic building blocks for practical and efficient protocols he readily passed to me.

I would like to thank Brandon Broadnax with whom I had the pleasure to co-author another publication. He taught me a lot of technical tricks and was a reliable oracle for any kind of UC-related questions.

I had the pleasure of working with a lot of wonderful colleagues. Out of many, three stand out in particular. Dirk Achenbach was an excellent mentor during my first year at the institute. Jeremias Mechler was an awesome partner in many projects which happen to arise at an institute beyond crypto. And last but not least, I want to thank my roommate Rebecca Schwerdt for her support, for her friendship, for backup in times of hardship, for fruitful discussions on cryptography as well as a lot of enjoyable non-crypto conversations, for being co-author and for a myriad amount of tea.

Contents

Abstract

In numerous user-centric, cyber-physical systems, point collection and redemption mechanisms are a core component. Loosely speaking, this component or building block may be viewed as personal “piggy bank” that allows users to deposit and disburse points. Depending on the context, points might be interpreted in numerous ways: monetary units (e.g. Euro cents), loyalty rating points, reliability credits, etc. This thesis deals with the problem of *anonymous* point collection.

Applications which are currently deployed in practice typically bind the stored value to some ID (e.g. the serial number of a card) or even worse to a user account. In other words, existing systems do not provide anonymity for the participating users, are at best only pseudonymous and allow to link transactions that belong to the same user. This enables tracing a user’s movements. In the literature, several privacy-preserving solutions have been proposed which target specific scenarios: inter alia (anonymous) e-cash, anonymous reputation systems, loyalty systems as well as incentive systems. None of these consider anonymous point collection as a generic, multi-purpose building block. While the latter does not need to be a disadvantage per se, the proposed solutions are typically very restricted (e.g. only look at the specific aspect of point deposition), or completely ignore important features (e.g. blacklisting) which might be required for practical deployment. Moreover, a majority of them lack formal security models, not to mention security proofs and rely on the hope that some vague notion of security and/or privacy is satisfied.

This thesis aims at two goals.

First and foremost, this thesis is a comprehensive, formal treatment of anonymous point collection as a generic building block together with a rigorous security model and proof. To this end, a definition of anonymous point collection is carved out which does not only provide a strong notion of security and privacy, but also covers features which are essential for practical use. Thereby, the proposed definition broadens the applicability of such a building block in real-world scenarios. As a pure definition is hollow, if it cannot be fulfilled, this thesis includes a practically efficient realization which also has been implemented on real-world hardware. This realization is rigorously proven to be secure with respect to the proposed definition.

Despite the formal methodology, the prospect of a practical efficient realization is already reflected by the definition of the envisioned building block. Cryptography has shown that—in principle—any computable function whose inputs might be distributed across mutual distrustful parties can be securely evaluated using so-called secure multi-party computation (MPC). However, generic MPC techniques are too inefficient for real-world applications and also come with a number of other drawbacks. Hence, research on the intersection between IT security and cryptography considers tailor-made building blocks which allow both a practically efficient realization but are also provably secure with respect to a precise definition. Therefore, the main challenge is to find a definition of security that is not overly idealized and thus cannot be realized on the one hand, but still captures a meaningful concept of security and is not too weak on the other hand, while allowing for a practically efficient realization at the same time.

The most important contribution of this thesis is to find that definition. Even in disregard of the extended features, the resulting building block is the first one that

(1) allows for anonymous two-way transactions,

(2) has (periodic) offline capabilities,

(3) requires only constant storage size (with respect to the stored value), and

(4) is provably secure.

The second and much more subtle goal of this thesis is to contribute to the question how security for complex systems should be defined. Besides game-based security definitions, simulation-based security definitions have turned out to be particularly prolific. In modern cryptography, new schemes or improved realization for existing schemes nearly always come together with a precise definition of their security and a corresponding proof. However, the building blocks which are considered in cryptography are traditionally rather simple objects (e.g. encryption schemes, signature schemes, commitment schemes, etc.). At least, they are much simpler than a building block for anonymous point collection which we deem a complex system. Conversely, in the field of IT security, which considers larger systems, strict security proofs in the cryptographic sense are frequently missing. This thesis aims at having a share in closing this gap. To this end, the traditional way to define a list of certain desired properties of the envisioned system is combined with the simulation-based Universal Composability (UC) framework. Evidence is given throughout the thesis that using this combined approach leads to improved security guarantees compared to a plain game-based approach. On the one hand side, this combined approach thus seems to be the right choice and might serve as a blueprint for comparably complex systems. On the other hand side, it also becomes obvious that a UC-based definition happens to be viable but yields cumbersome and bulky proofs. The thesis broaches the question, if this effect has a more fundamental cause which might be the starting point of further research.

Zusammenfassung

Das Sammeln und Einlösen von Punkten stellt in unzähligen nutzerzentrierten, cyber-physikalischen Systemen eine zentrale Komponente dar. Salopp ausgedrückt kann diese Komponente oder dieser Baustein als ein persönliches „Sparschwein" betrachtet werden, welches dem Nutzer ein Ein- und Auszahlen von Punkten ermöglicht. Je nach Anwendungsfall ergeben sich verschiedene Interpretationen der Punkte: als Geldeinheiten (z.B. Eurocent), Loyalitätsbonuspunkte, Zuverlässigkeitsbewertung, etc. Die vorliegende Arbeit beschäftigt sich mit dem Problem des *anonymen* Punktesammelns.

Derzeit in der Praxis eingesetzte Anwendungen verknüpfen den gespeicherten Punktestand typischerweise mit einer ID (z.B. der Seriennummer einer Karte) oder sogar direkt mit einem Nutzerkonto. Damit bieten existierende Systeme dem teilnehmenden Nutzer keinerlei Anonymität, sondern im besten Fall lediglich Pseudonymität und erlauben, einzelne Transaktionen, die zum selben Nutzer gehören, miteinander zu verketten. Dies ermöglicht, ein Bewegungsprofil des Nutzers zu erstellen. In der kryptographischen Literatur sind verschiedene, privatsphäreschützende Lösungen für spezifische Szenarien vorgeschlagen worden: unter anderem (anonymes) E-Cash, anonyme Reputationssysteme, Loyalitätssysteme und Anreizsysteme. Keine der vorgeschlagenen Lösungen betrachtet anonymes Punktesammeln als einen generischen Mehrzweckbaustein. Auch wenn Letzteres nicht per se nachteilig ist, sind die Lösungen häufig sehr beschränkt (bspw. wird nur der spezifische Aspekt der Punkteinzahlung betrachtet) und wichtige Zusatzfunktionen (bspw. das gezielte Ausschließen von Nutzern), die jedoch für die praktische Verwendbarkeit notwendig sind, bleiben unberücksichtigt. Darüber hinaus lässt eine Mehrheit der Vorschläge formale Sicherheitsmodelle, geschweige denn Sicherheitsbeweise, vermissen. Sie basieren vielmehr auf der Hoffnung, dass ein nur vage spezifizierter Sicherheits-/ Privatsphärebegriff irgendwie erfüllt sei.

Diese Arbeit verfolgt zwei Ziele.

In erster Linie ist diese Arbeit eine umfassende, formale Betrachtung des anonymen Punktesammelns als generischer Baustein inkl. eines präzisen Sicherheitsmodells und -beweises. Zu diesem Zweck wird eine Definition für anonymes Punktesammeln herausgearbeitet, die nicht nur einen starken Sicherheits- und Privatsphärebegriff bietet, sondern auch praktisch relevante Leistungsmerkmale abdeckt. Damit erweitert die vorgeschlagene Definition die Anwendbarkeit eines solchen Bausteins in realen Szenarien. Da eine reine Definition, welche nicht erfüllt werden kann, substanzlos ist, beinhaltet diese Arbeit auch eine praktisch effiziente Realisierung, die auf realer Hardware implementiert wurde. Diese Realisierung wird als sicher bzgl. der vorgeschlagenen Definition bewiesen.

Trotz der formalen Methodik zeigt sich das Ziel einer praktisch effizienten Realisierung bereits in der Definition. Die Kryptographie hat gezeigt, dass es prinzipiell möglich ist, jede beliebige, berechenbare Funktion, deren Eingabe über verschiedene, sich paarweise misstrauende Parteien verteilt sein kann, mit Hilfe sog. sichererer Mehrparteienberechnung (MPC) auszuwerten. Generische MPC-Techniken sind jedoch zu ineffizient für reale Systeme. Die Forschung an der Schnittstelle zwischen IT-Sicherheit und Kryptographie betrachtet daher maßgeschneiderte Bausteine, die sowohl eine praktisch effiziente Umsetzung erlauben, als auch beweisbar sicher bezüglich einer präzisen Definition sind. Die wesentliche Herausforderung ist somit, eine Definition zu finden, die auf der einen Seite nicht überidealisiert und somit unerfüllbar ist, aber auf der anderen Seite dennoch einen sinnvollen Sicherheitsbegriff bietet, der zudem auch eine praktisch effiziente Realisierung ermöglicht.

Der wichtigste Beitrag dieser Arbeit ist, eine solche Definition zu finden. Auch ohne Berücksichtigung der zusätzlichen Leistungsmerkmale ist der resultierende Baustein der erste seiner Art, der gleichzeitig

(1) anonyme Zwei-Wege-Transaktionen ermöglicht,

(2) konstanten Speicherbedarf besitzt (bzgl. des gespeicherten Werts),

(3) offline einsatzbar

(4) und beweisbar sicher ist.

Das zweite und deutlich subtilere Ziel dieser Arbeit leistet einen Beitrag zu der Frage, wie Sicherheit für komplexe Systeme definiert werden sollte. Neben spielebasierten Sicherheitsdefinitionen haben sich simulationsbasierte Sicherheitsdefinitionen als besonders fruchtbar herausgestellt. In der modernen Kryptographie werden neue Verfahren oder verbesserte Realisierungen vorhandener Verfahren nahezu immer zusammen mit einer präzisen Definition ihrer Sicherheit und einem zugehörigen Beweis vorgeschlagen. Allerdings sind die von der Kryptographie betrachteten Bausteine traditionell eher einfache Objekte (z.B. ein Verschlüsselungsverfahren, ein Signaturverfahren, ein Commitment-Verfahren, etc.), zumindest deutlich einfacher als ein Baustein für anonymes Punktesammeln, welcher im Folgenden als komplexes System betrachtet wird. Im Gegenzug fehlen im Bereich der IT-Sicherheit, welche größere Systeme betrachtet, häufig strenge Sicherheitsbeweise im Sinne der kryptographischen Methodik. Diese Arbeit möchte einen Beitrag dazu leisten, diese Lücke zu schließen. Zu diesem Zweck wird der traditionelle Ansatz, eine Liste wünschenswerter Eigenschaften des anvisierten

Systems zu definieren, mit dem simulationsbasierten UC-Framework kombiniert. Anhand verschiedener Aspekte des Systems wird diskutiert, wie dieser kombinierte Ansatz gegenüber einer rein-spielebasierten Modellierung zu verbesserten Sicherheitsgarantien führt. Einerseits scheint dieser Ansatz somit grundsätzlich der richtige Weg zu sein und könnte als Blaupause für vergleichbar-komplexe Systeme dienen. Andererseits wird jedoch auch offensichtlich, dass eine UC-basierte Definition zwar grundsätzlich ein gangbarer Weg ist, jedoch zu sperrigen, schlecht-handhabbaren Beweisen führt. Die Frage, ob diesem Effekt ein grundsätzlicheres Problem zugrunde liegt, wird andiskutiert und könnte Ausgangspunkt für weitere Forschung sein.

1 Introduction

This thesis proposes a flexible security model and cryptographic protocol framework designed for a new cryptographic building block that enables anonymous point collection. To the best of the author's knowledge, this work is the first with a rigorous security definition and proof which capture all aspects of such a building block in an integrated model. Furthermore, it is unarguably the most comprehensive formal treatment of anonymous point collection overall. The framework is very flexible in the sense that auxiliary features (e.g. blacklisting of users, selective unveil of individual transactions) which might be required in certain applications are included in the definition, but each can just as well be omitted individually, without changing any other part of the system or sacrificing security.

The need for such a building block is obvious from the multitude possible applications. The abstract notion of points can be interpreted as monetary units (e.g. Euro cents), loyalty rating points, reliability credits, etc.

In the scope of loyalty programs prominent examples are the German Payback system [PAY16] or the UK-based Nectar program [Aim16].

Complementary currencies are commonly used by providers of physical services to restrict access on a pre-payment basis. Typical examples are trading cards for regional public transportation systems, like the Oyster Card for the London underground railway [Tra19], access cards for natatoriums, or campus payment systems for canteens and alike [ven19; Cou19]. Here, customers first top-up their wallet (typically in form of an ID-1 card) which is then charged per usage. But also, post-payment variants exist, in which the users collect debt first and clear it later. In the scope of cashless payment systems, electronic toll collection (ETC) is of particular interest. ETC is already deployed in many countries all over the world with an estimated annual turnover of 10.6 billion US dollars by 2022 [Mar17]. The EU plans to introduce the first implementation of a fully interoperable tolling system (EETS) by 2027 [EC17].

Reliability (or reputation) assessment is used in various interactive systems to curtail riot behavior. When entering the system, new users only have a limited choice of options how to interact with the system, but long-term users can gain access to more advanced options (and more harmful options if misused) depending on their reputation level. Basic examples are Internet forums where new users can post new messages and edit their own ones, but must not edit or even delete other posts until they have demonstrated responsible behavior. In Vehicle-to-Grid scenarios [KT05], owners of e-vehicles are not only paid for the buffer capacity which the batteries of their e-vehicle provide to the grid when cars are parked at the mall, office, etc., but the grid operator also needs to rate the soundness of users' declarations how long their cars will be connected to the grid in order to predict their availability and to create precise forecasts for the grid management. This requires means to rate the reliability of (anonymous) individuals in order to spot owners of e-vehicles which frequently leave before the stated time.

Lastly, the same mechanism is used to incentify particular behavior. For instance, in envisioned mobile sensing scenarios [Chr+11], users should be encouraged to collect environmental or health data measured with their smart devices and provide this data (enhanced by location and time information) to some operator. In exchange, users receive micropayments they can use to pay for services based on the collected data.

Unfortunately, the systems in use today do not protect the privacy of their users and are identifying or only pseudonymous at best. The latter still allows transactions to be traced and linked to the same user. Surely, in some scenarios (e.g. loyalty programs), identification and traceability of users is part of the business interest in order to enable other business relevant purposes like, e.g., personalized advertising. But in many scenarios personal information is only a by-product which is (falsely) deemed unavoidable to manage individual wallets or accounts. For example, in the cases of campus cashless payment systems, the ETC scenarios or access cards, the operator of such a system, e.g. the caterer of the canteen or the operator of the natatorium, is interested into what has been purchased how often, but is usually not interested (or should not be interested) who has done the purchase. Having the personal information nonetheless encourages abuse or accidental theft of data. Thus, an efficient and cost-effective privacy-preserving mechanism which avoids data collection in the first place, but still enables the billing functionality, should be of interest to the providers as well. In this way, there is no need to deploy costly technical and organizational measures to protect a large amount of sensitive data and there is no risk of a data breach resulting in costly law suits, fines, and loss of customer trust. This is especially interesting in view of the new EU General Data Protection Regulation (GDPR) [EC18] which is in effect since May 2018. The GDPR stipulates comprehensive protection measures and heavy fines in case of non-compliance.

1.1 Related Work

When considering the related work of our anonymous point collection scheme, the collection of work to be looked at heavily depends on what perspective on the anonymous point collection scheme is chosen. The more application-oriented way is to directly look at the anonymous point collection system as some kind of anonymous e-cash system or at a concrete scenario which involves a specific kind of points, e.g. in the scope of a customer loyalty program or an anonymous reputation program. However, we would like to focus more on the aspects of anonymous point collection as a generic, multi-purpose building block. From this point of view our anonymous point collection scheme can be used to build the aforementioned systems but is not exclusively limited to these applications.

1.1.1 Application-specific Proposals

Except for [JR16; Mil+15] which are discussed in Section 1.1.3 the cryptographic literature has not considered anonymous point collection as a generic building block before. In the following, a brief overview of rather application-centric work is given. Among the proposed solutions for scenarios comparable to our goal the literature on (anonymous) e-cash and payment systems [CHL05; Bal+15; Rup+15; AIR01; Bel+08; ILV11; Gar+08; KHG08; Gar+09], anonymous reputation systems [AK12; AKS12], anonymous loyalty systems [EFS04; BD15] and anonymous incentive systems [Mil+15; Gon+15] is most notable. For the specific task of privacy-preserving, electronic toll collection (ETC) many ideas have been proposed as well [JCV15; Jar+14; Jar+16; Day+11; Bar+16; PBB09; Bal+10; Mei+11].

At first sight, the problem of anonymous point collection might appear easily solvable using (offline) e-cash, if each point is assumed to correspond to a single e-coin. In order to collect points, the users and the operator may execute the protocol to withdraw one e-coin repeatedly for each point. All collected coins may later be redeemed using the protocol for spending coins (multiple times). However, besides being inefficient, because coins typically cannot be aggregated, this also violates user privacy as in traditional offline e-cash, e.g. [CHL05], the withdrawal of e-coins is identifying. This is an unavoidable necessity, because a user's identity needs to be encoded into an e-coin during withdrawal to enable double-spending detection. Even transferable e-cash, e.g. [Bal+15], does not achieve the anonymity goal of this work. In such a scheme, the ownership of an e-coin can be transferred anonymously and unlinkably between users multiple times without the help of the bank. However, an impossibility result by Canard and Gouget [CG08] implies that an adversary impersonating the operator and the point-of-sale would be able to link a user's transactions. Moreover, transferable e-cash allows users to transfer e-coins arbitrarily among each other, a property which is undesirable in some of our envisioned scenarios as users would be able to pool their points.

A loyalty system is meant to reward users (most often a customer) for being steady partners of some other party (usually a merchant). In the easiest case users collect points for their participation in some action and later redeem those points. Enzmann, Fischlin, and Schneider II [EFS04] introduce two privacy-friendly loyalty systems for electronic market places. Their counter-based solution builds on RSA blind signatures. Blanco-Justicia and Domingo-Ferrer [BD15] propose a loyalty system which uses partially-blind signatures in pairing-based groups to ensure anonymity. Milutinovic et al. [Mil+15] present an unlinkable multi-purpose incentive scheme. The scheme draws from zero-knowledge proofs, commitment schemes, and partially blind signatures. Recently, Gong et al. [Gon+15] propose a privacy-preserving incentive-based demand and response scheme building on identity-based signatures, partially blind signatures as well as proofs of knowledge.

A reputation system provides the means to rate the behavior of parties in a system in order to support other parties in deciding whom to trust. In the simplest case, reputation equals the sum of (positive and negative) individual rating values. Systems providing rater and ratee privacy in peer-to-peer systems can be built from e-cash and anonymous credentials as, e.g., shown by [And+08]. Building on blacklistable anonymous credentials [Tsa+07], several papers (e.g., [AK12; AKS12]) have been published, dealing with TTP-free reputation-based blacklisting, where a central authority (like Wikipedia) may score the actions of its anonymous users.

Unfortunately, a lot of the aforementioned work frequently lacks a formal security model, a precise statement of what security goal is archived and/or rigorous proofs of security. Moreover, some of the papers were written with a particular use case in mind and implicitly assume that parties exhibit a particular behavior, i.e. they do not consider maliciously acting adversaries in the cryptographic sense but "rational" adversaries. Yet another set of applications which benefit from stronger security, offline capabilities, and negative points, are pre- or post-payment systems. In practice, such payment systems are typically implemented using simple RFID-transponder or smartcard-based solutions like the MiFARE Classic [NXP14], which essentially offers no security and privacy at all [Gar+08; KHG08; Gar+09, and more], or the MiFARE DESFire [NXP16; OP11] also allowing to link all transactions. Therefore, we prefer to look at anonymous point collection as an application-independent building block with a proper formalization of its functionality, its security and its privacy properties. For details how to use anonymous point collection to build some of the applications see Section 2.3. For a discussion of the long list of proposals for the electronic toll collection (ETC) scenario [JCV15; Jar+14; Jar+16; Day+11; Bar+16; PBB09; Bal+10; Mei+11; DDS12; Che+13] the reader is referred to Nagel et al. [Nag+20], which has been co-authored by the author of this thesis. There, the authors demonstrate how the proposed anonymous point collection scheme can be used to construct an ETC system. In summary, it seems fair to say that previous solutions for that domain have mostly been proposed by practitioners and also lack—apart from a few exceptions [DDS12; Che+13; Bal+10]—any formal security analysis.

1.1.2 Proposals with Similar Constructions

Our proposed anonymous point collection scheme shares some resemblance with the notion of a priced oblivious transfer (POT). POT was introduced by Aiello, Ishai, and Reingold [AIR01] as a tool to allow a customer to purchase digital goods from a merchant without leaking the "what, when and how much". However, privacy of the customer (or user in our scenario) is not granted and the original POT scheme is inherently limited to a single point-of-sale. A POT is a two-party protocol between the customer and the merchant. The merchant owns a set of messages and tags each of the messages with a price. The customer is allowed to receive a subset of the messages such that their total price does not exceed a specific limit. A POT scheme guarantees that the customer does not learn anything about the messages which have not been picked and that the merchant does not learn anything at all. The envisioned scenario is the purchase of a set of cryptographic keys which in a later step allow the customer to access a DRM-protected digital good (i.e. software licenses, video-on-demand, etc.). Camenisch, Dubovitskaya, and Neven [CDN10] extend POTs by anonymity of the customer and unlinkability of individual transactions which brings it closer to our scheme. The protocol is based on two different signature schemes [ASM06; BB04], the set membership protocol from [CCs08] and zero-knowledge proofs. Nonetheless, the scheme is still limited to a single merchant (but with multiple users). Moreover, [CDN10] lacks a full rigorous formal treatment. Rial and Preneel [RP10] extend POTs by optimistic fairness such that both parties can appeal to a third party in case of a dispute.

In some other aspects our anonymous point collection scheme exhibits similarities to P-signatures [Bel+08; ILV11] which have been introduced by Belenkiy et al. [Bel+08] as a tool to construct anonymous credentials. The scheme involves a set of users and an issuer. The scheme combines the algorithms of a commitment scheme and a signature scheme and extends them by two algorithms that allow the user to prove that (1) two commitments contain the same message, and (2) the user knows a valid signature under the issuer's private key on a message inside the commitment, resp. The scheme in [Bel+08] builds on weak Boneh-Boyen signatures [BB04], Groth-Sahai commitments and Groth-Sahai NIZK proofs [GS08]. Although their construction shares many ideas with ours, there are at least two major differences: (1) Our building block allows to homomorphically modify the commitments and obtain new signatures which is essential for "depositing points" while [Bel+08] only allows to re-randomize commitments. (2) P-signatures do not include a mechanism to prevent users from showing different commitments to the same message twice. Skipping ahead, such a mechanism is required for double-spending detection (see later) but is not required for standard anonymous credentials.

1.1.3 Generic Proposals—uCentive and BBA

Besides [JR16], only [Mil+15] appears to consider a point collection mechanism as a multi-purpose building block on its own. However, the proposed protocol—called uCentive—targets a simpler scenario than we do: incentives are not accumulatable on the user's side but stored and redeemed individually, negative points are not supported, and double-spending detection is done online rather than offline. uCentive also differ regarding the use of cryptographic building blocks: uCentive makes use of anonymous credentials and partially blind signatures. Unfortunately, the security and privacy properties of their protocol are again only informally stated and no proofs are given.

Jager and Rupp [JR16] have recently introduced BBA (Black-Box Accumulator) as a generic building-block for a curtailed variant of anonymous point collection. They formalized the core functional, security, and privacy requirements for a variety of user-centric protocols such as loyalty, refund, and incentive systems. As their work is the starting point for [Nag+17; Nag+20], which in turn are the base of this thesis, [JR16] is discussed in more detail. Differences between [JR16] and this work are also detailed out in Section 1.2.

BBA consists of a set of non-interactive algorithms to generate, manipulate, and show statements about BBA tokens (aka piggy banks or wallets). The scheme stipulates four types of parties: a set of users, an issuer, a set of accumulators and a verifier. However, as the issuer, all accumulators and the verifier share the same public-private key pair and must completely trust each other, they are better regarded as a single party. BBA allows a user to collect *positive* points (representing incentives) in an anonymous and unlinkable fashion. In the beginning, a user receives a BBA token generated by the issuer which is bound to a unique serial number known to both parties. This serial number remains constant during the lifetime of a token.[1] All points are collected using this single, constant-size accumulation token. To this end, a user blinds and unblinds the token before and after every transaction with an accumulator. When redeeming the token, the sum of all collected points as well as the *initial* serial number is revealed to the verifier. Obviously, obtaining and redeeming a BBA token is a linkable operation as the serial number of the token is revealed in both operations. After a token has been redeemed, it must not be used again. A permanent connection to a database containing serial numbers of tokens already redeemed is required in order to prevent double-redemption (aka double-spending) of tokens. Hence, BBA schemes are online systems. Also, users can re-use an old state of their token when points are accumulated without being detected. For this reason, "negative" points are not supported as users could easily get rid of them. Jager and Rupp [JR16] assume that positive points (i.e. incentives) are beneficial for users and thus a "rational" adversary has no interest in re-using an old state of a token.

[1] We stress that a serial number in [JR16] must not be confused with a serial number in this thesis. The serial numbers of [JR16] are better compared to wallet ID in this work. Both remain constant during the lifetime of a token or wallet, resp., and thus are identifying for the token/wallet. Serial numbers in the sense of this work denote single transactions, i.e. the deposition or disbursement of points, and do not exist in [JR16].

Moreover, the authors formalize a rather weak form of security, by only demanding that a collusion of malicious users may not be able to redeem more points than the total amount of points issued to them. In particular, this does not rule out that users may transfer points arbitrarily between their BBA tokens (without help). Normally, non-interactive schemes are a highly desired goal in cryptography, because non-interactive schemes have little communication complexity and are therefore typically very efficient. But the (non-interactive) algorithms of [JR16] are rather artificial. For example, the activity of adding points to a BBA token is not a single protocol, but willfully split into three algorithms which are (forcibly) non-interactive. First, users locally mask their tokens (to enable anonymity) using the first algorithm, then the blinded token is handed over to the accumulator outside the scope of the model, the accumulator locally manipulates the token using the second algorithm, the new token is given back to the users outside the scope of the model, and finally users locally unmask their tokens again using the third algorithm. This approach yields non-interactive algorithms at the cost of a direct semantic interpretation of these algorithms and it is not immediately clear what kind of security is achieved.

To summarize, the original BBA framework suffers from a number of serious restrictions including:

(1) fairly weak security guarantees,

(2) the need of a permanent database connection,

(3) the lack of mechanisms to enforce the collection of negative points, and

(4) the linkability of token creation and redemption.

These shortcomings limit the applicability of BBA as a building block. For instance, operators of loyalty or reputation systems do not want their users to pool or trade their points. Also, in certain scenarios negative points might be required. To realize this feature with a BBA scheme, one would need to redeem all points on a token, create a new one, and charge it with the remaining (unspent) points. However, in this way all partial redemptions of a user are linkable. Finally, BBA does not provide any of the auxiliary features (like blacklisting, etc.) which are required for practical use.

In [Nag+17], Nagel et al. propose BBA+ (Black-Box Accumulator Plus) which rectifies many of the drawbacks of the original BBA scheme [JR16]. But [Nag+17] still misses an integrated security model which captures both security for the operator and privacy for the users in a unified model. This and other issues are addressed by Nagel et al. in [Nag+20]. Both are discussed in the following section.

1.2 Contribution

This thesis is mostly based on [Nag+17; Nag+20], but also goes beyond those. Before the combined contribution of [Nag+17; Nag+20] and this work over previous proposals will be described, we shortly sketch their evolution.

BBA+ [Nag+17] improved over BBA [JR16] by offline capabilities, the support for negative points, the prevention against the pooling of points between users and a double-spending mechanism. Also, the definitional part has mostly been rewritten. BBA+ considers interactive protocols which leads to more intuitive definitions and broadens the class of possible instantiations. For example, the definition of a BBA+ scheme imposes less restrictions on an instantiation, as the definition only stipulates a single protocol for the deposition of points instead of three non-interactive algorithms. This also allows to formalize the security properties of BBA+ in a more natural as well as stronger way. However, in [Nag+17] security (incl. correctness) for the operator on the one hand and privacy for the users are still considered to be distinct aspects. Security is still defined by a list of properties that are individually proven in a game-based approach which has been inspired by the definition for a pre-payment with refunds scheme proposed in [Rup+15]. Privacy for users is defined by a simulation-based approach in [Nag+17].

In [Nag+20], Nagel et al. use BBA+ to construct a privacy-preserving ETC system. This enhances BBA+ by additional features that are essential for such a scenario. With respect to practical deployments the lack of these properties is a significant shortcoming of BBA+ and the enhancements are also beneficial for other applications of anonymous point collection. Also, Nagel et al. [Nag+20] uses the UC-framework to define all security aspects incl. privacy as an ideal functionality.

In this thesis, the functional extensions of [Nag+20] are backported and presented as part of a generic building block for anonymous point collection. Moreover, many subtle details in [Nag+20] are not formally spelled out, but are only sketched. This mostly concerns the channel model (i.e. in which cases communication is anonymous or authenticated and—if authenticated—at which point during the execution the identities are learned) and the synchronization of the distributed state between the different parties. In this thesis these seemingly minor details are straightened out as well. This has not only been a pure formality for the sake of completeness, but unveiled several oversights in [Nag+20]. Fixing these flaws necessitated modifications on the protocol level but also adjustments to the security model.

1.2.1 System Definition, Security Model and Proof

This thesis presents a framework for anonymous point collection which addresses the restrictions of BBA discussed in Section 1.1.3, thereby significantly strengthening its security and broadening its applicability. For the scenario which is detailed out in Chapter 2, we propose an ideal functionality $\mathcal{F}_{apc}$ for anonymous point collection based on the UC framework [Can01]. Typically, the standard approach is to cast a complex system like $\mathcal{F}_{apc}$ as an MPC problem and then resort to *generic but inefficient* UC-secure MPC [IPS08; Can+02]. Our work is one of very few combining a complex, yet practical crypto system with a thorough UC security analysis.

Our framework improves over previous work in the following aspects:

(1) The definition of anonymous point collection is captured as a single ideal functionality $\mathcal{F}_{apc}$ in the UC-framework with (polynomially) many parties that reactively participate in (polynomially) many transactions. This leads to a very precise demarcation of the system with a clean interface and thus yields numerous advantages:

  (a) The security of BBA [JR16] (and even BBA+ [Nag+17]) has been modeled by formalizing each security property individually as it is usually done in a game-based setting. This approach bears the intrinsic risk that important and expedient security aspects are overlooked, e.g., the list is incomplete. This danger is eliminated by the UC-approach where we do not aim to formalize a list of individual properties but rather how an ideal system should look like.

  (b) The definition $\mathcal{F}_{apc}$ allows interactive protocols, and thus poses less restrictions on possible realizations.

  (c) A single ideal functionality $\mathcal{F}_{apc}$ which encompasses a complete sequence of transactions allows for a very "strong" variant of security and privacy with an intuitive, semantic interpretation.

(2) The definition formalizes a stronger and more natural security property which demands that the balance of a wallet must be exactly the amount legitimately collected with this wallet. In other words, the pooling of points between wallets is ruled out.

(3) The definition supports the deposition of *negative* points and stipulates a mechanism to identify users who do not use the most recent state of their wallet.

(4) The definition covers offline realizations in the sense that there does not need to be a permanent connection to a database to check whether a presented wallet has already been robbed.

(5) We define a strong form of privacy, namely *forward and backward unlinkability* of transactions: A malicious adversary, including a collusion with the system operator, must neither be able to associate transactions to a particular wallet of an honest user nor be able to link preceding and succeeding transactions with each other. This even holds in

case a user commits double-spending (for those realization that allow double-spending with subsequent identification). The set of unlinkable transactions not only includes the deposition but also disbursement of points.

(6) The definition stipulates different parties with whom users can interact. Inter alia, an operator who runs the network and issues wallets to users and PoSes which deposit/disburse points to/from the wallets of users. Opposed to [JR16], the definition indeed enforces these parties to be actually distinct through the corruption model, i.e. by limiting what an adversary learns if, for example, a single PoS is corrupted. In other words, the definition of $\mathcal{F}_{\text{apc}}$ rules out realizations which use a shared secret key for all non-user parties and which assume complete trust among these parties. To this end $\mathcal{F}_{\text{apc}}$ envisions the certification of individual PoSes.

(7) To broaden the practical applicability $\mathcal{F}_{\text{apc}}$ functionally extends [JR16] in several ways.

   (a) The definition demands the existence of several auxiliary features which deal with potential "real-world" issues like broken hardware, legal disputes and so on: (i) A blacklisting mechanism that allows to exclude individual wallets or all wallets of a user from the network. (ii) A recalculation mechanism that allows to recalculate or restore the "true" balance of a wallet in case of a dissent, in case of double-spending or broken hardware. (iii) A prove-participation mechanism that allows users to selectively unveil a single transaction and thereby prove their participation without compromising the unlinkability of other transactions (including their own). Note that some of these features either premise the consent of the user (otherwise the operator could break unlinkability on its own) or a third party which serves as a dispute resolver and enables a key-escrow mechanism.

   (b) To enforce the collection of negative points which users may not voluntarily collect, the system optionally includes a party called violation enforcer to re-establish fairness.

   (c) Lastly, as a minor detail, $\mathcal{F}_{\text{apc}}$ allows user and PoS attributes on which the price of a transaction may depend. Also, the attribute can be used to bind wallets to a billing period which is encoded in the attribute. Although this extension seems trivial it has a great impact in practice. It does not only allow more complex pricing models but additionally increases real-world performance. By making PoSes only accept wallets from the current period, the size of the blacklist checked by the PoS can be limited to enable fast transactions. Similarly, the database needed to recalculate balances can be kept small.

A major challenge in designing $\mathcal{F}_{\text{apc}}$ was to combine provable security and practicality, where the latter includes practical performance figures. Hence, the difficulty was to find a definition that yields a reasonable trade-off between various aspects: On the one hand, it needs to be sufficiently abstract to represent the semantics of anonymous point collection which allows the formalization strong security features. If $\mathcal{F}_{\text{apc}}$ was aligned more closely to a concrete realization, this would artificially restrict the set of admissible realization, introduce unnatural artifacts and thereby weaken the provided security guarantees. On the other hand, while in principle every computationally solvable problem can be cast as an MPC problem, a definition that is completely agnostic of a potential realization would certainly lead to very inefficient solutions.

As stated above, the proposed definition captures the problem of anonymous point collection within a single ideal functionality $\mathcal{F}_{\text{apc}}$ with polynomial many parties. This makes the security analysis and proof highly non-trivial and cumbersome, because a high number of combinations which parties are corrupted needs to be considered in the proof. At first sight, it seems tempting to follow a different approach: In many tasks[2] of the system only specific parties interact with each other while the majority of parties is not involved. For example, a single user and a single PoS interact with each other in order to deposit points to the user's wallet. In a similar spirit, most tasks only involve two parties. This observation makes it temping to de-compose the system into a set of two-party tasks, define an ideal functionality for each of these tasks, realize each of them by a protocol, analyze their security separately and deduce the security of the system using the UC composition theorem. However, this entails a slew of technical subtleties due to the shared state between the individual two-party protocols which cannot easily be solved.

Moreover, although our system uses cryptographic building blocks for which UC formalizations exist (commitments, signatures, NIZK), these abstractions cannot be used. For example, UC-commitments are non-transferable, i.e., the commitment message cannot be passed to a different party, but we exploit this property heavily. Abstract UC-signatures are just random strings that are information-theoretic independent of the message they sign. Thus, it is impossible to prove in zero-knowledge any statement about message-signature-pairs. Hence, our security proof has to start almost from scratch. Although parts of it are inspired by proofs from the literature, it is very complex and technically demanding.

1.2.2 Protocols and Implementation

Besides the definitional framework, this thesis includes a realization π_{P5C} (Provably-Secure yet Practical Privacy-Preserving Point Collection) of $\mathcal{F}_{\text{apc}}$ using advanced cryptographic building

[2] The term "task" has no formal definition. However, we assume that the reader has some intuitive understanding of it. For an informal definition see Definition 2.1.

blocks and presents promising results of a prototypical implementation on real-world hardware. They show that the proposed realization may already be useable in practice, allowing to run transactions within a second.

At a high level, the construction is fairly intuitive and draws from techniques also commonly used in any privacy-preserving protocols including e-cash, P-signatures, and anonymous credentials. However, there are technical differences to these concepts as explained in Section 1.1.1. Moreover, a major challenge was to twist and combine all these techniques to achieve simulation-based security, practicality and efficiency *at the same time*. The concrete selection of the right instantiation of building blocks and the fine-tuning how they interplay has to be credited to the co-authors of [Nag+17; Nag+20] and not the author of this thesis.

This proposed realization is a semi-generic construction using public-key encryption, homomorphic trapdoor commitments, digital signatures, and Groth-Sahai non-interactive zero-knowledge proofs over bilinear groups for which the SXDH assumption holds. To achieve freshness of tokens, we draw from techniques typically used in offline e-cash systems, namely double-spending tags.

To realize the blacklisting mechanism of users we adopt and adjust an idea from the e-cash literature [CHL05]. On a high level this technique is a key escrow mechanism on a per wallet basis which allows to link all transactions of the affected wallet with the help of a trusted dispute resolver. Skipping ahead, this requires on a technical level to encrypt the seed of a PRF under the key of the dispute resolver. This part is tricky due to the use of Groth-Sahai NIZKs for efficiency reasons and the lack of a compatible (i.e., algebraic) encryption scheme whose message space is in turn compatible with the space of the seed. The author of this thesis contributed to this problem in so far that the author adopted a CCA-secure, structure-preserving encryption scheme [Cam+11] to the SXDH hardness assumption.

Other technical challenges arise from building on the Groth-Sahai (GS) proof system. GS-proofs are efficient and secure in the CRS model but require particular care, as they are no proper proofs-of-knowledge for witness components over $\mathbb{Z}_p$ and not always zero-knowledge. For example, to prove statements about shrinking multi-commitments over $\mathbb{Z}_p$, which we use to obtain compact tokens and proofs, the employed commitment scheme needs to satisfy a non-standard binding property.

In order to assess the suitability of the proposed realization for real-world applications, several variants have been implemented. The user side of the protocols in [Nag+17] has been implemented on a commercial off-the-shelf (COTS) smartphone, while the PoS side has been implemented on an embedded PC of a turnstile. The proposed protocol in [Nag+20] for the ETC system has specifically been implemented on an embedded processor which is known to be used in currently available on-board-units such as the Savari MobiWAVE [Sav17]. The biggest advantage for real-world deployment originates in the use of non-interactive zero-knowledge proofs, where major parts of the proofs can be precomputed and verification equations can be batched efficiently. This effectively reduces the computations which have to be performed by the user and the PoS during an actual protocol run. The implementation results show that the most time critical task—the deposition of points at a PoS on a user's wallet—can be executed within 510 ms.

1.2.3 Concomitant Contributions

Our proposed definition of security and privacy of our building block follows the simulation-based paradigm and especially builds on top of the so-called UC-framework [Can01]. However, common saying occasionally states that the UC framework is incompatible with privacy and does not allow to define privacy-preserving building blocks. We do away with this tale. To this end we first clarify a typical misconception how privacy should be looked at in UC. Second, we introduce a new messaging functionality to get rid of the communication model which uses identity-based messaging—as we call it—and which is hard-coded into the original UC framework without breaking compatibility with the rest of the model.

In this thesis, the security and privacy of our building block are not considered distinct features but captured by a single, uniform definition. With respect to security, the simulation-based paradigm is usually contrasted with the game-based approach. The game-based approach is sometimes considered to be more natural as each security game is typically associated to a single desired objective of the final building block.[3] With respect to privacy, several notions like k-anonymity [Swe02] or ε-differential privacy [Dw006; Dw009; Dw010] have been proposed. This thesis suggests an approach which combines all these paradigms. Instead of defining a single game for each desired security objective and then applying the game to a concrete (cryptographic) realization, the ideal functionality is shown to meet the list of objectives. Likewise, the privacy assessment should not be conducted on a concrete realization, but on the ideal functionality. The ideal functionality abstracts away the cryptographic complexity and "pulls it out of the equation". As such, the approach followed in this thesis can serve as a blueprint for the analysis of similar systems.

1.3 Organization of the Thesis

In Chapter 2 the envisioned scenario is detailed out. The involved parties and their major interactions with each other are introduced. As the features of a building block for anonymous

[3] One of the (anonymous) reviewer of [Nag+20] declared to feel more confident about the security of the scheme, if there was a list of individual security games instead of a single ideal abstraction, because he/she admitted not to be able to tell what security the simulation-based definition provides.

point collection are dictated by the applications within which the building block is eventually deployed, some of these possible applications are discussed in more detail. The chapter concludes with a list of desired properties one might expect from a building block for anonymous point collection.

As our security model is UC-based, Chapter 3 is an introduction into Universal Composability for those readers who are not familiar with this framework. This chapter does not contain any own contribution, but is included for self-completeness of this thesis. Also, some very common, so-called setup assumptions are provided from the literature. Only, the messaging functionality on which the proposed protocol relies is not a pure reproduction, but a merge of existing functionalities.

Given the scenario from Chapter 2, the definition of the proposed building block for anonymous point collection is presented in Chapter 4. The building block is defined as an ideal functionality within the UC framework. The functionality is highly non-trivial and nearly a protocol on its own as many "real world artifacts" have to be considered.

Due to its complexity, the definition is reviewed in Chapter 5. This chapter argues why the stipulated definition captures the "right definition" of security and privacy for the involved parties. Also, we show that the identified properties from Chapter 2 are indeed met by the definition. We stress, that this is *not* the security proof for the proposed protocol as (1) a definition cannot be proven and (2) the protocol has yet to be defined. Rather, Chapter 4 bridges the more traditional gamed-based approach with the simulation-based paradigm.

Chapter 6 introduces the hardness assumptions, all building blocks (encryption, digital signatures, commitments, and alike) and their usual security definitions (IND-CCA, EUF-CMA, and alike) are defined. Similar to Chapter 3 this chapter contains no own contribution. Reader who are familiar with these building blocks can safely skip this chapter.

In Chapter 7 a realization of the ideal functionality defined in Chapter 4 is proposed. This realization is given in pseudo-code and uses the building blocks from Chapter 6 as black boxes.

Chapter 8 gives the security proof which shows that the proposed protocol from Chapter 7 is actually a realization of the definition from Chapter 4. The proof follows the typical approach to define a sequence of hybrids and is rather bulky due to the complexity of the definition.

Chapter 9 reports figures for a real implementation of the pseudo-code on real-world hardware.

Finally, this thesis concludes with Chapter 10. The thesis is summarized, some of the encountered difficulties revisited and discussed how they might stimulate further research. Also, we sketch some straightforward improvements of this work which are trivial on their own but entail a slew of changes in all parts of this work.

2 Considered Scenario

In a nutshell, anonymous point collection refers to a variety of scenarios in which a set of parties—the users—collect or redeem points inside a personal wallet. The system is managed by an operator which typically is some kind of legal entity (e.g. a company) whose business interest usually is to have as many users as possible using its system.[1] Users interact with the system at points-of-sale (PoSes) which are setup and maintained by the operator.

Our proposed scheme P5C (Provably-Secure yet Practical Privacy-Preserving Point Collection) is highly flexible and can easily be adopted to different applications. The main design parameter is whether the addition and subtraction of points are treated uniformly by the same interactive task or if both interactions are treated separately. Another, but strongly related design parameter is whether wrap-arounds (i.e. a change of sign of the balance of a wallet) and/or under-/overflows needs to be specially considered or can be ignored. Both design parameters heavily influence which tasks are supported by the system, which parties interact in these tasks and which "level" of security—or more precisely anonymity—is provided. More, but decoupled design decisions relate to the support of optional features like blacklisting.

For the ease of presentation, we preliminary concentrate on a specific embodiment that keeps the addition of points—called *deposition*—separated from the subtraction of points—called *disbursement*. Also, deposition is anonymous and is carried out between a user and a PoS while disbursement is identifying and takes place between a user the operator. We discuss the alternatives in Section 2.3. Also, we shortly sketch what needs to be changed for the protocols to realize these alternative embodiments whenever convenient during the thesis.

2.1 Involved Parties

Our scheme P5C involves the following parties:

- The *Operator* which usually is a legal entity and runs the system. It owns and maintains the PoSes. Also, it manages a database of users who have registered for participation in

[1] Please note, that the users normally do not pay the operator directly in order to participate in the system, but the operator is typically reimbursed by some third party for its service.

the system and who own a legitimately issued wallet. We stress, the operator *does not* manage the wallets.

- A *User* participates in the system by means of a (digital) wallet that is kept on a portable, personal device. Typically, this is a smartphone or a smartcard, but other devices are possible, too. A suitable device must be able to store a few hundred bytes, have some[2] computational power and be able to communicate with the PoSes over some sort of local link (e.g. NFC, DSRC, ...). We stress that a permanent online connection is not required. Depending on the application, P5C supports multiple wallets per user. In this case a user may own several smartcards (one for each wallet) or the application on the smartphone allows to select a wallet.

- A *Point-of-Sale (PoS)* interacts with a user and is managed by the operator. To enable fast and reliable transactions with a user, we do *not* require PoSes to have a permanent connection to the operator. We only assume that it is periodically online for a short duration to exchange data with the operator. Optionally, it also needs to trigger the violation enforcer.

- The *Dispute Resolver* is an optional party that is necessary, if blacklisting and/or re-calculation of a wallet's balance is a required feature. Please remember, that users are anonymous when interacting with PoSes. Hence, after users have enrolled for the system and have legitimately received a valid wallet, there is no way to prevent a user from interacting with a PoS in a user-targeted manner. Also, individual transactions are unlinkable with each other or with a particular wallet. If a user claims that the balance of his wallet does not match his past transactions or that a particular PoS has applied a wrong value to his wallet, there is no way to trace the transactions. If there was, this would contradict anonymity. The dispute resolver is an optional third party that implements some kind of key escrow mechanism and supports the operator to de-anonymize a specific wallet. The dispute resolver must be trusted by the users not to collude with the operator.

- The *Violation Enforcer* is another optional party that might be instrumental in some special applications only in case a transaction fails. Please keep in mind, that users are anonymous when interacting with PoSes. The question whether a violation enforcer is needed or not depends on the kind of application and how the transaction of points is interleaved with the outer application. If the kind of application ensures that the

[2] Our implementation (cp. Chapter 9) clearly demonstrates that even low-end smartphones have sufficient computational power to run our protocol.

transaction of points has successfully terminated before users gain whatever benefit is traded in exchange, then a violation enforcer is probably not needed. However, if the kind of application is such that users may trick the PoS (or operator) to grant them access to the application-specific benefit before points have been exchanged, then a violation enforcer might be required in order to re-establish equity. See Section 2.3 and in particular Section 2.3.3 for an example.

2.2 Main Tasks

In the following, we sketch the main tasks of the system to foster a better understanding of the life cycle of the system.

The term "task" has no precise definition. Also, it seems very difficult to give a formal definition which captures the accurate meaning in all cases. On a colloquial level, a task could be called a protocol, but this is formally wrong as in the context of the UC-framework (cp. Chapter 3), the term "protocol" denotes to the whole system, i.e. a (UC-)protocol is synonymous to a scheme from the more traditional game-based point of view. In our sense, "task" means "phase" which is another term without a generally applicable, precise definition but commonly used in the literature. For example, a commitment protocol (aka scheme) consists of a commitment phase and an unveil phase, or an encryption scheme[3] consists of an encryption phase and a decryption phase. Here, we intentionally coined the term "task" and avoid the word "phase" as the latter suggests a predefined order/number of executions which is something we do not want to stipulate. An informal definition is

Definition 2.1 (Task (informal)) *Within a cryptographic protocol or scheme, a task is an interaction between a fixed subset of parties, which is bounded, i.e. has a defined starting and termination point, and which can be given some semantic interpretation. The subset of parties can also encompass only one single party.*

For example, the issuance of a wallet is a task. Figure 2.1 provides an overview of the most important tasks. A detailed description that also includes all tasks can be found in Chapter 4.

Remember, that we tentatively concentrate on a specific embodiment that keeps the deposition and disbursement of points separated in two tasks that also exhibit different features.

Party Registration In order to participate in the system, all parties (users, PoSes, operator, etc.) must first create a public key and publish it. The public key is used to identify a party in

[3] In the context of encryption the term "protocol" instead of scheme is rarely used, as encryption is assumed to be non-interactive.

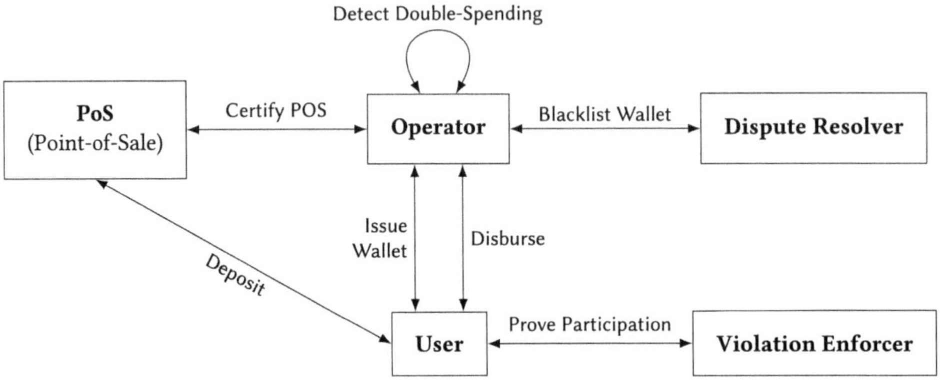

Figure 2.1: The P5C System Model

the system and is assumed to be bound to the party's (physical) identity such as a passport number, social security number, companies' register number etc. This is done once and makes the party accountable in case they cheat. For the majority of parties, namely users and PoSes, the operator can act as the registration authority. Details are discussed later on.

Wallet Issuing The operator issues wallets to users. A wallet is bound to the user's key and a set of user attributes (discussed later on). The wallet is used to deposit and/or disburse points, stores the accumulated balance and thus constitutes the essential object to participate in the system.

Point-of-Sale Certification In order to be able to manipulate wallets in the scope of Deposit or Disburse each PoS needs a certificate that is signed by the operator. This certificate also contains a set of PoS attributes (discussed later on).

Deposition This task is executed between a user and an (offline) PoS to deposit points on the user's wallet. The user is always anonymous and the previous balance of the wallet remains secret. The value to be added may depend on publicly verifiable factors from outside the protocol (e.g. the good that is traded, the current time of day, ...) as well as a combination of the user's, the current and previous PoS' attributes. Please note, that the operator can also play the role of a PoS as the operator can use a self-signed PoS-certificate. To put it in another way, the operator delegates some of its capabilities to manipulate a wallet to PoSes by issuing certificates.

Disbursement This task complements Deposit to enable users to disburse points. Disburse is not a mere "inverse" of Deposit, but has some distinct properties that set it apart from

Deposit. The concrete changes depend on the application. For most parts of this thesis, Deposit is executed between a user and the operator (instead of a PoS), the previous balance is unveiled (instead of being kept secret), and users are identified. Also, users do not receive an updated wallet (with a lower balance), but wallets are invalidated. However, users can obtain a new wallet by rerunning IssueWallet afterwards. A discussion why Disburse differs from Deposit is given in Section 2.3. There, also other variants of Disburse are presented.

Double-Spending Detection As the system is an offline scheme, malicious users might re-use an old state of their wallet instead of the most recent one. In other words, malicious users are not directly detained from rewinding to a previous, more expedient snapshot of their wallet and thus commit double-spending. To elude this problem IssueWallet, Deposit and Disburse generate double-spending tags that are eventually collected by the operator. The operator periodically runs DetectDS on its database to find pairs of matching double-spending tags and to identify fraudulent users.

Wallet Blacklisting With the help of the trusted dispute resolver, the operator is able to blacklist users. We assume that the dispute resolver convinces itself that either the user is fraudulent (e.g. by validating a proof of double-spending) or that the user has volunteered to be blacklisted (e.g. due to a lost wallet) out-of-band, before the dispute resolver consents to blacklist a user.

Prove of Participation In special scenarios that include a violation enforcer it might be necessary that users are able to prove their participation in a specific execution of Deposit without unveiling their complete internal state. See Section 2.3.3 for such a scenario.

2.3 Applications

Before we proceed to further describe the scenario and eventually formally define the system, we take an excursion and bring forward some applications of anonymous point collection. Although many details of P5C are still left unspecified, we deem this necessary, as many of the functional features and their security properties are inspired from practical requirements. Hence, some definitions can only be understood with the "right" application in mind. In the following, we sketch important aspects when applying P5C in some selected applications. From a high-level perspective, applying P5C to these applications seems mostly straightforward. Nonetheless, there are some technical subtleties that needs to be considered:

- The representation of integers values in a finite group and the connected problem of over-/ underflows or wraparounds. This results into the asymmetry of Deposit vs. Disburse

- Depending on the application users need to be forced to actually run Deposit or Disburse, if doing so is not for their benefit despite the fact that they are anonymous.

Before we discuss some concrete applications and how the tasks of P5C are specifically used, we elaborate more on the asymmetry of Deposit vs. Disburse. First, we pin down the precise meaning of two colloquial terms in our context.

Definition 2.2 (Price, Balance)

(1) *The* price *denotes the value of a* single transaction, *i.e. the amount of points that are deposited to or disbursed from a wallet in a single invocation of the tasks* Deposit *or* Disburse. *We use the term price for positive and negative values. The term shall not imply whether the transaction is beneficial for the user or not. Also, even if a price is specified as positive or negative, the sign shall not have an inherent signification. This is solely left to the application-specific interpretation of the term point.*

(2) *The* balance *is the amount of points that are stored in a wallet. The balance is the accumulated sum over the prices of all transactions that have been conducted with the wallet.*

In P5C the price and the balance are both encoded as elements of $\mathbb{Z}_\mathfrak{p}$ with $\mathfrak{p}$ being the prime-order of the used elliptic curve. An encoding of integers from $\mathbb{Z}$ in $\mathbb{Z}_\mathfrak{p}$ only makes sense relative to a fixed representation of $\mathbb{Z}_\mathfrak{p}$. Two obvious representations are $\mathbb{Z}_\mathfrak{p} \triangleq \{0, \dots, \mathfrak{p} - 1\} \subset \mathbb{Z}$ or $\mathbb{Z}_\mathfrak{p} \triangleq \left\{-\frac{\mathfrak{p}-1}{2}, \dots, 0, \dots, \frac{\mathfrak{p}-1}{2}\right\} \subset \mathbb{Z}$. This poses the well-known problem of wraparounds and over-/underflows. We use the terms in the following meaning.

Definition 2.3 (Over-/Underflow, Wraparounds (informal))

(1) *If we have fixed the representation* $\left\{-\frac{\mathfrak{p}-1}{2}, \dots, 0, \dots, \frac{\mathfrak{p}-1}{2}\right\}$ *or* $\{0, \dots, \mathfrak{p} - 1\}$ *and have a balance* $b \leq \frac{\mathfrak{p}-1}{2}$ *or* $b \leq \mathfrak{p} - 1$ *resp. and add a price* $p \geq 0$ *such that for the resulting balance* $b' = b + p > \frac{\mathfrak{p}-1}{2}$ *or* $> \mathfrak{p} - 1$ *holds, resp., we call this an* overflow.

(2) *If we have fixed the representation* $\left\{-\frac{\mathfrak{p}-1}{2}, \dots, 0, \dots, \frac{\mathfrak{p}-1}{2}\right\}$ *and have a balance* $b \geq -\frac{\mathfrak{p}-1}{2}$ *and subtract a price* $p \geq 0$ *such that* $b' = b - p < -\frac{\mathfrak{p}-1}{2}$ *holds, we call this an* underflow.

(3) *If we have fixed the representation* $\{0, \dots, \mathfrak{p} - 1\}$ *and have a balance* $b \geq 0$ *and subtract a price* $p \geq 0$ *such that* $b' = b - p < 0$ *holds, we call this a* wraparound.

Shortly, for the scope of this thesis, an over-/underflow denotes an unintended change of sign due to passing an interval limit in the magnitude of $\mathfrak{p}$, while a wraparound denotes an unintended change of sign due to passing the interval limit at zero.

For a minimum of 80 Bit of security, $\mathfrak{p}$ is a prime in the magnitude of 2^{254}. For most applications a wallet typically starts with a balance of zero. If we assume that the price of each transaction can be bounded by some reasonable value and there are only polynomially many transactions, then the event of an over-/underflow can be safely ignored. For example, if a point represents one cent, then a wallet has to conduct transactions with a total worth of 10^{75} € before an over-/underflow happens. Hence, we do not consider any special precautions against over-/underflows. However, depending on the application, wraparounds might be a concern.

Surely, the trivial scenario is an application which allows arbitrary transactions in both directions without giving any importance to the sign of the balance of a wallet as long as the sign is correct. In this case, the representation $\mathbb{Z}_p \triangleq \left\{-\frac{p-1}{2}, \dots, 0, \dots, \frac{p-1}{2}\right\}$ is the right choice and deposition and disbursement of points can be unified in the same task without further checks.

But for most application the range of acceptable balances is bounded at one side. For example, users must not disburse more points than they have previously deposited and thereby unnoticeable pile debt. In this case there is one "safe" direction leading away from the bound and one "unsafe" direction that needs some more precautions. This yields an asymmetry which is reflected by the two distinct tasks Deposit and Disburse. In the following we always use Deposit for the "safe" direction and Disburse for the "unsafe" direction. We deposit points by addition of positive values and disburse points by *subtraction* of positive values.

The task Deposit is conceptionally simpler and provides a very high level of secrecy. As Deposit represents the "safe" direction, a user always remains anonymous and the previous balance of the used wallet is never unveiled, when depositing points on the wallet.

The task Disburse must deal with potential wraparounds. In its simplest variant Disburse unveils the current balance of the wallet to the PoS (or operator) and the PoS (or operator) aborts, if more points shall be disbursed than are deposited on the wallet. Obviously, this may infringe upon privacy and there are a variety of applications where it might be desirable not to reveal the current balance. To overcome this issue, the Disburse protocol could alternatively be extended by a range proof system such as [CCs08; CLZ12]. Range proofs are formally defined in Section 6.2.7 and allow the user to prove in zero-knowledge that the current balance is higher than the amount of disbursed points. Although there has been great progress to increase the efficiency of those proof systems, they considerably slow down the execution on low-end hardware like mobile devices (cp. Chapter 9). Depending on possible real-time restrictions they are not always applicable. Please note, that even range-proofs are zero-knowledge, the PoS (or operator) learns the statement that the wallet's balance is sufficiently high, and thus Disburse is "less private" than Deposit. Additionally, for some applications it might also be expedient or even necessary, that Disburse unveils the user's identity to the PoS/operator. In Sections 2.3.1 to 2.3.3 we sketch applications for all these options.

2.3.1 Customer Loyalty Systems

Disburse unveils balance:	yes	Dispute resolver required/expedient:	no
Disburse unveils user-identity:	no	Violation enforcer required/expedient:	no
Disburse uses range-proof:	no		

As the most basic application, we outline how P5C can be used to create a privacy-preserving loyalty system for customer retention. We stress that we do not aim to imitate the modern loyalty programs such as Payback [PAY16] or Nectar [Aim16] whose primary focus is to analyze their customer's behavior, train a sales-response model and sell targeted advertisement. Here, we present a very basic loyalty program that resembles the classic trading stamps, i.e. a system that realizes a "buy n, get one for free"-approach.

The operator is the merchant or an association of several merchants who jointly run the loyalty system. The roles of PoSes and users are obvious. To participate in the program users register themselves first and then obtain a wallet. Users collect points using Deposit which is completely anonymous and does not unveil the current balance. In order to redeem points (in exchange for some benefit) users run Disburse which unveils the total balance of collected points. The latter ensures that users cannot redeem too many points and obtain a negative balance.

In this scenario, we assume that there are many depositions prior to each disbursement. Hence, we assume that unveiling the balance during disbursement is a not a severe loss of privacy, especially if the majority of users disburse points when they have reached similar balances.

In this scenario a dispute resolver is not necessarily required. Keeping the idea of trading stamps in the back of our mind, we do not see a good reason why blacklisting should be necessary. Also, an expiration date could be used and encoded into the user attributes as an alternative to blacklisting. In this case, wallets that are not renewed drop out of the system after a short time period. Of course, a dispute resolver could be used to offer users an additional "backup service" that allows to restore their wallets in case of a loss or similar. However, using our full recalculation-mechanism for this issue feels like an overdone solution. A simple backup of the most recent state of the wallet at the user-side would do as well.

Also, a violation enforcer is not required. We assume users to voluntarily participate in Deposit, because they benefit from point collection. Vice versa, we assume users to obtain their reward (e.g. a free good) only *after* they have successfully completed Disburse.

Simple Extensions The basic application can simply be extended in several ways: Instead of a single "type" of points, multiple types of points can used to differentiate between different types of goods. In this case a wallet does not store a single counter but a vector. Also, the user attributes that are attached to a wallet could be used to distinguish between different types of customers and let the pricing function depend on that. On top, the user attributes can be used to limit the wallet's lifetime and encourage customers to collect and redeem points faster.

2.3.2 Pre-Payment Systems

Disburse unveils balance:	no	Dispute resolver required/expedient:	yes
Disburse unveils user-identity:	no	Violation enforcer required/expedient:	no
Disburse uses range-proof:	yes		

A common application of pre-payment systems are micro-payments. First, users top up their wallet in exchange for real money and then successively spend their deposit. Typical examples are canteen systems, vending machines at work places, natatoriums or public transportation. Again, the roles of operator, PoSes and users are quite obvious.

Typically, user either present their wallet *once*, e.g. at a vending machine, or present their wallet *twice*, e.g. at a PoS upon entering *and* leaving. The latter allows the price to depend on the duration of the stay or the distance that has been traveled. To this end, the entry-PoS sets the attributes of the previous PoS in the wallet, but does not disburse any price. The exit-PoS reads the previous PoS attributes, clears them, calculates a price that may depend on user attributes, previous PoS attributes as well as its own attributes and disburses the price from the wallet. Of course, this way a pair of transactions between entry and exit becomes linkable, but not with other transactions. For the role of attributes and a detailed discussion see Section 2.4.

In a pre-payment scenario, topping up a wallet represents the "safe" direction and is realized by Deposit. As in Section 2.3.1 spending points is the "unsafe" direction and realized by Disburse. But contrary to the previous example, a single Deposit transaction that is privacy-preserving per default is followed by a (long) sequence of Disburse transactions. Hence, unveiling the previous balance during each Disburse to vouch sufficient funds might allow to link individual transactions. Especially, if there is a small and fixed set of admissible prices and fractional balances. A more privacy-friendly solution are so-called range proofs that show in zero-knowledge that the previous balance is higher than the price to be withdrawn.

Including a dispute resolver into this scenario is at least useful, could foster the acceptance of an anonymous payment system or might even by required by legal regulations. Typically, the PoSes are unmanned turnstiles or similar physical barriers. In case a user has already lost points, i.e. Disburse completed successfully, but the barrier fails to open, a dispute can usually not be settled on the spot. Instead, users simply try a second time (at a different turnstile), provisionally volunteer to pay twice and file a claim afterwards. Here, a recalculation mechanism that selective lifts the anonymity of the questionable transactions is expedient. Also, a lost wallet can be blacklisted such that a potential finder cannot use it and the legitimated owner can be compensated for the remaining balance.

A violation enforcer is not required. As in Section 2.3.1 user will likely not prematurely abort Deposit, because they (physically) paid for the price to be deposited. In case of Disburse, the vending machine or turnstile physically ensures that access is only granted after the price has successfully been withdrawn.

2.3.3 Post-Payment Systems

Disburse unveils balance:	yes	Dispute resolver required/expedient:	yes
Disburse unveils user-identity:	yes	Violation enforcer required/expedient:	yes
Disburse uses range-proof:	no		

A post-payment system is not simply the inversion of a pre-payment system as presented in the previous section. Post-payment systems are preferable over pre-payment system, if a high throughput of users is vital. In these scenarios, the speed of admissions must not drop either because users have simply forgotten to sufficiently top up their balance (as it might be the case in a pre-payment system) or because a transaction fails for other reasons. In some scenarios it might be even impossible or undesirable to prevent users from access to the good/service without paying first. In order to make this example more interesting and set it further apart from a pre-payment system, we focus on this special kind of scenarios.

This being said, a post-payment system differs from a pre-payment system in two aspects (despite the fact that the meaning of points is "inverted"). Firstly, users must be enforced to eventual clear their collected debt. Opposed to the previous examples, there is no inherent incentive for the users to do so. Secondly, "free-riders" who are able to gain admission at no charge must be pursued after the fact. Both aspects conflict with the anonymity of users.

In order to solve the first issue, a limited lifetime is encoded into a user's wallet as part of the user attributes. We assume that the system uses fixed billing periods, e.g. monthly billing periods, which are the same for all users. Prior to the beginning of a billing period, users obtain a fresh wallet from the operator using IssueWallet. As IssueWallet is identifying, the operator records which user owns a wallet for a particular billing period. Within a billing period, users collect debt at PoSes using Deposit. Please note, that adding points to the wallet actually means increasing the owed debt. Again, deposition is the "safe" direction, does not unveil the previous balance and is non-identifying. At the end of a billing period, users are requested to clear their owed debt by running Disburse with the operator. In this scenario, Disburse unveils the total balance and the user's identity such that the operator can invoice the user. As in Section 2.3.1 we assume that the total balance sufficiently masquerades the individual Deposit transactions. A successful disbursement invalidates the wallet. After having cleared the owed debt (in the real world using a traditional payment method), users may run IssueWallet again to obtain a new wallet for the next billing period.

The dispute resolver is necessary, if users refuse to clear their last wallet and accept not to get issued a new one. In this case, the operator and the dispute resolver can jointly recover all transactions of the outstanding wallet and the operator can then pursue the debtor. Also, a dispute resolver is expedient for the same reasons as in Section 2.3.2, e.g. lifting privacy in case of a dispute or immediate blacklisting of lost or stolen wallets with the consent of the user.

In order to pursue free-riders that refuse to collect debt, but gain access to the service nonetheless, the involved PoS triggers the violation enforcer which persecutes and punishes the free-rider, if found guilty. To this end, the violation enforcer needs to identity the user out-of-band. Typically, this involves taking a photo of the suspect using a camera that is mounted on every PoS but is owned and operated by the violation enforcer. We stress that we used the term "trigger" on purpose: The assume the communication between the PoS (or operator, resp.) and the violation enforcer to be one-way. Otherwise, a curious PoS/operator might be tempted to exploit the cameras in order to lift the privacy in each and every transaction. Due to technical limitations, it might be impossible to exactly determine which user triggered the camera. To settle this situation, the violation enforcer summons all users under investigation to run the task ProveParticipation. This task allows all innocent users to prove their participation in a matching Deposit task with the particular PoS.

We illustrate the scenario using electronic toll collection (ETC) in an open-road setting as a concrete example. This scenario is considered by Nagel et al. [Nag+20]. In this setting the violation enforcer is typically a police authority or another law enforcement agency. Moreover, users correspond to vehicles and PoSes to toll gantries. The dispute resolver could be an NGO or another public authority, like the data protection authority, a court or the department of justice. In an open-road setting, vehicles pass through toll gantries at normal travel speed and are tolled in transit. Due to a variety of reasons, a vehicle might simply pass the toll gantry without collecting debt. In these cases, the toll gantry triggers a camera. Especially in case of multi-lane roads, several photos of more than one vehicle being in the range of the toll gantry are taken or a single photo might show several suspects driving close to each other [Kap18].

We like to stress two aspects: Firstly, a user only needs to participate in ProveParticipation, if something has failed and if the user is in the set of suspects. Secondly, we assume that all erroneously suspected users volunteer to run ProveParticipation. Moreover, in any case, users always have the option to appeal to the dispute resolver and thereby unveil its successful participation in a transaction at the PoS under audit. But, the dispute resolver unveils *all* transaction of a particular wallet, while a ProveParticipation only proves the participation in a *single* transaction. This means, ProveParticipation is more selective and less privacy infringing.

Simple Extensions The user attribute can not only be used to limit the wallet's lifetime, but could encode further attributes to distinguish between different classes of users as in Section 2.3.1. Also, the previous PoS attribute could be encoded into the wallet as in Section 2.3.2 to realize distance-based tolling. Then, the pricing function may be dynamic and depend on different factors like the current time and congestion, the number of axles (recognized by sensors attached to the PoS), some user attributes attached to the wallet as well as some attributes of the previous PoS the user drove by.

2.3.4 Further Applications and Running Prime Example

The aforementioned examples are by far not a complete list. For example, in an anonymous reputation system with discrete reputation levels that correspond to intervals of reputation points, e.g. 0–9 corresponds to novice, 10–19 is beginner, up to 90–99 for expert, the range of admissible points is bounded at both sides. This peculiarity is not covered by any of the examples above. In [Nag+17] we sketched how this can be realized without using range-proofs if combined with an anonymous reputation system. Nonetheless, we deem this list a sufficient indication how to apply anonymous point collection to further applications.

For the remainder of this thesis, we use the post-payment system from Section 2.3.3 as our prime example and baseline. The sketched post-payment system requires the most features (such as a violation enforcer) from all examples. This also implies that—if not stated otherwise—we consider a variant of Deposit that is executed between a user and the operator, unveils the balance and identifies the user. This variant is used to formally define anonymous point collection in Chapter 4 and to realize P5C in Chapter 7. Concentrating on a single variant keeps the presentation simpler than tedious case-by-case distinctions.

2.4 Attributes, Pricing Function and Privacy Leakage

Our system involves two types of attribute vectors: user attributes $a_{\mathcal{U}}$ as well as PoS attributes $a_{\mathcal{P}}$. User attributes are stored in the wallet and are set when the wallet is issued. PoS attributes are part of the PoS certificate and set when the PoS is certified. Moreover, the attributes of the participating PoS are written to the wallet when the wallet is issued[4] and when points are deposited or disbursed. In other words, a wallet carries the attributes of the previous PoS it has interacted with besides its own user attributes. As a trivial generalization the attributes of a PoS could be split into a "full" attribute vector that is attached to the PoS' certificate and a sub-vector of attributes that is carried by the wallet as the (partial) attributes of the previous PoS. For the ease of notation, we only consider a single vector.

[4] In IssueWallet the operator plays the role of a PoS using a self-signed PoS certificate

We do not stipulate which kind of attributes or how many of them are used. Those details depend on the concrete pricing model of the application with a pricing function $p := f_{\text{price}}(a_{\mathcal{U}}, a_{\mathcal{P}}, a_{\mathcal{P}}^{\text{prev}}, aux)$ depending on the user attributes, the current and previous PoS attributes $a_{\mathcal{P}}, a_{\mathcal{P}}^{\text{prev}}$ and auxiliary, publicly verifiable input aux (e.g., time of day, weather conditions, ...). However, we expect that for most scenarios very little information needs to be encoded into these attributes. Typical examples have been sketched in Sections 2.3.1 to 2.3.3. For instance, limiting the validity of a wallet is quite common. Either to animate users to increase the volume of sales or—if points on a wallet represent some kind of debt—to actually force users to eventually clear their debt. Clearly, for privacy reasons, unique expiration dates in attributes need to be avoided. In case of unattended PoSes, one might want PoSes to also have an expiration date which is periodically renewed and encoded as a PoS attribute. As the secrets of a PoS allow to tamper with a wallet's balance, such an expiration date mitigates the damage of a stolen or compromised PoS. Also pricing models that are based on a distance between two PoSes or the duration of admission can be realized by using PoS attributes to distinguish between entry and exit PoSes.[5]

Obviously, the concrete content of the attributes affects the "level" of user privacy in an instantiation of our system. In case of our running prime example (cf. Sections 2.3.3 and 2.3.4) the goal is to provide provable privacy up to what can be possibly be deduced by

(1) an operator/PoS who *explicitly* learns those attributes as part of its input to the pricing function f_{price}, and

(2) an operator who *explicitly* learns the balance b of a user at the end when points are disbursed.

Our framework guarantees that protocol runs of honest users do not leak anything (useful) beyond that (cp. Chapter 5). In Section 5.3, we analyze the impact of these attributes on the privacy leakage of our system in more detail.

Item (1) of the previous paragraph already indicates that in our design of an anonymous point collection system the price of a transaction is determined by the PoS[6] that unilaterally evaluates the pricing function f_{price} and thus needs to know the attributes of the user and previously visited PoS. This design might seem not as "ideal" as it could be and comes with two obvious cutbacks at first glance. It may needlessly infringe upon the user's privacy and the PoS could deviate from the "right" price. This has been an intentional design decision with respect to real-world applicability.

[5] In this way, the entry and exit point can be linked. Still, our system ensures that the user is anonymous and multiple entry/exit pairs are unlinkable.

[6] In the next few lines, we only use the term PoS, but what is said also applies to the operator.

Please remember, that the PoS and user must efficiently evaluate the pricing function f_{price} themselves in the real implementation without the help of a third party due to offline capabilities. Ultimately, this boils down to two options: Either the pricing function is evaluated in the clear which implies that both parties learn their mutual inputs, or the PoS and user run some sort of secure two-party computation (2PC).

Depending on the complexity of the pricing function general 2PC techniques might be too inefficient to meet the real-time requirements of most applications, especially if low-end devices like smart phones are involved. Note that it does not suffice to pass the attributes as input to the 2PC and merely evaluate the pricing function, but the 2PC must also ensure that the "correct" inputs are used, i.e. those that are attached to the wallet and the PoS certificate. Skipping ahead to the implementation, this would imply—among other things—to validate signatures inside of 2PC. Of course, there might be extremely simple pricing functions that also exhibit some kind of "structural compatibility" with the building blocks of an instantiation of our scheme such that one can abstain from general 2PC technique but resort to tailored techniques that nicely interplay with the other building blocks in a white-box fashion. However, these cases are presumably rare. Also, evaluating the pricing function with 2PC and keeping the inputs secret has only a beneficial impact on the achieved "level" of privacy, if the pricing function is sufficiently intricate. If the pricing function allows to infer the inputs from the price, using 2PC yields no benefits. In summary, we conjecture that most application fall into one of the following three categories:

(1) The pricing function is extremely simple (e.g. a constant admission fee), especially it does not depend on user attributes. In this case the user attributes are trivial, too, (e.g. a zero-length vector) and handing over $a_{\mathcal{U}}$ to the PoS does not harm privacy.

(2) The pricing function is moderately simple and only depends on a few user attributes such that it is suitable for tailor-made 2PC in principle. For example, there are different, but fixed prices for a finite set of user classes (e.g. "newcomers", "regulars", "patrons"). In this case 2PC is of no practical benefit, because the resulting price unveils the original input anyway.

(3) The pricing function is complex, depends on various attributes and especially is not injective, i.e. maps large sets of different attribute values to the same price. In this case, 2PC could increase the "practically" achieved level of privacy, but 2PC is typically too inefficient.

In conclusion, we are convinced that evaluating the pricing function in the clear, is the right choice.

Also, with the timing-constraints of typical applications in mind, we assume that users preliminarily accept any price willingly in order to proceed and (in case of a dispute) file an out-of-band claim later. To this end, $\mathcal{F}_{\text{apc}}$ outputs all relevant information about the transaction to the users. This enables them to check the price themselves and to appeal afterwards if the wrong amount of points is deposited. In the real world, this detectability will deter PoSes from manipulation.

In order to allow users to assess the privacy of a particular instantiation of our framework, we recommend that all attributes, all possible values for those attributes and how they are assigned, as well as the pricing function are fixed in advance and public. In this way, the operator is also discouraged from running trivial attacks by tampering with an individual's attribute values (e.g., by assigning a billing period value not assigned to any other user). To this end, a user needs to check if the assigned attribute values appear reasonable. Such checks could also be conducted (at random) by a regulatory authority or often also automatically by the user's device. Likewise, a PoS could try to break the privacy of a user by charging a peculiar price. However, these "attacks" cannot be ruled out by cryptographic means but are immanent to the application. Again, we assume that watchful users file a claim in such a case which may lead to an audit.

2.5 Handling of Aborts

To enable offline capabilities IssueWallet, Deposit and Disburse all generate double-spending tags which are eventually collected by the operator. If the operator encounters a pair of matching double-spending tags the associated, fraudulent user is identified. If Deposit is aborted after this double-spending tag has been generated but before the user has received a new wallet state, the user is left with an already used wallet state. In this case users have two options: (1) Either they re-use this wallet state in the next transaction and thus deliberately commit double-spending, or (2) they contact the operator to be issued a new wallet. In both cases the user is identified. Thus, an abort during Deposit allows to partly lift privacy. We stress two points here: Firstly, privacy is only lifted for one particular transaction. All remaining past and future transactions are unaffected. Secondly, privacy-under-abort is a well-known open problem and not specific to our system.[7]

We expect unintentional aborts to only occur infrequently and hence result in an acceptable level of privacy infringement. Furthermore, the operator and PoSes have very little reason

[7] Without perfect fair exchange, either the double-spending tag is created before the users obtain a new, valid state of their wallet or vice versa. In the first case, it is always possible to abort such that users are left with an invalid wallet. In the second case, a malicious user could purposely abort before a double-spending tag is generated. This would foil double-spending detection altogether.

to abort purposely: They cannot target specific users, as the user is completely anonymous during Deposit. Only *after* an PoS aborts will the operator learn which user's privacy they have infringed upon. Hence, PoSes would have to abort a substantial amount of transactions in order to gain useful information. Doing so would draw attention, certainly lead to an audit of the operator and thus be contrary to their business interests.

In the opposite direction, the system or the surrounding application must ensure that a user does not benefit from an abort:

(1) A user has an intrinsic benefit to complete an advantageous transaction, e.g. top up a pre-payment card, gain more reputation points, etc.

(2) A user is (physically) prevented from gaining an extrinsic benefit before a disadvantageous transaction has successfully completed, e.g. by a turnstile, vending machine, etc.

(3) A user is externally identified by a violation enforcer and prosecuted.

In any case, if a user aborts too late, they are identified by the double-spending mechanism.

Aborts of any task other than Deposit are trivially handled by repetition, as the involved parties are non-anonymous anyway. In the remainder of this thesis we ignore aborts.

2.6 Desired Properties

With the applications from Section 2.3 at the back of our mind, the following list summarizes some exemplary, informal and desirable high-level properties that one would reasonably expect from anonymous point collection. These properties inspire the eventual definition of the ideal functionality in Chapter 4. Note that the ideal functionality (and not this list) is meant to formally conceive the security of our proposed protocol. Nonetheless, this list may help to better understand the scenario and concludes this chapter. In Chapter 5 we demonstrate how these high-level goals are reflected in the ideal functionality. We stress that some of these goals are not immediately achieved by the ideal functionality alone (for example property (P5)), but only make sense in combination with the outer application. For these cases, our system exports appropriate interfaces to enable the outer application to implement this feature.

(P1) *Owner-binding:* A user may only use a wallet legitimately issued to him.

(P2) *Attribute-binding:* A user cannot pretend a wallet to bear other attributes than those that were legitimately attached to it; be it user attributes or be it previous PoS attributes.

(P3) *Balance-binding:* A user cannot unveil a different balance (in Disburse) than the amount added to the wallet unless the user has committed double-spending.

(P4) *Double-spending Detection:* If a user reuses an old state of a wallet, the user will be identified.

(P5) *Participation Enforcement:* If a user fails to participate in Deposit, he will be identified.

(P6) *Blacklisting:* The operator is able—with a hint from the dispute resolver—to efficiently blacklist wallets of individual users.

(P7) *Accountability:* The operator is able—with a hint from the dispute resolver—to efficiently trace the transactions of an individual user. This allows to determine the actual balance of a double-spender. Also, in a dispute, a user may request a detailed invoice listing of the visited PoSes the associated transactions.

(P8) *Renegade Expulsion:* As the secrets of an PoS allow to tamper with a wallet's balance, the system supports a mechanism to mitigate the financial loss due to a compromised PoS.

(P9) *Unlinkability:* If user attributes and (previous) PoS attributes are ignored, a collusion of operator and PoSes may not be able to link a set of IssueWallet, Deposit and Disburse transactions of an honest user given that the user is neither blacklisted nor has committed double-spending. More precisely, IssueWallet, Deposit and Disburse do not reveal any information (except for user attributes, PoS attributes and the final balance in case of Disburse) that may help in linking transactions.

(P10) *Participation Provability:* ProveParticipation enables the violation enforcer to deanonymize a single transaction of an honest user in case of an incident. The remaining transactions stay unlinkable.

(P11) *Protection Against False Accusation:* The user is protected against false accusation of having committed double-spending (cp. (P4)).

3 The UC Model

We model P5C within the UC-framework by Canetti [Can01], which is a simulation-based security notion. The UC-framework carries forward the tradition of simulation-based security definitions for general protocols in an arbitrary context ([GMW86; Bea92; MR92]).

Simulation-based security notions come with the great advantage over other kinds of security notion that they usually explicate the achieved "level" of security very clearly. This stands in contrast with game-based definitions, where security is expressed by a number of games. A set of individual security games always bears the inherent danger that an important aspect is overlooked, thus not captured by any game and thereby inadvertently claiming an insecure system as secure. Guarantees expressed in a simulation-based notion usually have more evident semantics, obtained from directly considering how a protocol is used, rather than a hypothetical interaction of an adversary with a simplified game that encodes excluded attacks. More importantly, simulation-based security notions are also very good at making explicit what *cannot* be achieved.

The great advancement of the UC-framework over previous work is its general composition theorem. Security under (universal) composition is a very strong notion. The guarantees are provided even if a protocol is executed in an arbitrary environment, alongside other protocols. Moreover, composable frameworks facilitate modularity. One can define components with clean abstraction boundaries and use their idealized versions in a higher-level protocol. The overall security of the composed protocol follows from the composition theorem.

After its first publication the UC-framework and the independent, but conceptionally very similar work by Pfitzmann and Waidner [PW01] have spawned a long series of further research on security definitions. Besides major revisions [Can00; Can05; Can13; Can18] extended frameworks either for generalized settings or for broadened problem definitions [Can+07; CV12; CR03] were proposed. Pass [Pas03], Prabhakaran and Sahai [PS04], Barak and Sahai [BS05], Canetti, Lin, and Pass [CLP10], and Broadnax et al. [Bro+17] analyzed relaxations of the UC-framework that require less assumptions but still yields a meaningful, (somewhat) composable security notion. Katz [Kat07] investigated alternative setup assumptions. Moreover, UC-compatible security definitions for most cryptographic primitives have been formalized (see [Can05] for an overview). There are other conceptionally very similar frameworks that also come with a general composition theorem [BPW04; Küs06; HS15; Mau11; MR11]. Nonetheless, the UC-framework remains the de-facto standard to prove security of a protocol.

This chapter is organized as follows. In Section 3.1 we give a condense overview and line out the "big" picture. Sections 3.2 and 3.3 proceed with a formal definition. This formal definition is based on a compilation of [Can05; Can13] with some backported fixes from [Can18; HS15]. Although we slightly deviate from the original UC framework and also clarify some aspects where the original framework is ambiguous, these details are not crucial and thus the Sections 3.2 and 3.3 do not contain new information for readers who are familiar with the UC framework. Hence, the expert reader may skip these sections and proceed with Section 3.4. Nonetheless, we deem a formal foundation necessary, in order to soundly discuss the communication model. Shortly stated, the original UC-framework uses—what we call—"identity-based" addressing to send messages between parties. Clearly, this foils any attempt to define a protocol with anonymous parties right on the definitional level. We clarify this and related issues in Section 3.4. Also, we define some custom ideal functionalities for secure and anonymous communication in Section 3.4. This chapter concludes with Section 3.5 on setup assumptions, some well-known functionalities from the literature and implicit writing conventions for ideal functionalities.

3.1 Overview on the UC Framework

In the UC-framework, an ideal functionality $\mathcal{F}$ (acting as TTP) is defined that plainly solves the problem at hand in a secure and privacy-preserving manner. A protocol π is said to be a (secure) *realization* of this ideal functionality $\mathcal{F}$ if no PPT-machine $\mathcal{Z}$, called the *environment*, can distinguish between two experiments: the *real experiment* (running π) and the *ideal experiment* (using $\mathcal{F}$).

In the *real experiment*, $\mathcal{Z}$ interacts with parties running the actual protocol π and is supported by a real adversary $\mathcal{A}$. The environment $\mathcal{Z}$ specifies the input of the honest parties, receives their output and determines the overall course of action. The adversary $\mathcal{A}$ is instructed by $\mathcal{Z}$ and represents $\mathcal{Z}$'s interface to the network, e.g., $\mathcal{A}$ reports all messages generated by any party to $\mathcal{Z}$ and can manipulate, reroute, inject and/or suppress messages on $\mathcal{Z}$'s order. Moreover, $\mathcal{Z}$ may instruct $\mathcal{A}$ to corrupt parties. In this case, $\mathcal{A}$ takes over the role of the corrupted party, reports its internal state to $\mathcal{Z}$ and from then on may arbitrarily deviate from the protocol π in the name of the corrupted party as requested by $\mathcal{Z}$.

In the *ideal experiment*, on the other hand, the protocol parties are mere dummies that pass their input to a trusted third party $\mathcal{F}$ and hand over $\mathcal{F}$'s output as their own output. The ideal functionality $\mathcal{F}$ executes the task at hand in a trustworthy manner and is incorruptible. The real adversary $\mathcal{A}$ is replaced by a simulator $\mathcal{S}$. The simulator must mimic the behavior of

$\mathcal{A}$, e.g., simulate appropriate network messages (there are no network messages in the ideal experiment), and come up with a convincing internal state for corrupted parties (dummy parties do not have an internal state).

If no environment $\mathcal{Z}$ can tell executions of the real and the ideal experiment apart, then any successful attack existing in the real experiment would also exist in the ideal experiment. Therefore, the real protocol π guarantees the same level of security as the (inherently secure) ideal functionality $\mathcal{F}$.

Regarding privacy, the situation in UC is somewhat unsatisfying. As far as *input privacy* is concerned, the UC framework perfectly suitable. Note that all parties (incl. the simulator) use the ideal functionality as a black-box and only know what it explicitly allows them to know as part of their prescribed output. The output to the simulator is called leakage. This makes UC suitable to reason about input privacy in a very nice way. As no additional information is unveiled, the achieved level of input privacy can directly be deduced from the defined output of the ideal functionality. In other words, the privacy assessment can be conducted onto the ideal functionality and is completely decoupled from the analysis of the protocol implementation. The proof of indistinguishability asserts that any secure realization of the functionality provides the same level of privacy.

With respect to *sender privacy*—or anonymity—the UC framework is somewhat flubbed. Strictly speaking, it is impossible to achieve anonymity in UC due to the way how message routing and transportation is formally defined in [Can00; Can13; Can18]. If a party wants to send a message to another party, the actual message has to be prefixed with the sender's and receiver's identity which are used as addressing information. The message is then handed over to the adversary for delivery who may alter the message (including the addressing information) unless authenticated channels are assumed. But even in the plain model without authenticated channels the addressing information still exists as a prefix to the message and thus is learned by the receiver. We cope with this issue by unhinging the (implicit) message transportation from the UC-framework, defining a couple of ideal functionalities and thereby making message transportation explicit.

3.2 The Formal Model of Computation

In UC, the basic entity of computation is a Turing machine (TM). Conceptionally, UC distinguishes between interactive Turing machines (ITMs) and interactive Turing machine instances (ITIs). An ITM is an intangible and static object, while an ITI is a concrete instantiation of an ITM. The ITM defines all common characteristics, especially the code. An ITI is the runnable realization of an ITM and has a well-defined internal state (given by the content of its tapes, see below).

Definition 3.1 (Interactive Turing Machine (ITM)) *An* interactive Turing machine *is a probabilistic Turing machine with the following properties. Besides its usual working tape, it has the following tapes:*

- An identity tape: *This tape contains two strings prg and id. prg is the code of the TM and id the identity.* $\overline{id} = (prg, id)$ *is called the extended identity. This tape is read-only.*
- An outgoing message tape: *This tape contains a sequence of all generated message of the form* $\overline{m} = (\overline{id}_{\text{snd}}, \overline{id}_{\text{rcv}}, m)$. *m is called the (actual) message and* $\overline{m}$ *the extended message. This tape represents the outbox for messages that are supposed to be sent to other parties over the network.*
- An output tape: *Syntactically, identical to the outgoing message tape. This tape represents the outbox for messages that are locally passed to other ITI's within the same party.*
- *Two externally writable tapes:*

  (1) An incoming message tape

  (2) An input tape

  They are the counterparts to the outgoing message tape and output tape, resp. They serve as inboxes and are non-writable with respect to the possessing ITM.
- A random tape *A read-only tape that contains a uniformly drawn bit string of sufficient length. We assume that this tape cannot be exhausted.*

An ITM has two additional instructions:

- write-external*: The ITM writes a new message on its outgoing message tape or output tape and halts. The destination tape and the message are parameters of the instruction.*
- read-next*: The ITM reads the next, unread message from the incoming message tape or input tape. The source tape is specified as a parameter of the instruction.*

Please note, that an ITM supports two different halt states: a) The usual halt state identical to an ordinary TM. The ITM transits into this halt state if prescribed by its program. In this case the ITM cannot be activated again, but is "dead". b) A temporary halt state adopted by the ITM due to a write-external. In this state, the ITM "sleeps" until it is activated again.

Definition 3.2 (Interactive Turing Machine Instance (ITI)) *An instance* $\mathcal{M}$ *of an ITM is defined by its extended identity* $\overline{id} = (prg, id)$.

The number and names of the different tapes related to messaging have evolved over the different revisions of UC [Can00; Can05; Can13; Can18]. For Definition 3.1 we chose a variant that we believe to be the "Best-Of". The number of tapes is the same as in [Can00]. Here, we have a pair of two tapes for passing local data (input/output tape) and a pair of tapes for network messaging (incoming/outgoing message tape). We slightly changed their names such that their pairwise association becomes more evident.

We now define a system of ITIs. The following definition can be thought of as a set of rules how ITIs are allowed to interact with each other. To increase the flexibility and to enable different models of computation [Can13; Can18] takes a two-step approach and introduces a so-called global control function as an intermediate step. To put it simple, this global control function is a bit-valued function $\{0,1\}^* \rightarrow \{0,1\}$ that determines whether a write-external-command is allowed (or not) depending on the content of the tapes of the involved TMs. In the second step, [Can13; Can18] concretely instantiates this global control function. However, the Universal Composition Theorem (implicitly) assumes that the global control function is exactly instantiated as is. We do not define such a function separately but incorporate it into the definition of a system of ITIs.

Moreover, we push forward a definition on the identification of ITIs.

Definition 3.3 (Party Identifier (PID), Session Identifier (SID)) *We assume that the identity string of an ITI is structured as $id = (pid, sid)$. The first part is called the party identifier (PID) and the second part is called session identifier (SID) of the ITI.*

The reason for this convention becomes clear after the next definition. The following definition appears to be very long-winded and cumbersome. An intuitive explanation that makes this definition actually trivial follows below.

Definition 3.4 (System of Interactive Turing Machine Instances) *A system $\mathfrak{S} = \langle \mathcal{Z}, \mathcal{A} \rangle$ of ITIs is defined by two ITIs $\mathcal{Z}$ and $\mathcal{A}$ that generate the system. $\mathcal{Z}$ is called the initial ITI or the environment. $\mathcal{A}$ is called the adversary. More ITIs $\mathcal{M} \in \mathfrak{S}$ are invoked while the system is executed. If an ITI $\mathcal{M}$ invokes (i.e. creates) a new ITI $\mathcal{M}'$, $\mathcal{M}$ is called the direct parent of $\mathcal{M}'$ and $\mathcal{M}'$ is called the direct subsidiary of $\mathcal{M}$. In the following let $\overline{m} = (\overline{id}_{\text{snd}}, \overline{id}_{\text{rcv}}, m)$ denote the extended message that has been passed as the parameter to* write-external. *Also let $\overline{id}_{\text{snd}} = (prg_{\text{snd}}, id_{\text{snd}})$ and $id_{\text{snd}} = (pid_{\text{snd}}, sid_{\text{snd}})$ denote the extended ID, the code, the ID, the PID and SID of the* claimed *sender. Likewise, $\overline{id}_{\text{rcv}} = (prg_{\text{rcv}}, id_{\text{rcv}})$ and $id_{\text{rcv}} = (pid_{\text{rcv}}, sid_{\text{rcv}})$ denote the same for the* claimed *receiver. Moreover, $\overline{id} = (prg, id)$ and $id = (pid, sid)$ belong to the* true *sender and $\overline{id}' = (prg', id')$ and $id' = (pid', sid')$ belong to the* true *receiver. Beware, that the claimed sender/receiver does not necessarily equal the true sender/receiver. If we say the execution fails, the system $\mathfrak{S}$ immediately holds and outputs a special failure symbol. Then, the execution of $\mathfrak{S}$ on input x is governed by the following rules:*

- *$\mathcal{Z}$ is activated with x on its input tape*
- *$\mathfrak{S}$ halts, if $\mathcal{Z}$ halts finally; the output of $\mathfrak{S}$ is the output of $\mathcal{Z}$.*
- *If $\mathcal{Z}$ calls* write-external*:*
  (1) *If $\mathcal{Z}$ uses the outgoing message tape, the execution fails.*
  (2) *If $\mathcal{Z}$ uses the output tape:*
    (a) *If $pid_{\text{snd}} \neq pid_{\text{rcv}}$ holds, the execution fails.*
    (b) *If the destination ITI $\mathcal{M}'$ with $id' = id_{\text{rcv}}$ does not exist, a new ITI $\mathcal{M}'$ with $\overline{id}' = (prg', id')$ is invoked and $\overline{m}$ is written on its input tape. The new ITI $\mathcal{M}'$ becomes a direct subsidiary of $\mathcal{Z}$ and $\mathcal{Z}$ its direct parent.*
    (c) *If the destination ITI $\mathcal{M}'$ with $id' = id_{\text{rcv}}$ exists:*
      (i) *If $prg' \neq prg_{\text{rcv}}$, the execution fails.*
      (ii) *If id' is not a direct subsidiary of $\mathcal{Z}$, the execution fails.*
      (iii) *If $\overline{id}_{\text{snd}}$ does not equal the extended identity that has been used by $\mathcal{Z}$ as the sender's identity when* write-external *was called the first time for this particular receiver, the execution fails.*
      (iv) *Else, $\overline{m}$ is written on the input tape of $\mathcal{M}'$.*
- *If $\mathcal{A}$ calls* write-external*:*
  (1) *If $\mathcal{A}$ uses the outgoing message tape, and the destination ITI $\mathcal{M}'$ with $id' = id_{\text{rcv}}$ exists, $\overline{m}$ is written onto its incoming message tape, else the execution fails.*
  (2) *If $\mathcal{A}$ uses the output tape and id_{rcv} is the identity of $\mathcal{Z}$, $\overline{m}$ is written on the input tape of $\mathcal{Z}$, else the execution fails.*
- *If any $\mathcal{M} \in \mathfrak{S} \setminus \{\mathcal{Z}, \mathcal{A}\}$ calls* write-external*:*
  (1) *If $\mathcal{M}$ uses the outgoing message tape and $id_{\text{snd}} = id$ and $sid_{\text{snd}} = sid_{\text{rcv}}$ holds, then $\overline{m}$ is written onto the incoming message tape of $\mathcal{A}$, the execution fails.*
  (2) *If $\mathcal{M}$ uses the output tape:*
    (a) *If $\overline{id}_{\text{snd}} \neq \overline{id}$ or $pid_{\text{snd}} \neq pid_{\text{rcv}}$ holds, the execution fails.*
    (b) *If the destination ITI $\mathcal{M}'$ with $id' = id_{\text{rcv}}$ does not exist, a new ITI $\mathcal{M}'$ with $\overline{id}' = (prg', id')$ is invoked and $\overline{m}$ is written on its input tape. The new ITI $\mathcal{M}'$ becomes a direct subsidiary of $\mathcal{M}$ and $\mathcal{M}$ its direct parent.*
    (c) *If the destination ITI $\mathcal{M}'$ with $id' = id_{\text{rcv}}$ exists:*

(i) If $prg' \neq prg_{\mathrm{rcv}}$*, the execution fails.*

(ii) If $\mathcal{M}'$ *is not a direct subsidiary nor a direct parent of* $\mathcal{M}$*, the execution fails.*

(iii) Else, $\overline{m}$ *is written on the input tape of the destination ITI. If* $\overline{id}_{\mathrm{rcv}}$ *is the extended identity of* $\mathcal{Z}$ *that has been used by* $\mathcal{Z}$ *to invoke this ITI, then the code field of the claimed sender is erased before the message is passed onto* $\mathcal{Z}$*'s input tape, i.e.* $\overline{id}_{\mathrm{snd}} = (\bot, id_{\mathrm{rcv}})$.

- *If* write-external *has successfully been called, the senders halts and the receiver is activated next.*
- *If an ITI halts without having called* write-external, *the environment* $\mathcal{Z}$ *is activated again.*

We discuss this definition on two counts: Firstly, we give a graphical explanation that makes the definition more memorable, secondly, we highlight the differences to the original definition(s).

We start with "normal" ITIs (cp. Fig. 3.1). A "normal" ITI—neither the environment nor the adversary—can best be depicted as a single process running on a usual physical computer. The subset of all ITIs that share the same PID are located on the same machine, i.e. they constitute

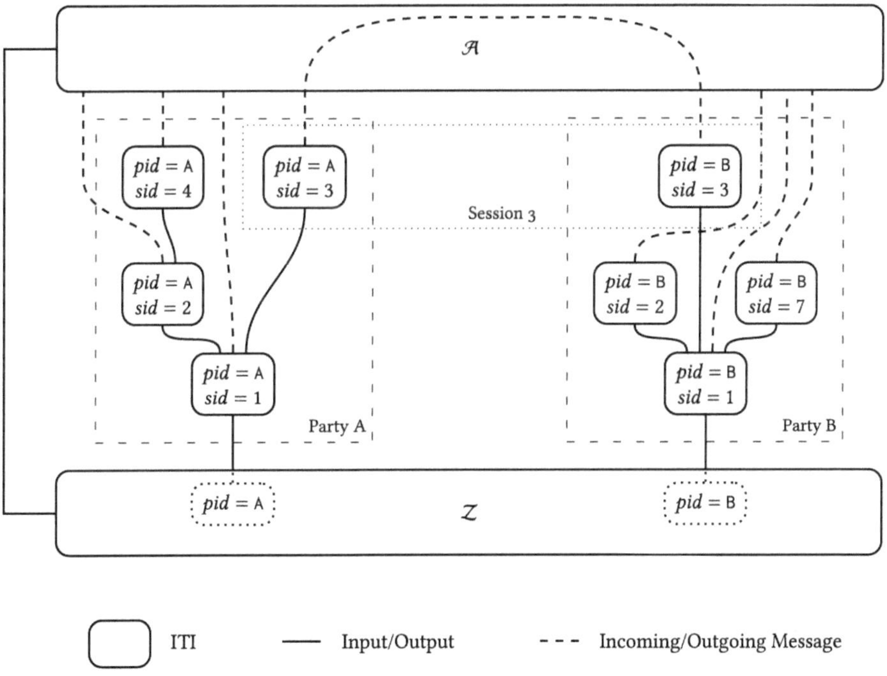

Figure 3.1: A System of ITIs

a party (framed by dashed line in Fig. 3.1). Within a party the involved ITIs communicate via their input/output tapes; the input/output tapes must not be used for communication with ITIs belonging to other parties (cp. Item (2a)). This kind of communication is secret, trustworthy, reliable and immediate. Especially, the ITIs know each other's code (cp. Item (2c-i)). This models the fact that some "main process" usually knows the called "subroutine function". Moreover, the caller must not lie about its own identity (cp. Item (2a)). The only exception to this rule affects the output of the root ITIs to the environment $\mathcal{Z}$ (cp. Item (2c-iii)). Here, the environment that initially has invoked the root ITIs and thus has determined their code *prg* has no guarantee that the ITI returning output to the environment actually runs the stipulated code.[1] New subsidiary ITIs (e.g. "subroutine functions") are implicitly created, if they are called for the first time (cp. Item (2b)). Communication is only allowed along the calling graph, i.e. the hierarchy of ITIs within a party forms a tree (cp. Item (2c-ii)).

While parties group ITIs "vertically", sessions group ITIs "horizontally" (cp. framed by dotted line in Fig. 3.1). ITIs belonging to the same session can best depicted as the different legs of a communication channel (e.g. the initiator and the target of a TLS connection). ITIs of the same session use the incoming/outgoing message tapes for communication. Again, the sender must not lie about its identity and is only allowed to send messages to other ITIs of the same session (cp. Item (1)). However, there are no security guarantees whatsoever as all incoming/outgoing messages are routed through the adversary $\mathcal{A}$ who represents an unreliable and untrustworthy network.

The environment $\mathcal{Z}$ is the initial ITI of the whole system. It binds together all parties and creates their root ITIs. As its name suggests, $\mathcal{Z}$ constitutes the environment in which the parties are executed and also incorporates any other processes that run concurrently. Intuitively, $\mathcal{Z}$ represents the "mastermind" that controls all parties by purporting their input and processing their output. Also, $\mathcal{Z}$ is allowed to communicate with the adversary $\mathcal{A}$ via input/output, but must not participate in the network itself (cp. Item (1)). If $\mathcal{Z}$ wishes to do so, it may request $\mathcal{A}$ for that (see below). To enable $\mathcal{Z}$ to be the parent of root ITIs of different parties, the restrictions on using its input/output tape are relaxed compared to "normal" parties. The environment $\mathcal{Z}$ is allowed to impersonate different parties. If $\mathcal{Z}$ originally invokes the root ITI of a not yet existing party it must do so using the designated PID (cp. Item (2a)) of the new party. Note, that neither Item (2a) nor Item (2b) demand that the "claimed" extended identity $\overline{id}$ of $\mathcal{Z}$ as a sender must be $\mathcal{Z}$'s true identity. However, if $\mathcal{Z}$ has called an ITI once, it has to do so consistently (Item (2c-iii)).

[1] This detail becomes important for the definition of protocol simulation.

The adversary $\mathcal{A}$ represents the network. As such, it must not use (local) input/output except for the communication with $\mathcal{Z}$ (cp. Item (2)). Any message that is written by any ITI M onto its outgoing message tape is handed over to $\mathcal{A}$. Although, M is not allowed to claim any other sender than itself, there are no restriction on how the message is handled by $\mathcal{A}$. Hence, $\mathcal{A}$ may arbitrarily manipulate, reroute, inject and/or suppress messages. $\mathcal{A}$ may send any (extended) message to any incoming message tape of any (existing) ITI with no restrictions on the claimed sender identity (cp. Item (1)).

Finally note that the model of asynchronous execution in UC is conceptionally very similar to what is called *preemptive multitasking* in the field of operating systems. At every point of the execution only a single ITI is active and the scheduling is message-driven. In other words, an ITI remains active until it voluntarily waives activation by passing a message to another ITI.

Deviations from the original UC framework The above definition enforces that the hierarchy of ITIs belonging to the same party is a tree and ensures that passing local input/output is only allowed along this hierarchy. As other aspects of the framework the concrete details have evolved over time and [Can05; Can13] explicitly claims[2] to allow arbitrary local communication among ITIs of the same party in order not to unnecessarily exclude certain models of computation. However, a non-hierarchical system of ITIs turns out to be problematic with respect to the composition theorem and corruption. Hofheinz and Shoup [HS15] showed that the composition theorem as originally be stated in [Can00] does not hold and therefore only consider trees for their own GNUC framework. To remedy this problem, Canetti [Can05] introduces the concept of *subroutine-respecting protocols*[3] in a first step. In a second step, [Can18] additionally demands protocols to be *compliant*. In order to avoid these technicalities all together, we follow the approach of Hofheinz and Shoup [HS15] and simply restrict the framework to parties with a tree-like calling hierarchy.

Moreover, Definition 3.4 clarifies that a new ITI is only allowed to be created by its parent via passing (local) input to it for the first time. In the original UC framework, a new ITI is created on-the-fly whenever a message of any kind is delivered to it, i.e. a new ITI may also be created by the adversary delivering an incoming (network) message to a non-existing ITI. Again, this flexibility raises some definitional problems. In Definition 3.4 the adversary's attempt to deliver an incoming (network) message to a non-existing recipient simply fails. Considering real computers and real programs we deem this clarification sufficient. The system of ITIs belonging to the same party must be created bottom-up from its root and the receiving end of a communication needs to be created first and then wait for incoming messages.

[2] However, this is not reflected by the formal definition of the control function

[3] Subroutine-respecting protocols do not necessarily adhere to a tree-like hierarchy but must not be arbitrary neither.

3.3 UC Protocols and Protocol Emulation

After having defined the computational model in the previous section this section defines how to use it to model interactive computer programs and define their security through *emulation.*

Definition 3.5 (Protocol, Protocol Instance)

(1) *A* protocol π *is an ITM running the code* π*.*

(2) *A* protocol instance *of* π *is a set of ITIs running* π *that all share the same SID but have pairwise different PIDs.*

In the UC framework the terms "code", "protocol" and ITM are somewhat synonymous and frequently used interchangeably. If one would like to discriminate, one might say that an ITM defines what can be computed in principle (i.e. defines the limits of the computational model), a code defines how something is computed (i.e. a list of instructions) and a protocol is both combined together (i.e. a code that is compatible with the capabilities of an ITM). If a protocol comprises different roles (e.g. the sender and receiver of a commitment protocol), the code π includes the code for all roles and the particular role of an ITI within the session is selected through appropriate input upon invocation. Please note, that a non-interactive program that is executed on a single ITI is also called a protocol.

The UC framework defines security as a relative concept by comparison of a protocol to some other protocol and stating that the former is secure simply means that it is as least as secure as the latter. Hence, in order get any useful results, we need something that we assume to be inherently secure as our comparison object. These objects are called *ideal functionalities* and are defined next.

Definition 3.6 (Ideal Functionality) *An ideal functionality* $\mathcal{F}$ *is an ITM with the following special properties:*

(1) *For each instance of* $\mathcal{F}$ $pid = \bot$ *holds.*

(2) *Dissenting from Definition 3.4* $\mathcal{F}$ *is allowed to pass output to (and obtain input from) ITIs with* $pid' \neq pid$ *if they belong to the same session and run the code of the dummy party (see below).*

Definition 3.7 (Ideal Protocol, Dummy Party) *A* ideal protocol $\mathsf{IDEAL}_{\mathcal{F}}$ *consists of an ideal functionality* $\mathcal{F}$ *together with an ITM, the so-called dummy party.*[4] *An instance of an ideal protocol*

[4] Canetti sometimes uses the term party synonymic for a single ITM or ITI. Although the dummy party is a particular ITM (and not a set of ITIs sharing the the same PID) we keep this term.

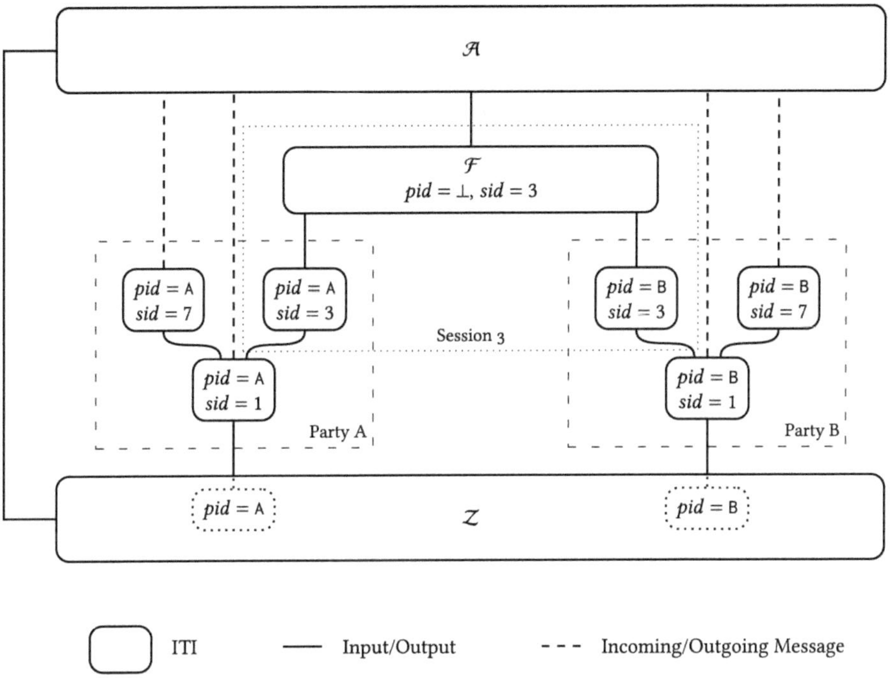

Figure 3.2: A System of ITIs with an ideal functionality $\mathcal{F}$

consists of an instance of $\mathcal{F}$ and one instance of the dummy party for each PID that $\mathcal{F}$ passes output to. The instances of the dummy party have the same SID as the instance of $\mathcal{F}$. If an ITI $\mathcal{M}$ invokes an ITI with the code of $\mathcal{F}$ with $id = (pid, sid)$ for the first time, an instance of $\mathcal{F}$ with $id_{\mathcal{F}} = (\bot, sid)$ and an instance of the dummy party with $id_{\text{dummy}} = (pid, sid)$ is invoked. The dummy party becomes a subsidiary of $\mathcal{M}$. If another ITI $\mathcal{M}'$ belonging to a different party passes input to an instance of $\mathcal{F}$ with $id = (pid', sid)$ and there is already an ITI with the code of $\mathcal{F}$ and SID sid, then only a suitable dummy party with $id'_{\text{dummy}} = (pid', sid)$ is invoked. Dummy parties simple pass input/output between their parent ITI and the instance of $\mathcal{F}$.

Sloppily, ideal functionalities are thought to span across multiple parties and be part of each party via one dummy party (cp. Fig. 3.2). This allows ideal functionalities to conduct distributed tasks using (local) input/output only and evading the adversary for remote messaging.

A reasonable security framework also requires a mechanism for the adversary to corrupt ITIs.

Definition 3.8 (Corruption) *The adversary $\mathcal{A}$ is allowed to* corrupt *ITIs with $pid \neq \bot$. In this case the content of all tapes of the corrupted ITI is handed over to $\mathcal{A}$. From then on, $\mathcal{A}$ impersonates* *the corrupted ITI. Whenever (local) input is passed to the corrupted ITI from its parent or from one of its subsidiaries via* write-external, *the message is written onto the input tape of $\mathcal{A}$ and $\mathcal{A}$ gets activated. Vice versa, the adversary $\mathcal{A}$ is allowed to pass input to the parent or the subsidiaries of the corrupted ITI as if the message came from the particular ITI.*

Descriptively, corruptions can be depicted as if the adversary incorporates the corrupted ITI and all communication lines from or to the ITI are re-attached to the adversary.

Please note, that the condition $pid \neq \bot$ prevents ideal functionalities from being corrupted. However, dummy parties are corruptible and thus the adversary learns all past input/output of the ideal functionality for the particular party. Moreover, the ideal functionality is notified that the dummy party is corrupted. We stress, that the code of an ideal functionality may depend on the corruption status of its associated dummy parties.

Deviations from the original UC framework Again, Definition 3.8 is more restrictive than the original corruption mechanism. In [Can00; Can05; Can13; Can18] the adversary corrupts an ITI through sending a special corrupt message to the ITI's incoming message tape in order to express its wish to corrupt the recipient. The ITI can then decide to ignore the request, to surrender completely (as above) or to do something else; typically, this means to alter some parts of its tapes (e.g. erase secret keys) before handing over the tape's content to the adversary. This enables different kinds of corruption models. The corruption model underlying Definition 3.8 in case of "normal" ITIs (not a dummy nor an ideal functionality) is called the *Byzantine corruption model* in [Can00; Can05; Can13; Can18] and is the mostly used one. The fact that the adversary learns all past input/output upon corruption of a dummy party, is called *standard corruption* in [Can05]. All ideal functionalities in [Can05] are of this type. We deem Byzantine corruption sufficient for two reasons. Firstly, considering real software it seems peculiar that an ITI should have the power to object to corruption. Normally, "programs" do not know if they are corrupted and allowing ITIs to run arbitrary code upon corruption might encourage the definition of protocols (in pseudo-code) that turn out to be unimplementable in the "real world" using real programming languages. Secondly, the UC framework provides an alternative approach to model incorruptible elements. Of course, there might be valid use cases where a more fine-grained reaction to corruption is desirable and is an essential part of the security concept. If certain parts of an ITI should withstand corruption and other parts not, then the system should be re-factored with the incorruptible parts being outsourced to an independent component that is modeled as an ideal functionality. We deem this alternative approach to be "the right one" as it spells out the required trust assumptions more explicitly.

Finally, we are ready to define the UC experiment and UC security.

Definition 3.9 (The UC Experiment) *Let the environment $\mathcal{Z}$ and the adversary $\mathcal{A}$ be two ITMs as in Definition 3.4 and π a protocol as in Definition 3.5. Then* $\mathsf{EXEC}_{\pi,\mathcal{A},\mathcal{Z}}(1^n)$ *is defined as the execution of the system $\langle \mathcal{Z}, \mathcal{A} \rangle$ on input 1^n with the additional restriction that any ITI invoked by $\mathcal{Z}$ must have the same SID and the code of the ITI is (silently) enforced to be π. The output of* $\mathsf{EXEC}_{\pi,\mathcal{A},\mathcal{Z}}(1^n)$ *is the output of $\langle \mathcal{Z}, \mathcal{A} \rangle$. The protocol π is called the* challenge protocol.

Definition 3.10 (Protocol Emulation, UC Realization, UC Security) *Let π, φ be two protocols. We define*

$$\pi \geq_{\mathrm{UC}} \varphi \qquad :\Leftrightarrow \qquad \forall \mathcal{A}\, \exists \mathcal{S}\, \forall \mathcal{Z} : \mathsf{EXEC}_{\pi,\mathcal{A},\mathcal{Z}}(1^n) \stackrel{c}{\equiv} \mathsf{EXEC}_{\varphi,\mathcal{S},\mathcal{Z}}(1^n) \tag{3.1}$$

In this case we say π emulates φ or π is a (UC-)secure realization of φ. The ITI $\mathcal{S}$ is called the simulator. Likewise, the left UC-experiment $\mathsf{EXEC}_{\pi,\mathcal{A},\mathcal{Z}}(1^n)$ *is called the* real game *and the right UC-experiment* $\mathsf{EXEC}_{\varphi,\mathcal{S},\mathcal{Z}}(1^n)$ *the* simulated game *or* ideal game.

Sloppily, π UC-realizes φ means that no environment $\mathcal{Z}$ is able to distinguish if it is interacting with an instance of the protocol π and a (real) adversary $\mathcal{A}$ or if it is interacting with an instance of the protocol φ and a simulator $\mathcal{S}$ mimicking the behavior of $\mathcal{A}$. The order of quantifiers is important, i.e. the simulator $\mathcal{S}$ may depend an $\mathcal{A}$ but must not depend on the environment $\mathcal{Z}$. We highlight to definitional issues: As the environment $\mathcal{Z}$ believes to interact with instances of π Definition 3.9 enforces the challenge protocol to run the correct code agnostic to $\mathcal{Z}$. Hence, the challenge session is an instance of φ in the ideal game although $\mathcal{Z}$ believes to invoke π-instances. For the same reason, Item (2c-iii) in Definition 3.4 ensures that the sender's identity (which encodes the sender's code) is erased if instances of the challenge protocol pass output to $\mathcal{Z}$. Otherwise $\mathcal{Z}$ could trivially distinguish the games.

Definition 3.10 quantifies over two adversarial entities: the adversary $\mathcal{A}$ and the environment $\mathcal{Z}$. The definition of UC-emulation can equivalently be rephrased such that only one specific adversary, the so-called dummy adversary $\mathcal{D}$, needs to be considered. This greatly simplifies the application of Definition 3.10, as consequently only a specific simulator $\mathcal{S}_{\mathcal{D}}$ for the prescribed adversary needs to be defined.

Definition 3.11 (Dummy Adversary) *The dummy adversary is an ITM with the following code:*

(1) *If $\mathcal{D}$ is activated by a message $\overline{m}$ on its incoming message tape, or by an input $\overline{m}$ on its input tape that has not been passed by $\mathcal{Z}$, $\mathcal{D}$ forwards the $\overline{m}' = (\overline{id}_{\mathcal{D}}, \overline{id}_{\mathcal{Z}}, \overline{m})$ as output to $\mathcal{Z}$.*

(2) *If $\mathcal{D}$ is activated by an input $\overline{m}' = (\overline{id}_{\mathcal{Z}}, \overline{id}_{\mathcal{D}}, m)$ with $m = (\text{corrupt}, id)$ from $\mathcal{Z}$, $\mathcal{D}$ corrupts the designated ITI and forwards the received internal state of the corrupted ITI back to $\mathcal{Z}$.*

(3) *If $\mathcal{D}$ is activated by an input $\overline{id}' = (\overline{id}_{\mathcal{Z}}, \overline{id}_{\mathcal{D}}, \overline{m})$ from $\mathcal{Z}$ with $\overline{m} = (\overline{id}_{\text{snd}}, \overline{id}_{\text{rcv}}, m)$, then $\mathcal{D}$ passes $\overline{m}$ as output or sends $\overline{m}$ as an outgoing message. Please note: $\mathcal{D}$ can only use the (local) output tape in the name of $\overline{id}_{\text{snd}}$, if it has previously corrupted this ITI and thus $\mathcal{D}$ incorporates this ITI.*

The next theorem states, that any protocol is already UC-secure, if it is secure with respect to the dummy adversary.

Theorem 3.12 (Completeness of the Dummy Adversary) *Let π and φ be protocols and $\mathcal{D}$ the dummy adversary. Then π emulates φ in the sense of Definition 3.10 if and only if π emulates φ with respect to the dummy adversary. Formally:*

$$\begin{aligned} &\forall \mathcal{A} \exists \mathcal{S} \forall \mathcal{Z} : \mathsf{EXEC}_{\pi,\mathcal{A},\mathcal{Z}}(1^n) \stackrel{c}{\equiv} \mathsf{EXEC}_{\varphi,\mathcal{S},\mathcal{Z}}(1^n) \\ :\Leftrightarrow \quad &\exists \mathcal{S}_{\mathcal{D}} \forall \mathcal{Z} : \mathsf{EXEC}_{\pi,\mathcal{D},\mathcal{Z}}(1^n) \stackrel{c}{\equiv} \mathsf{EXEC}_{\varphi,\mathcal{S}_{\mathcal{D}},\mathcal{Z}}(1^n) \end{aligned} \tag{3.3}$$

Informally, the dummy adversary is simply a thin communication wrapper around $\mathcal{Z}$ and helps $\mathcal{Z}$ to access the network. All "adversarial logic" has been put into the environment $\mathcal{Z}$. For a proof, see [Can00; Can05; Can13; Can18].

Before we conclude this section, we re-consider corruption. Both the scope of corruption and the time of corruption can be further restricted. The corruption mechanism as defined in Definition 3.8 allows ITIs belonging to the same party to be corrupted individually. Hofheinz and Shoup show that the UC Composition Theorem as stated in [Can05] does not hold for this general type of corruption, but needs further restrictions. To keep matters simple, we only consider PID-wise corruption from now on. As the name suggests, this means the adversary is allowed to either corrupt no ITI of a party or must corrupt all ITIs at once.

Definition 3.13 (PID-wise Corruption) *A UC-experiment $\mathsf{EXEC}_{\pi,\mathcal{A},\mathcal{Z}}(1^n)$ or a system of ITIs $\langle \mathcal{Z}, \mathcal{A} \rangle$ uses PID-wise corruption, if either all ITIs sharing the same PID are uncorrupted or corrupted.*

Additionally, the corruption model can be distinguished with respect to at what point of time the adversary is allowed to corrupt an ITI.

Definition 3.14 (Static vs. Adaptive Corruption)

(1) *A UC-experiment $\mathsf{EXEC}_{\pi,\mathcal{A},\mathcal{Z}}(1^n)$ or a system of ITIs $\langle \mathcal{Z}, \mathcal{A} \rangle$ uses* static corruption, *if the adversary is only allowed to corrupt ITIs* before *they receive their first input.*

(2) *A UC-experiment or a system of ITIs uses* adaptive corruption, *if it is not static, i.e. the adversary is allowed to corrupt an ITI at any time.*

A common misunderstanding is to deem adaptive corruption the more realistic model. The rationale behind this statement is that real programs or computers are usually not initially corrupted. However, this motivation falls short. First note, that UC-security quantifies over all adversarial strategies. This includes adversaries that statically corrupt a party but then follow the prescribed protocol honestly first and may deviate from the protocol later. From the perspective of another honest party this behavior is indistinguishable from a party that is honest first and then corrupted adaptively. Hence, for all scenarios in which security is only guaranteed to permanently honest parties and security for eventually corrupted parties is deemed irrelevant, static corruption is the adequate model.

Instead, adaptive corruption is tightly related to deniability. Simplified, the simulator must simulate protocol messages without knowing the input/output of the honest party in the beginning and then upon corruption (when the simulator learns the party's input/output) contrive appropriate secrets that consistently explain the party's past messages. Typically, this means that the simulator has an algorithm that computes a consistent randomness given the actual past input/output, the transcript of messages and the keys. Then, this randomness is handed over to the environment by the simulator as the pretended randomness of the corrupted party. As the algorithm works for any tuple of input/output, transcript and keys, a modification of this algorithm can also be used by honest parties to plausible deny a particular input/output to any third party.

For the sake of completeness, we shortly define the universal composition operator and state the composition theorem which lends the UC framework its name.

Definition 3.15 (Universal Composition Operator) *Let π, φ and ρ be protocols. The protocol*

$$\rho^{\frac{\pi}{\varphi}} \tag{3.4}$$

is identical to ρ with the following modifications:

(1) *Whenever ρ contains a* write-external *instruction with an extended identity $\overline{id} = (\varphi, (pid, sid))$ for the recipient, the instruction is replaced by an identical instruction with $\overline{id} = (\pi, (pid, sid))$.*

(2) *Whenever $\rho^{\frac{\pi}{\varphi}}$ receives an input from an ITI with extended identity $\overline{id} = (\pi, (pid, sid))$, $\rho^{\frac{\pi}{\varphi}}$ proceeds as ρ would do, if the input came from $\overline{id} = (\varphi, (pid, sid))$.*

Theorem 3.16 (The UC-Theorem) *Let π, φ and ρ be protocols and let $\pi \geq_{\mathrm{UC}} \varphi$ hold. Then $\rho^{\frac{\pi}{\varphi}} \geq_{\mathrm{UC}} \rho$ holds.*

For a proof see [Can13]. The theorem stated there additionally demands π and φ to be subroutine-respecting. This is implicit here, as Definition 3.4 only allows this kind of protocols. Instead of

$\rho^{\frac{\pi}{\varphi}} \geq_{\mathrm{UC}} \rho$ one usually writes $\rho^{\pi} \geq_{\mathrm{UC}} \rho^{\varphi}$. The following corollary illustrates the most frequent application of Theorem 3.16.

Corollary 3.17 (UC Composition) *Let $\mathcal{F}$ and $\mathcal{G}$ be ideal functionalities and π, φ be protocols. Then*

$$\varphi^{\mathsf{IDEAL}_{\mathcal{F}}} \geq_{\mathrm{UC}} \mathsf{IDEAL}_{\mathcal{G}}, \pi \geq_{\mathrm{UC}} \mathsf{IDEAL}_{\mathcal{F}} \implies \varphi^{\pi} \geq_{\mathrm{UC}} \mathsf{IDEAL}_{\mathcal{G}} \tag{3.5}$$

or more sloppily

$$\varphi^{\mathcal{F}} \geq_{\mathrm{UC}} \mathcal{G}, \pi \geq_{\mathrm{UC}} \mathcal{F} \implies \varphi^{\pi} \geq_{\mathrm{UC}} \mathcal{G} \tag{3.6}$$

holds.

3.4 Communication Model and Anonymity

As described in the previous section there are two types of channels being hard-coded into the framework:

(1) The first type is called input/output and provides reliable, immediate, confidential communication between ITIs of the same party. This type is inspired by communication between individual processes that are executed within the same trust domain, i.e. typically a computer.

(2) The second type is called incoming/outgoing messaging and provides communication between ITIs of the same session across different parties. This type does not provide any security properties and shall represent an unreliable network.

Both types use the same kind of addressing mechanism: The actual message m is prefixed by the extended identity of the sender and the receiver. These extended identities contain the PID, the SID and the code of the respective party. We call this *identity-based addressing*. While this method seems adequate for inner-party (i.e. local) communication and suffices for our purposes, this method is problematic for cross-party (i.e. network) communication. Identity-based addressing does not appropriately capture how addressing is implemented real-world networks and thus does not only fall short to be a realistic model, but also prevents anonymous communication.

There are three related issues:

(1) The adversary/simulator always leans the sender's true identity.

(2) Even if the adversary/simulator erased the sender's identity from the extended message (or replaced it by a fixed, fake identity), the recipient still would require the originator's identity in order to send a reply.

(3) The communication model of the UC framework implicitly assumes, that the involved parties already have agreed beforehand upon what protocol they are going to run, who has what role using which PID and what SID they are going to use.

Apart from the inability to adequately model real computer networks one might be tempted to argue that the issues (2) and (3) are only of minor concern. As the description of subordinated ITIs is included in their parent's code, the environment $\mathcal{Z}$ (implicitly) invokes all ITIs. As $\mathcal{Z}$ gives input to the parties and therefore controls their participation in a session, there is no anonymity with respect to $\mathcal{Z}$. Hence, one might say that directly using identities instead of addresses is an acceptable simplification of the model that avoids an additional level of indirection. From this point of view the avoidance of additional network addresses is at most a blemish of the model and one might assume that all the technicalities of real networks such as session setup or address resolution are pulled back into $\mathcal{Z}$. In particular, with respect to issue (2) a receiver could even reply to the correct originator of an anonymous message, if the environment wants so, because the environment knows the sender's identity and could pass the reply address as input to the receiver.[5] Probably, issues (2) and (3) are part of the reason why common saying states that it is impossible to model privacy within the UC-framework. If the environment $\mathcal{Z}$ triggers two parties to interact with each other and then asks the dummy adversary $\mathcal{D}$ to report the observed messages, $\mathcal{Z}$ knows to whom the messages belong. We claim, however, that this is a misconception of anonymity. The question is whether in the ideal model the simulator $\mathcal{S}$—without using any information about the parties' identities—is able to simulate messages that are indistinguishable from messages that $\mathcal{D}$ reports to $\mathcal{Z}$ in the real model. If the ideal functionality only outputs non-identifying information to the simulator and the simulator is still able to generate a convincing transcript (from $\mathcal{Z}$'s viewpoint), then anonymity is provided. But this is formally impossible due to issue (1). Remember that the dummy adversary in the real experiment receives an extended message $\overline{m} = (\overline{id}_{\text{snd}}, \overline{id}_{\text{rcv}}, m)$. Even if the simulator was able to simulate the actual message m independent of the sender's identity, the simulator still needs to report a convincing extended message containing the sender's identity to $\mathcal{Z}$.

To solve these issues, we explicitly introduce an ideal functionality $\mathcal{F}_{\text{msg}}$ for cross-party communication and completely give up on using the incoming/outgoing messaging that is hard-coded into the UC-framework. Our new messaging functionality $\mathcal{F}_{\text{msg}}$ ensures the anonymity we require. Consequently, our real P5C protocol lives in a $\mathcal{F}_{\text{msg}}$-hybrid model.

[5] Of course, the environment could lie about the originator's identity and input the wrong reply address to the recipient, such that the recipient sends its outgoing reply to the wrong destination. However, the network is under control of the adversary anyway and thus providing the recipient with the wrong originator's identity gives no additional power to $\mathcal{Z}$.

As the real dummy adversary and the environment in the real game are aware of $\mathcal{F}_{\mathrm{msg}}$ and thus do not expect to receive the sender's identity, the simulator in the ideal model does not need to provide one neither. Using an ideal functionality allows us to stay in line with the original UC-framework and also makes our requirements on the communication very explicit. (Alternatively, we had to redefine the messaging mechanism which we feel to be the conceptually wrong way.)

$\mathcal{F}_{\mathrm{msg}}$ is a multi-party functionality that supports polynomially many communication sub-sessions (within one UC session) between pairs of parties. A multi-party functionality that supports multiple sub-sessions allows a distinguished party[6] to announce its "existence" once in the beginning and from then on can be reached by other parties upon those parties' will. If we modeled $\mathcal{F}_{\mathrm{msg}}$ as a two-party functionality that only supported a single communication instead, a new instance of $\mathcal{F}_{\mathrm{msg}}$ would have to be instantiated for each communication and this would again rise the question how the involved parties "find" each other in the first place. Several formulations for similar functionalities, e.g. $\mathcal{F}_{\mathrm{auth}}$ (authenticated communication), $\mathcal{F}_{\mathrm{smt}}$ (secure message transfer), $\mathcal{F}_{\mathrm{scs}}$ (secure communication sessions), $\mathcal{F}_{\mathrm{rsc}}$ (relaxed secure channels), exist in the literature [Can03; Can05; CK02; NMO05]. $\mathcal{F}_{\mathrm{auth}}$ provides bi-lateral authentication, but only supports a single (one-shot) message and no confidentiality. $\mathcal{F}_{\mathrm{scs}}$ captures the idea that communication is divided into three phases: first, a session is established utilizing some kind of communication identifier, second, several messages are exchanged in both direction and last the communication session is teared down again. However, $\mathcal{F}_{\mathrm{scs}}$ does not provide any kind of security. $\mathcal{F}_{\mathrm{smt}}$ provides confidential communication, but only support a single (one-shot) message again.

Our functionality $\mathcal{F}_{\mathrm{msg}}$ can be depicted as a merge of these functionalities and is defined in Figs. 3.3 and 3.4. A party that becomes the *initiator* can establish a communication session that is identified by a *sub-session identifier* (SSID) *ssid* throughout its lifetime. A party that becomes the *responder* of the communication session can then accept the communication. Please note, that the term "responder" does not state anything about the direction of communication. The terms "initiator" and "responder" are only used to distinguish who started the session. Initiators can determine whether they want to stay anonymous or be identified by appropriately setting the mode $\mathit{mode} \in \{\mathtt{anon}, \mathtt{ident}\}$ when they establish a session. A session is always identifying for the responder. After a session has been established, polynomially many messages can be sent in both directions. If both parties are honest, the adversary only learns the length $|m|$ and direction $\mathit{dir} \in \{\mathtt{request}, \mathtt{response}\}$ of each message. Again, please note, that the terms "request" and "response" shall not stipulate any communication structure, especially requests

[6] This particular party is the operator in P5C, see later.

Functionality $\mathcal{F}_{\text{msg}}$

I. State

A (partial) mapping $f_{\text{comm-state}}$ assigning a triple of initiator PID $pid_{\text{initiator}}$, responder PID $pid_{\text{responder}}$ and communication state to a sub-session identifier (SSID) *ssid*:

$$f_{\text{comm-state}} : \mathcal{SSID} \to \mathcal{PID} \times \mathcal{PID} \times \{\texttt{pending}, \texttt{active}, \texttt{closed}\}$$

II. Behavior

(1) Upon obtaining input ($\texttt{establish-session}$, *mode*, $pid_{\text{responder}}$, *what*) from a party with PID $pid_{\text{initiator}}$, proceed as follows ...
  (a) Draw a fresh sub-session identifier (SSID) *ssid* that has not been used previously.
  (b) Set $f_{\text{comm-state}}(ssid) := (pid_{\text{initiator}}, pid_{\text{responder}}, \texttt{pending})$.
  (c) If $mode = \text{anon}$, redefine $pid_{\text{initiator}} := \bot$.
  (d) Leak ($\texttt{establishing-session}$, *ssid*, $pid_{\text{initiator}}$, $pid_{\text{responder}}$) to the adversary.
  (e) Output ($\texttt{establishing-session}$, *ssid*, $pid_{\text{initiator}}$, *what*) to party $pid_{\text{responder}}$.

(2) Upon obtaining input ($\texttt{accept}$, *ssid*) from a party with PID $pid_{\text{responder}}$ and there exists $pid_{\text{initiator}}$ such that $f_{\text{comm-state}}(ssid) = (pid_{\text{initiator}}, pid_{\text{responder}}, \texttt{pending})$ holds, proceed as follows ...
  (a) Redefine $f_{\text{comm-state}}(ssid) := (pid_{\text{initiator}}, pid_{\text{responder}}, \texttt{active})$.
  (b) Leak/output ($\texttt{accepted}$, *ssid*) to the adversary and party $pid_{\text{initiator}}$.

(3) Upon obtaining input ($\texttt{send}$, *ssid*, *m*) from a party with PID pid_{snd}, and there exists $pid_{\text{initiator}}, pid_{\text{responder}}$ such that $f_{\text{comm-state}}(ssid) = (pid_{\text{initiator}}, pid_{\text{responder}}, \texttt{active})$ and $pid_{\text{snd}} \in \{pid_{\text{initiator}}, pid_{\text{responder}}\}$ hold, proceed as follows ...
  (a) If $pid_{\text{snd}} = pid_{\text{initiator}}$, then set $pid_{\text{rcv}} := pid_{\text{responder}}$ and $dir = \texttt{request}$, else set $pid_{\text{rcv}} := pid_{\text{initiator}}$ and $dir := \texttt{response}$.
  (b) If pid_{snd} and pid_{rcv} are honest:
    (i) Leak ($\texttt{sending}$, *ssid*, *dir*, $|m|$) to the adversary.
  Else (pid_{snd} or pid_{rcv} is corrupted):
    (i) Leak ($\texttt{sending}$, *ssid*, *dir*, *m*) to the adversary.
    (ii) Obtain alternative value for *m* from the adversary.
  (c) Output ($\texttt{sent}$, *ssid*, *m*) to party pid_{rcv}.

Figure 3.3: The Functionality $\mathcal{F}_{\text{msg}}$

Functionality $\mathcal{F}_{\text{msg}}$ (cont.)

(4) Upon obtaining input (`close`, *ssid*) from a party with PID *pid*, and there exists $pid_{\text{initiator}}, pid_{\text{responder}}$ such that $f_{\text{comm-state}}(ssid) = (pid_{\text{initiator}}, pid_{\text{responder}}, \texttt{active})$ and $pid \in \{pid_{\text{initiator}}, pid_{\text{responder}}\}$ hold, proceed as follows ...
   (a) Redefine $f_{\text{comm-state}}(ssid) := (pid_{\text{initiator}}, pid_{\text{responder}}, \texttt{closed})$.
   (b) Leak/output (`closed`, *ssid*) to the adversary, and parties $pid_{\text{initiator}}$, $pid_{\text{responder}}$.

Figure 3.4: The Functionality $\mathcal{F}_{\text{msg}}$ (cont. from Fig. 3.3)

and responses do not need to come in pairs. They are only used to leak the direction of the message to the adversary without breaking the initiator's anonymity. If one of the parties is corrupted, the adversary learns the whole message m and may alter it. Finally, any of the involved parties may close the communication session.

$\mathcal{F}_{\text{msg}}$ provides the following high-level security properties (if both communication partners are honest): Messaging is either bilateral *authenticated* or one-sided authenticated and one-sided anonymous. Even if the initiator is anonymous, *integrity* of messages is always ensured. Also, $\mathcal{F}_{\text{msg}}$ ensures that within a single session the initiator is always the same party despite being anonymous. Lastly, messaging with $\mathcal{F}_{\text{msg}}$ is *confidential*.

We conclude this section with some final remarks on the realizability of $\mathcal{F}_{\text{msg}}$ by a real protocol. Of course, $\mathcal{F}_{\text{msg}}$ is trivially unrealizable in the first place due to its anonymity feature (see above). However, this is more of a definitional problem of the UC model. Assume for a moment that we only consider authenticated communication and only use $\mathcal{F}_{\text{msg}}$ with *mode* = `ident`. Canetti [Can05, Claim 20] shows that $\mathcal{F}_{\text{auth}}$ is unrealizable in the plain model. Obviously, $\mathcal{F}_{\text{auth}}$ can be realized by $\mathcal{F}_{\text{msg}}$ plus a wrapper protocol that restricts $\mathcal{F}_{\text{msg}}$ to a single sub-session and a single message. In conclusion, $\mathcal{F}_{\text{msg}}$ is also unrealizable in the plain model even in disregard of anonymity.

3.5 Setup Assumptions and Writing Conventions

Security under universal composition is a very strong notion and thus faces impossibility results in the plain model. Especially, Canetti and Fischlin [CF01] show that UC-secure commitments are impossible without setup assumptions. Setup assumptions are modeled as ideal functionalities that are facilitated by the real protocol in order to bootstrap security. In other words, in the real security experiment the protocol is still a hybrid with some components being

Functionality $\mathcal{F}_{\text{CRS}}$

Public parameters: Security parameter n, PPT-algorithm Setup

I. Receive CRS

Party $\mathcal{P}$ input: (`retrieve`)

(1) If no crs has been internally recorded, run $crs \leftarrow \text{Setup}(1^n)$ and store crs internally.
(2) Load the internally recorded crs.

Party $\mathcal{P}$ output: (crs)

Figure 3.5: The CRS Functionality $\mathcal{F}_{\text{CRS}}$

left idealized. These setup assumptions enable a security proof, because the ideal functionality implementing the setup assumption is a subordinate of the real protocol and thus is not directly accessible by the environment. This provides the simulator in the ideal experiment with a lever to lie about the setup assumption, e.g. to embed a trapdoor, and thereby avoids the impossibility results.

3.5.1 The Common-Reference String Model

A typical and widely used setup assumption is the CRS (common-reference string) model. A CRS is a short piece of information, i.e. a bit-sequence, that is shared among all parties and has been trustworthily generated. The ideal CRS-functionality $\mathcal{F}_{\text{CRS}}$ is depicted in Fig. 3.5.

We like to elaborate on the usefulness of the CRS-model. Depending on the way how the CRS is utilized, the model is more or less realistic. For example, following a modular approach where first a real protocol is defined using commitments as idealized UC-functionalities $\mathcal{F}_{\text{com}}$ and then these commitments are replaced by real commitment protocols in the CRS-model using the composition theorem, a fresh instance of $\mathcal{F}_{\text{CRS}}$ is required for each commitment. This stems from the requirement of the composition theorem that protocols must be subroutine-respecting and that $\mathcal{F}_{\text{CRS}}$ is local to each commitment. Hence, this approach is highly wasteful on the CRS and it is questionable where a sufficiently long CRS should come from. We stress that it is impossible to generate the CRS with plain cryptographic means by the parties themselves without violating the impossibility result and thus sacrificing security. As the CRS must come from outside the model the CRS should be succinct and efficiently used by the protocol. This applies to our scheme. A single instance of P5C supports polynomial many parties in polynomial many interactions using the same small CRS. In other words, in our particular case

Functionality $\mathcal{F}_{\text{bb}}$

I. Register

Party $\mathcal{P}$ input: (register, $(key_1, key_2, ...)$)

(1) Send (registering, $pid_{\mathcal{P}}, (key_1, key_2, ...)$) to the adversary.
(2) Upon receiving OK from the adversary proceed, else abort.
(3) If another entry $(pid_{\mathcal{P}}, (\dots))$ has already been registered for $pid_{\mathcal{P}}$, abort.
(4) If $\exists\, pid_{\mathcal{P}'}$ and i, j such that $(pid_{\mathcal{P}'}, (\dots, key'_i, ...))$ has been recorded and $key'_i = key_j$ holds, abort.
(5) Internally record the pair $(pid_{\mathcal{P}}, (key_1, key_2, ...))$.

Party $\mathcal{P}$ output: (OK)

II. Retrieve

Party $\mathcal{P}$ input: (retrieve, pid)

(1) Look up $(pid, (key_1, key_2, ...))$ internally; set $(key_1, key_2, ...) = \perp$ if no record exists

Party $\mathcal{P}$ output: $(pid, (key_1, key_2, \dots))$

III. Reverse Retrieve (Partial, reverse lookup)

Party $\mathcal{P}$ input: (reverse_retrieve, j, key)

(1) Look up $(pid, (key_1, key_2, \dots, key_j, \dots))$ with $key_j = key$ internally; set $(key_1, key_2, ...) = \perp$ if no record exists

Party $\mathcal{P}$ output: $(pid, (key_1, key_2, \dots))$

Figure 3.6: The Bulletin Board Functionality $\mathcal{F}_{\text{bb}}$

it is plausible to assume that the CRS is generated by some trustworthy state authority or by some standardization committee beforehand.

3.5.2 The Bulletin Board or Key Registration Service

Moreover, our scheme makes use of a bulletin board $\mathcal{F}_{\text{bb}}$ [CSV16, Fig. 3], which is sometimes also referred to as a key registration service [Cano7; Bar+04]. A bulletin board can be depicted as a database which associates party identifiers (PIDs) with (cryptographic) public keys. The assumptions about $\mathcal{F}_{\text{bb}}$ are that upon registration the operator of the bulletin board checks the identity of the registering party in a trustworthy way and that every party can retrieve information from $\mathcal{F}_{\text{bb}}$ trustworthily. $\mathcal{F}_{\text{bb}}$ is depicted in Fig. 3.6. We slightly enhanced $\mathcal{F}_{\text{bb}}$ over the usual definitions. This modification is not significant and does not have any impact on how $\mathcal{F}_{\text{bb}}$ can be realized in principle. The modification is only required for syntactical purposes. $\mathcal{F}_{\text{bb}}$ does not only allow a single opaque bit-string to be registered as the only key per party, but a vector of bit strings. This is necessary as the reverse lookup allows to search for a particular component and not only for a complete string. Intuitively, this captures the fact that in complex systems the key is actually a composed key for several building blocks, i.e. one key for a particular instantiation of an encryption scheme, another key for a particular signature scheme, and so on. The reverse lookup allows to identify a party, given only one component of the key. To this end pairwise inequality of keys must not only hold for complete keys, but for every component of a key. Having realistic building blocks in mind this is not a severe restriction.

$\mathcal{F}_{\text{bb}}$ is unrealizable in the plain model without authenticated channels, i.e. without another setup-assumption [Can03, Sec. 3.2]. However, the other way around $\mathcal{F}_{\text{bb}}$ can also be used to realize authenticated channels $\mathcal{F}_{\text{auth}}$ or our messaging functionality $\mathcal{F}_{\text{msg}}$. In this case, a real-world implementation of $\mathcal{F}_{\text{bb}}$ needs to trusted that it correctly verifies the PID of a party outside the model. In our scenario the PIDs of users could be a passport number, SSN, a customer ID or any other reasonable, verifiable and unique attribute. For PoSes the geo-location could be used as a PID.

Again, we like to shortly sketch how $\mathcal{F}_{\text{bb}}$ could be implemented in our scenario. Looking ahead, P5C puts us in the lucky situation that the scheme only exhibits a restricted communication pattern. Users only communicate with PoSes and the operator but never with each other. Vice versa, the inverse holds for the PoSes, with the additional benefit that users remain anonymous. Moreover, there is only a unique operator of the system that stays the same all the time and the set of PoSes is rather static. Only the set of users is relatively dynamic. Hence, $\mathcal{F}_{\text{bb}}$ could be implemented as a simple list that is locally (and partially) stored at each party and infrequently updated. This frees us from the problem that the bulletin board needs to remotely accessible over an online connection, which itself would require some sort of authentication again. Each PoS only needs to know the key of the operator. This could be set upon deployment of the PoS and updated during maintenance, if necessary. Users need the key of the operator and a list of keys of valid PoSes. Again, this list could be installed/updated at the user's side when the user wallet is issued. Inversely, the operator needs a list of keys of all users and PoSes. But this is not a problem at all, because the operator owns/maintains the PoSes and users must register with the operator which we assume to happen in person. At the bottom line, the security assumption boils down to the ability of the parties to mutually verify their (physical) identities and to exchange their public keys over a local connection (e.g. an NFC reader) when meeting face-to-face without a man-in-the-middle. In summary, we deem this a very mild trust assumption.

3.5.3 Some Writing Conventions

Lastly, we assume our functionality also uses the implicit writing conventions for ideal functionalities [Can01]. In the real experiment parties need to communicate over the network. Hence, a party that expects to receive a message does usually not proceed nor output anything until the adversary delivers the message. Contrary, ideal functionalities use local input/output and thus normally react immediately per definition. In order to enable indistinguishability, the ideal functionality must provide the simulator with a lever to delay output. Formally, an ideal functionality asks the simulator for permission to pass output to a party. To this end the ideal functionality sends its a suitable request to the simulator. This request does not contain the actual output (which remains secret) but is equipped with a unique "output ID" that uniquely identifies this output. When the simulator replies with the same output ID, the associated output is eventually passed to the party. The output IDs also allow to re-order outputs to some extent. For example, if a sender broadcasts a message to several recipients in the real experiment and the ideal functionality passes output to the same set of recipients, the simulator must be able to re-order the sequence of outputs in correspondence to the order of delivered messages in the real experiment.

As this entails a lot of boilerplate code that does not provide any insight, we simply assume this mechanism to be implicit to all ideal functionalities and that they "just do the right thing". In particular, our simulator can delay outputs and abort the current tasks of the ideal functionality at any point.

4 System Definition

In this chapter we formally define our ideal functionality $\mathcal{F}_{\text{apc}}$. Usually, ideal functionalities are rather simple objects and immediately evince that they capture the "right" definition of security. At least this is true for ideal functionalities that define cryptographic primitives like commitments, encryption or oblivious transfer. But here, $\mathcal{F}_{\text{apc}}$ defines security and privacy for a complex, real-world system and is almost a protocol on its own. Therefore, we also try to motivate why the definition is the way it is and why seemingly "insecure"[1] choices are the best we can hope for. An explicit mapping of the properties identified in Section 2.6 onto the ideal model is given in Chapter 5. A summary of the used variables is listed in the appendix as a quick reference.

We do not formalize each task (e.g., IssueWallet, Deposit, ...) as an individual ideal functionality, but the whole system as a monolithic, highly reactive functionality $\mathcal{F}_{\text{apc}}$ with polynomially many parties as users and PoSes. A monolithic functionality allows for a shared state between the individual interactions and to define correctness, security and privacy more easily. We will therefore first explain this state in Section 4.1 before we go on to describe the behavior of $\mathcal{F}_{\text{apc}}$. The ideal function $\mathcal{F}_{\text{apc}}$ provides twelve different tasks in total which we divide up into three categories: "Setup Tasks" (comprising all party registration and CertifyPOS) are defined in Section 4.2. "Main Tasks" (IssueWallet, Deposit and Disburse) are defined in Section 4.3. Finally, "Utility Tasks" (ProveParticipation, DetectDS, VerifyGuilt and BlacklistWallet) are covered in Section 4.4.

4.1 The Internal State

The key idea of $\mathcal{F}_{\text{apc}}$ is to internally keep track of all conducted transactions in a pervasive transaction database *TRDB* (see Fig. 4.1). Note that in this case "transaction" refers to the tasks IssueWallet, Deposit or Disburse, not just Deposit. Each transaction entry $trdb \in TRDB$ is of the form

$$trdb = (s^{\text{prev}}, s, \varphi, x, \lambda, pid_{\mathcal{U}}, pid_{\mathcal{P}}, p, b, \omega_{\text{ds}}, \omega_{\text{rc}}, \omega_{\text{pp}}). \tag{4.1}$$

[1] N.b.: The ideal functionality cannot be insecure per definitionem. However, it could capture a concept of security that does not coincide with the intuitive perception of security.

Functionality $\mathcal{F}_{\text{apc}}$

I. *State*

- Set $TRDB = \{trdb\}$ of transactions

$$
\begin{aligned}
trdb = (&s^{\text{prev}}, s, \varphi, x, \lambda, pid_{\mathcal{U}}, pid_{\mathcal{P}}, p, b, \omega_{\text{ds}}, \omega_{\text{rc}}, \omega_{\text{pp}}) \\
&\in S \times S \times \Phi \times \mathbb{N}_0 \times \mathcal{L} \times \mathcal{PID}_{\mathcal{U}} \times \mathcal{PID}_{\mathcal{P}} \times \mathbb{Z}_p \times \mathbb{Z}_p \\
&\quad \times \{0,1\}^* \times \{0,1\}^* \times \{0,1\}^*.
\end{aligned}
$$

- A (partial, injective) mapping f_{Φ} assigning a fraud-detection ID φ to a pair of wallet ID λ and counter x:

$$f_{\Phi} : \mathcal{L} \times \mathbb{N}_0 \to \Phi, (\lambda, x) \mapsto \varphi$$

- A (partial) mapping $f_{\mathcal{A}_{\mathcal{U}}}$ assigning user attributes to a wallet ID λ:

$$f_{\mathcal{A}_{\mathcal{U}}} : \mathcal{L} \to \mathcal{A}_{\mathcal{U}}, \lambda \mapsto a_{\mathcal{U}}$$

- A (partial) mapping $f_{\mathcal{A}_{\mathcal{P}}}$ assigning PoS attributes to a PoS PID $pid_{\mathcal{P}}$:

$$f_{\mathcal{A}_{\mathcal{P}}} : \mathcal{PID}_{\mathcal{P}} \to \mathcal{A}_{\mathcal{P}}, pid_{\mathcal{P}} \mapsto a_{\mathcal{P}}$$

- A (partial) mapping f_{π} assigning a validity bit to a pair of user PID $pid_{\mathcal{U}}$ and proof of guilt π:

$$f_{\pi} : \mathcal{PID}_{\mathcal{U}} \times \Pi \to \{\mathsf{OK}, \mathsf{NOK}\}$$

- A injective mapping $f_{\Omega_{\text{bl}}}$ assigning a blacklisting tag ω_{bl} to a wallet ID λ:

$$f_{\Omega_{\text{bl}}} : \mathcal{L} \to \Omega_{\text{bl}}, \lambda \mapsto \omega_{\text{bl}}$$

II. *Behavior*

- *Dispute Resolver Registration* (Fig. 4.4)
- *Operator Registration* (Fig. 4.5)
- *Point-of-Sale Registration* (Fig. 4.6)
- *User Registration* (Fig. 4.7)
- *Point-of-Sale Certification* (Fig. 4.8)
- *Wallet Issuing* (Fig. 4.9)
- *Deposition* (Figs. 4.10 and 4.11)
- *Disbursement* (Fig. 4.12)
- *Double-Spending Detection* (Fig. 4.13)
- *Guilt Verification* (Fig. 4.14)
- *Wallet Blacklisting* (Fig. 4.15)
- *Balance Recalculation* (Fig. 4.16)
- *Prove of Participation* (Fig. 4.17)

Figure 4.1: The Functionality $\mathcal{F}_{\text{apc}}$ – Internal State and Overview of Tasks

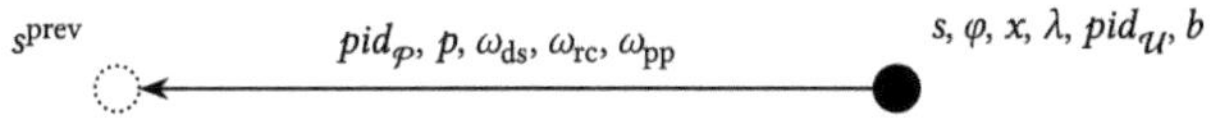

Figure 4.2: An entry $trdb \in TRDB$ visualized as an element of a directed graph

It contains the identities $pid_{\mathcal{U}}$ and $pid_{\mathcal{P}}$ of the involved user and PoS (or operator in the case of IssueWallet and Disburse), the wallet ID λ of the wallet that was used as well as the price p associated with this particular transaction and the total balance b of the user's wallet after this transaction, i.e., the accumulated sum of all prices so far including the current transaction. In other words, $\mathcal{F}_{\text{apc}}$ implements a trustworthy global bookkeeping service that manages the wallets of all users. Each transaction entry is uniquely identified by a serial number s and links via s^{prev} to the previous transaction $trdb^{\text{prev}}$ which corresponds to the wallet state prior to $trdb$. Additionally, each entry contains a counter x indicating the number of subsequent transactions of a wallet since its generation, i.e. $x = x^{\text{prev}} + 1$ always holds, and a fraud-detection ID φ which is required for double-spending detection.

The database *TRDB* can best be visualized as a directed graph with each *trdb* entry representing a node together with an edge pointing to its predecessor (see Fig. 4.2 for a depiction). Each node represents the state of a wallet *after* the respective transaction, i.e., at the end of an execution of IssueWallet, Deposit or Disburse, and the edges correspond to the transition from the previous to the next state. Nodes are identified by serial numbers s and additionally labeled with $(\varphi, x, \lambda, pid_{\mathcal{U}}, b)$. The edge to the predecessor is identified by (s^{prev}, s) and additionally labeled with $(pid_{\mathcal{P}}, p, \omega_{\text{ds}}, \omega_{\text{rc}}, \omega_{\text{pp}})$.

Also, each transaction, or more precisely each transition from one wallet state to the next, is associated with various tags: the double-spending tag ω_{ds}, the recalculation tag ω_{rc} and the prove-participation tag ω_{pp}. A forth tag, the blacklisting tag ω_{bl}, is not depicted here. The latter is only generated, when a wallet is issued and thus belongs to the "imaginary transition" from the void to the root node. Therefore, ω_{bl} is not recorded in *trdb* but separately kept by $\mathcal{F}_{\text{apc}}$ in the map $f_{\Omega_{\text{bl}}}$ (cp. Fig. 4.1). In short, these tags serve as a kind of receipt or "evidence" for certain aspects of a transaction and store implementation-specific information. Their description is postponed to Section 4.1.2. But first some explanations are in order with respect to the different IDs that are attached to each transaction, namely the serial number s, the wallet ID λ and the fraud-detection ID φ.

4.1.1 Transaction Identifiers

In a truly ideal world, $\mathcal{F}_{\text{apc}}$ would use the user's identity $pid_{\mathcal{U}}$ and a wallet ID λ to look up its most recent entry in the database and append a new entry. Such a scheme, however, could only be implemented by an online system. Since we require offline capabilities—allowing a user and

PoS to interact without the help of other parties and without permanent access to a central authority—the inherent restrictions of such a setting must be reflected in the ideal model:

- (Even formally honest) users can misbehave and commit double-spending without being noticed *instantly*. We call these users honest, but misbehaving.
- Double-spending is eventually detected after-the-fact.

In order to accurately define security, these technicalities have to be incorporated into $\mathcal{F}_{\text{apc}}$, which causes the bookkeeping to be more involved.

To ease the upcoming definition of $\mathcal{F}_{\text{apc}}$ we bring forward some properties of the transaction database *TRDB*. In Section 5.1 we show that *TRDB* is a directed forest with labels as described above and prove some invariants. But there we reverse the train of thought, take the definition of $\mathcal{F}_{\text{apc}}$ as a starting point and then prove that $\mathcal{F}_{\text{apc}}$ actually yields a graph with the desired properties. Here, we start from our goal and describe our intention behind the transaction database to enable an intuitive understanding.

A user's wallet is represented by the subgraph of all nodes with the same wallet ID λ and forms a tree inside the forest (see Fig. 4.3). If a new wallet is issued, IssueWallet creates a new entry of the form

$$(\bot, s, \varphi, 0, \lambda, pid_{\mathcal{U}}, pid_{\mathcal{O}}, 0, 0, \omega_{\text{ds}}, \omega_{\text{rc}}, \omega_{\text{pp}}). \tag{4.2}$$

These transactions have no predecessor and are root nodes of new wallets. Therefore, $s^{\text{prev}} = \bot$ and also $p = 0$ holds. Deposit and Disburse extend a tree. The task Disburse clears a wallet's balance and the corresponding entries are leaf nodes of their tree with the restricted form

$$(s^{\text{prev}}, s, \varphi, x, \lambda, pid_{\mathcal{U}}, pid_{\mathcal{O}}, -b^{\text{bill}}, 0, \omega_{\text{ds}}, \omega_{\text{rc}}, \omega_{\text{pp}}) \tag{4.3}$$

Every other task than IssueWallet, Deposit and Disburse does not alter *TRDB* but only queries it.

Unless a user commits double-spending with a wallet the particular subgraph is a linked, linear list. If a user misbehaves and reuses an old wallet state (i.e., there are edges (s^{prev}, s) and (s^{prev}, s')), the corresponding subgraph becomes a directed tree. The counter x equals the depth of a node in a tree and the fraud-detection ID φ is an injective, random function $f_{\Phi} : \mathcal{L} \times \mathbb{N}_0 \to \Phi, (\lambda, x) \mapsto \varphi$ of the pair (λ, x) of wallet ID and counter. If and only if a node is not part of a double-spending, the pair (λ, x) is globally unique and therefore φ. Otherwise, all transaction entries that constitute a double-spending, i.e., all nodes with the same predecessor, share the same counter value x and the same fraud-detection ID φ.

Although the database *TRDB* and the mapping f_{Φ} contains most of the required information, $\mathcal{F}_{\text{apc}}$ stores four more partially defined mappings. $f_{\mathcal{A}_{\mathcal{U}}} : \mathcal{L} \to \mathcal{A}_{\mathcal{U}}$ and $f_{\mathcal{A}_{\mathcal{P}}} : \mathcal{PID}_{\mathcal{P}} \to \mathcal{A}_{\mathcal{P}}$

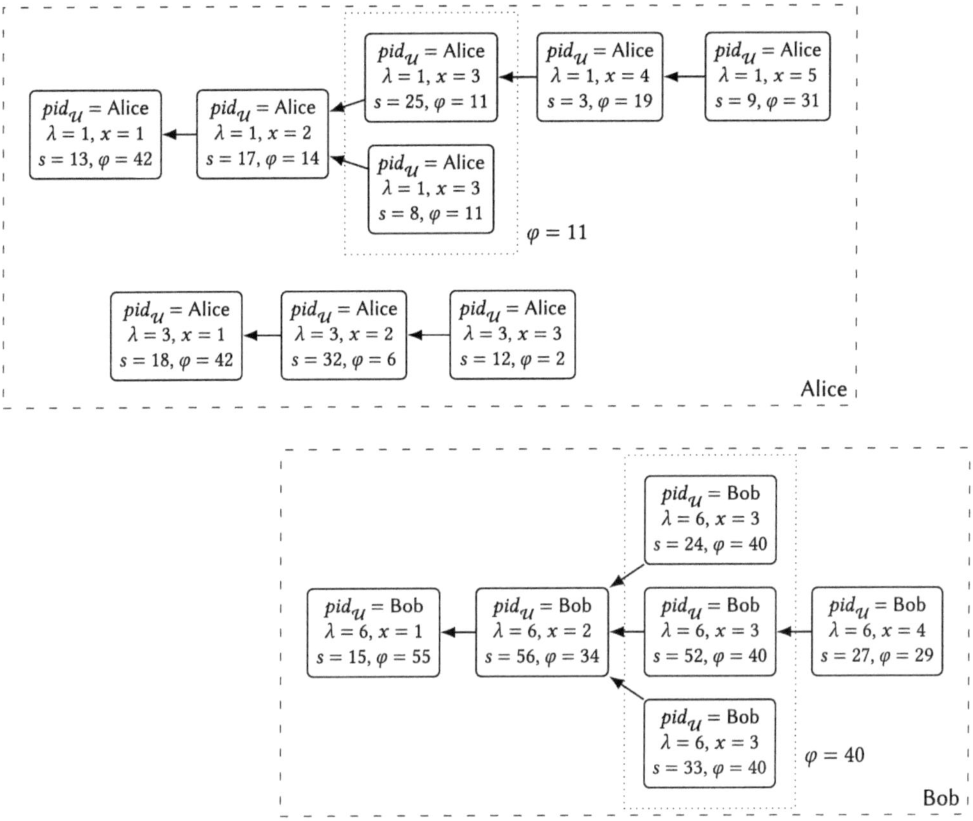

Wallets that belong to the same user a grouped by a dashed line. The serial number s is *globally unique* for a node. Nodes that belong to the same tree (aka wallet) share the same wallet ID λ (here: 1, 3 or 6). The counter x equals the depth of a node. The fraud-detection ID φ is an injective, random function of the pair (λ, x). Unless double-spending occurred, (λ, x) is also *globally unique* and thus φ, too. Nodes that belong to the same double-spending sharing the same fraud-detection ID φ are grouped by a dotted line.

Figure 4.3: The transaction database *TRDB* visualized as a directed forest keeps tracks of parties' attributes by internally storing PoS attributes $a_{\mathcal{P}}$ upon certification and user attributes $a_{\mathcal{U}}$ when a wallet is issued. The mapping f_{π} keeps track of proofs of guilt that are issued or queried in the context of double-spending detection. The already mentioned mapping $f_{\Omega_{\text{bl}}}$ keeps track of blacklisting tags that are generated when a new wallet is issued.

4.1.2 Tags and the Synchronization of State

As already briefly touched in the introduction of this section each transaction is associated to a collection of so-called "tags" that are stored in the transaction database alongside the actual information about the transaction. Their common characteristic is that they serve as a sort of digital receipt and each type of tag goes with one of the utility tasks:

- Double-spending tags $\omega_{\text{ds},i}$ are generated when points are deposited to or disbursed from a wallet and later used by DetectDS to enable the operator to check if users have used the same wallet state repeatedly.
- Prove-participation tags $\omega_{\text{pp},i}$ are generated when points are deposited to a wallet and alter used by ProveParticipation and allow users to prove that they have participated in a particular transaction when they are summoned by the violation enforcer despite being primarily anonymous.
- Recalculation tags $\omega_{\text{rc},i}$ are generated when points are deposited to or disbursed from a wallet and later used by RecalculateBalance to enable the operator to recalculate the balance of a wallet.
- Blacklisting tags $\omega_{\text{bl},i}$ are generated when a new wallet is issued and later used by BlacklistWallet to exclude a particular wallet from further participation in the system.

The same that is being said about the different identifiers in Section 4.1.1 also applies to the tags. In a truly ideal world, none of these tags would be required and $\mathcal{F}_{\text{apc}}$ could be defined without them. For example, in order to prove participation in a particular transaction the user and violation enforcer could simply input the whereabouts of the transaction into $\mathcal{F}_{\text{apc}}$ and $\mathcal{F}_{\text{apc}}$ merely uses its global transaction database to undoubtedly acknowledge (or deny) if such a transaction has been recorded. Similarly, in order to recalculate the balance of a particular wallet, the operator could input the wallet ID λ into $\mathcal{F}_{\text{apc}}$ and $\mathcal{F}_{\text{apc}}$ easily sums over the prices p for all recorded transactions with that wallet ID. Unfortunately, this would be an overly idealized model and could not be realized, at least not by a system in that information is stored in a decentralized way with offline capabilities. In such a system inconsistencies naturally arise. For example, when a user and a PoS have completed a transaction but the PoS has not yet sent the accounting information to the operator, the operator incapable of considering this transaction when a balance needs to be recalculated. These technicalities must be accurately modeled by the ideal functionality to let the security proof go through. An alternative approach instead of using tags is discussed in Section 5.4.1. That section also points out some of the errors in [Nag+20].

We stress, that the ideal model does not stipulate how theses tags look like nor what they encode. These details are left to the eventual realization. From the perspective of $\mathcal{F}_{\text{apc}}$ these tags are treated as opaque bit strings that are "placeholders" to be filled out by the simulator in the security proof. The ideal functionality uses the tags only in so far to "flag" which transaction is known by which party. For $\mathcal{F}_{\text{apc}}$ the global transaction database *TRDB* is the only authoritative source of information.

Typically, the tags are only passed through as output to a party and later re-input. This raises the problem that the environment can also input tags which have never been output by any task of the ideal functionality before but are made-up by the environment. We coin the following terms.

Definition 4.1 (Genuine vs. Fake Tags) *If a tag is input to a task of $\mathcal{F}_{\text{apc}}$ by any party and the tag has been output before, we call it a* genuine *tag. A tag that is not genuine is called a* fake *tag.*

Skipping ahead to the definition of all tasks of $\mathcal{F}_{\text{apc}}$ a tag is genuine, if and only if it is recorded in *TRDB* (in case of ω_{ds}, ω_{pp}, ω_{rc}) or if $f_{\Omega_{\text{bl}}}^{-1}(\omega_{\text{bl}})$ is defined (in case of ω_{bl}). In other words, all tasks of $\mathcal{F}_{\text{apc}}$ are defined such that they never output a tag without recording it in the internal state.

4.2 Setup Tasks

To set up the system two things are required: All parties—the dispute resolver, operator, PoS and users—have to register to be able to participate in the toll collection system. As all of these registration tasks are similar, we will not describe them separately. In addition, PoSes needs to be certified by the operator.

4.2.1 Registrations

The tasks of RegisterDR, RegisterOp, RegisterPOS and RegisterUser (cp. Figs. 4.4 to 4.7) are straightforward and analogous. Upon invocation by the respective party through the input `register`, these tasks notify the adversary about the registration. This model that the information whether a particular party participates in the system is public. In case of the operator, the respective task additionally receives an attribute vector a_O which defines the PoS-attributes

Functionality $\mathcal{F}_{\text{apc}}$ (cont.) – Task RegisterDR

Dispute resolver input: (`register`)

(1) Leak (`registering_dr`, pid_{DR}) to the adversary.

Dispute resolver output: (`registered`)

Figure 4.4: The Functionality $\mathcal{F}_{\text{apc}}$ (cont. from Fig. 4.1) – Task RegisterDR

Functionality $\mathcal{F}_{\text{apc}}$ (cont.) – Task RegisterOp

Operator input: (`register`, $a_{\mathcal{O}}$)

(1) Leak (`registering_op`, $pid_{\mathcal{O}}, a_{\mathcal{O}}$) to the adversary.

(2) If $f_{\mathcal{A}_{\mathcal{P}}}(pid_{\mathcal{O}})$ is undefined, set $f_{\mathcal{A}_{\mathcal{P}}}(pid_{\mathcal{O}}) := a_{\mathcal{O}}$.

Operator output: (`registered`)

Figure 4.5: The Functionality $\mathcal{F}_{\text{apc}}$ (cont. from Fig. 4.1) – Task RegisterOp

Functionality $\mathcal{F}_{\text{apc}}$ (cont.) – Task RegisterPOS

PoS input: (`register`)

(1) Leak (`registering_pos`, $pid_{\mathcal{P}}$) to the adversary.

PoS output: (`registered`)

Figure 4.6: The Functionality $\mathcal{F}_{\text{apc}}$ (cont. from Fig. 4.1) – Task RegisterPOS

Functionality $\mathcal{F}_{\text{apc}}$ (cont.) – Task RegisterUser

User input: (`register`)

(1) Leak (`registering_user`, $pid_{\mathcal{U}}$) to the adversary.

User output: (`registered`)

Figure 4.7: The Functionality $\mathcal{F}_{\text{apc}}$ (cont. from Fig. 4.1) – Task RegisterUser

Functionality $\mathcal{F}_{\text{apc}}$ (cont.) – Task CertifyPOS

PoS input: (certify_pos)

(1) If RegisterOp or RegisterPOS have not yet been run, output $\perp$ and abort.

Operator output: $(\texttt{certifying\_pos}, pid_{\mathcal{P}})$

Operator input: $(\texttt{certifying\_pos}, a_{\mathcal{P}})$

(2) Leak $(\texttt{certifying\_pos}, pid_{\mathcal{P}}, a_{\mathcal{P}})$ to the adversary.

(3) Set $f_{\mathcal{A}_{\mathcal{P}}}(pid_{\mathcal{P}}) := a_{\mathcal{P}}$.

PoS output: $(\texttt{certified\_pos}, a_{\mathcal{P}})$

Operator output: (certified_pos)

Figure 4.8: The Functionality $\mathcal{F}_{\text{apc}}$ (cont. from Fig. 4.1) – Task CertifyPOS

that are used by the operator when acting like a PoS, for example in the tasks IssueWallet and Disburse. For a discussion of the attributes see Section 2.4.

4.2.2 Point-of-Sale Certification

CertifyPOS (cp. Fig. 4.8) is a two-party task between the operator and an PoS in which the PoS is assigned an attribute vector $a_{\mathcal{P}}$. Again, we refer to Section 2.4 for a discussion on these attributes. The attribute vector $a_{\mathcal{P}}$ is chosen by the operator after it has learned the PoS' identity, while the PoS only inputs its desire to be certified. $\mathcal{F}_{\text{apc}}$ (re-)defines the partial mapping $f_{\mathcal{A}_{\mathcal{P}}}(pid_{\mathcal{P}}) := a_{\mathcal{P}}$ which internally stores all PoS attributes. The identity $pid_{\mathcal{P}}$ and attributes $a_{\mathcal{P}}$ are leaked to the adversary before the attributes are output to the PoS.

Please note, that the proposed definition of CertifyPOS is extremely simple and enables effects that are probably undesirable in a real-world application. In order to model re-certification of a PoS $\mathcal{F}_{\text{apc}}$ allows to overwrite $f_{\mathcal{A}_{\mathcal{P}}}$ and thereby annihilate a previous version of the attributes. Skipping ahead, let's assume that the number of points a user gains in Deposit depends on $f_{\mathcal{A}_{\mathcal{P}}}$. Further assume that the balance of a user's wallet is recalculated by the operator at some later point of time and that the PoS' attributes have been changed in the meantime. In this case the re-calculated balance and the balance that is stored in the wallet won't match. This is even true, if all parties have been honest.

To remedy this problem in the ideal model, we would need to introduce a sequence of "versions" of $f^{\xi}_{\mathcal{A}_{\mathcal{P}}}$ for a version counter ξ and log the temporal order of all transactions, i.e. equip each transaction with ξ to indicate which version has been in effect at the time of the transaction. This would complicate the ideal functionality even more. Also note, that a secure realization would be quite involved, too. It would not suffice, if the operator locally stored a history of all past certifications, because a malicious operator had the power to lie about it. If a consistent re-calculation of the balance under intermittently changing attributes was one of the security properties, a secure realization would at least require that the attributes are irreversible logged in a publicly verifiable way, before they become effective. To keep matters simple, we ignore this problem.

4.3 Main Tasks

Now we describe the main tasks one would expect from any anonymous point collection system: IssueWallet, Deposit and Disburse. As mentioned before, these are the only tasks in which transaction entries are created.

4.3.1 Wallet Issuing

IssueWallet (cp. Fig. 4.9) is a two-party task between a user and the operator in which a new wallet is created for the user. After the operator has learned the user's identity, the operator inputs an attribute vector $a_{\mathcal{U}}$. The operator is free to abort at this point, if users shall not obtain a new wallet, e.g. because they have been identified as fraudsters in a previous run of DetectDS. First, $\mathcal{F}_{\text{apc}}$ randomly picks a (previously unused) serial number s for the new transaction entry *trdb*. A new wallet ID λ and fraud-detection ID φ are uniquely and randomly picked, unless the user is corrupted in which case the adversary chooses φ. This may infringe upon the unlinkability of the user's transactions and we do not give any privacy guarantees for corrupted users. Finally, a transaction entry

$$trdb := (\bot, s, \varphi, 0, \lambda, pid_{\mathcal{U}}, pid_{\mathcal{O}}, 0, 0, \bot, \bot, \bot) \tag{4.4}$$

corresponding to the new wallet is stored in *TRDB* and the wallet's attributes $f_{\mathcal{A}_{\mathcal{U}}}(\lambda) := a_{\mathcal{U}}$ are appended to the partial mapping $f_{\mathcal{A}_{\mathcal{U}}}$. $\mathcal{F}_{\text{apc}}$ asks the adversary to provide a blacklisting tag ω_{bl} which internally recorded as being associated to the wallet through the partial mapping $f_{\Omega_{\text{bl}}}$. The blacklisting tag is re-used in the utility task BlacklistWallet. Both parties get the serial number s as output. The user also receives the attribute vector $a_{\mathcal{U}}$ to check out-of-band that it has been assigned correctly and more importantly does not contain any identifying information. The operator receives the blacklisting tag ω_{bl}.

We stress that $\mathcal{F}_{\text{apc}}$ does not really use the blacklisting tag ω_{bl}, but only passes it through. For a discussion of the tags see Section 4.1.2.

Functionality $\mathcal{F}_{\text{apc}}$ (cont.) – Task IssueWallet

User input: (`issue_wallet`)

(1) If RegisterOp, RegisterUser or RegisterDR have not yet been run, output $\bot$ and abort.

Operator output: (`issuing_wallet`, $pid_{\mathcal{U}}$)
Operator input: (`issuing_wallet`, $a_{\mathcal{U}}$)

(2) Pick serial number $s \xleftarrow{R} S$ and wallet ID $\lambda \xleftarrow{R} \mathcal{L}$ that has not previously been used.
(3) If $pid_{\mathcal{U}} \in \mathcal{PID}_{\text{corr}}$ or $pid_{\mathcal{O}} \in \mathcal{PID}_{\text{corr}}$, leak (`issuing_wallet`, $s, a_{\mathcal{U}}$) to the adversary.[a]
(4) Pick fraud-detection ID $\varphi \xleftarrow{R} \Phi$ that has not previously been used, or—if $pid_{\mathcal{U}} \in \mathcal{PID}_{\text{corr}}$—leak (`issuing_wallet`) to the adversary and ask for fraud-detection ID φ that has not previously been used.[b]
(5) Append $f_{\Phi}(\lambda, 0) := \varphi$ to f_{Φ}.
(6) Leak (`issuing_wallet`) to the adversary and ask for a blacklisting tag ω_{bl} that has not previously been used.
(7) Append $trdb := (\bot, s, \varphi, 0, \lambda, pid_{\mathcal{U}}, pid_{\mathcal{O}}, 0, 0, \bot, \bot, \bot)$ to $TRDB$
(8) Set $f_{\mathcal{A}_{\mathcal{U}}}(\lambda) := a_{\mathcal{U}}$.
(9) Set $f_{\Omega_{\text{bl}}}(\lambda) := \omega_{\text{bl}}$.

User output: (`issued_wallet`, $s, a_{\mathcal{U}}$)
Operator output: (`issued_wallet`, s, ω_{bl})

[a] N.b., this leakage does not weaken the "actual" security at all. The serial number s is output to both parties (see below), and the attribute vector $a_{\mathcal{U}}$ is input by the operator and output to the user. Hence, if any of these parties is corrupted, the adversary learns this information anyway. This early leakage ahead of time is only a concession to the final implementation to enable the simulation of messages in the correct order.

[b] Picking the upcoming fraud-detection IDs randomly asserts untrackability for honest users. For corrupted users, we do not (and cannot) provide such a guarantee and the fraud-detection ID might be chosen adversarially (cp. text body).

Figure 4.9: The Functionality $\mathcal{F}_{\text{apc}}$ (cont. from Fig. 4.1) – Task IssueWallet

4.3.2 Deposition

This two-party task (cp. Figs. 4.10 and 4.11) is conducted whenever a user interacts with a PoS and serves the main purpose of depositing points on a user's wallet.

This task is by far the most complicated and it is not straightforward to see why it captures a sane definition of security. For the ease of presentation, we first describe the behavior of $\mathcal{F}_{\text{apc}}$ in the completely honest case without misbehaving, i.e. all parties (user, PoS and operator) are honest, and the user is neither blacklisted nor commits double-spending. After that we describe the restrictions and conditional branches of code which are required to obtain a definition that is actually realizable under corruption in our setting. Please note, although the operator seems not to be immediately involved in the task Deposit as a participating party, the definition still depends on the corruption status of the operator. Remember that within a single instantiation of $\mathcal{F}_{\text{apc}}$ polynomial many parties can interact within polynomial many tasks and thus the operator is implicitly involved. This has been one of the oversights in [Nag+20].

To start a deposition of points, users input a serial number s^{prev}, indicating which past wallet state they wish to use and the identity of the PoS they want to interact with. Of course, well-behaving users always use the most recent state of a wallet. The participating PoS in turn inputs a blacklist bl_{Φ} of fraud-detection IDs.

Firstly, $\mathcal{F}_{\text{apc}}$ looks up if a wallet state $trdb^{\text{prev}}$ in $TRDB$ corresponds to the provided serial number s^{prev} and belongs to the correct user with PID $pid_{\mathcal{U}}$. This guarantees that users can only deposit points on a wallet which has been legitimately issued to them. The ideal functionality uses part of the information from the previous wallet state

$$trdb^{\text{prev}} = (\cdot, s^{\text{prev}}, \varphi^{\text{prev}}, x^{\text{prev}}, \lambda^{\text{prev}}, pid_{\mathcal{U}}, pid_{\mathcal{P}}^{\text{prev}}, \cdot, b^{\text{prev}}, \cdot, \cdot, \cdot) \tag{4.5}$$

to determine those parts of the new transaction entry $trdb$ which remain constant for transactions within the same wallet. $\mathcal{F}_{\text{apc}}$ randomly picks a fresh serial number s for the upcoming transaction, the user PID $pid_{\mathcal{U}}$ and wallet ID λ stay the same, $pid_{\mathcal{P}}$ is set to the identity of the participating PoS and the transaction counter ($x := x^{\text{prev}} + 1$) is increased by one. In the completely honest case without misbehaving, the map $f_{\Phi}(\lambda, x)$ is always undefined (cp. Step 6 in Fig. 4.10). $\mathcal{F}_{\text{apc}}$ ties a fresh, uniformly and independently drawn fraud-detection ID $((\lambda, x) \mapsto \varphi)$ to the x'th transaction of the wallet λ. This fraud-detection ID φ is checked against the blacklist bl_{Φ}. Note, that the probability to blacklist a freshly drawn fraud-detection ID is negligible. Moreover, $\mathcal{F}_{\text{apc}}$ looks up the user's attributes bound to this particular wallet ($a_{\mathcal{U}} := f_{\mathcal{A}_{\mathcal{U}}}(\lambda)$) and the attributes of the current and previous PoS ($a_{\mathcal{P}} := f_{\mathcal{A}_{\mathcal{P}}}(pid_{\mathcal{P}})$, $a_{\mathcal{P}}^{\text{prev}} := f_{\mathcal{A}_{\mathcal{P}}}(pid_{\mathcal{P}}^{\text{prev}})$). The current serial number s, the current fraud-detection ID φ together with the attributes of the user and the previous PoS are output to the PoS which chooses the price p of this transaction. We refer the reader to Section 2.4 for a justification why the PoS chooses the price unilaterally.

Functionality $\mathcal{F}_{\text{apc}}$ (cont.) – Task Deposit, **Part 1**

User input: ($\texttt{deposit}, s^{\text{prev}}, pid_{\mathcal{P}}$)

(1) If RegisterOp or RegisterPOS have not yet been run, output $\perp$ and abort.

(2) Select $(\cdot, s^{\text{prev}}, \varphi^{\text{prev}}, x^{\text{prev}}, \lambda^{\text{prev}}, pid_{\mathcal{U}}, pid_{\mathcal{P}}^{\text{prev}}, \cdot, b^{\text{prev}}, \cdot, \cdot, \cdot) \in TRDB$ with $(s^{\text{prev}}, pid_{\mathcal{U}})$ being the uniqe key.$^{\perp}$

PoS output: ($\texttt{depositing}$)

PoS input: ($\texttt{depositing}, bl_{\Phi}$)

(3) Pick serial number $s \stackrel{R}{\leftarrow} S$ that has not previously been used.

(4) If $pid_{\mathcal{U}} \in \mathcal{PID}_{\text{corr}}$ or $pid_{\mathcal{P}} \in \mathcal{PID}_{\text{corr}}$, leak ($\texttt{depositing}, s, a_{\mathcal{U}}$) to the adversary.[a]

(5) Set $\lambda := \lambda^{\text{prev}}$ and $x := x^{\text{prev}} + 1$.

(6) If $f_{\Phi}(\lambda, x)$ is already defined:

  (a) Set $\varphi := f_{\Phi}(\lambda, x)$.

  (b) Leak ($\texttt{depositing}, pid_{\mathcal{U}}, \Omega_{\text{ds}}^{\varphi}$) with $\Omega_{\text{ds}}^{\varphi} := \{\omega_{\text{ds}}^{\varphi} \mid (\cdot, \cdot, \varphi, \cdot, \cdot, \cdot, \cdot, \cdot, \cdot, \omega_{\text{ds}}^{\varphi}, \cdot, \cdot) \in TRDB\}$ to the adversary[b] and ask for a proof of guilt $\pi \in \Pi$ for that $f_{\pi}(pid_{\mathcal{U}}, \pi) = \texttt{NOK}$ has not yet been defined.

  (c) Set $f_{\pi}(pid_{\mathcal{U}}, \pi) = \texttt{OK}$.

Else:

  (a) Pick fraud-detection ID $\varphi \stackrel{R}{\leftarrow} \Phi$ that has not previously been used, or—if $pid_{\mathcal{U}} \in \mathcal{PID}_{\text{corr}}$—leak ($\texttt{depositing}$) to the adversary and ask for fraud-detection ID φ that has not previously been used.[c]

  (b) Append $f_{\Phi}(\lambda, x) := \varphi$ to f_{Φ}.

(7) If $\varphi \in bl_{\Phi}$, output $\texttt{blacklisted\_wallet}$ to both parties and abort.

(8) Set $a_{\mathcal{U}} := f_{\mathcal{A}_{\mathcal{U}}}(\lambda)$, $a_{\mathcal{P}} := f_{\mathcal{A}_{\mathcal{P}}}(pid_{\mathcal{P}})$, and $a_{\mathcal{P}}^{\text{prev}} := f_{\mathcal{A}_{\mathcal{P}}}(pid_{\mathcal{P}}^{\text{prev}})$.$^{\perp}$

PoS output: ($\texttt{depositing}, s, a_{\mathcal{U}}, a_{\mathcal{P}}^{\text{prev}}$)

$^{\perp}$ If this does not exist, abort.

[a] N.b., this leakage does not weaken the "actual" security at all. The serial number s is output to both parties (see below), and the attribute vector $a_{\mathcal{U}}$ is input by the operator and output to the user. Hence, if any of these parties is corrupted, the adversary learns this information anyway. This early leakage ahead of time is only a concession to the final implementation to enable the simulation of messages in the correct order.

[b] This unveils the user's identity, but we do not guarantee that for double-spenders (cp. text body).

[c] Picking the upcoming fraud-detection IDs randomly asserts untrackability for honest users. For corrupted users, we do not (and cannot) provide such a guarantee and the fraud-detection ID might be chosen adversarially (cp. text body).

Figure 4.10: The Functionality $\mathcal{F}_{\text{apc}}$ (cont. from Fig. 4.1) – Task Deposit, Part 1

Functionality $\mathcal{F}_{\text{apc}}$ (cont.) – Task Deposit**, Part 2**

PoS input: $(\texttt{depositing}, p)$

(9) $b := b^{\text{prev}} + p$.

(10) If $O \notin \mathcal{PID}_{\text{corr}}$, leak $(\texttt{depositing}, s, \varphi, pid_{\mathcal{P}})$ to the adversary,[a] else leak $(\texttt{depositing}, s, \varphi, pid_{\mathcal{P}}, p)$ to the adversary,[b] and (in both cases) ask for tags $(\omega_{\text{ds}}, \omega_{\text{rc}}, \omega_{\text{pp}})$ that have not previously been used, or—if $pid_{\mathcal{P}} \in \mathcal{PID}_{\text{corr}}$—also accept a non-unique ω_{ds}.[c]

(11) Append $(s^{\text{prev}}, s, \varphi, x, \lambda, pid_{\mathcal{U}}, pid_{\mathcal{P}}, p, b, \omega_{\text{ds}}, \omega_{\text{rc}}, \omega_{\text{pp}})$ to *TRDB*.

User output: $(\texttt{deposited}, s, a_{\mathcal{P}}, p, b, \omega_{\text{pp}})$

PoS output: $(\texttt{deposited}, \omega_{\text{ds}}, \omega_{\text{rc}}, \omega_{\text{pp}})$

[a] N.b., for honest users φ is a mere random number. The identity of the PoS cannot remain secret, because even an honest user might eventually be asked by the violation enforcer to prove its participation in this transaction.

[b] N.b., the corrupted operator eventually collects all recalculation tags and thus the adversary learns the price.

[c] If the PoS is corrupted, we cannot guarantee double-spending detection.

Figure 4.11: The Functionality $\mathcal{F}_{\text{apc}}$ (cont. from Fig. 4.1) – Task Deposit, Part 2

The new balance b is calculated and the adversary is asked to provide a double-spending tag ω_{ds}, a recalculation tag ω_{rc} and a prove-participation tag ω_{pp}. These tags may depend on the current serial number s, the current fraud-detection ID φ and the identity of the involved PoS $pid_{\mathcal{P}}$. We stress that both IDs (s, φ) have been freshly and uniformly drawn and thus do not unveil anything useful information-theoretically. Finally, the new transaction record *trdb* is stored in *TRDB*. Note that all information leading to the new wallet state except for the price p and the tags $(\omega_{\text{ds}}, \omega_{\text{rc}}, \omega_{\text{pp}})$ came from data internally stored in $\mathcal{F}_{\text{apc}}$ itself and can therefore not be compromised. The serial number s, the current PoS' attributes $a_{\mathcal{P}}$, the price p and the updated balance b are output to the users so they may check they received the expected amount of points. As before, $\mathcal{F}_{\text{apc}}$ does not really use the tags, but only records and outputs them again. For a discussion of the tags see Section 4.1.2.

We now discuss the omitted cases of the task Deposit, which deal with corruption or misbehavior.

If in Step 6 the map $f_{\Phi}(\lambda, x)$ is undefined as above, but the user is corrupted, the fraud-detection ID φ is not independently and uniformly drawn, but chosen adversarially. Similar to the task IssueWallet (cp. Section 4.3.1), this may infringe upon the unlinkability of the user's transactions. But we do not give any such guarantees for corrupted users. Also, this may lead to a premature abort (cp. Step 7), if the adversary chooses a $\varphi \in bl_{\Phi}$ which is blacklisted.

In Step 6 the map $f_\Phi(\lambda, x)$ will be defined, if the user commits double-spending or if fraud-detection IDs have been precalculated and prefilled for blacklisting purposes (cp. Section 4.4.2). Remember, the wallet ID λ and transaction counter x corresponds to the tree and depth of a transaction node. In this, case $\mathcal{F}_{\text{apc}}$ assigns the same fraud-detection ID φ to the current transaction record in order to preserve consistency. Also, the set of all previous double-spending tags $\Omega_{\text{ds}}^{\varphi}$ which have been recorded for transactions of the same wallet and transaction counter together with the user's identity are leaked to the adversary. The adversary replies with a proof of guilt π which is internally recorded by $\mathcal{F}_{\text{apc}}$.

The latter two steps fix an oversight in [Nag+20]. To understand them we need to skip ahead. The proof of guilt π is some kind of digital "evidence" which allows the operator to prove to any other party that the particular user is a fraudster and has committed double-spending. To enforce soundness, consistency and protection against false accusation of innocent users, $\mathcal{F}_{\text{apc}}$ internally manages the map f_π which records pairs of user identities and proofs of guilt. Usually, these proofs of guilt are not directly obtained via Deposit in case of a double-spending, but their generation is deferred to the utility task DetectDS (cp. Section 4.4.1). The validity of the proofs of guilt can be checked by any party using VerifyGuilt (cp. Section 4.4.1). This three-step approach is necessary, because misbehaving users might commit double-spending at different PoSes which are offline and only after these PoSes have synchronized their state with the operator, the operator is actually capable of detecting double-spending later. However, in a real implementation (at least in our implementation) the environment which guides all parties can create a valid proof of guilt as soon as a (even honest) user has committed double-spending. The environment simply runs the real code of DetectDS in its own head without actual calling DetectDS. The proof of guilt is perfectly valid and does not contradict the protection against false accusation (because the user has indeed committed double-spending), but has nevertheless not been output by DetectDS. On a high-level the environment can do so, because it instantly knows which users commit double-spending and does not depend on a periodically synchronization of information. To enable consistent replies by VerifyGuilt for these yet valid and legitimate but not system-generated proofs, $\mathcal{F}_{\text{apc}}$ also needs to generate such a proof of guilt at the very moment when double-spending occurs. We stress that (1) this proof is not being output but only kept internally (direct output would preclude offline capabilities) and (2) misbehaving users immediately loose their anonymity as soon as they commit double-spending and not until DetectDS is invoked. This has been overlooked in [Nag+20] as the synchronization of state has not formally been defined but explained on a hand-waving level.

Lastly, if the operator is corrupted $\mathcal{F}_{\text{apc}}$ will not only leak $(s, \varphi, pid_{\mathcal{P}})$ to the adversary but also the price p (cp. Step 10 in Fig. 4.11). Opposed to the leakage of the random numbers s,

φ, this might lead to an actual loss of unlinkability,[2] but it is the best we can hope for, if the operator is corrupted. Although we do not stipulate how a recalculation tag ω_{rc} looks like, because this is specific to the implementation, the recalculation tag enables the operator to recalculate the balance of a wallet, i.e. it acts like a digital invoice (see also RecalculateBalance in Section 4.4.3). Hence, it is quite reasonable that this tag encodes the price of a transaction among other things. If the operator is corrupted, the price cannot be kept secret from the adversary. Admittedly, the additional leakage of the price is a rather small detail, but again, has been overlooked in [Nag+20] as the synchronization of state has not spelled out and thus has not been part of the simulation-based proof.

4.3.3 Disbursement

As Disburse (cp. Fig. 4.12) is very similar to the task of Deposit, we will refrain from describing it again in full detail but rather just highlight the differences to Deposit.

Please remind, that Disburse is designed with the post-payment scenario from Section 2.3.3 in mind. In other words, disbursement of points means to clear the recent balance and invalidate the wallet. Alternative definitions are discussed below.

The first difference is that it is conducted with the operator rather than an PoS and no blacklist is taken as input as we do not want to prevent any user from clearing the balance. Disburse is identifying for the users to allow the operator to invoice them and check if they (physically) pay the correct amount. Also, the users do not obtain a new serial number as part of their output, because the transaction entry is supposed to be a leaf node. Nonetheless, a serial number is internally drawn and associated with the transaction. Instead of obtaining a price from the operator the recent balance is used and the price $p := -b^{\mathrm{bill}}$ is part of the output to the operator. The prove-participation tag is omitted, but double-spending tag and recalculation tag are still kept, because Disburse is identifying for the user and hence there is no point in a separate prove-participation tag. Also note, that the leakage to the adversary is asymmetric to the leakage in Deposit and does not consider an extra case for a corrupted operator, because the operator directly participates in Disburse and learns the current price $p = -b^{\mathrm{bill}}$ as part of the output (cp. Step 7 in Fig. 4.12 vs. Step 10 in Fig. 4.11).

Alternative Definitions To realize the other scenarios from Sections 2.3.1 to 2.3.3 Disburse could be modified in several aspects. Each of these options make Disburse more similar to Deposit:

---

[2] Of course, this depends on the pricing model. If there is only a single, constant price, the additional leakage does not bear any information.

Functionality $\mathcal{F}_{\text{apc}}$ (cont.) – Task Disburse

User input: ($\texttt{disburse}, s^{\text{prev}}$)

(1) If RegisterOp has not yet been run, output $\bot$ and abort.

(2) Select $(\cdot, s^{\text{prev}}, \varphi^{\text{prev}}, x^{\text{prev}}, \lambda^{\text{prev}}, pid_{\mathcal{U}}, pid_{\mathcal{P}}^{\text{prev}}, \cdot, b^{\text{prev}}, \cdot, \cdot, \cdot) \in \mathit{TRDB}$ with $(s^{\text{prev}}, pid_{\mathcal{U}})$ being the unique key.[⊥]

Operator output: ($\texttt{disbursing}, pid_{\mathcal{U}}$)

Operator input: ($\texttt{disbursing}$)

(3) Pick serial number $s \xleftarrow{R} S$ that has not previously been used.

(4) Set $\lambda := \lambda^{\text{prev}}$ and $x := x^{\text{prev}} + 1$.

(5) If $f_{\Phi}(\lambda, x)$ is already defined:

  (a) Set $\varphi := f_{\Phi}(\lambda,x)$.

  (b) Leak ($\texttt{disbursing}, pid_{\mathcal{U}}, \Omega_{\text{ds}}^{\varphi}$) with $\Omega_{\text{ds}}^{\varphi} := \{\omega_{\text{ds}}^{\varphi} \mid (\cdot, \cdot, \varphi, \cdot, \cdot, \cdot, \cdot, \cdot, \cdot, \omega_{\text{ds}}^{\varphi}, \cdot, \cdot) \in \mathit{TRDB}\}$ to the adversary[a] and ask for a proof of guilt $\pi \in \Pi$ for that $f_{\pi}(pid_{\mathcal{U}}, \pi) = \mathsf{NOK}$ has not yet been defined.

  (c) Set $f_{\pi}(pid_{\mathcal{U}}, \pi) = \mathsf{OK}$.

Else:

  (a) Pick fraud-detection ID $\varphi \xleftarrow{R} \Phi$ that has not previously been used, or—if $pid_{\mathcal{U}} \in \mathcal{PID}_{\text{corr}}$—leak ($\texttt{disbursing}$) to the adversary and ask for fraud-detection ID φ that has not previously been used.[b]

  (b) Append $f_{\Phi}(\lambda, x) := \varphi$ to f_{Φ}.

(6) $b^{\text{bill}} := b^{\text{prev}}$.

(7) Leak ($\texttt{disbursing}, s, \varphi$) to the adversary[c] and ask for tags $(\omega_{\text{ds}}, \omega_{\text{rc}})$ that have not previously been used, or—if $pid_{\mathcal{O}} \in \mathcal{PID}_{\text{corr}}$—also accept a non-unique ω_{ds}.[d]

(8) Append $(s^{\text{prev}}, s, \varphi, x, \lambda, pid_{\mathcal{U}}, pid_{\mathcal{O}}, -b^{\text{bill}}, 0, \omega_{\text{ds}}, \omega_{\text{rc}}, \bot)$ to TRDB.

User output: ($\texttt{disbursed}, b^{\text{bill}}$)

Operator output: ($\texttt{disbursed}, b^{\text{bill}}, \omega_{\text{ds}}, \omega_{\text{rc}}$)

⊥ If this does not exist, abort.

a Leaking previous double-spending tags of sibling nodes is a concession to enable consistent simulation. This may infringe on a user's privacy, but we do not guarantee that for double-spenders (cp. text body).

b Picking the upcoming fraud-detection IDs randomly asserts untrackability for honest users. For corrupted users, we do not (and cannot) provide such a guarantee and the fraud-detection ID might be chosen adversarially (cp. text body).

c N.b., for honest users φ is a mere random number. Also the leakage here is asymmetric to Deposit, because the operator itself participates in this task.

d If the operator is corrupted, we cannot guarantee double-spending detection.

Figure 4.12: The Functionality $\mathcal{F}_{\text{apc}}$ (cont. from Fig. 4.1) – Task Disburse

(1) Disburse could also be executed with a PoS.

(2) Instead of being identifying for the user, only the user's attributes could be output to the operator/PoS. Surely, in this case the blacklist should again be re-included into the input and checked. Also, the prove-participation tag is required again.

(3) Instead of using the previous balance as the new price, the price could be determined by the operator/PoS the same way as in Disburse. In this case the next item also needs to be considered.

(4) To ensure that the wallet is not overdrawn, the previous balance is output to the operator/PoS before the operator/PoS inputs the price and the operator/PoS aborts, if the previous balance is no sufficiently high. Alternatively, $\mathcal{F}_{\text{apc}}$ internally checks that the balance is high enough after operator/PoS has input the price and outputs a special error message to both parties. However, this requires costly range proofs [CLZ12; CCs08] in the implementation (cp. Section 6.2.7).

4.4 Utility Tasks

To obtain a feature complete anonymous point collection system we also provide the utility tasks DetectDS, VerifyGuilt, BlacklistWallet and ProveParticipation. All of those tasks deal with different aspects arising from fraudulent user behavior.

4.4.1 Double-Spending Detection and Guilt Verification

Due to our requirement to allow offline PoSes, misbehaving users are able to fraudulently deposit points on outdated states of their wallets. This double-spending cannot be prevented but must be detected afterwards. To ensure this, $\mathcal{F}_{\text{apc}}$ provides the tasks DetectDS (cp. Fig. 4.13) and VerifyGuilt (cp. Fig. 4.14).

DetectDS is a one-party task executed by the operator and takes two double-spending tags ω_{ds}, ω'_{ds} as input. Again, we first describe the case in which all parties are honest and in which the environment only inputs genuine double-spending tags, i.e. tags that have been output by Deposit or Disburse before (cp. Definition 4.1).

First $\mathcal{F}_{\text{apc}}$ looks up the corresponding transaction nodes *trdb*, *trdb'*. These exist, because ω_{ds}, ω'_{ds} are genuine. The condition in Step 2 in Fig. 4.13 simplifies to the question whether the fraud-detection IDs φ, φ' match or not. If they are not equal, the given double-spending tags do not belong to transactions that have a common predecessor, in other words the double-spending tags do not attest double-spending. In this case the adversary is asked for a user identity $pid_{\mathcal{U}}$, a proof of guilt π and a result bit *result*. However, the result bit it not used at

Functionality $\mathcal{F}_{\text{apc}}$ (cont.) – Task DetectDS

Operator input: (detect_ds, $\omega_{\text{ds}}, \omega'_{\text{ds}}$)

(1) Pick $trdb \neq trdb'$ in $TRDB$ such that $trdb = (\cdot, \cdot, \varphi, \cdot, \cdot, pid_{\mathcal{U}}, pid_{\mathcal{P}}, \cdot, \cdot, \omega_{\text{ds}}, \cdot, \cdot)$ and $trdb' = (\cdot, \cdot, \varphi', \cdot, \cdot, pid'_{\mathcal{U}}, pid'_{\mathcal{P}}, \cdot, \cdot, \omega'_{\text{ds}}, \cdot, \cdot)$.
If no record $trdb, trdb' \in TRDB$ for $\omega_{\text{ds}}, \omega'_{\text{ds}}$, resp., exists or $\omega_{\text{ds}} = \omega'_{\text{ds}}$, set $trdb := trdb' := \bot$.

(2) If $trdb = \bot$ or $trdb' = \bot$ or $\varphi \neq \varphi'$:
  (a) Leak (detecting_ds, $\omega_{\text{ds}}, \omega'_{\text{ds}}$) to the adversary and obtain $(pid_{\mathcal{U}}, \pi, result)$.
  (b) If $f_\pi(pid_{\mathcal{U}}, \pi)$ has already been defined, do nothing, else if $f_\pi(pid_{\mathcal{U}}, \pi)$ is undefined and $pid_{\mathcal{U}} \in \mathcal{PID}_{\text{corr}}$, set $f_\pi(pid_{\mathcal{U}}, \pi) := result$, else overwrite $(pid_{\mathcal{U}}, \pi) := (\bot, \bot)$.

  Else (i.e. distinct $trdb, trdb'$ exist and $\varphi = \varphi'$ holds):
  (a) Leak (detecting_ds, $pid_{\mathcal{U}}$) to the adversary[a] and ask for a proof $\pi \neq \bot$ for that $f_\pi(pid_{\mathcal{U}}, \pi) =$ NOK has not yet be defined previously.
  (b) Set $f_\pi(pid_{\mathcal{U}}, \pi) :=$ OK.

Operator output: (detected_ds, $pid_{\mathcal{U}}, \pi$)

[a] N.b., $pid_{\mathcal{U}} = pid'_{\mathcal{U}}$ holds.

Figure 4.13: The Functionality $\mathcal{F}_{\text{apc}}$ (cont. from Fig. 4.1) – Task DetectDS

Functionality $\mathcal{F}_{\text{apc}}$ (cont.) – Task VerifyGuilt

Party input: (verify_guilt, $pid_{\mathcal{U}}, \pi$)

(1) If $f_\pi(pid_{\mathcal{U}}, \pi)$ is defined, then set $result := f_\pi(pid_{\mathcal{U}}, \pi)$.
(2) If $f_\pi(pid_{\mathcal{U}}, \pi)$ is not defined and $pid_{\mathcal{U}} \in \mathcal{PID}_{\text{corr}}$, then leak (verifying_guilt, $pid_{\mathcal{U}}, \pi$) to the adversary and obtain result *result*.
(3) In any other case, set $result :=$ NOK.
(4) Append $(pid_{\mathcal{U}}, \pi) \mapsto result$ to f_π.

Party output: (verified_guilt, *result*)

Figure 4.14: The Functionality $\mathcal{F}_{\text{apc}}$ (cont. from Fig. 4.1) – Task VerifyGuilt all, but $\mathcal{F}_{\text{apc}}$ unconditionally returns the invalid output $(\bot, \bot)$. Note, we assume the user to be honest, i.e. $pid_{\mathcal{U}} \notin \mathcal{PID}_{\text{corr}}$ holds. This branch asserts protection against false accusation for honest users. If the fraud-detection IDs are equal, there has indeed been a double-spending incident. In this case the user's identity is leaked to the adversary and the adversary is asked to provide a proof of guilt π. This proof of guilt is then recorded as being valid for the fraudulent user. This branch asserts completeness.

We now discuss the remaining corner cases. If no transaction exists for at least one of the given double-spending tags, i.e. at least one of the double-spending tags is a fake tag, the first branch is applied and the adversary may decide about the user and the result. Also, if the denoted user is corrupted, the result is adopted unaltered. This may result into a valid proof of guilt although the user has not committed double-spending, but protection against false accusation is not guaranteed for corrupted users. Moreover, if $f_\pi(pid_{\mathcal{U}}, \pi)$ has already been defined, the result is not changed. This asserts consistency across multiple invocation and a proof of guilt that has been invalid for a particular user cannot spontaneously become valid and vice versa.

Double-spending detection is complemented by VerifyGuilt. It is also a one-party task but can be performed by any party. To put it simply, VerifyGuilt checks if the given proof of guilt π is internally recorded as being valid for the particular user ID $pid_{\mathcal{U}}$. Again, this over-simplification turns out to be unrealizable, because consistency with respect to fake proofs and corruption of parties must be taken into account.

First, VerifyGuilt checks if this particular pair $(pid_{\mathcal{U}}, \pi)$ has already been defined and outputs whatever has been output before. This ensures consistent answers across different invocations. If $(pid_{\mathcal{U}}, \pi)$ has neither been issued nor queried before *and* the affected user is corrupted, the adversary is allowed to decide if this proof of guilt should be accepted. This reflects that we do not protect corrupted users from false accusations of guilt. If the user is honest and $(pid_{\mathcal{U}}, \pi)$ has neither been issued nor queried before, then the proof of guilt is marked as invalid. This protects honest users from being accused by fake proofs which have not been issued by the ideal functionality itself. Finally, the result is recorded for the future and output to the party. This possibility of public verification is vital to prevent the operator from wrongly accusing any user of double-spending and should for instance be utilized by the dispute resolver before it agrees to blacklist and therefore deanonymize a user on the basis of double-spending.

4.4.2 Wallet Blacklisting

The task BlacklistWallet (cp. Fig. 4.15) is run between the operator and dispute resolver. The operator inputs a blacklisting tag ω_{bl} which the operator has obtained at the end of IssueWallet to denote the wallet the operator wishes to blacklist. If BlacklistWallet succeeds, the operator

Functionality $\mathcal{F}_{\text{apc}}$ (cont.) – Task BlacklistWallet

Operator input: (blacklist_wallet, ω_{bl})

(1) Set $\lambda := f_{\Omega_{\text{bl}}}^{-1}(\omega_{\text{bl}})$.
(2) Let $pid_{\mathcal{U}}$ the user PID that is associated to any $(\cdot,\cdot,\cdot,\cdot,\lambda, pid_{\mathcal{U}},\cdot,\cdot,\cdot,\cdot,\cdot,\cdot) \in TRDB$.[a]
(3) If O is corrupted and $(pid_{\mathcal{U}}, \lambda)$ is undefined, leak blacklisting_wallet to the adversary and ask for $(pid_{\mathcal{U}}, \lambda)$ with a λ not used in *TRDB*.[b]
(4) If $(pid_{\mathcal{U}}, \lambda)$ is undefined, output (blacklisted_wallet, $\emptyset$) to operator and halt.

Dispute resolver output: (blacklisting_wallet)

Dispute resolver input: (blacklisting_wallet, $pid'_{\mathcal{U}}$)

(5) If $pid_{\mathcal{U}} \neq pid'_{\mathcal{U}}$, output (blacklisted_wallet, $\emptyset$) to operator and halt.
(6) $x_\lambda := \max\{x \mid f_\Phi(\lambda, x) \text{ is already defined}\}$.
(7) For $x \in \{x_\lambda + 1, \ldots, x_{\text{bound}}\}$:
   (a) Pick $\varphi \xleftarrow{R} \Phi$ that has not previously been used, or—if $pid_{\mathcal{U}} \in \mathcal{PID}_{\text{corr}}$—leak (blacklisting_wallet, λ, x) to the adversary and ask for fraud-detection ID φ that has not previously been used.
   (b) Append $(\lambda, x) \mapsto \varphi$ to f_Φ.
(8) $bl_{\Phi_\lambda} := \{f_\Phi(\lambda, x) \mid 0 \leq x \leq x_{\text{bound}}\}$.

Dispute resolver output: (blacklisted_wallet)

Operator output: (blacklisted_wallet, bl_{Φ_λ})

[a] N.b.: $pid_{\mathcal{U}}$ is constant across each $trdb \in TRDB$ for a fixed wallet ID λ, hence $pid_{\mathcal{U}}$ is well-defined.
[b] Only an honest operator is guaranteed to get a blacklist for the "correct" wallet. N.b., λ is never output anywhere, hence the chance to meet an actually existing λ is neglible.

Figure 4.15: The Functionality $\mathcal{F}_{\text{apc}}$ (cont. from Fig. 4.1) – Task BlacklistWallet

receives a set of past and upcoming fraud-detection IDs bl_{Φ_λ} as output so it may add them to the PoS blacklist bl_Φ. The dispute resolver inputs a user identity $pid'_{\mathcal{U}}$ to signal its consent to blacklist a wallet of that user. We assume that both parties negotiated on the user identity out-of-band before the task starts. For example, the operator might have presented a valid proof of guilt to the dispute resolver for that user or the user agreed to be blacklisted due to a lost wallet. Note, that IssueWallet (cp. Section 4.3.1 and Fig. 4.9) is identifying for the user. Hence, the operator knows which blacklisting tag are associated to which user.

Again, we start the description for the "good" case, i.e. for an honest operator that inputs a genuine blacklisting tag and an honest user. (N.b.: The dispute resolver is assumed to be always honest.) In a nutshell, $\mathcal{F}_{\text{apc}}$ first determines the wallet ID λ the blacklisting tag has been output for and looks up the associated user ID $pid_{\mathcal{U}}$ from the transaction database. If the

Functionality $\mathcal{F}_{\text{apc}}$ (cont.) – Task RecalculateBalance

Operator input: (`recalculate_balance`, $bl_\Phi, \Omega_{\text{rc}}$)

(1) If RegisterOp has not yet been run, output $\perp$ and abort.
(2) $\Omega_{\text{rc}}^{\text{genuine}} := \{\omega_{\text{rc}} \in \Omega_{\text{rc}} \mid \exists\, trdb = (\cdot,\cdot,\cdot,\cdot,\cdot,\cdot,\cdot,\cdot,\cdot,\omega_{\text{rc}},\cdot) \in TRDB\}$
(3) $\Omega_{\text{rc}}^{\text{fake}} := \Omega_{\text{rc}} \setminus \Omega_{\text{rc}}^{\text{genuine}}$.
(4) $\Xi := \{(s,p) \mid \exists\, trdb = (\cdot, s, \varphi, \cdot,\cdot,\cdot,\cdot, p, \cdot,\cdot, \omega_{\text{rc}}, \cdot) \in TRDB \wedge \omega_{\text{rc}} \in \Omega_{\text{rc}}^{\text{genuine}} \wedge \varphi \in bl_\Phi\}$
(5) Set $b^{\text{bill}} := \sum_{(s,p)\in\Xi} p$.
(6) If $\Omega_{\text{rc}}^{\text{fake}} = \emptyset$, then set $p^{\text{deviate}} := 0$, else leak (`recalculating_balance`, $bl_\Phi, \Omega_{\text{rc}}^{\text{fake}}$) to the adversary and obtain deviating price p^{deviate}.
(7) $b^{\text{bill}} := b^{\text{bill}} + p^{\text{deviate}}$

Operator output: (`recalculated_balance`, b^{bill})

Figure 4.16: The Functionality $\mathcal{F}_{\text{apc}}$ (cont. from Fig. 4.1) – Task RecalculateBalance

dispute resolver inputs the same user ID, $\mathcal{F}_{\text{apc}}$ checks how many values of $f_\Phi(\lambda,\cdot)$ are already defined and extends f_Φ to the first x_{bound} fraud-detection IDs, with x_{bound} being a parameter we assume to be greater than the number of transactions a user would be involved in within one billing period. To that end, yet undefined fraud-detection IDs $f_\Phi(\lambda, x)$ with $x \leq x_{\text{bound}}$ are uniquely and randomly drawn. This ensures that upcoming transactions use predetermined fraud-detection IDs that are actually blacklisted.

If a corrupted operator inputs a fake blacklisting tag the adversary is asked to provide a user ID $pid_{\mathcal{U}}$ and a wallet ID λ which must not belong to an existing wallet. In this case the operator might eventually receive a set bl_{Φ_λ} of x_{bound} random fraud-detection IDs, but these are never used in any task. If the user is corrupted, the adversary is allowed to choose the fraud-detection IDs.

4.4.3 Balance Recalculation

The task RecalculateBalance (cp. Fig. 4.16) is a one-party task executed by the operator. The operator inputs a set of fraud-detection IDs bl_Φ and a set of recalculation tags Ω_{rc}. The result is the accumulated sum of all transaction for which an associated recalculation tag has been provided and which are selected by a matching fraud-detection ID. Note that although the sum may contain the prices of transactions and wallets that have already been cleared, this does not falsify the value of b^{bill} as every successful execution of Disburse creates an entry with the amount that was disbursed as negative price.

The *intended* usage is to recalculate the balance b^{bill} of individual wallets or all wallets of a particular user. To this end, the operator needs to input a set bl_{Φ} of fraud-detection IDs that equals a complete or otherwise unaltered set bl_{Φ_λ} as it has been output by BlacklistWallet (cp. Section 4.4.2) or a union thereof. Figuratively spoken, the intention is that operator handles the output set bl_{Φ_λ} of BlacklistWallet as monolithic, opaque blocks and the input set bl_{Φ} is a union of these. Still, there is no guarantee that the operator inputs the union of "complete" sets bl_{Φ_λ}. Moreover, the set bl_{Φ} and the set Ω_{rc} could also contain fake entries. In the latter case, the adversary is allowed to modify the result by an offset p^{deviate} without any restrictions.

In [Nag+20] the tasks BlacklistWallet and RecalculateBalance are a combined single task (called BlacklistUser there). The task has been split, because the dispute resolver is only required for the actual blacklisting part, but not for the recalculation part and keeping these parts separately make this clear.

4.4.4 Prove of Participation

This is a two-party task involving a user and the violation enforcer (cp. Fig. 4.17) and assumed to be conducted with every user which has been physically identified by the violation enforcer's and is suspected of having avoid Deposit. It allows well-behaving users to prove their successful participation in a transaction with the PoS at which the identification took place, while the fraudulent user will not be able to do so.

The violation enforcer inputs the identity of the suspected user $pid_{\mathcal{U}}$, the identity of the PoS $pid_{\mathcal{P}}$ and a set Ω_{pp} of prove-participation tags which are related to the investigated transaction in a timely and spatial manner and must be provided by the PoS which reported the incident. The user inputs a single prove-participation tags ω_{pp} after having learned which PoS and potential transactions are under investigation. Using the "right" ω_{pp} allows users to prove their innocence.

Again, we describe the "good" case (all parties are honest, the input tags are genuine) first. If the provided prove-participation tag ω_{pp} is in the set of investigated prove-participation tags Ω_{pp} and if the recorded user and PoS identities $pid'_{\mathcal{U}}, pid'_{\mathcal{P}}$ of the transaction which is associated to ω_{pp} match the identities under investigation, then the violation enforcer obtains a positive result, else a negative result.

If the prove-participation tag is a fake tag and if both the user and the PoS are corrupted, then the adversary may decide on the result. This may lead to a false positive result, but this is an inherent restriction of our setting with offline capabilities. Remember that the task Deposit is a two-party task between the user and the PoS. If the suspected user and the PoS are both corrupted and collude, the PoS is able to give a false testimony.

If the violation enforcer is corrupted, the prove-participation tag ω_{pp} is leaked to the adversary. We like to stress that this is not only a peculiarity of our proposed implementation,

Functionality $\mathcal{F}_{\text{apc}}$ (cont.) – Task ProveParticipation

Violation enforcer input: (prove_participation, $pid_{\mathcal{U}}, pid_{\mathcal{P}}, \Omega_{\text{pp}}$)

(1) If RegisterUser for $pid_{\mathcal{U}}$ or RegisterPOS for $pid_{\mathcal{P}}$ have not yet been run, output $\perp$ and abort.

User output: (proving_participation, $pid_{\mathcal{P}}, \Omega_{\text{pp}}$)
User input: (proving_participation, ω_{pp})

(2) If $\omega_{\text{pp}} \notin \Omega_{\text{pp}}$, then output (proved_participation) to $\mathcal{U}$, output (proved_participation, NOK) to VE and halt.
(3) Let $trdb = (\cdot, \cdot, \cdot, \cdot, \cdot, pid'_{\mathcal{U}}, pid'_{\mathcal{P}}, \cdot, \cdot, \cdot, \cdot, \omega_{\text{pp}}) \in \mathit{TRDB}$.
(4) If $pid_{\mathit{VE}} \in \mathcal{PID}_{\text{corr}}$, leak (proving_participation, ω_{pp}) to the adversary.
(5) If $trdb$ is undefined and $\{pid_{\mathcal{U}}, pid_{\mathcal{P}}\} \in \mathcal{PID}_{\text{corr}}$:
   (a) Leak (proving_participation) to the adversary and obtain *result*.
   Else (i.e. $trdb$ is defined or $pid_{\mathcal{U}}$ or $pid_{\mathcal{P}}$ is honest):
   (a) If $pid_{\mathcal{U}} = pid'_{\mathcal{U}}$ and $pid_{\mathcal{P}} = pid'_{\mathcal{P}}$ hold,[a] then set $result :=$ OK, else $result :=$ NOK.

User output: (proved_participation)
Violation enforcer output: (proved_participation, *result*)

[a] N.b., if $trdb$ is undefined, then $pid'_{\mathcal{U}} = \perp$ holds which implies that $pid_{\mathcal{U}} \neq pid'_{\mathcal{U}}$ and $result =$ NOK follow.

Figure 4.17: The Functionality $\mathcal{F}_{\text{apc}}$ (cont. from Fig. 4.1) – Task ProveParticipation

but inherent to the task. Assume that the user is able to successfully prove its participation. Although the violation enforcer only learns a single result bit, this is sufficient to find out which $\omega_{\text{pp}} \in \Omega_{\text{pp}}$ the user has input. The violation enforcer could repeatedly run the task and summon the user to prove its participation for a descending sequence of bi-sected sets until the last set only contains a single tag. Nonetheless, this does not affect the anonymity or unlinkability of any other transactions.

We are aware of the fact that this definition leaves room for an "attack" or more precisely an abuse by the PoS. The PoS triggers the violation enforcer to identify the offending user out-of-band (e.g. by taking a photo) and the same PoS also provides the set Ω_{pp} of prove-participation tags. Of course, the intended idea is that this set encompasses prove-participation tags which are somehow[3] related to the whereabouts of the incident. However, the PoS could intentionally provide a wrong set Ω_{pp} which misses the relevant tags and thus make it impossible for the (innocent) user to exculpate themselves. This flaw cannot be fully resolved, but mitigated. A

[3] We are intentionally vague here, because what the precise meaning of "whereabouts" depends on the concrete deployment.

possible solution requires the introduction of another ideal functionality[4] and would very much deviate from [Nag+20]. This extension is discussed in Chapter 10. Moreover, note that a PoS cannot use this "attack" to target a specific user and the strategy poses the risk that not only a single, but multiple users are (falsely) found guilty. (Because the PoS cannot know which prove-participation tags should be omitted from Ω_{pp} and thus may drop too many.) However, as for a single transaction only one user can have been cheating, such an impossible result should be noticed and lead to an audit of the system. But this out of the scope of the security model.

[4] This functionality needs to encapsulate the concept of "whereabouts".

5 System Discussion

In this chapter we discuss some aspects of the definition of $\mathcal{F}_{\text{apc}}$ from Chapter 4.

Most importantly, we argue why $\mathcal{F}_{\text{apc}}$ captures an ideal model of a secure and privacy-preserving anonymous point collection scheme. Especially, we illustrate how the high-level objectives of an anonymous point collection scheme (cp. Section 2.6) are reflected in $\mathcal{F}_{\text{apc}}$. The properties (P1) to (P8) are consolidated under the term Operator Security and Correctness and discussed in Section 5.1, while properties (P9) to (P11) are summed up under User Security and Privacy in Section 5.2. Instead of defining a game-based security definition for each of these properties and then show that the yet to be defined implementation fulfills these games, we formalize the properties and show that the ideal functionality fulfills the properties.

Section 5.3 discusses some aspects of the user/PoS attributes, the leakage and the pricing function with a focus on anonymity. This section clarifies what kind of anonymity is considered in this thesis and likewise important what is *not* guaranteed.

Finally, Section 5.4 regards two aspects of the definition with nearby alternative approaches.

5.1 Operator Security and Correctness

At the bottom line, operator security, especially correctness of billing, follows from the fact that $\mathcal{F}_{\text{apc}}$ represents an incorruptible accountant which manages all wallets and their associated transactions in a single, pervasive database *TRDB*. For example, in Deposit and Disburse a (possibly malicious) user only inputs a serial number to indicate which previous wallet state should be used. All relevant information is then looked up by $\mathcal{F}_{\text{apc}}$ internally. Similar observations hold for all other tasks.

Typically, an ideal functionality is a rather simple object (e.g., a commitment, an oblivious transfer, a coin toss) and it is mostly obvious from its definition that it captures the right notion of security and correctness. In contrast, our ideal functionality $\mathcal{F}_{\text{apc}}$ is already a complex system on its own with polynomially many parties that can reactively interact forever, i.e., $\mathcal{F}_{\text{apc}}$ itself has no inherent exit point except that at some point the polynomially bounded runtime of the environment is exhausted.

As already described in Section 4.1 the set of transactions *TRDB* is best visualized as a description of a directed graph with labeled nodes and edges. Section 4.1 has also brought forward the intended interpretation of particular structural properties of this graph (e.g. wallets correspond to trees; see there and in particular cf. Fig. 4.3). In this section we show that the definition of $\mathcal{F}_{\text{apc}}$ (cp. Sections 4.2 to 4.4) actually fulfills this intention. We give a series of graph-theoretic lemmas to prove that the desired structural properties hold after each invocation of a task of $\mathcal{F}_{\text{apc}}$ as a sort of invariant and thereby assert that there is no execution of $\mathcal{F}_{\text{apc}}$ which can deviate. These lemmas include that the graph as a whole is a directed forest where each tree corresponds to a wallet ID λ, double-spending corresponds to branching and different wallet states have the same fraud-detection ID φ if and only if they have the same depth in the same tree. Moreover, these lemmas a closely associated to the desired properties of an anonymous point collection scheme (cp. Section 2.6).

Definition 5.1 (Ideal Transaction Graph) *The transaction database $TRDB = \{trdb_i\}$ with*

$$trdb = (s^{\text{prev}}, s, \varphi, x, \lambda, pid_{\mathcal{U}}, pid_{\mathcal{P}}, p, b, \omega_{\text{ds}}, \omega_{\text{rc}}, \omega_{\text{pp}}) \in TRDB \tag{5.1}$$

is a directed, labeled graph with vertices identified by s, edges identified by (s^{prev}, s), vertex labels given by $(\varphi, x, \lambda, pid_{\mathcal{U}}, b)$ and edge labels given by $(pid_{\mathcal{P}}, p, \omega_{\text{ds}}, \omega_{\text{rc}}, \omega_{\text{pp}})$. This graph is called the Ideal Transaction Graph.

Lemma 5.2 (Forest Structure of the Ideal Transaction Graph) *The Ideal Transaction Graph TRDB is a forest.*

Proof *TRDB* is a forest, if and only if it is cycle-free and every node has in-degree at most one. A new node is only inserted in the scope of IssueWallet, Deposit or Disburse. Proof by Induction: The statement is correct for the empty *TRDB*. If IssueWallet (cp. Fig. 4.9) is invoked, a new node with no predecessor is inserted. Moreover, the serial number s of the new node is randomly chosen from the set of unused serial numbers, i.e., it is unique and no existing node can point to the new node as its predecessor. If Deposit (cp. Figs. 4.10 and 4.11) or Disburse (cp. Fig. 4.12) is invoked, a new node is inserted that points to an existing node. Again, the serial number s of the new node is randomly chosen from the set of unused serial numbers, i.e., it is unique and no existing node can point to the new node as its predecessor. Hence, no cycle can be closed. Since the only incoming edge of a node is defined by the stated predecessor s^{prev} (which may also be $\perp$), each vertex has in-degree at most one. ∎

Lemma 5.3 (Tree-wise Uniqueness of the Wallet Identifier) *The wallet ID λ maps one-to-one and onto a connected component (i.e., tree) of the Ideal Transaction Graph.*

Proof "$\Longleftarrow$": Let $trdb_i$ be an arbitrary node in *TRDB* and λ be its wallet ID. Furthermore, let $trdb_i^*$ be the root of the tree containing $trdb_i$. Then on the (unique) path from $trdb_i^*$ to $trdb_i$, every node apart from $trdb_i^*$ was inserted by means of either Deposit (cp. Figs. 4.10 and 4.11) or Disburse (cp. Fig. 4.12), both of which ensure the inserted node has the same λ as its predecessor. By induction over the length of the path, $trdb_i$ has the same wallet ID as $trdb_i^*$ and hence the wallet ID is a locally constant function on *TRDB*.

" $\Longrightarrow$ ": For contradiction assume there are two nodes $trdb_i$ and $trdb_j$ with equal wallet IDs $\lambda_i = \lambda_j$ in two different connected components. Pick the root nodes $trdb_i^*$ and $trdb_j^*$ of their respective trees. By " $\Longleftarrow$ " it we get $\lambda_i^* = \lambda_i = \lambda_j = \lambda_j^*$, i.e., the root nodes have equals wallet IDs, too. Both root nodes are inserted in the scope of IssueWallet and the wallet ID is randomly drawn from the set of *unused* wallet IDs, i.e., they cannot both have the same wallet ID. Contradiction! ∎

Lemma 5.4 (Tree-wise Constness of the User PID) *Within a tree of the Ideal Transaction Graph the PID $pid_{\mathcal{U}}$ of the corresponding user is constant.*

Proof Same proof as " $\Longleftarrow$ " in the proof of Lemma 5.3. ∎

In other words, Lemma 5.4 states that a wallet (a tree in *TRDB*) is always owned by a distinct user. But a user can own multiple wallets.

Lemma 5.5 (Layer-wise Uniqueness of the Fraud-Detection Identifier)

(1) *Within a tree of TRDB, every node $trdb = (s^{\text{prev}}, s, \varphi, x, \lambda, pid_{\mathcal{U}}, pid_{\mathcal{P}}, p, b, \omega_{\text{ds}}, \omega_{\text{rc}}, \omega_{\text{pp}})$ has depth x and all nodes of the same depth in the same tree have the same fraud-detection ID φ. Conversely, nodes with the same fraud-detection ID are in the same tree and have the same depth within this tree.*

(2) *f_Φ is injective.*

Proof Proof by Induction. The statement is true for the empty *TRDB*. In the scope of IssueWallet (cp. Fig. 4.9) a new root node is inserted, IssueWallet sets $x := 0$ and an unused φ is chosen. In the scope of Deposit or Disburse, x is calculated as $x := x^{\text{prev}} + 1$, where by induction x^{prev} is the depth of its predecessor. With respect to φ we note that when inserted, every node gets as fraud-detection ID the value stored in $f_\Phi(\lambda, x)$ which only depends on the node's wallet ID and depth. When this value is set (in either IssueWallet, Deposit, Disburse or BlacklistWallet, cp. Figs. 4.9 to 4.12 and 4.15) it is chosen from the set of *unused* fraud-detection IDs and therefore unique for given λ and x. ∎

So far, the lemmas above have not had a concrete semantic interpretation in terms of an anonymous point collection scheme. This changes for the upcoming lemmas.

Lemma 5.6 (Billing Correctness) *Let trdb* $= (s^{\text{prev}}, s, \varphi, x, \lambda, pid_{\mathcal{U}}, pid_{\mathcal{P}}, p, b, \omega_{\text{ds}}, \omega_{\text{rc}}, \omega_{\text{pp}})$ *be an arbitrary but fixed node. If trdb is not a root let* $trdb^{\text{prev}} = (s^{\text{prev,prev}}, s^{\text{prev}}, \varphi^{\text{prev}}, x^{\text{prev}}, \lambda, pid_{\mathcal{U}}, pid_{\mathcal{P}}^{\text{prev}}, p^{\text{prev}}, b^{\text{prev}}, \omega_{\text{ds}}^{\text{prev}}, \omega_{\text{rc}}^{\text{prev}}, \omega_{\text{pp}}^{\text{prev}})$ *be its predecessor. Then* $b = b^{\text{prev}} + p$ *holds for non-root nodes and* $p = \perp, b = 0$ *for root nodes.*

Proof Same induction argument as in proof of Lemma 5.5. ∎

Lemma 5.7 (Double-Spending Detection Completeness) *Let the operator be honest and let a user (possible malicious) with PID* $pid_{\mathcal{U}}$ *have committed double-spending while interacting with two honest PoSes with PIDs* $pid_{\mathcal{P}}$ *and* $pid'_{\mathcal{P}}$.[1] *Let* $\omega_{\text{ds}}, \omega'_{\text{ds}}$ *denote the corresponding double-spending tags that are output at the PoS' side.*

(1) *The task* DetectDS *outputs* $(pid_{\mathcal{U}}, \pi)$ *with* $\pi \neq \perp$ *upon input of* $(\omega_{\text{ds}}, \omega'_{\text{ds}})$.

(2) *The task* VerifyGuilt *returns* OK *upon input of* $(pid_{\mathcal{U}}, \pi)$.

Proof (1) The honest PoSes imply that $\omega_{\text{ds}}, \omega'_{\text{ds}}$ are unique, especially $\omega_{\text{ds}} \neq \omega'_{\text{ds}}$ holds (cp. Step 10 in Fig. 4.11). Let *trdb*, *trdb'* denote the recorded transaction entries and φ, φ' the associated fraud-detection IDs. Lemma 5.5 implies $\varphi = \varphi'$. Hence, the else-branch of DetectDS (cp. Step 2 in Fig. 4.13) applies, $f_\pi(pid_{\mathcal{U}}, \pi) :=$ OK is set and the statement follows.

(2) Due to Item (1) $f_\pi(pid_{\mathcal{U}}, \pi) :=$ OK holds. This is the return value of VerifyGuilt (cp. Fig. 4.14). ∎

Lemma 5.8 (Correctness of Wallet Blacklisting and Balance Recalculation) *Let* ω_{bl} *an arbitrary but fixed blacklisting tag which O has received as output from* IssueWallet *for a wallet with ID* λ. *Let the operator O and all PoSes which interacts with this wallet be honest. Under the assumption that the wallet is used in less than* x_{bound} *transactions, i.e., in less than* x_{bound} *invocations of* IssueWallet, Deposit *and* Disburse, *the following two statements hold:*

(1) *The set* bl_{Φ_λ} *returned to O by* BlacklistWallet *on input* ω_{bl} *for a successful execution*[2] *contains all fraud-detection IDs that have ever been used for the wallet.*

(2) *Any invocation of* Deposit *on input of a serial number* s^{prev} *which belongs to this wallet and on input of a blacklist* $bl_\Phi \supseteq bl_{\Phi_\lambda}$ *aborts with* `blacklisted_wallet`.

1 The PoS might be the same in both interactions.
2 We postulate that the dispute resolver agrees to blacklist the affected user.

(3) RecalculateBalance *returns the accumulated sum of all transaction of the wallet within* Deposit *and* Disburse, *if* RecalculateBalance *is called with input* $(bl_{\Phi_\lambda}, \Omega_{\mathrm{rc}})$ *for a set* Ω_{rc} *which contains at least all recalculation tags that have been output to the PoSes and no fake recalculation tags.*

PROOF (1) As ω_{bl} is genuine, i.e. is output of a successful execution of IssueWallet, $\lambda := f_{\Omega_{\mathrm{bl}}}^{-1}(\omega_{\mathrm{bl}})$ is defined and the set $TRDB_\lambda \subseteq TRDB$ of all transaction entries $trdb = (\dots, \lambda, \dots)$ corresponding to λ is not empty. The statement is a consequence of Lemma 5.5. The depth of the tree described by $TRDB_\lambda$ is given by $x_\lambda := \max\{x \mid f_\Phi(\lambda, x) \neq \bot\}$. If the associated wallet hast been used in less than x_{bound} transaction, then the depth x_λ is smaller than x_{bound}. The set of used fraud-detection IDs is given by $\{f_\Phi(\lambda, x) \mid 0 \leq x \leq x_\lambda\}$ which is a subset of $bl_{\Phi_\lambda} := \{f_\Phi(\lambda, x) \mid 0 \leq x \leq x_{\mathrm{bound}}\}$.

(2) Let s^{prev} denote the serial number for which Deposit is invoked and let $trdb^{\mathrm{prev}} = (\cdot, s^{\mathrm{prev}}, \varphi^{\mathrm{prev}}, x^{\mathrm{prev}}, \lambda, \dots)$ be the corresponding transaction entry. By assumption $x^{\mathrm{prev}} < x_{\mathrm{bound}}$ holds. As BlacklistWallet has previously been called, $\varphi = f_\Phi(\lambda, x^{\mathrm{prev}} + 1)$ is already fixed. Moreover, $\varphi \in bl_{\Phi_\lambda} \subseteq bl_\Phi$ holds and thus Deposit aborts.

(3) By assumption $\Omega_{\mathrm{rc}}^{\mathrm{fake}} = \emptyset$ holds in RecalculateBalance and thus $p^{\mathrm{deviate}} = 0$ follows (cp. Step 6 in Fig. 4.16). Let

$$\Xi_\lambda := \{(s, p) \mid trdb = (\cdot, s, \cdot, \lambda, \cdot, \cdot, \cdot, p, \cdot, \cdot, \cdot, \cdot) \in TRDB\} \tag{5.2}$$

the set of all (s, p)-pairs for the wallet with wallet ID λ under consideration. Let

$$\Xi := \{(s, p) \mid \exists\, trdb = (\cdot, s, \varphi, \cdot, \cdot, \cdot, \cdot, p, \cdot, \cdot, \omega_{\mathrm{rc}}, \cdot) \in TRDB \wedge \omega_{\mathrm{rc}} \in \Omega_{\mathrm{rc}}^{\mathrm{genuine}} \wedge \varphi \in bl_\Phi\} \tag{5.3}$$

be as in Step 4 of Fig. 4.16. We have to show that $\Xi_\lambda = \Xi$ holds.

"$\Xi_\lambda \subseteq \Xi$": Let $(s^*, p) \in \Xi_\lambda$ and let $trdb^* = (\cdot, s^*, \varphi, \lambda, \cdot, \cdot, \cdot, p, \cdot, \cdot, \omega_{\mathrm{rc}}, \cdot) \in TRDB$ be the corresponding transaction entry. $\varphi \in bl_\Phi = bl_{\Phi_\lambda}$ follows by Item (1) and $\omega_{\mathrm{rc}} \in \Omega_{\mathrm{rc}}^{\mathrm{genuine}}$ follows by assumption. This yields $trdb^* \in \Xi$.

"$\Xi_\lambda \supseteq \Xi$": Assume there is a $(s^*, p) \in \Xi \setminus \Xi_\lambda$ and let $trdb^* = (\cdot, s^*, \varphi, \lambda', \cdot, \cdot, \cdot, p, \cdot, \cdot, \omega_{\mathrm{rc}}, \cdot) \in TRDB$ the corresponding transaction entry. $trdb^* \notin \Xi_\lambda$ implies $\lambda \neq \lambda'$. However, this means there exists $x, x' \in \{0, \dots, x_{\mathrm{bound}}\}$ s.t. $f_\Phi(\lambda, x) = \varphi = f_\Phi(\lambda', x')$ and there exist $trdb = (\cdot, \cdot, \cdot, \lambda, \cdot, \cdot, \cdot, \cdot, \cdot, \cdot, \omega_{\mathrm{rc}}, \cdot) \in TRDB$ for the "correct" λ and identical ω_{rc}. Each of the condition is impossible and an immediate contradiction: f_Φ is injective (cp. Lemma 5.5) and in Deposit as well as Disburse a unique recalculation tag ω_{rc} is selected (cp. Step 10 in Fig. 4.11 and Step 7 in Fig. 4.12). ∎

We now discuss why the properties properties (P1) to (P8) are fulfilled by $\mathcal{F}_{\text{apc}}$.

(P1) *Owner-binding:* Given the serial number s^{prev} of a previous wallet state, $\mathcal{F}_{\text{apc}}$ checks that the associated wallet actually belongs to the calling user and thus has been legitimately issued to this user.

(P2) *Attribute-binding:* As the attributes $a_{\mathcal{U}}, a_{\mathcal{P}}^{\text{prev}}$ associated to the indicated transaction, resp. wallet, are internally managed by $\mathcal{F}_{\text{apc}}$, the user is unable to claim his wallet contains any other information than it actually does.

(P3) *Balance-binding:* This is a direct consequence of Lemma 5.6.

(P4) *Double-spending Detection:* Follows from Lemma 5.7.

(P5) *Participation Enforcement:* This is handled outside the scope of $\mathcal{F}_{\text{apc}}$. As discussed in Chapter 2, we assume users to be physically identified by cameras, if they do not properly participate in Deposit.

(P6) *Blacklisting:* A consequence of Lemma 5.8, Items (1) and (2).

(P7) *Accountability:* Follows from Lemma 5.8, Item (3).

(P8) *Renegade Expulsion:* This is handled outside the scope of $\mathcal{F}_{\text{apc}}$ by encoding a limited time of validity into the PoS' attributes (cp. Section 2.4).

5.2 User Security and Privacy

In this section we argue why $\mathcal{F}_{\text{apc}}$ implements the properties (P9) to (P11). As in the previous section, we first show two lemmas.

Lemma 5.9 (Double-Spending Detection Soundness) *Let the user with $pid_{\mathcal{U}}$ be honest and not have committed double-spending.*

(1) The task DetectDS *never outputs $(pid_{\mathcal{U}}, \pi)$ with $\pi \neq \bot$.*

(2) For all π the task VerifyGuilt *returns* NOK *on input $(pid_{\mathcal{U}}, \pi)$.*

Proof (1) The user has not committed double-spending. Lemma 5.5 implies that $\varphi \neq \varphi'$ holds for all pairs of transactions $trdb \neq trdb'$ which are associated to $pid_{\mathcal{U}}$. Hence, in Fig. 4.13 the first branch of Step 2 applies and $\mathcal{F}_{\text{apc}}$ outputs $(\bot, \bot)$.

(2) The task VerifyGuilt first checks if $f_\pi(pid_\mathcal{U}, \pi)$ has already been defined. $f_\pi(pid_\mathcal{U}, \pi)$ is only defined in Deposit (cp. Step 6 in Fig. 4.10), Disburse (cp. Step 5 in Fig. 4.12), DetectDS (cp. Fig. 4.13) or VerifyGuilt (cp. Fig. 4.14). The assumption that the user has not committed double-spending immediately rules out the first two options and the Item (1) rules out the third option. If $f_\pi(pid_\mathcal{U}, \pi)$ has been defined by VerifyGuilt, then VerifyGuilt outputs the same result as in the previous invocation. Hence, w.l.o.g. it suffices to consider first time invocations of VerifyGuilt and to assume that $f_\pi(pid_\mathcal{U}, \pi)$ is undefined. In this case, VerifyGuilt returns NOK irrespective of the input (cp. Step 3 in Fig. 4.14). ■

Lemma 5.10 (Prove of Participation Completeness) *Let the user be honest and ω_{pp} the prove-participation tag which the user has obtained as output from* Deposit *in an interaction with a (possibly malicious) PoS. Then,* ProveParticipation *returns* OK *upon input $(pid_\mathcal{U}, pid_\mathcal{P}, \Omega_{\text{pp}})$ for a Ω_{pp} with $\omega_{\text{pp}} \in \Omega_{\text{pp}}$.*

Proof As the user is honest and ω_{pp} genuine, a corresponding $trdb \in TRDB$ has been recorded by an execution of Deposit. The statement follows from the definition of ProveParticipation (cp. else-branch of Step 5 in Fig. 4.17). ■

The information leakage that needs to be considered for an assessment of user privacy directly follows from the in- and output as well as the explicit leakage of the ideal functionality. We stress that we only care about privacy for honest, well-behaving, non-blacklisted[3] users.

(P9) *Unlinkability:* First note that the serial number of the previous transaction s^{prev} is a private input of the user and never output to any party. After Deposit the PoS only learns the serial number s and fraud-detection ID φ of the current transaction which are both freshly, uniformly and independently drawn by $\mathcal{F}_{\text{apc}}$. IssueWallet only outputs s and Disburse additionally outputs the final balance b^{bill} (cp. Figs. 4.9 and 4.12). Hence, it is *information-theoretically impossible* to track an honest and well-behaving user across any pair of transactions using any of these numbers. The only "real" information leakage in Deposit is determined by the user's and the previous PoS' attributes $a_\mathcal{U}$ and $a_\mathcal{P}^{\text{prev}}$ which need to be assessed separately (see Section 5.3).

(P10) *Participation Provability:* As discussed in Chapter 2 we assume that if users do not properly participate in Deposit, they are physically identified outside the scope of $\mathcal{F}_{\text{apc}}$.

[3] Note that the operator may only blacklist users with the help of the incorruptible dispute resolver who only cooperates if the user has agreed or misbehaved.

Task	Leakage					
	$pid_{\mathcal{U}}$	$a_{\mathcal{U}}$	$a_{\mathcal{P}}/a_{\mathcal{O}}$	$a_{\mathcal{P}}^{\text{prev}}$	p	b^{bill}
RegisterUser	•					
IssueWallet	•	•	•			
Deposit		•	•	•	•	
Disburse	•	(•)		•		•
ProveParticipation	•					

Table 5.1: Information an adversary learns about honest users.

Lemma 5.10 asserts that suspected but inculpable users who successfully completed Deposit and are accidentally part of the investigation can prove their innocence. In ProveParticipation $\mathcal{F}_{\text{apc}}$ only outputs a single bit whether the user has successfully participated or not. The violation enforcer who does not learn anything about any of the user's transactions beyond that.

(P11) *Protection Against False Accusation:* Follows from Lemma 5.9.

5.3 Impact of the Attributes and Leakage on the Privacy Level

The ideal functionality provides unlinkability of transactions (cp. property (P9)) up to what can be deduced from user and PoS attributes and the leakage of the ideal functionality. As already discussed in Section 2.4, we assume these attributes to be sufficiently indistinct that they do not enable tracking of the user. This is not ensured within the scope of $\mathcal{F}_{\text{apc}}$, apart from outputs to the users, which enable them to check themselves that they are not identifying. Since we prove our realization π_{P5C} to be indistinguishable from the ideal functionality $\mathcal{F}_{\text{apc}}$, it is ensured that an adversary attacking π_{P5C} in the real world can only learn as much about a user as an adversary in the ideal model.

Table 5.1 summarizes what an adversary learns about the users in each task. We omitted the serial number s and the fraud-detection ID φ in the table as these are independently and uniformly drawn randomness and thus cannot be exploited (see (P9) in Section 5.2). In all tasks except Deposit the user's identity $pid_{\mathcal{U}}$ is leaked. The variables $a_{\mathcal{U}}$, $a_{\mathcal{P}}$, $a_{\mathcal{P}}^{\text{prev}}$ and $a_{\mathcal{O}}$ refer to attributes of the participating parties. The variable p denotes the price of a Deposit transaction, and b^{bill} is the total debt the user owes at the end of the task Disburse.

Let's call the period from the point of time at which a wallet is issued until the point of time at which its points are disbursed, the lifetime of a wallet.[4] For every wallet's lifetime, the operator collects all transaction information from every PoS. Hence, the operator eventually possesses two datasets:

(1) A database of users that are identified by their PID $pid_{\mathcal{U}}$ together with their attributes and total balance b^{bill} at the end of a wallet's lifetime. This dataset comprises all information from every conducted task but Deposit.

(2) A database of anonymous transactions during the wallet's lifetime. This dataset stems from the Deposit tasks (cp. Table 5.1).

With respect to practical privacy considerations one can naturally pose several questions: Can a single transaction be linked to a specific user? Has a user deposited points at a particular PoS? Can a user be mapped to a complete sequence of consecutive transactions? A final answer to these questions crucially depends on the concrete instantiation of the attributes $a_{\mathcal{U}}$, $a_{\mathcal{P}}$ and the pricing function but also on "environmental" parameters that cannot be chosen by the system designer such as the total number of registered users, the average number of transactions within the lifetime of a wallet, etc. An in-depth analysis would require plausible and justifiable assumptions about probability distributions for these parameters, and would constitute a separate line of research in its own right.

In the following, however, we would like to elaborate a bit on the general aspects of the question, how a user can be linked to a wallet's transactions. This problem can be depicted as a graph-theoretical problem of finding a path in a directed graph. In short, the problem is to reconstruct the (unknown) ideal transaction graph *TRDB* from a given set of nodes without the edges. More precisely, a problem instance is given by a graph which consists of initial nodes, inner nodes and terminal nodes. Initial nodes correspond to root nodes of *TRDB*, represent IssueWallet transactions and are linked to users. Terminal nodes correspond to leaf nodes of *TRDB*, represent Disburse transactions and are also linked to users and final balances b^{bill}. Inner nodes represent the anonymous Deposit transactions in between. A directed edge connects two nodes if the target node is a plausible successor of the source node. Hence, the set of examined edges is a superset of the edges in *TRDB*. Especially, the graph is not a directed forest and the problem is to select a subset of those edges such that the "true" *TRDB* is reconstructed.

The complexity of the task obviously depends on how much larger the superset of edges is compared to the size of the true set. Assuming that transactions can only occur at discrete

[4] N.b., the explanations are written with the running prime example of a post-payment scheme (cf. Sections 2.3.3 and 2.3.4) in mind. Adopted considerations hold for the other scenarios.

points in time, the inner nodes can be ordered in layers. As a bare minimum, an edge is only plausible and thus contained in the superset, if the connected nodes have equal user attributes $a_{\mathcal{U}}$, the attribute $a_{\mathcal{P}}^{\text{prev}}$ of the target node equal $a_{\mathcal{P}}$ of the source node and the target node is in a later layer than the source node (because time can only increase). Additionally, background knowledge such as the geo-position of the PoSes, etc. can be utilized to further reduce the superset of plausible edges and thereby simplify the search problem.

For privacy, two characteristics are important: How many solutions do exist and what is the computational complexity to find one (or all) solutions? This results in a trade-off between two borderline cases:

(1) There is exactly one unique solution. At first glance, this contradicts privacy. However, the mere existence of a unique solution is worthless, if it is computationally infeasible to find it.

(2) Finding a solution is easy but there are many equally valid solutions. In this case privacy is preserved as well.

If additional background information is omitted, the problem can be cast as a specialized instance of various NP-complete problems, e.g., the parallel-version of the KNAPSACK problem or a generalized version of the PARTITION SUM problem with variable partition sizes. For general instances, these problems are NP-complete. This is beneficial as it implies that finding a solution is generally believed to be intractable. However, there might be good heuristics for all "natural" instances. Moreover, depending on the concrete parameters (e.g., an upper bound on the maximum price p or the balance b^{bill}) the problem might become fixed-parameter tractable [Alb+18]. In other words, although solving the general problem is assumed to have super-polynomial runtime in the instance size, it might still be practically solvable for "real world" instances. We stress again, that an in-depth analysis requires to look at concrete distributions of these parameters which may be the basis for an independent work.

Nonetheless, there are indicators that—if finding one solution is easy—there might be a myriad of solutions, which again yields privacy. In [Nag+20], the authors sketch such estimation for the German Toll Collect System which indicates that the solution space for mapping a particular user (there: truck) to a specific wallet (there: trip) might be vast.

In practice, several privacy notions like k-anonymity are established. For several reasons these notions are not directly applicable here. First of all, these notions evaluate the privacy level of a concrete dataset and we stress again that this is out of the scope of this work. While at first glance the calculations above might suggest that our system features k-anonymity [Swe02] for some yet to be determined k, the notion of k-anonymity is actually not applicable due to formal reasons. The definition of k-anonymity requires the database to have exactly one entry for each individual, but our transaction database features several entries per user. Therefore, the notion of k-anonymity is syntactically not applicable to the users of our system. While we could still discuss k-anonymity in this setting if the operator combined all entries that pertain to the same user into one single entry, privacy of our system largely stems from the operator not being able to link transactions of the same user in this way and hence such a discussion would largely undervalue the privacy protection P5C provides.

5.4 Alternative Approaches

In this section we would like to discuss alternatives for two aspects of the definition. The first section sketches a different approach to model the distributed state of the system and the resulting inconsistencies instead of using tags. The second section does actually not present a proper alternative, because the approach turns out to be non-working. However, it is still presented, because it seems to be a very obvious approach at first glance.

5.4.1 An Alternative to Tags and the Case of [Nag+20]

In order to accurately model a distributed system with inconsistent knowledge of the individual parties, two nearby solutions exist:

(1) (The proposed approach) The ideal functionality additionally outputs some administrative meta-information—called tags here—alongside the actual output in certain tasks. Later these tags are re-input into those tasks that need them. On a conceptional level this implies that the ideal functionality assumes the existence of a framing protocol which transports information between parties and is played by the environment.

(2) (Alternative approach) The ideal functionality manages an array of indices (or some other kind of reference pointers) to represent which piece of information is known by which party. The parties' in-/output only consists of information that have a straightforward semantic interpretation in the context of the task at hand. The ideal functionality provides an explicit Sync operation that allows parties to mutually update their state of knowledge. Under the hood, an invocation of Sync let $\mathcal{F}_{\text{apc}}$ update which piece of information is accessible by which party.

The main advantage of the alternative approach is that it provides a cleaner interface as honest parties do not export any internal information to the caller protocol. Also, this definitional approach seems to be better decoupled from a particular implementation at first glance. However, this first impression fails and it has turned out that getting the definition right under this approach ends up in an incomprehensible clutter of indices. This runs contrary to the idea that the ideal functionality should grasp a plausible definition of security.

We argue that both approaches are mostly equivalent and more a question of style. In both cases, a potential implementation would most likely use some sort of tags in the one or other way to synchronize the parties' state from time to time. The main difference is that these tags are either (1) transported over the usual communication channel using incoming/outgoing message tapes, or (2) transported with the help the environment using input/output. In both cases, the environment has the same set of possibilities to maliciously manipulate these tags either directly by itself or with the help of the dummy adversary.[5]

Using the proposed approach, it is rather evident that $\mathcal{F}_{\text{apc}}$ must not make any assumptions about how the framing protocol, i.e. the environment, forwards the tags. For example, there is even no guarantee that a tag that is later input into a task has ever been output before by another task. Making the tags an explicit part of the ideal functionality enables to formalize conditions on non-excludable attacks in more comprehensible way. Hiding away these tags under the cover of an indirect indexing scheme leads to more artificial conditions that are not easily justifiable.

The approach taken in [Nag+20] lies somewhere in the middle of both approaches. Tags are not part of the ideal functionality, i.e. the in-/output interfaces are very clean, but the ideal functionality does not keep track of what is known by which party neither. Instead, the real implementation provides tags, but keeps them in the local state of each party and assumes that the internal state of one party is "magically" transported to another party by some not explicated mechanism of synchronization that is spontaneously executed when favorable. In some sense, the protocol in [Nag+20] implicitly re-introduces the assumption of globally available and perfectly consistent state. Strictly spoken, it does not realize the proposed ideal functionality there. Unfortunately, the problems have not only been a lack of thorough formalism, but as it has turned out the protocol in [Nag+20] actually contains some insecurities that have been overlooked. These insecurities have been unveiled during the write-up of this thesis and fixed.

5.4.2 Balance Recalculation

The task RecalculateBalance is defined as a one-party task which is conducted by the operator who exclusively provides the input. If the operator provides faulty input, the calculated balance is wrong (cp. Section 4.4.3). In essence, the task RecalculateBalance provides very little correctness guarantees. This corresponds to the typical "bogus-in-bogus-out" principle. At

5 Formally, this is not completely true. Using the alternative approach, the environment might be required to formally corrupt one of the communication parties first, before gaining all the options it immediately has under the approach used here. But this technicality is irrelevant for the point we want to make.

first glance it might seem that this only affects the operator itself but has no security impact on other parties. This is true on a technical level within the scope of the security model. However, a wrong balance might have an impact in the “real world”, if the result is used to file a claim against a user. Hence, a more practical solution should also provide evidence that the result is correct or allow the user to appeal against it.

In [Nag+20] the definition of the ideal task BlacklistUser (including the recalculation part[6]) provides stronger guarantees than what is actually fulfilled by the implementation in [Nag+20]. Again, the root of the problem is that the synchronization of states is not modeled in [Nag+20]. In contrast to other fixes between this thesis and [Nag+20], this problem has been fixed by unilaterally weakening $\mathcal{F}_{\text{apc}}$ and not tackling the implementation.

We are convinced, that a stronger (and more useful) variant of the task RecalculateBalance could be provided, but at the costs of major rework of the implementation. In a nutshell, the prove-participation tags and recalculation tags have to be fused into one kind of tag and the implementation Deposit/Disburse require an additional round of communication. Moreover, RecalculateBalance needs to be converted into an optional[7] two-party task between the operator and user. The presentation here mostly follows [Nag+20] and the envisioned improvements are discussed in Chapter 10.

5.4.3 The Commitment Problem and the Lack of Modularity

As stated in Chapter 3 the UC framework does not only provide strong security guarantees under concurrent execution in arbitrary environments, but comes with two great promises: composition and modularity. However, the definition of $\mathcal{F}_{\text{apc}}$ in Chapter 4 captures anonymous point collection in a monolithic functionality and only makes little use of modularity. Section 1.2 touches a tempting alternative: define an ideal functionality for each of the tasks, realize each of them by a protocol, analyze their security separately and deduce the security of the system using the UC composition theorem. If this was possible, this would make the proofs much easier and give higher confidence that they are correct.

This raises the question why such a modular approach has not been used. Chapter 4 argues that a monolithic definition allows to define the security of anonymous point collection more evidently, because a global database that keeps track of all transactions conveys a direct semantic interpretation and avoids a slew of technical subtleties due to the distributed state between the individual tasks that would arise otherwise. However, the problem is actually more than a skin-deep technicality. The rest of this section does not try to present an alternative approach, but argues why this alternative approach turns out to be infeasible.

[6] In [Nag+20] BlacklistUser combines the tasks BlacklistWallet and RecalculateBalance.

[7] The participation of the user must be optional in order to cover those cases in which the user refuses to participate.

Although UC promises modular proofs, complex protocols which have been proposed with a UC-proof rarely use this feature. Instead they are formalized as monolithic entities and proven secure from scratch. $\mathcal{F}_{\mathrm{apc}}$ is no exception. Other examples are UC-formalizations of P-signatures [Cam+15] or commit-and-prove [Lin03]. We encounter the so-called "commitment problem" [CDT19] of simulation-based security definitions.

For the rest of the discussion, we need push forward some of the cryptographic building blocks, namely commitments as well as ZK-proofs (cp. Section 6.2), and how they are used in the realization (cp. Chapter 7). Readers who are completely unfamiliar with these building blocks should skip the rest of this section on a first reading.

A typical structure found in many complex protocols is a commit-and-prove construction, which is also widely used in our proposed realization. A party commits to a secret message m and proves in zero-knowledge that the message hidden inside the commitment c fulfills some predicate P. In other words, the receiver of the commitment is not only asserted that the sender is bound to a value, but that this value fulfills certain constraints given by P. Although abstract UC-functionalities $\mathcal{F}_{\mathrm{com}}$ and $\mathcal{F}_{\mathrm{ZK}}$ for commitments and zero-knowledge proofs, resp., exist [e.g., cp. Can05], these functionalities cannot be used to modularly construct a UC-functionality $\mathcal{F}_{\mathrm{cp}}$ which in turn captures commit-and-prove. The underlying reason is that the actual primitives, i.e. real commitments and real ZK-proofs, offer interfaces which do not exist in the ideal functionalities. This allows to assemble these primitives in the real model in a way that cannot be achieved in the ideal model. For the scenario at hand, e.g., the commit-and-prove construction, the problem is also illustrated in Fig. 5.1.

The ideal functionality $\mathcal{F}_{\mathrm{ZK}}$ for zero-knowledge proofs is parameterized by a statement-witness relation $R_{gp} = (stmnt, wit)$. When the prover inputs a tuple $(stmnt, wit)$, $\mathcal{F}_{\mathrm{ZK}}$ checks if R_{gp} is fulfilled and only outputs the decision bit to the verifier. For the commit-and-prove construction, the concrete ZK-relation is $R_{gp} := \{(c, (m, d)) \mid P(m) \wedge \mathsf{Open}(m, c, d) = 1\}$ with the commitment $c = stmnt$ as the statement and the secret message together with the opening information $(m, d) = wit$ as the witness.

The ideal functionality $\mathcal{F}_{\mathrm{com}}$ for a commitment receives the message m from the committer, stores m internally and only outputs a notification bit to the receiver. Later, when the committer decides to unveil the message, $\mathcal{F}_{\mathrm{com}}$ forwards m to the receiver. Please note, that the receiver does not learn anything beyond a single bit in the commitment phase. Especially, there is no commitment message c. $\mathcal{F}_{\mathrm{com}}$ is information-theoretically secure. There is no decommitment d neither, not even at the committer's side.

But this is exactly the point, where the step-by-step transition from the real to the ideal model fails. $\mathcal{F}_{\mathrm{ZK}}$ expects c and d as part of its input, which are output by the real commitment scheme, but not by its ideal counterpart.[8] Interestingly, the (completely) real construction is a UC-secure realization of $\mathcal{F}_{\text{cp}}$[9] nonetheless, but this can only be proven in a monolithic way not by composition.

Figure 5.1 shows a commuting diagram which illustrates the favored, but failing construction. The upper left corner represents a completely real protocol consisting of a real commitment scheme π_{com}, a real ZK-scheme π_{ZK} and a base protocol π_{cp}. The base protocol receives a message m from the environment, input m into π_{com}, receives a decommitment d, feeds this into π_{ZK} and finally outputs what π_{ZK} outputs. Please note, that the construction only works, because the base protocol exploits π_{com}. The base protocol access π_{com} in a whitebox-fashion and directly utilizes the commit message and decommitment information c, d from the underlying commitment primitive, although c, d is not part of the prescribed output of $\mathcal{F}_{\text{com}}$ (illustrated by the curly line). The lower left corner represents the ideal functionality $\mathcal{F}_{\text{cp}}$. Going down from upper left to lower left is possible and represents the monolithic proof. However, the preferred, modular proof would first go the upper right. The upper right corner represents a hybrid in which π_{ZK} has been replaced by $\mathcal{F}_{\text{ZK}}$. This step is (syntactically) possible and the proof (using suitable building blocks) also holds. However, replacing π_{com} by $\mathcal{F}_{\text{com}}$ is impossible, as the decommitment d is lost. I.e., the construction in the lower right corner does not even exist.

At first glance, the problem arises from the fact that $\mathcal{F}_{\text{com}}$ provides information-theoretic security, while a UC-secure real commitment only provides computational security.[10] Having in mind, that the completely real construction is indeed UC-secure, one might conjecture that the ideal formalizations of the building blocks are overly strong beyond what is required for security. To address this problem, a number of approaches have been proposed—none of them, however, being able to fully satisfactorily formalize the weaker guarantees achieved by regular schemes. First, the notion of non-information oracles [CK02] has been proposed that essentially embeds a game-based definition in a composable abstraction module. Unfortunately, it remains unclear what "kind" of security this new notion implies. In essence, a non-information oracle provides the missing piece of information. But there is no sound justification why the facilitated construction remains secure, especially why it does not fail under arbitrary composition.

[8] Note that we are deliberately lying at this point. Of course, the real UC-commitment scheme π_{com} must not output the decommitment d to the committer, because otherwise it would not even syntactically realize $\mathcal{F}_{\text{com}}$ due to a different IO interface. The crucial point is that the commit-and-prove construction uses the game-based notion of a commitment scheme or makes white box access into π_{com}.

[9] Again, we are deliberately lying. Of course, there is no automatism that all combinations of a real commitment scheme and a real ZK-protocol which are composed this way, yield a UC-secure commit-and-prove scheme. The commitment scheme and the ZK-protocol still needs to be carefully chosen.

[10] This is so, as a UC-commitment needs to be extractable.

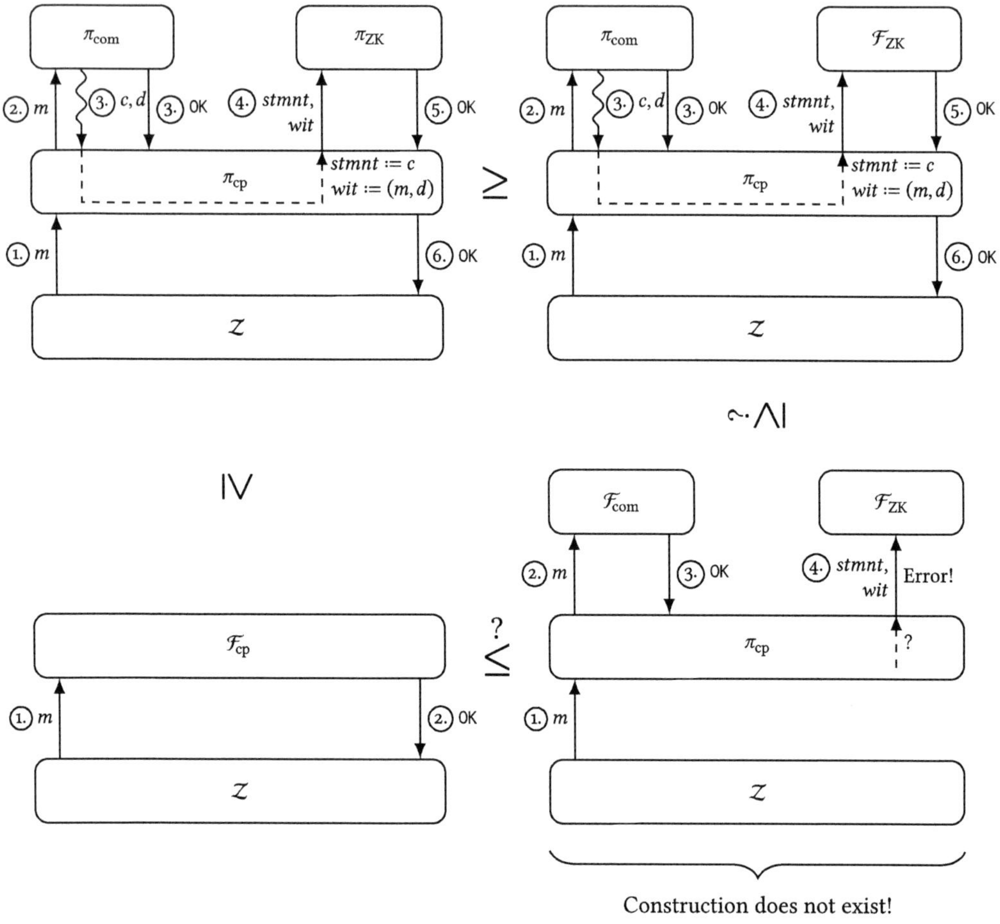

Figure 5.1: The commitment problem in case of commit-and-prove

Only very recently, Camenisch, Drijvers, and Tackmann [CDT19] have captured this lack of modular proofs as a generic problem and proposed a new framework called multi-protocol UC. The essential trick is not to consider a single challenge protocol π_{com} or π_{ZK} and replace them step-by-step, but consider a set of challenge protocols $(\pi_{\text{com}}, \pi_{\text{ZK}})$ and replace them en bloc. The obvious drawback is that one must still separately prove that $(\pi_{\text{com}}, \pi_{\text{ZK}})$ jointly realize $(\mathcal{F}_{\text{com}}, \mathcal{F}_{\text{ZK}})$. Hence, the approach is not completely modular but still somewhat modular. Moreover, it is not completely clear, whether the construction is flawed. For the proof Camenisch, Drijvers, and Tackmann [CDT19] assume the verifier to be incorruptible which is a very strong and unrealistic assumption. They only argue that this condition can be dropped.

On top, our proposed construction requires a feature which has not been addressed so far. We require *homomorphic* commitments. This make the problem of modularity even worse.

6 Assumptions and Building Blocks

In this chapter we introduce the algebraic setting and building blocks we make use of. In particular, the latter includes non-interactive zero-knowledge proofs, commitments, signatures, encryption and pseudo-random functions. Due to efficiency reasons our building blocks are not completely generic and do not work over sets of arbitrary (unstructured) bit strings, but are algebraic and share particularly related groups as their common definitional space. In Section 6.1 we describe this common framework. In Section 6.2 we define the building blocks, describe possible instantiations for these building blocks and explain how these primitives are used in our system.

6.1 Algebraic Setting and Hardness Assumptions

The following definitions are adopted from [Nag+17].

Definition 6.1 (Pairing)

(1) *Let* $G_1 = \langle g_1 \rangle, G_2 = \langle g_2 \rangle, G_T = \langle g_T \rangle$ *be three cyclic groups of prime order* $\mathfrak{p}$ *and* g_1, g_2, g_T*, resp., their generators. A map* $e : G_1 \times G_2 \to G_T$ *with*

$$\forall a \in G_1, b \in G_2, x, y \in \mathbb{Z}_\mathfrak{p} : e(a^x, b^y) = e(a, b)^{xy} \tag{6.1}$$

is called bilinear *or a* pairing.

(2) *A pairing e is called* non-degenerated *if and only if* $e(g_1, g_2)$ *generates* G_T.

Please note, that the co-domain of a pairing e is a sub-group of G_T. Hence, for prime order groups, e is either trivial, i.e. $e(a, b) = 1 \; \forall a \in G_1, b \in G_2$ or non-degenerated, i.e. generates the whole target group.

Moreover, e is called efficiently computable, if there is an efficient algorithm that evaluates e on its inputs. In cryptography, we are only interested in "useful" pairings that are non-degenerated and efficient. From here and below the term "pairing" always implicitly denotes this particular kind of pairing.

Definition 6.2 (Prime-order Bilinear Group Generator) *A* prime-order bilinear group generator *is a PPT algorithm* Setup *that on input of a security parameter* 1^n *outputs a tuple of the form*

$$gp := (G_1, G_2, G_T, e, \mathfrak{p}, g_1, g_2) \leftarrow \mathsf{Setup}(1^n) \tag{6.2}$$

with G_1, G_2, G_T *being descriptions of cyclic groups of prime order* $\mathfrak{p}$, $\log \mathfrak{p} = \Theta(n)$, g_1 *being a generator of* G_1, g_2 *being a generator of* G_2, *and* $e : G_1 \times G_2 \rightarrow G_T$ *being a (non-degenerated, efficient) pairing. W.l.o.g we assume* $g_T = e(g_1, g_2)$. *We call gp a (prime-order) bilinear group description.*

A bilinear group description can be typed according to how the involved groups relate to each other with respect to computational complexity.

Definition 6.3 (Types of Bilinear Group Setting) *Let* $gp := (G_1, G_2, G_T, e, \mathfrak{p}, g_1, g_2)$ *be a bilinear group description as above.*

Type 1: gp is said to be of Type 1, if and only if an efficiently computable isomorphism between G_1 *and* G_2 *exists. Type 1 is also called the* symmetric case.

Type 2: gp is said to be of Type 2, if and only if an efficiently computable homomorphism $\psi : G_2 \rightarrow G_1$ *exists, but the inverse* $\psi^{-1} : G_1 \rightarrow G_2$ *is computationally hard.*

Type 3: gp is said to be of Type 3, if and only if there is no efficiently computable homomorphism between G_1 *and* G_2 *neither way. Type 3 is also called the* asymmetric case.

In the remainder of this thesis, we only consider the asymmetric setting.

Most of our building blocks make use of a particular projection $F_{gp} : \mathbb{Z}_\mathfrak{p}^* \times G_1^* \times \mathbb{Z}_\mathfrak{p}^* \times G_2^* \rightarrow G_1^* \times G_2^*$ with $*$ denoting an arbitrary number of components. For lack of a better name we simply call it the F_{gp}-mapping.

Definition 6.4 (F_{gp}-mapping) *Let* $G_1 = \langle g_1 \rangle$ *and* $G_2 = \langle g_2 \rangle$ *as before. For* $\alpha, \beta, \gamma, \delta \in \mathbb{N}$ *let the family of functions* $\left\{F_{gp}^{(\alpha,\beta,\gamma,\delta)}\right\}_{\alpha,\beta,\gamma,\delta}$ *be defined as*

$$F_{gp}^{(\alpha,\beta,\gamma,\delta)} : \begin{cases} \mathbb{Z}_\mathfrak{p}^\alpha \times G_1^\beta \times \mathbb{Z}_\mathfrak{p}^\gamma \times G_2^\delta \rightarrow G_1^{\alpha+\beta} \times G_2^{\gamma+\delta} \\ (n_1, \dots, n_\alpha, h_{1,1}, \dots, h_{1,\beta}, m_1, \dots, m_\gamma, h_{2,1}, \dots, h_{2,\delta}) \mapsto \\ \qquad (g_1^{n_1}, \dots, g_1^{n_\alpha}, h_{1,1}, \dots, h_{1,\beta}, g_2^{m_1}, \dots, g_2^{m_\gamma}, h_{2,1}, \dots, h_{2,\delta}) \end{cases} \tag{6.3}$$

Informally, $F_{gp}^{(\alpha,\beta,\gamma,\delta)}$ *maps* $\mathbb{Z}_\mathfrak{p}$*-elements to* G_1 *and* G_2*, resp., by exponentiation and acts on* G_1 *and* G_2 *as the identity function.*

Then, F_{gp} is defined as the "union" over this family, or more precisely $F_{gp}(x) := F_{gp}^{(\alpha,\beta,\gamma,\delta)}(x)$ for $x \in \mathbb{Z}_p^\alpha \times G_1^\beta \times \mathbb{Z}_p^\gamma \times G_2^\delta$.

Beware, that $F_{gp}^{(\alpha,0,\gamma,\delta)}$ and $F_{gp}^{(\alpha',0,\gamma',\delta)}$ are syntactically indistinguishable for $\alpha + \gamma = \alpha' + \gamma'$ and $\beta = 0$, but in the following the correct domain is always clear from the context. F_{gp} is indeed a projection as $F_{gp} \circ F_{gp} = F_{gp}$ (for matching choices of dimensions). Moreover, if the domain is fixed (i.e. for given $\alpha, \beta, \gamma, \delta$), then F_{gp} is injective and thus invertible[1] on the restricted domain. (This is important in the later definition of proof of knowledge.)

We are now ready to present the hardness assumptions which the instantiations of our building block rely upon. This concludes this section.

The co-CDH assumption is defined as follows

Definition 6.5 (Co-CDH Assumption) *Let $gp := (G_1, G_2, G_T, e, p, g_1, g_2) \leftarrow \mathsf{Setup}(1^n)$. We say that the* co-CDH assumption *holds with respect to gp, if the advantage $\mathsf{Adv}_{gp,\mathcal{A}}^{\mathsf{CO-CDH}}(1^n)$ defined by*

$$\Pr\left[a = g_2^x \;\middle|\; \begin{array}{c} x \stackrel{R}{\leftarrow} \mathbb{Z}_p \\ a \leftarrow \mathcal{A}(1^n, gp, g_1^x) \end{array}\right] \tag{6.4}$$

is negligible in n for all PPT algorithms $\mathcal{A}$.

The SXDH assumption essentially asserts that the DDH assumption holds in both source groups G_1 and G_2 and is formally defined as:

Definition 6.6 (SXDH Assumption) *Let $gp := (G_1, G_2, G_T, e, p, g_1, g_2) \leftarrow \mathsf{Setup}(1^n)$.*

(1) We say that the DDH assumption *holds with respect to gp over G_i if the advantage $\mathsf{Adv}_{gp,i,\mathcal{A}}^{\mathsf{DDH}}(1^n)$ defined by*

$$\left|\Pr\left[b = b' \;\middle|\; \begin{array}{c} x, y, z \stackrel{R}{\leftarrow} \mathbb{Z}_p; h_0 := g_i^{xy}; h_1 := g_i^z \\ b \stackrel{R}{\leftarrow} \{0,1\} \\ b' \leftarrow \mathcal{A}(1^n, gp, g_i^x, g_i^y, h_b) \end{array}\right] - \frac{1}{2}\right| \tag{6.5}$$

is negligible in n for all PPT algorithms $\mathcal{A}$.

(2) We say that the SXDH assumption *holds with respect to gp, if the above holds for both $i = 1$ and $i = 2$.*

[1] N.b., we do not require F_{gp} to be efficiently invertible.

The n'-DDHI assumption (Decisional Diffie-Hellman Inversion assumption) states that no efficient adversary can distinguish $g_1^{1/x}$ from a random group element after having seen n' consecutive group elements for increasing powers of x.

Definition 6.7 (n'-DDHI Assumption) *Let G_1 be a prime-order group with $\mathfrak{p} \in \Theta(2^n)$ and generator g_1. We say that the n'-DDHI assumption holds with respect to G_1 if the advantage $\mathsf{Adv}^{\mathsf{DDHI}}_{G_1,n',\mathcal{A}}(1^n)$ defined by*

$$\left| \Pr\left[b = b' \;\middle|\; \begin{array}{c} x \overset{R}{\leftarrow} \mathbb{Z}_{\mathfrak{p}}; h_0 := g_1^{1/x}; h_1 \overset{R}{\leftarrow} G_1 \\ b \overset{R}{\leftarrow} \{0,1\} \\ b' \leftarrow \mathcal{A}\left(1^n, G_1, \{g_1, g_1^x, g_1^{x^2}, \ldots, g_1^{x^{n'}}\}, h_b\right) \end{array} \right] - \frac{1}{2} \right| \tag{6.6}$$

is negligible in n for all PPT algorithms $\mathcal{A}$.

The co-DLIN assumption is defined as follows:

Definition 6.8 (co-DLIN Assumption) *Let $gp := (G_1, G_2, G_T, e, \mathfrak{p}, g_1, g_2) \leftarrow \mathsf{Setup}(1^n)$. We say that the co-DLIN assumption holds with respect to gp, if the advantage $\mathsf{Adv}^{\mathsf{CO-DLIN}}_{gp,\mathcal{A}}(1^n)$ defined by*

$$\Pr\left[b = b' \;\middle|\; \begin{array}{l} \alpha, \beta, \gamma \overset{R}{\leftarrow} \mathbb{Z}_{\mathfrak{p}} \\ b \overset{R}{\leftarrow} \{0,1\} \\ \check{h}_1 := g_1^{\alpha}, \check{h}_2 := g_1^{\beta}, \check{h}_3 := g_1^{\alpha+\beta+b\gamma} \\ \hat{h}_1 := g_2^{\alpha}, \hat{h}_2 := g_2^{\beta}, \hat{h}_3 := g_2^{\alpha+\beta+b\gamma} \\ b' \leftarrow \mathcal{A}(1^n, gp, \check{h}_1, \check{h}_2, \check{h}_3, \hat{h}_1, \hat{h}_2, \hat{h}_3) \end{array} \right] \tag{6.7}$$

is negligible in n for all PPT algorithms $\mathcal{A}$.

Our construction relies on the co-CDH assumption and the security of our building blocks (cp. Section 6.2). For our special instantiation of the building blocks, security holds under the SXDH and co-DLIN assumption. The former implies the co-CDH assumption.

6.2 Cryptographic Building Blocks

Our semi-generic construction makes use of various cryptographic primitives including (F_{gp}-extractable) NIZK proofs, equivocal and extractable homomorphic commitments, digital signatures, public-key encryption, symmetric encryption and pseudo-random functions. All building blocks are aligned to a bilinear group setting in the type 3 case, i.e. they do not require an efficiently computable homomorphism between the involved groups. On the contrary, the security of their instantiation relies on the fact that such an homomorphism does not exist. In the following, $gp := (G_1, G_2, G_T, e, \mathfrak{p}, g_1, g_2) \leftarrow \mathsf{Setup}(1^n)$ denotes a suitable bilinear group description (cp. Definition 6.2).

Additionally, the latter building blocks need to be efficiently and securely combinable with the chosen NIZK proof system, which is Groth-Sahai (GS) in our case. In the following, we formally define these building blocks and describe possible instantiations.

6.2.1 Non-Interactive Zero-Knowledge Proofs

Let R_{gp} be a witness relation for some NP language

$$L_{gp} = \left\{ stmnt \,\middle|\, \exists\ wit \text{ s.t. } (stmnt, wit) \in R_{gp} \right\}. \tag{6.8}$$

A zero-knowledge proof allows a prover $\mathcal{P}$ to convince a verifier $\mathcal{V}$ that some *stmnt* is contained in L_{gp} without $\mathcal{V}$ learning anything beyond that fact. In a non-interactive zero-knowledge proof (NIZK), only one message, namely the proof π, is sent from $\mathcal{P}$ to $\mathcal{V}$ for that purpose.

More precisely, a (group-based) NIZK scheme is defined as:

Definition 6.9 (Non-Interactive Zero-Knowledge Proof Scheme) *Let $gp := (G_1, G_2, G_T, e, \mathfrak{p}, g_1, g_2) \leftarrow \mathsf{Setup}(1^n)$ be as usual and F_{gp} the projection as in Definition 6.4. Let R_{gp} be an efficiently verifiable relation containing tuples $(stmnt, wit)$. We call stmnt the statement, and wit the witness. Let L_{gp} be the language containing all statements stmnt such that $(stmnt, wit) \in R_{gp}$. Let $\mathsf{POK} := (\mathsf{Setup}, \mathsf{Prove}, \mathsf{Vfy})$ be a tuple of PPT algorithms such that*

- Setup *takes as input gp and outputs a (public) CRS crs_{pok}.*
- Prove *takes as input the CRS crs_{pok}, a statement stmnt, and a witness wit with $(stmnt, wit) \in R_{gp}$ and outputs a proof π.*
- Vfy *takes as input the CRS crs_{pok}, a statement stmnt, and a proof π and outputs* 1 *or* 0.

POK *is called a NIZK proof scheme for R_{gp} with F_{gp}-extractability, if the following properties are satisfied:*

(1) Perfect completeness: *For all $crs_{\mathsf{pok}} \leftarrow \mathsf{Setup}(gp)$, $(stmnt, wit) \in R_{gp}$, and $\pi \leftarrow \mathsf{Prove}(crs_{\mathsf{pok}}, stmnt, wit)$ we have that $\mathsf{Vfy}(crs_{\mathsf{pok}}, stmnt, \pi) = 1$.*

(2) Perfect soundness: *For all (possibly unbounded) adversaries $\mathcal{A}$ we have that*

$$\Pr\left[0 \leftarrow \mathsf{Vfy}(crs_{\mathsf{pok}}, stmnt, \pi) \,\middle|\, \begin{array}{c} crs_{\mathsf{pok}} \leftarrow \mathsf{Setup}(gp) \\ (stmnt, \pi) \leftarrow \mathcal{A}(crs_{\mathsf{pok}}) \\ stmnt \notin L_{gp} \end{array} \right] \tag{6.9}$$

is 1.

(3) Perfect F_{gp}-extractability: *There exists a polynomial-time extractor* (SetupExt, Extract) *such that for all (possibly unbounded) adversaries* $\mathcal{A}$

(a) *we have that the advantage* $\mathsf{Adv}^{\mathsf{pok-setup-ext}}_{\mathsf{POK},\mathcal{A}}(gp)$ *defined by*

$$\Big|\Pr\big[1 \leftarrow \mathcal{A}(crs_{\mathsf{pok}}) \,\big|\, crs_{\mathsf{pok}} \leftarrow \mathsf{Setup}(gp)\big] \\ - \Pr\big[1 \leftarrow \mathcal{A}(crs'_{\mathsf{pok}}) \,\big|\, (crs'_{\mathsf{pok}}, td_{\mathsf{epok}}) \leftarrow \mathsf{SetupExt}(gp)\big]\Big| \tag{6.10}$$

is zero.

(b) *we have that the probability* $\mathsf{Succs}^{\mathsf{pok-ext}}_{\mathsf{POK},\mathcal{A}}(gp)$ *of a successful extraction defined by*

$$\Pr\left[\begin{array}{c|c} & (crs'_{\mathsf{pok}}, td_{\mathsf{epok}}) \leftarrow \mathsf{SetupExt}(gp) \\ \exists\, wit : F_{gp}(wit) = Wit \wedge & (stmnt, \pi) \leftarrow \mathcal{A}(crs'_{\mathsf{pok}}, td_{\mathsf{epok}}) \\ (stmnt, wit) \in R_{gp} & 1 \leftarrow \mathsf{Vfy}(crs'_{\mathsf{pok}}, stmnt, \pi) \\ & Wit \leftarrow \mathsf{Extract}(crs'_{\mathsf{pok}}, td_{\mathsf{epok}}, stmnt, \pi) \end{array}\right] \tag{6.11}$$

is 1.

(4) Composable zero-knowledge: *There exists a polynomial-time simulator* (SetupSim, ProveSim) *such that for all PPT adversaries* $\mathcal{A}$

(a) *we have that the advantage* $\mathsf{Adv}^{\mathsf{pok-setup-sim}}_{\mathsf{POK},\mathcal{A}}(gp)$ *defined by*

$$\Big|\Pr\big[1 \leftarrow \mathcal{A}(crs_{\mathsf{pok}}) \,\big|\, crs_{\mathsf{pok}} \leftarrow \mathsf{Setup}(gp)\big] \\ - \Pr\big[1 \leftarrow \mathcal{A}(crs'_{\mathsf{pok}}) \,\big|\, (crs'_{\mathsf{pok}}, td_{\mathsf{spok}}) \leftarrow \mathsf{SetupSim}(gp)\big]\Big| \tag{6.12}$$

is negligible in n.[2]

[2] N.b., the terms implicitly depend on n, because $gp \leftarrow \mathsf{Setup}(1^n)$ does and we require $\log p \in \Theta(1^n)$ for the group modulus

(b) *we have that the advantage* $\mathsf{Adv}^{\mathsf{pok-zk}}_{\mathsf{POK},\mathcal{A}}(gp)$ *defined by*

$$\Big|\Pr\big[1 \leftarrow \mathcal{A}^{\mathsf{ProveSim}(crs'_{\mathsf{pok}},td_{\mathsf{spok}},\cdot,\cdot)}(crs'_{\mathsf{pok}}, td_{\mathsf{spok}}) \big| (crs'_{\mathsf{pok}}, td_{\mathsf{epok}}) \leftarrow \mathsf{SetupExt}(gp)\big] \\ - \Pr\big[1 \leftarrow \mathcal{A}^{\mathsf{Prove}(crs'_{\mathsf{pok}},\cdot,\cdot)}(crs'_{\mathsf{pok}}, td_{\mathsf{spok}}) \,\big|\, (crs'_{\mathsf{pok}}, td_{\mathsf{epok}}) \leftarrow \mathsf{SetupExt}(gp)\big]\Big| \tag{6.13}$$

is negligible in n. Here, $\mathcal{A}$ *has oracle access either to* $\mathsf{ProveSim}(crs'_{\mathsf{pok}}, td_{\mathsf{spok}}, \cdot, \cdot)$ *or* $\mathsf{Prove}(crs'_{\mathsf{pok}}, \cdot, \cdot)$. *Both* ProveSim *and* Prove *return* $\perp$ *on input* $(stmnt, wit) \notin R_{gp}$.

We wish to point out some remarks.

Remark 6.10

(1) F_{gp}*-extractability actually implies soundness: If there was a false statement stmnt which verifies and thus violates soundness, then there is obviously no witness wit for stmnt, which violates extractability.*

(2) *Extractability essentially means that* Extract*—given a trapdoor* td_{epok}*—is able to extract* $F_{gp}(wit)$ *for an NP-witness wit for stmnt* $\in L_{gp}$ *from any valid proof* π*. If* F_{gp} *is the identity function, then the actual witness is extracted and the scheme is called a* proof of knowledge.

Our Instantiation

We choose the SXDH-based Groth-Sahai (GS) proof system [EG14; GS08] as our NIZK scheme. On the one hand, it allows for very efficient proofs under standard assumptions. On the other hand, GS comes with two drawbacks which makes using it sometimes pretty tricky:

- Extract only extracts an F_{gp}-mapping $F_{gp}(wit)$ of the witness and thus GS is not a real proof of knowledge, if the witness contains $\mathbb{Z}_p$-elements.
- GS does not support arbitrary relations R_{gp} over the underlying groups but only systems of certain restricted types of equations.

We work around both issues by carefully choosing the remaining building blocks and the languages of NP-statements we need to prove. Also, in many places, the proof of security for our system does not require This holds indeed, if the co-domain of F_{gp} is restricted to the particular NP-language under consideration. a true proof of knowledge. The existence of a unique witness suffices. This holds indeed, if the co-domain of F_{gp} is restricted to the particular NP-language under consideration.

For the sake of completeness, we summarize what types of equations are supported by GS. In the following, let $X_1, X_2, \ldots \in G_1$, $x_1, x_2, \ldots \in \mathbb{Z}_p$, $Y_1, Y_2, \ldots \in G_2$, as well as $y_1, y_2, \ldots \in \mathbb{Z}_p$ denote secret variables, i.e. the witnesses, and let $A, A_1, A_2, \ldots \in G_1$, $a_1, a_2, \ldots \in \mathbb{Z}_p$, $B, B_1, B_2, \ldots \in G_2$, $b_1, b_2, \ldots \in \mathbb{Z}_p$, $C \in G_T$ as well as $c, c_{1,1}, c_{1,2}, c_{2,1}, \ldots \mathbb{Z}_p$ denote public constants.

- *Pairing-Product Equation (PPE):*

$$\prod_i e(A_i, Y_i) \prod_j e(X_j, B_j) \prod_i \prod_j e(X_i, Y_j)^{c_{i,j}} = C \tag{6.14}$$

  if there is a known decomposition for $C = \prod_k e(A'_k, B'_k)$ with public constants $A'_1, A'_2, \ldots \in G_1$ and $B'_1, B'_2, \ldots \in G_2$.

- *Multi-Scalar Equation (MSE) over G_1:*

$$\prod_i A_i^{x_i} \prod_j X_j^{a_j} \prod_i \prod_j X_j^{c_{i,j} x_j} = A \tag{6.15}$$

- *Multi-Scalar Equation (MSE) over G_2:*

$$\prod_i B_i^{y_i} \prod_j Y_j^{b_j} \prod_i \prod_j Y_j^{c_{i,j} y_i} = B \tag{6.16}$$

- *Quadratic Equation (QE) over $\mathbb{Z}_p$:*

$$\sum_i a_i x_i + \sum_j b_j y_j + \sum_i \sum_j c_{i,j} x_i y_j = c \tag{6.17}$$

6.2.2 Commitments

A commitment scheme is a two-party protocol between a sender and a receiver. In the first phase—called the commit phase—the sender commits itself to a message m such that the message remains hidden to the receiver. Later, in the second phase—called the unveil phase—the sender unveils the message to the receiver and the receiver is convinced that the sender has been bound to the original message and is unable to claim a different message. A commitment scheme is called non-interactive, if committing and unveiling only requires a single message from the sender to the receiver. Let $gp := (G_1, G_2, G_T, e, p, g_1, g_2) \leftarrow \mathsf{Setup}(1^n)$ be as usual and F_{gp} the projection as in Definition 6.4. A commitment scheme is called an (group-based) commitment scheme with F_{gp}-binding, if the sender commits to a message m but unveils the commitment using $F_{gp}(m)$. We call the codomain of F_{gp} the implicit message space.

Definition 6.11 ((Group-Based, Non-Interactive) Commitment Scheme)
A (group-based) commitment scheme $\mathsf{COM} := (\mathsf{Setup}, \mathsf{Commit}, \mathsf{Open})$ *with F_{gp}-binding consists of three algorithms:*

- Setup *is a PPT algorithm, which takes gp as input and outputs public parameters* crs_{com}.

- Commit *is a PPT algorithm, which takes as input parameters* crs_{com} *and a message* $m \in \mathcal{M}$ *and outputs a commitment c to m and some decommitment value d.*

- Open *is a deterministic polynomial-time algorithm, which takes as input parameters* crs_{com}, *a commitment c, an implicit message* $M \in \mathcal{M}'$, *and a decommitment value d. It returns either* 0 *or* 1.

COM *is* correct *if* $\mathsf{Open}(crs_{\mathsf{com}}, F_{gp}(m), c, d) = 1$ *holds for all* $crs_{\mathsf{com}} \leftarrow \mathsf{Setup}(gp)$, $m \in \mathcal{M}$, *and* $(c,d) \leftarrow \mathsf{Commit}(crs_{\mathsf{com}}, m)$.

We say that COM *is* hiding, F_{gp}-binding, equivocal *and* extractable, *if it the following properties hold:*

(1) Hiding: *For all PPT adversaries* $\mathcal{A}$ *it holds that the advantage* $\mathsf{Adv}^{\mathsf{Hiding}}_{\mathsf{COM},\mathcal{A}}(gp)$ *defined by*

$$\left| \Pr\left[b = b' \;\middle|\; \begin{array}{c} crs_{\mathsf{com}} \leftarrow \mathsf{Setup}(gp) \\ (m_0, m_1, state) \leftarrow \mathcal{A}(crs_{\mathsf{com}}) \\ b \overset{R}{\leftarrow} \{0,1\} \\ (m,d) \leftarrow \mathsf{Commit}(crs_{\mathsf{com}}, m_b) \\ b' \leftarrow \mathcal{A}(c, state) \end{array} \right] - \frac{1}{2} \right| \tag{6.18}$$

is negligible in n. The scheme is called statistically hiding *if* $\mathsf{Adv}^{\mathsf{Hiding}}_{\mathsf{COM},\mathcal{A}}(gp)$ *is negligible even for an unbounded adversary* $\mathcal{A}$.

(2) F_{gp}-binding: *For all PPT adversaries* $\mathcal{A}$ *it holds that the advantage* $\mathsf{Adv}^{F_{gp}\text{-binding}}_{\mathcal{A}}(gp)$ *defined by*

$$\Pr\left[\begin{array}{c} \mathsf{Open}(crs_{\mathsf{com}}, M, c, d) = 1 \wedge \\ \mathsf{Open}(crs_{\mathsf{com}}, M', c, d') = 1 \wedge \\ M \neq M' \end{array} \;\middle|\; \begin{array}{c} crs_{\mathsf{com}} \leftarrow \mathsf{Setup}(gp) \\ (c, M, d, M', d') \leftarrow \mathcal{A}(1^n, crs_{\mathsf{com}}) \end{array} \right] \tag{6.19}$$

is negligible in n.

(3) Equivocal: *There exist PPT algorithms* SetupSim, CommitSim *and* Equivoke *such that for all PPT adversaries* $\mathcal{A}$

(a) *we have that the advantage* $\mathsf{Adv}^{\mathsf{SetupSim}}_{\mathsf{COM},\mathcal{A}}(gp)$ *defined by*

$$\Big|\Pr\big[1 \leftarrow \mathcal{A}(crs_{\mathsf{com}}) \,\big|\, crs_{\mathsf{com}} \leftarrow \mathsf{Setup}(gp)\big] \\ - \Pr\big[1 \leftarrow \mathcal{A}(crs'_{\mathsf{com}}) \,\big|\, (crs'_{\mathsf{com}}, td_{\mathsf{eqcom}}) \leftarrow \mathsf{SetupSim}(gp)\big]\Big| \tag{6.20}$$

is negligible in n.

(b) *we have that the advantage* $\mathsf{Adv}^{\mathsf{Equiv}}_{\mathsf{COM},\mathcal{A}}(gp)$ *defined by*

$$\left|\Pr\left[1 \leftarrow \mathcal{A}\begin{pmatrix} crs'_{\mathsf{com}}, td_{\mathsf{eqcom}}, \\ m, c, d \end{pmatrix} \middle| \begin{array}{c} (crs'_{\mathsf{com}}, td_{\mathsf{eqcom}}) \leftarrow \mathsf{SetupSim}(gp), \\ m \leftarrow \mathcal{M}, \\ (c,d) \leftarrow \mathsf{Commit}(crs'_{\mathsf{com}}, m) \end{array}\right] \right. \\ \left. - \Pr\left[1 \leftarrow \mathcal{A}\begin{pmatrix} crs'_{\mathsf{com}}, td_{\mathsf{eqcom}}, \\ m, c', d' \end{pmatrix} \middle| \begin{array}{c} (crs'_{\mathsf{com}}, td_{\mathsf{eqcom}}) \leftarrow \mathsf{SetupSim}(gp), \\ (c', r) \leftarrow \mathsf{CommitSim}(gp), \\ m \leftarrow \mathcal{M}, \\ d' \leftarrow \mathsf{Equivoke}(crs'_{\mathsf{com}}, td_{\mathsf{eqcom}}, m, r) \end{array}\right]\right| \tag{6.21}$$

is zero.

(4) F_{gp}-Extractable: *There exist PPT algorithms* SetupExt *and* Extract *such that for all PPT adversaries* $\mathcal{A}$

(a) *we have that the advantage* $\mathsf{Adv}^{\mathsf{SetupExt}}_{\mathsf{COM},\mathcal{A}}(gp)$ *defined by*

$$\Big|\Pr\big[1 \leftarrow \mathcal{A}(crs_{\mathsf{com}}) \,\big|\, crs_{\mathsf{com}} \leftarrow \mathsf{Setup}(gp)\big] \\ - \Pr\big[1 \leftarrow \mathcal{A}(crs'_{\mathsf{com}}) \,\big|\, (crs'_{\mathsf{com}}, td_{\mathsf{extcom}}) \leftarrow \mathsf{SetupExt}(gp)\big]\Big| \tag{6.22}$$

is negligible in n.

(b) *we have that the advantage* $\mathsf{Adv}^{\mathsf{Ext}}_{\mathsf{COM},\mathcal{A}}(n)$ *defined by*

$$\Pr\left[\begin{array}{c} \exists\, m, r\colon\ c = \mathsf{Commit}(crs'_{\mathsf{com}}, m; r) \wedge \\ \mathsf{Extract}(crs'_{\mathsf{com}}, td_{\mathsf{extcom}}, c) \neq F_{gp}(m) \end{array} \middle| \begin{array}{c} (crs'_{\mathsf{com}}, td_{\mathsf{extcom}}) \leftarrow \mathsf{SetupExt}(gp), \\ c \leftarrow \mathcal{A}(crs'_{\mathsf{com}}) \end{array}\right] \tag{6.23}$$

is zero.

Furthermore, assume that the message space of COM *is an additive group. Then* COM *is called* additively homomorphic, *if there exist additional PPT algorithms* $c \leftarrow \mathsf{AddC}(crs_{\mathsf{com}}, c_1, c_2)$ *and*

$d \leftarrow$ AddD*($crs_{\text{com}}, d_1, d_2$) which on input of two commitments and corresponding decommitment values $(c_1, d_1) \leftarrow$* Commit*(crs_{com}, m_1) and $(c_2, d_2) \leftarrow$* Commit*(crs_{com}, m_2), output a commitment c and decommitment d, respectively, such that* Open$(crs_{\text{com}}, c, F_{gp}(m_1 + m_2), d) = 1$.

Finally, we call COM opening complete *if for all $M \in \mathcal{M}'$ and arbitrary values c, d with* Open$(crs_{\text{com}}, m, c, d) = 1$ *holds that there exists $m \in \mathcal{M}$ and randomness r such that $(c, d) \leftarrow$* Commit$(crs_{\text{com}}, m; r)$.

Our Instantiation

We will make use of two commitment schemes that are both based on the SXDH assumption. We first use the shrinking α-message-commitment scheme from Abe et al. [Abe+15]. This commitment scheme has message space $\mathbb{Z}_p^\alpha$, commitment space G_2 and opening value space G_1. It is statistically hiding, additively homomorphic, equivocal, and F'_{gp}-Binding, for $F'_{gp}(m_1, \dots, m_\alpha) := (g_1^{m_1}, \dots, g_1^{m_\alpha})$. We use this commitment scheme as C1 with CRS $crs_{\text{com}}^{(1)}$ and C2 with CRS $crs_{\text{com}}^{(2)}$ in the following ways in our system:

- In IssueWallet and ProveParticipation we use C2 for messages from $\mathbb{Z}_p$.
- In IssueWallet we use C1 for messages from $\mathbb{Z}_p$, $\mathbb{Z}_p^2$ and $\mathbb{Z}_p^4$.
- In Deposit task we use C1 for messages from $\mathbb{Z}_p$ and $\mathbb{Z}_p^4$.

We also use the (dual-mode) equivocal and extractable commitment scheme from Groth and Sahai [GS08]. This commitment scheme has message space G_1, commitment space G_1^2 and opening value space $\mathbb{Z}_p^2$. It is equivocal, extractable, hiding and F'_{gp}-Binding for $F'_{gp}(m) := m$. In our system, we use this commitment scheme as C4 with CRS $crs_{\text{com}}^{(4)}$ in IssueWallet and Deposit.

6.2.3 Digital Signatures

A signature allows a signer to issue a signature σ on a message m using its secret signing key sk such that anybody can publicly verify that σ is a valid signature for m using the public verification key pk of the signer but nobody can feasibly forge a signature without knowing sk. Again, we only consider a group-based setting. The standard definition of signature scheme security, EUF-CMA, has been introduced by Goldwasser, Micali, and Rivest [GMR88].

Definition 6.12 ((Group-Based) Signature Scheme) *A* digital signature scheme SIG := (Gen, Sign, Vfy) *consists of three PPT algorithms:*

- Gen *takes gp as input and outputs a key pair (pk, sk). The public key and gp define a message space $\mathcal{M}$.*

- Sign *takes as input the secret key sk and a message $m \in \mathcal{M}$, and outputs a signature σ.*
- Vfy *takes as input the public key pk, a message $m \in \mathcal{M}$, and a purported signature σ, and deterministically outputs a bit.*

We call SIG *correct if for all $m \in \mathcal{M}$, $(pk, sk) \leftarrow \mathsf{Gen}(gp)$, $\sigma \leftarrow \mathsf{Sign}(sk, m)$ we have $1 \leftarrow \mathsf{Vfy}(pk, \sigma, m)$.*

We say that SIG *is EUF-CMA secure if for all PPT adversaries $\mathcal{A}$ it holds that the advantage $\mathsf{Adv}^{\mathsf{EUF-CMA}}_{\mathsf{SIG},\mathcal{A}}(1^n)$ defined by*

$$\Pr\left[\mathsf{Vfy}(pk, \sigma^*, m^*) = 1 \;\middle|\; \begin{array}{c} gp \leftarrow \mathsf{Setup}(1^n) \\ (pk, sk) \leftarrow \mathsf{Gen}(gp) \\ (m^*, \sigma^*) \leftarrow \mathcal{A}^{\mathsf{Sign}(sk,\cdot)}(1^n, pk) \\ m^* \notin \{m_1, \dots, m_q\} \end{array}\right] \tag{6.24}$$

is negligible in n, where $\mathsf{Sign}(sk, \cdot)$ is an oracle that, on input m, returns $\mathsf{Sign}(sk, m)$, and $\{m_1, \dots, m_q\}$ denotes the set of messages queried by $\mathcal{A}$ to its oracle.

Our Instantiation

As we need to prove statements about signatures, the signature scheme has to be algebraic. For our construction, we use the structure-preserving signature scheme of Abe et al. [Abe+11], which is currently the most efficient structure-preserving signature scheme. Its EUF-CMA security proof is in the generic group model, a restriction we consider reasonable with respect to our goal of constructing a highly efficient BBA+ scheme. An alternative secure in the plain model would be [KPW15]. For the scheme in [Abe+11], one needs to fix two additional parameters $\mu, \nu \in \mathbb{N}_0$ defining the actual message space $G_1^\nu \times G_2^\mu$. Then $sk \in \mathbb{Z}_p^{\mu+\nu+2}$, $pk \in G_1^{\mu+2} \times G_2^\nu$ and $\sigma \in G_2^2 \times G_1$.

We use the signature scheme SIG from Abe et al. [Abe+11] in the following ways in our system:

- For messages from $G_2 \times G_1^j$ ($\nu = j$ and $\mu = 1$) to sign the fixed part of a wallet in IssueWallet.
- For messages from $G_2 \times G_1$ ($\nu = 1$ and $\mu = 1$) to sign the updatable part of a wallet in IssueWallet and Deposit.
- For messages from G_1^3 ($\nu = 3$ and $\mu = 0$) to sign recalculation tags in IssueWallet and Deposit.
- For messages from $(G_1^3 \times G_2) \times (G_1^2 \times G_2^3) \times G_1^y$ ($\nu = 5 + y$ and $\mu = 4$) to sign the public key and the attributes of a PoS in the CertifyPOS and RegisterOp.

6.2.4 Asymmetric Encryption

We use the standard definitions for asymmetric encryption schemes and corresponding security notions, except that the algorithms take $gp := (G_1, G_2, G_T, e, p, g_1, g_2) \leftarrow \mathsf{Setup}(1^n)$ as an additional parameter to fit our algebraic setting.

Definition 6.13 (Asymmetric Encryption) *An* asymmetric encryption scheme $\mathsf{ENC} :=$ $(\mathsf{Gen}, \mathsf{Enc}, \mathsf{Dec})$ *consists of three PPT algorithms:*

- $\mathsf{Gen}(gp)$ *outputs a pair* (pk, sk) *of keys, with pk being the (public) encryption key and sk being the (secret) decryption key.*
- $\mathsf{Enc}(pk, m)$ *takes a key pk and a plaintext message* $m \in \mathcal{M}$ *and outputs a ciphertext c.*
- $\mathsf{Dec}(sk, c)$ *takes a key sk and a ciphertext c and outputs a plaintext message m or* $\perp$. *We assume that* Dec *is deterministic.*

Correctness is defined in the usual sense.

An asymmetric encryption scheme ENC *is* IND-CCA2*-secure if for all PPT adversaries* $\mathcal{A}$ *it holds that the advantage* $\mathsf{Adv}^{\mathsf{IND-CCA-asym}}_{\mathsf{ENC},\mathcal{A}}(gp)$ *defined by*

$$\left| \Pr\left[b = b' \;\middle|\; \begin{array}{c} (pk, sk) \leftarrow \mathsf{Gen}(gp) \\ (state, m_0, m_1) \leftarrow \mathcal{A}^{\mathsf{Dec}(sk,\cdot)}(1^n, pk) \\ b \overset{R}{\leftarrow} \{0,1\} \\ c^* \leftarrow \mathsf{Enc}(pk, m_b) \\ b' \leftarrow \mathcal{A}^{\mathsf{Dec}'(sk,\cdot)}(state, c^*) \end{array} \right] - \frac{1}{2} \right| \tag{6.25}$$

is negligible in n, with $|m_0| = |m_1|$, $\mathsf{Dec}(sk, \cdot)$ *being an oracle that gets a ciphertext c from the adversary and returns* $\mathsf{Dec}(sk, c)$ *and* $\mathsf{Dec}'(sk, \cdot)$ *being the same, except that it returns* $\perp$ *on input* c^*.

An asymmetric encryption scheme ENC *is* NM-CCA2*-secure if for all PPT adversaries* $\mathcal{A}$ *it holds that the advantage* $\mathsf{Adv}^{\mathsf{NM-CCA}}_{\mathsf{ENC},\mathcal{A}}(1^n)$ *defined by*

$$\left| \mathsf{Succs}^{\mathsf{NM-CCA}}_{\mathsf{ENC},\mathcal{A},\mathrm{real}}(1^n) - \mathsf{Succs}^{\mathsf{NM-CCA}}_{\mathsf{ENC},\mathcal{A},\mathrm{random}}(1^n) \right| \tag{6.26}$$

is negligible with

$$\mathsf{Succs}^{\mathsf{NM-CCA}}_{\mathsf{ENC},\mathcal{A},\mathrm{real}}(1^n) := \Pr\left[\begin{array}{c|c} & (pk,sk) \leftarrow \mathsf{Gen}(gp) \\ c \notin \boldsymbol{c} \wedge & (M, state) \leftarrow \mathcal{A}^{\mathsf{Dec}(sk,\cdot)}(1^n, pk) \\ \bot \notin \boldsymbol{m} \wedge & m \xleftarrow{R} M \\ R(m, \boldsymbol{m}) = 1 & c \leftarrow \mathsf{Enc}(pk, m) \\ & (R, \boldsymbol{c}) \leftarrow \mathcal{A}^{\mathsf{Dec}'(sk,\cdot)}(1^n, state, c) \\ & \boldsymbol{m} \leftarrow \mathsf{Dec}(sk, \boldsymbol{c}) \end{array}\right] \tag{6.27}$$

and

$$\mathsf{Succs}^{\mathsf{NM-CCA}}_{\mathsf{ENC},\mathcal{A},\mathrm{random}}(1^n) := \Pr\left[\begin{array}{c|c} & (pk,sk) \leftarrow \mathsf{Gen}(gp) \\ c \notin \boldsymbol{c} \wedge & (M, state) \leftarrow \mathcal{A}^{\mathsf{Dec}(sk,\cdot)}(1^n, pk) \\ \bot \notin \boldsymbol{m} \wedge & m, \widetilde{m} \xleftarrow{R} M \\ R(\widetilde{m}, \boldsymbol{m}) = 1 & c \leftarrow \mathsf{Enc}(pk, m) \\ & (R, \boldsymbol{c}) \leftarrow \mathcal{A}^{\mathsf{Dec}'(sk,\cdot)}(1^n, state, c) \\ & \boldsymbol{m} \leftarrow \mathsf{Dec}(sk, \boldsymbol{c}) \end{array}\right], \tag{6.28}$$

where M denotes a space of valid, equally long messages, $R \subseteq M \times M^*$ denotes an relation, $\mathsf{Dec}(sk,\cdot)$ *is an oracle that gets a ciphertext c from the adversary and returns* $\mathsf{Dec}(sk,c)$ *and* $\mathsf{Dec}'(sk,\cdot)$ *is the same, except that it returns $\bot$ on input c.*

An encryption is IND-CCA2 secure if and only if it is NM-CCA2 secure [Bel+98].

Our Instantiation

We will make use of two different IND-CCA2-secure encryption schemes:

- We use a variant of Camenisch et al. [Cam+11] to directly instantiate the explicit encryption scheme ENC1 for the deposit wallet IDs.
- We use the encryption scheme by Cash, Kiltz, and Shoup [CKS08] as the outer encryption of ENC2 for the encryption of the recalculation tags.
- We also implicitly use the same encryption [CKS08] to realize the secure channels of $\mathcal{F}_{\mathrm{msg}}$ which underlies our model.

The scheme by Cash, Kiltz, and Shoup [CKS08] is based on the twin-DH assumption. For efficiency reasons we utilize the typical hybrid approach and use the asymmetric scheme to setup a session key for a symmetric encryption of messages following the KEM/DEM pattern (cp. Section 6.2.5). Note that we don't require any algebraic properties, especially we don't need to prove anything about ciphertexts. For the ease of presentation, we act as if the message space of ENC2 was $G_1 \times G_1 \times \mathbb{Z}_p \times (G_1^2 \times G_2^3) \times (G_2^2 \times G_1)$, because this is the space of the recalculation tags ω_{rc}. However, the encryption scheme Cash, Kiltz, and Shoup [CKS08] does not depend on this, but treats plain messages and ciphertexts as opaque bit strings.

The scheme for ENC1 is an adapted variant of the structure-preserving, IND-CCA2 secure encryption scheme by Camenisch et al. [Cam+11]. Thus, some remarks are in order. The original scheme is formalized for a group setting of type 1, but we need a scheme that is secure in the asymmetric type 3 setting. For the conversion we followed the generic transformation proposed by Abe et al. [Abe+14] with some additional, manual optimizations. The transformed scheme encrypts vectors of G_1-elements and is secure under the co-DLIN assumption (cp. Definition 6.8) which holds in the generic group model. This follows automatically from [Abe+14] (or can also be easily seen by inspecting the original proof in [Cam+11]). We present the modified scheme in full detail.

Definition 6.14 (Type 3 Variant of Camenisch et al. [Cam+11]) *Let* $gp := (G_1, G_2, G_T, e, p, g_1, g_2) \leftarrow \mathsf{Setup}(1^n)$ *be as usual. Let* $\wp$ *be the dimension of the message space* $G_1^{\wp}$. *The algorithms* Gen, Enc *and* Dec *are depicted in Figs. 6.1 to 6.3.*

We instantiate this scheme with $\wp = \ell + 2$.

6.2.5 Symmetric Encryption

We use standard definitions for symmetric encryption schemes and corresponding security notions.

Definition 6.15 (Symmetric Encryption) *A* symmetric encryption scheme ENC := (Gen, Enc, Dec) *consists of three PPT algorithms:*

- Gen(1^n) *outputs a key sk.*
- Enc(sk, m) *takes a key sk and a plaintext message* $m \in \mathcal{M}$ *and outputs a ciphertext c.*
- Dec(sk, c) *takes a key sk and a ciphertext c and outputs a plaintext message m or* $\bot$. *We assume that* Dec *is deterministic.*

As for asymmetric encryption, we require correctness in the usual sense.

We now define a multi-message version of IND-CCA2 security. It is a well-known fact that IND-CCA2 security in the multi-message setting is equivalent to standard IND-CCA2 security. (This can be shown via a standard hybrid argument.)

Gen$(gp, \wp)$

$$
\begin{aligned}
&\text{parse } (G_1, G_2, G_T, e, \mathfrak{p}, g_1, g_2) := gp \\
&\alpha_1, \dots, \alpha_\wp, \beta_0, \dots, \beta_3, \gamma_1, \dots, \gamma_\wp \stackrel{R}{\leftarrow} \mathbb{Z}_\mathfrak{p}^3 \\
&sk := (\{\alpha_i\}_{i=1,\dots,\wp}, \{\beta_i\}_{i=0,\dots,3}, \{\gamma_i\}_{i=1,\dots,\wp}) \\
&\xi_1, \dots, \xi_3 \stackrel{R}{\leftarrow} \mathbb{Z}_\mathfrak{p}^* \\
&\check{h}_1 := g_1^{\xi_1}, \quad \check{h}_2 := g_1^{\xi_2}, \quad \check{h}_3 := g_1^{\xi_3} \\
&\hat{h}_1 := g_2^{\xi_1}, \quad \hat{h}_2 := g_2^{\xi_2}, \quad \hat{h}_3 := g_2^{\xi_3} \\
&x_{i,1} := \check{h}_1^{\alpha_{i,1}} \check{h}_3^{\alpha_{i,3}}, \quad x_{i,2} := \check{h}_2^{\alpha_{i,2}} \check{h}_3^{\alpha_{i,3}}, \quad \text{for } i = 1, \dots, \wp \\
&y_{i,1} := \hat{h}_1^{\beta_{i,1}} \hat{h}_3^{\beta_{i,3}}, \quad y_{i,2} := \hat{h}_2^{\beta_{i,2}} \hat{h}_3^{\beta_{i,3}}, \quad \text{for } i = 0, \dots, 3 \\
&z_{i,1} := \hat{h}_1^{\gamma_{i,1}} \hat{h}_3^{\gamma_{i,3}}, \quad z_{i,2} := \hat{h}_2^{\gamma_{i,2}} \hat{h}_3^{\gamma_{i,3}}, \quad \text{for } i = 1, \dots, \wp \\
&pk := (\check{h}_1, \check{h}_2, \check{h}_3, \hat{h}_1, \hat{h}_2, \hat{h}_3, \\
&\qquad \{x_{i,1}, x_{i,2}\}_{i=1,\dots,\wp}, \{y_{i,1}, y_{i,2}\}_{i=0,\dots,3}, \{z_{i,1}, z_{i,2}\}_{i=1,\dots,\wp}) \\
&\textbf{return } (pk, sk)
\end{aligned}
$$

Figure 6.1: The key generation algorithm Gen of the adapted CCA-secure encryption scheme by Camenisch et al. [Cam+11] with parameter $\wp$ and message space $G_1^\wp$

Enc(pk, m)

$$
\begin{aligned}
&\text{parse } (\check{h}_1, \check{h}_2, \check{h}_3, \hat{h}_1, \hat{h}_2, \hat{h}_3, \{x_{i,1}, x_{i,2}\}_{i=1,\dots,\wp}, \\
&\qquad \{y_{i,1}, y_{i,2}\}_{i=0,\dots,3}, \{z_{i,1}, z_{i,2}\}_{i=1,\dots,\wp}) := pk \\
&r, s \stackrel{R}{\leftarrow} \mathbb{Z}_\mathfrak{p} \\
&\check{u}_1 := \check{h}_1^r \quad \check{u}_2 := \check{h}_2^s \quad \check{u}_3 := \check{h}_3^{r+s} \\
&\hat{u}_1 := \hat{h}_1^r \quad \hat{u}_2 := \hat{h}_2^s \quad \hat{u}_3 := \hat{h}_3^{r+s} \\
&c_i = m_i x_{i,1}^r x_{i,2}^s \text{ for } i = 1, \dots, \wp \\
&v = \prod_{i=0}^{3} e(\check{u}_i, y_{i,1}^r y_{i,2}^s) \prod_{i=1}^{\wp} e(c_i, z_{i,1}^r z_{i,2}^s) \text{ with } \check{u}_0 := g_1 \\
&\mathfrak{c} := (u, c, v) \text{ with } u := (\check{u}_1, \check{u}_2, \check{u}_3, \hat{u}_1, \hat{u}_2, \hat{u}_3) \text{ and } c := (c_1, \dots, c_\wp) \\
&\textbf{return } (\mathfrak{c})
\end{aligned}
$$

Figure 6.2: The encryption algorithm Enc of the adapted CCA-secure encryption scheme by Camenisch et al. [Cam+11] with parameter $\wp$ and message space $G_1^\wp$

$\mathsf{Dec}(sk, \mathfrak{c})$
parse $(\{\alpha_i\}_{i=1,\dots,\wp}, \{\beta_i\}_{i=0,\dots,3}, \{\gamma_i\}_{i=1,\dots,\wp}) := sk$
parse $(u, c, v) := \mathfrak{c}$, $(\check{u}_1, \check{u}_2, \check{u}_3, \hat{u}_1, \hat{u}_2, \hat{u}_3) := u$ and $(c_1, \dots, c_\wp) := c$
$\check{u}_0 := g_1$
if $v \neq \prod_{i=0}^{3} e\left(\check{u}_i, \hat{u}_1^{\beta_{i,1}} \hat{u}_2^{\beta_{i,2}} \hat{u}_3^{\beta_{i,3}}\right) \prod_{i=1}^{\wp} e\left(c_i, \hat{u}_1^{\gamma_{i,1}} \hat{u}_2^{\gamma_{i,2}} \hat{u}_3^{\gamma_{i,3}}\right)$ abort
if $e(\check{u}_i, g_2) \neq e(g_1, \hat{u}_i)$ for any $i \in \{1, 2, 3\}$ abort
$m_i := c_i \check{u}_1^{-\alpha_{i,1}} \check{u}_2^{-\alpha_{i,2}} \check{u}_3^{-\alpha_{i,3}}$ for $i \in \{1, \dots, \wp\}$
$m := (m_1, \dots, m_\wp)$
return (m)

Figure 6.3: The decryption algorithm Dec of the adapted CCA-secure encryption scheme by Camenisch et al. [Cam+11] with parameter $\wp$ and message space $G_1^{\wp}$

Definition 6.16 (IND-CCA2-Security for Symmetric Encryption) *A symmetric encryption scheme* ENC *is* IND-CCA2*-secure if for all PPT adversaries $\mathcal{A}$ it holds that the advantage* $\mathsf{Adv}^{\mathsf{IND-CCA-sym}}_{\mathsf{ENC},\mathcal{A}}(1^n)$ *defined by*

$$\left| \Pr\left[b = b' \;\middle|\; \begin{array}{c} sk \leftarrow \mathsf{Gen}(1^n) \\ (state, j, \boldsymbol{m_0}, \boldsymbol{m_1}) \leftarrow \mathcal{A}^{\mathsf{Enc}(sk,\cdot),\mathsf{Dec}(sk,\cdot)}(1^n) \\ b \leftarrow \{0,1\} \\ \boldsymbol{c}^* \leftarrow (\mathsf{Enc}(sk, m_{b,1}), \dots, \mathsf{Enc}(sk, m_{b,j})) \\ b' \leftarrow \mathcal{A}^{\mathsf{Enc}(sk,\cdot),\mathsf{Dec}'(sk,\cdot)}(state, \boldsymbol{c}^*) \end{array} \right] - \frac{1}{2} \right| \tag{6.29}$$

is negligible in n, where $\boldsymbol{m_0}, \boldsymbol{m_1}$ are two vectors of $j \in \mathbb{N}$ bit strings each such that for all $1 \leq i \leq j$: $|m_{0,i}| = |m_{1,i}|$, $\mathsf{Enc}(sk, \cdot)$ *and* $\mathsf{Dec}(sk, \cdot)$ *denote oracles that return* $\mathsf{Enc}(sk, m)$ *and* $\mathsf{Dec}(sk, c)$ *for a m or c chosen by the adversary, and* $\mathsf{Dec}'(sk, \cdot)$ *is the same as* $\mathsf{Dec}(sk, \cdot)$*, except that it returns* $\perp$ *on input of any c_i^* that is contained in $\boldsymbol{c}^*$.*

Our Instantiation

We use an IND-CCA2-secure symmetric encryption scheme in our protocol to encrypt the exchanged protocol messages. To this end, we combine an IND-CCA2-secure asymmetric encryption (see Section 6.2.4) with an IND-CCA2-secure symmetric encryption in the usual KEM/DEM approach. The symmetric encryption can for example be instantiated with AES in CBC mode together with HMAC based on the SHA-256 hash function. The result will be

IND-CCA2-secure if AES is a pseudo-random permutation and the SHA-256 compression function is a PRF when the data input is seen as the key [Bel15].

6.2.6 Pseudo-Random Functions

A pseudo-random function (PRF)—more precisely a family of PRF's indexed in the seed λ—is a function $\mathsf{F} : \mathcal{L} \times \mathcal{X} \to \mathcal{Y}, (\lambda, x) \mapsto y$ that for a randomly chosen, but constant seed λ is computationally indistinguishable from a randomly chosen function $R : \mathcal{X} \to \mathcal{Y}$. In other words, any PPT adversary given oracle access to either $\mathsf{F}(\lambda, \cdot)$ or $R(\cdot)$ cannot distinguish between them with non-negligible probability. Formally, a PRF is defined as follows.

Definition 6.17 ((Group-Based) Pseudo-Random Function) *Let $gp := (G_1, G_2, G_T, e, p, g_1, g_2) \leftarrow \mathsf{Setup}(1^n)$ be as usual. The key space $\mathcal{L}$, the domain $\mathcal{X}$ and the co-domain $\mathcal{Y}$ may all depend on gp. A (group-based)* pseudo-random function *(PRF)* $\mathsf{PRF} := (\mathsf{Gen}, \mathsf{Eval})$ *consists of two PPT algorithms:*

- Gen *takes gp as input and outputs a seed $\lambda \in \mathcal{L}$.*
- Eval *is a deterministic algorithm which takes as input a seed $\lambda \in \mathcal{L}$ and a value $x \in \mathcal{X}$, and outputs some $y \in \mathcal{Y}$. By abuse of notation, we simply write $y = \mathsf{PRF}(\lambda, x)$ for short.*

We say that PRF *is secure if for all PPT adversaries $\mathcal{A}$ it holds that the advantage $\mathsf{Adv}^{\mathsf{prf}}_{\mathcal{A}}(1^n)$ defined by*

$$\left|\Pr\left[1 \leftarrow \mathcal{A}^{\mathsf{PRF}(\lambda,\cdot)}(gp) \,\middle|\, \lambda \leftarrow \mathsf{Gen}(gp)\right] - \Pr\left[1 \leftarrow \mathcal{A}^{R(\cdot)}(gp) \,\middle|\, R \stackrel{R}{\leftarrow} \{R : \mathcal{X} \to \mathcal{Y}\}\right]\right| \quad (6.30)$$

is negligible in n.

Our Instantiation

As we want to efficiently prove statements about PRF outputs, we use an efficient algebraic construction, namely the Dodis-Yampolskiy PRF [DY04]. This function is defined by $\mathsf{PRF}(\lambda, x) : \mathbb{Z}_p^2 \to G_1$, $(\lambda, x) \mapsto g_1^{\frac{1}{\lambda+x}}$, where $\lambda \stackrel{R}{\leftarrow} \mathbb{Z}_p$ is the random PRF seed. It is secure for inputs $\{0, \dots, n_{\mathsf{PRF}}\} \subset \mathbb{Z}_p$ under the n_{PRF}-DDHI assumption. This is a family of increasingly stronger assumptions which is assumed to hold for asymmetric bilinear groups.

6.2.7 Range Proofs

A range proof is not a real building block on its own, but rather a clever combination of a zero-knowledge scheme with a signature scheme. Nonetheless, in the rest of the thesis we treat range proofs as if there were building blocks and therefore present their construction in this chapter. A range proof asserts in zero-knowledge that some secret $\mathbb{Z}_p$-element w is contained within the range $\{m_l, \dots, m_u\}$. Clearly, such a statement only makes sense, if one pins down a fixed representation of $\mathbb{Z}_p$, reinterprets $\mathbb{Z}_p$-elements as ordinary $\mathbb{Z}$-elements and then resorts to the normal $\leq$-relation over the integers. For the ease of presentation, we fix the representation $\mathbb{Z}_p \triangleq \{0, \dots, p-1\} \subset \mathbb{Z}$ (see also Definitions 2.2 and 2.3). We need range proofs for two purposes:

- To enable the blacklisting mechanism the users must prove during IssueWallet that they have chosen a particular component of their secret smaller than some fixed system parameter. This is a technical necessity such that calculating the DLOG remains feasible in case the users might be blacklisted eventually.
- Also, a range proof could be included into a variant of Disburse such that the users are enabled to prove to have sufficient funds on their wallet without unveiling the actual balance. A scenario that might benefit from such an alternative variant of Disburse is described in Section 2.3.2 as a pre-payment system.

We realize range proofs using Groth-Sahai by applying the signature-based technique of Camenisch, Chaabouni, and shelat [CCs08].

The Trivial Approach

Firstly, we recap the trivial approach to prove that a secret w is within the range $\{m_l, \dots, m_u\}$. The verifier creates a signature for every element in $\{m_l, \dots, m_u\}$ under his secret key and publishes these signatures. Then, the prover proves in zero-knowledge that he knows a signature for his secret value. Obviously, this approach only works if the range $\{m_l, \dots, m_u\}$ is small to keep the number of signatures limited. If the size of the range is proportional to size of the underlying group $\mathbb{Z}_p$, this method requires exponentially many signatures as $\log p \in \Theta(n)$ holds.

An Approach for Aligned Intervals

Camenisch, Chaabouni, and shelat [CCs08] exploit a q-ary representation of the secret w with at most $\eta_{\max}$ positions to overcome this problem. For a fixed base

$$2 \leq q \leq p - 1 \tag{6.31}$$

the maximal admissible number of positions $\eta_{\max}$ is

$$\eta_{\max} := \lfloor \log_q p \rfloor . \tag{6.32}$$

and the largest integer that can be represented equals

$$N_{\max} := q^{\eta_{\max}} - 1. \tag{6.33}$$

The base $q \in \mathbb{N}$ and the maximum number of positions $\eta_{\max} \in \mathbb{N}$ are public design parameters and put into the CRS. Also, the verifier creates a signature for each of the possible digits $\{0, \dots, q-1\}$ in advance and publishes these signatures. For the actual range proof, the verifier and prover first agree on the number of positions $\eta \in \{1, \dots, \eta_{\max}\}$ they want to use. Then the prover secretly computes a representation $w = \sum_{j=0}^{\eta-1} w_j q^j$ with $w_j \in \{0, \dots, q-1\}$. The prover shows in zero-knowledge that equality holds and that he knows a signature for each w_j, i.e. that each w_j is indeed a valid digit in $\{0, \dots, q-1\}$. The actual value of each digit remains secret and the verifier only learns that w can be represented with $\eta \leq \eta_{\max}$ positions. Hence, the approach is only applicable to intervals whose upper limits is aligned to powers of q.

The General Case

In order to prove membership in an arbitrary interval $w \in \{m_{\mathrm{l}}, \dots, m_{\mathrm{u}}\}$ whose limits are not aligned to q-powers, the prover shifts the secret by a pertinent offset and then conducts two basic range proofs for two intervals that have properly aligned boundaries and whose intersection (after reverting the shifting) equals the original interval.

Let $\eta \in \{1, \dots, \eta_{\max}\}$ be defined as

$$\eta := \lfloor \log_q (m_{\mathrm{u}} - m_{\mathrm{l}}) \rfloor + 1 \quad \Leftrightarrow \quad q^{\eta-1} \leq m_{\mathrm{u}} - m_{\mathrm{l}} < q^{\eta} \tag{6.34}$$

and define an offset value as

$$o := q^{\eta} - 1, \tag{6.35}$$

i.e. $o + 1$ is the smallest q-power larger than the length $m_{\mathrm{u}} - m_{\mathrm{l}}$ of the interval. Please note, that q, $\eta_{\max}$ and the boundaries of the interval m_{l}, m_{u} are known by both the verifier and the prover. Hence, the number of needed positions η and the offset value o are public, too. It follows

$$\begin{aligned}
& w \in \{m_{\mathrm{l}}, \dots, m_{\mathrm{u}}\} \\
\Leftrightarrow\ & w - m_{\mathrm{l}} \in \{0, \dots, m_{\mathrm{u}} - m_{\mathrm{l}}\} \\
\Leftrightarrow\ & w - m_{\mathrm{l}} \in \{0, \dots, o\} \cap \{m_{\mathrm{u}} - m_{\mathrm{l}} - o, \dots, m_{\mathrm{u}} - m_{\mathrm{l}}\} \\
\Leftrightarrow\ & \begin{cases} w - m_{\mathrm{l}} \in \{0, \dots, o\} \wedge \\ o + w - m_{\mathrm{u}} \in \{0, \dots, o\} \end{cases}
\end{aligned} \tag{6.37}$$

$$\Leftrightarrow \begin{cases} \exists\, w'_0, \dots, w'_{\eta-1} \in \{0, \dots, q-1\} : w - m_l = \sum_{j=0}^{\eta-1} w'_j q^j \\ \exists\, w''_0, \dots, w''_{\eta-1} \in \{0, \dots, q-1\} : o + w - m_u = \sum_{j=0}^{\eta-1} w''_j q^j \end{cases} \tag{6.37}$$

Unfortunately, the final two lines of equation (6.37) cannot be directly proven in zero-knowledge. For our particular instantiations of the building blocks commitments to $\mathbb{Z}_\mathfrak{p}$-elements are unveiled to the F_{gp}-mapping of the committed value. This implies that equation (6.37) has to be projected by F_{gp} as well. We denote the first $\eta_{\max}$ q-powers of g_1 by

$$Q_j := g_1^{(q^j)} \qquad \text{for } j = 0, \dots, \eta_{\max} - 1. \tag{6.38}$$

These constants are an F_{gp}-mapping of all relevant magnitudes of the positional digit system. For an F_{gp}-mapped secret $W \in G_1$ the prover shows

$$\exists\, w'_0, \dots, w'_{\eta-1} \in \mathbb{Z}_\mathfrak{p} : W^{-1} \prod_{j=0}^{\eta-1} Q_j^{w'_j} = g_1^{-m_l} \tag{6.39}$$

$$\exists\, w''_0, \dots, w''_{\eta-1} \in \mathbb{Z}_\mathfrak{p} : W^{-1} \prod_{j=0}^{\eta-1} Q_j^{w''_j} = g_1^{o-m_u} \tag{6.40}$$

These are MSEs (cp. Section 6.2.1) and therefore perfectly fit into the Groth-Sahai proof system. Please remember, that besides Eqs. (6.39) and (6.40) the prover also has to show that $w'_0, \dots, w'_{\eta-1}, w''_0, \dots, w''_{\eta-1}$ are valid digits in the range $\{0, \dots, q\}$. Hence, the ZK-proof is additionally increased by 2η verifications of signatures that have been published by the verifier.

Final Remarks with Respect to the Implementation

Firstly, the efficiency of range proofs heavily depends on the representation of the elements with individual digits and then proofing statements about the digits in zero-knowledge. The design parameters q and $\eta_{\max}$ are a trade-off between the number of signatures and the size of the NIZK statement. Please note, that the signatures can be pre-computed and re-used for all NIZKs. Hence, a larger q and a smaller $\eta_{\max}$ is usually beneficial.

Secondly, due to rounding errors in $\eta_{\max} := \lfloor \log_q \mathfrak{p} \rfloor$ there is a "margin" of $\mathbb{Z}_\mathfrak{p}$-elements $\{N_{\max} + 1, \dots, \mathfrak{p} - 1\}$ with $N_{\max} := q^{\eta_{\max}} - 1$ that cannot be represented by the positional number system. These $\mathbb{Z}_\mathfrak{p}$-elements encode "illegal" integers.[3] Please note, that setting $\eta_{\max}$ (and $N_{\max}$,

[3] In practical terms this means that only a subset of $\mathbb{Z}_\mathfrak{p}$ can be used and "illegal" integers have to be avoided by the application. We claim, this does not pose a problem in practice. For a usual security level of 80 bit, the

resp.) to a larger value would foil the uniqueness of the representation $w = \sum_{j=0}^{\eta_{\max}-1} w_j q^j$ due to overflow issues. This would thwart the soundness of the range proof.

Thirdly, whenever a constant Q_j appears in a formula the party can compute $g_1^{(q^j)}$ by itself. In practice, it might be beneficial to pre-compute Q_j and include them into the CRS such that they can be looked up quickly when needed.

group order $\mathfrak{p}$ is a prime in the magnitude of 2^{254}. If the base $q = 16$ is used (as we do in our implementation), this yields $\eta_{\max} := \lfloor \log_{16} 2^{254} \rfloor = 63$ and $N_{\max} := 16^{63} = 2^{252}$. In other words, "only" integers between 0 and 2^{252} can be represented, while integers between 2^{252} and 2^{254} are "illegal". For any naturally appearing balances/prices the restricted space of representable elements is far more than sufficient. Although cleartext balances/prices are restricted to a smaller domain, this does not weaken security as randomness and therefore ciphertexts/commitments are still varying over the whole group.

7 System Instantiation

In this chapter we describe and define a real protocol π_{P5C} that realizes our anonymous point collection scheme $\mathcal{F}_{\text{apc}}$. We say

Definition 7.1 (Provably-Secure yet Practical Privacy-Preserving Point Collection Scheme) *A protocol* π_{P5C} *is called a* Provably-Secure yet Practical Privacy-Preserving Point Collection *scheme (P5C), if it UC-realizes* $\mathcal{F}_{\text{apc}}$.

The proof that π_{P5C} is a UC-realization of $\mathcal{F}_{\text{apc}}$ is given in Chapter 8.

The style of the presentation follows the same structure as the presentation of the ideal model $\mathcal{F}_{\text{apc}}$ in Chapter 4. First, we start to describe what information is stored locally be each party in Section 7.1 and then present a realization for each of the tasks in Sections 7.2 to 7.4. Again, an overview of all used variables can be found in the appendix for quick reference.

Although π_{P5C} is a single, monolithic protocol, the individual tasks are presented as if they were individual protocols. For typographic reasons we split their presentation into a *wrapper protocol* and a *core protocol.* Except for a few cases, there is a one-to-one correspondence between wrapper and core protocols. The wrapper protocols have the same input/output interfaces as their ideal counterparts and describe steps that are executed by each party locally before and after the respective core protocol. The wrapper protocols pre-process the inputs, parse the previously stored state from local memory which also includes to load individual keys, post-process the output after the core protocol has returned, persist the new state, and interact with other UC functionalities. The core protocols describe the actual interaction between parties and what messages are exchanged. This dichotomy between wrapper and core protocols is lifted in the following cases:

(1) We give an algorithm for the setup of the system (cf. Fig. 7.2) which explains how the CRS is generated. Naturally, there is no wrapper protocol, because setup of the CRS is not part of our protocol, but part of the setup assumption and provided by $\mathcal{F}_{\text{CRS}}$.

(2) We describe a helper algorithm VerifyWallet (cf. Fig. 7.30). This algorithm has no purpose on its own, but simple collects some shared code of multiple tasks.

(3) The tasks DetectDS, VerifyGuilt and ProveParticipation (cf. Figs. 7.23, 7.24 and 7.29) are not split, because they are so short that doing so would run contrary to a concise presentation.

The realization π_{P5C} lives in the $(\mathcal{F}_{\mathrm{msg}}, \mathcal{F}_{\mathrm{bb}}, \mathcal{F}_{\mathrm{CRS}})$-hybrid model. $\mathcal{F}_{\mathrm{msg}}$ is used for messaging between parties, $\mathcal{F}_{\mathrm{bb}}$ is used to publish public keys for the parties, and $\mathcal{F}_{\mathrm{CRS}}$ is a trustworthy source for a common reference string. We refer the reader to Sections 3.4 and 3.5 for more details. In the following, the wrapper protocol for each task typically interacts with these setup functionalities and passes/accepts required information to/from the core protocol. The core protocols have no knowledge about the setup functionalities, but they implicitly use the messaging capabilities of $\mathcal{F}_{\mathrm{msg}}$ which has appropriately been initialized by surrounding wrapper protocols in advance.

7.1 The Local State of the Parties

While in the ideal model all information is kept in a single, pervasive, trustworthy database *TRDB*, no such database exists in the real model. Instead, the state of the system is distributed across all parties. Figure 7.1 depicts what is stored by which party. After a description of each party's local state in Sections 7.1.1 to 7.1.3, the instantiation of the tags (cf. Section 4.1.2) is detailed out in Section 7.1.4. Although these tags are not a direct part of a party's local state, they are passed between parties for synchronization and thus contributes to the local state.

7.1.1 Local State of a User

We start with a description of the user's state because the *wallet* is the central concept of our P5C scheme. A wallet is created during IssueWallet locally stored by the user and subsequently updated. If the inner components of a wallet are understood, the rest follows naturally. A wallet is of the form

$$\tau := (s, \varphi, x^{\mathrm{next}}, \lambda, a_{\mathcal{U}}, c_{\mathrm{upd}}, d_{\mathrm{upd}}, \sigma_{\mathrm{upd}}, cert_{\mathcal{P}}, c_{\mathrm{fix}}, d_{\mathrm{fix}}, \sigma_{\mathrm{fix}}, b, u_1^{\mathrm{next}}). \tag{7.1}$$

Some of the components are fixed after issuing, some change after every transaction. The most essential elements are two signed commitments $c_{\mathrm{fix}}, c_{\mathrm{upd}}$ with c_{fix} binding the fixed part of a wallet and c_{upd} binding the updatable part.

The fixed part consists of the *wallet ID* λ, the *user attributes* $a_{\mathcal{U}}$, the *fixed commitment* c_{fix}, its corresponding opening d_{fix} and a signature σ_{fix} which created by the operator when the wallet

UC-Protocol π_{P5C}

I. *Local State*

(1) The operator internally records:

- A public and private key $(pk_{\mathcal{O}}, sk_{\mathcal{O}})$.
- A self-signed certificate $cert_{\mathcal{O}}$.
- A partial, set-valued and pairwise disjoint mapping $f_{bl_{\Phi_\lambda}}$ assigning a set of blacklisted fraud-detection IDs to a blacklisting tag:

$$f_{bl_{\Phi_\lambda}} : \Omega_{\text{bl}} \to \wp(\Phi), \omega_{\text{bl}} \mapsto bl_{\Phi_\lambda}$$

(2) Each PoS internally records:

- A public and private key $(pk_{\mathcal{P}}, sk_{\mathcal{P}})$.
- A certificate $cert_{\mathcal{P}}$ signed by the operator.

(3) Each user internally records:

- A public and private key $(pk_{\mathcal{U}}, sk_{\mathcal{U}})$.
- A set $\{\tau\}$ of the most recent states of all personal wallets.
- A mapping f_{pp} assigning the hidden part of a prove-participation tag ψ_{pp} to a prove-participation tag ω_{pp}:

$$f_{\text{pp}} : \Omega_{\text{pp}} \to \Psi_{\text{pp}}, \omega_{\text{pp}} \mapsto \psi_{\text{pp}}$$

(4) The dispute resolver internally records a public and private key (pk_{DR}, sk_{DR}).

II. *Behavior*

- *Dispute Resolver Registration* (Fig. 7.3)
- *Operator Registration* (Fig. 7.5)
- *Point-of-Sale Registration* (Fig. 7.7)
- *User Registration* (Fig. 7.9)
- *Point-of-Sale Certification* (Fig. 7.11)
- *Wallet Issuing* (Fig. 7.13)
- *Deposition* (Figs. 7.16 and 7.17)
- *Disbursement* (Fig. 7.21)
- *Double-Spending Detection* (Fig. 7.23)
- *Guilt Verification* (Fig. 7.24)
- *Wallet Blacklisting* (Fig. 7.25)
- *Balance Recalculation* (Fig. 7.27)
- *Prove of Participation* (Fig. 7.29)

Figure 7.1: The Protocol π_{P5C} – Local State of Parties and Overview of Tasks is issued. The fixed commitment $c_{\mathrm{fix}} = \mathsf{Commit}(\lambda, sk_{\mathcal{U}})$[1] pins users down to the wallet ID λ and their secret key $sk_{\mathcal{U}}$. The signature $\sigma_{\mathrm{fix}} \leftarrow \mathsf{SIG.Sign}(sk_{\mathcal{O}}^{\mathrm{fix}}, (c_{\mathrm{fix}}, a_{\mathcal{U}}))$ is initially created by the operator, ties together c_{fix} and $a_{\mathcal{U}}$ and also gives testimony that the wallet is valid.

The updatable part consists of the *serial number* s, the *fraud-detection ID* φ for the current transaction, the transaction counter x^{next} for the next interaction, the *updatable commitment* c_{upd}, its corresponding opening d_{upd}, a signature σ_{upd} which created by a PoS, a *PoS certificate* $cert_{\mathcal{P}}$, the *balance* b, and the *double-spending mask* u_1^{next} for the next transaction. The updatable commitment $c_{\mathrm{upd}} = \mathsf{Commit}(\lambda, b, u_1^{\mathrm{next}}, x^{\mathrm{next}})$ binds together the wallet ID λ, the balance b, some user-chosen mask u_1 to generate consistent double-spending tags in the next transaction and the future transaction counter x^{next}. The wallet ID λ is contained in the updatable commitment in order to link it with the fixed commitment. The signature $\sigma_{\mathrm{upd}} \leftarrow \mathsf{SIG.Sign}(sk_{\mathcal{O}}^{\mathrm{upd}}, (c_{\mathrm{upd}}, s))$ ties c_{upd} to a serial number s and is re-created by a PoS in every transaction. It is valid under the PoS' public key which is deposited in $cert_{\mathcal{P}}$ (cf. Section 7.1.2).

Note, that the fraud-detection ID φ itself is not contained in the updatable commitment as it is determined by (λ, x) and thus is pinned down indirectly. The wallet ID λ serves a PRF key and the fraud-detection ID of the current transaction is calculated as $\varphi := \mathsf{PRF}(\lambda, x^{\mathrm{next}} - 1)$. This choice of the fraud-detection ID has the advantage that the different states of a wallet are untraceable as long as λ remains secret, but becomes traceable if λ is unveiled.

The remaining information which is stored by a user is rather simple (cp. Fig. 7.1). A user stores a public-secret key pair $(pk_{\mathcal{U}}, sk_{\mathcal{U}})$ for the purpose of identification. Additionally, a user locally manages a lookup table f_{pp} which associates a hidden counterpart ψ_{pp} to each prove-participation tags ω_{pp} that has been created in the scope of Disburse (cp. Section 7.3.3). For details on this not yet introduced hidden complement ψ_{pp} see Section 7.1.4. Users have to look up the hidden counterpart ψ_{pp} when they are confronted with one of their previous prove-participation tag ω_{pp} in the scope of ProveParticipation (cp. Section 7.4.4) again.

7.1.2 Local State of a Point-of-Sale

The local state of a PoS is a subset of what the operator stores and therefore described first. A PoS stores a public-private key pair $(pk_{\mathcal{P}}, sk_{\mathcal{P}})$ and a certificate $cert_{\mathcal{P}}$. The key pair is of the form

$$pk_{\mathcal{P}} := (pk_{\mathcal{P}}^{\mathrm{upd}}, pk_{\mathcal{P}}^{\mathrm{rc}}, pk_{\mathcal{P}}^{\mathrm{pp}}) \qquad sk_{\mathcal{P}} := (sk_{\mathcal{P}}^{\mathrm{upd}}, sk_{\mathcal{P}}^{\mathrm{rc}}, sk_{\mathcal{P}}^{\mathrm{pp}}) \tag{7.2}$$

[1] By abuse of notation, we sometimes ignore the opening or decommitment value d_{fix} which is also an output of $\mathsf{Commit}(\cdot)$.

and consists of three key pairs of an EUF-CMA secure signature scheme: $(pk_{\mathcal{P}}^{\text{upd}}, sk_{\mathcal{P}}^{\text{upd}})$ to sign the updatable part of a wallet, $(pk_{\mathcal{P}}^{\text{rc}}, sk_{\mathcal{P}}^{\text{rc}})$ to sign recalculation tags and $(pk_{\mathcal{P}}^{\text{pp}}, sk_{\mathcal{P}}^{\text{pp}})$ to sign prove-participation tags. The certificate is of the form

$$cert_{\mathcal{P}} := (pk_{\mathcal{P}}, a_{\mathcal{P}}, \sigma_{\mathcal{P}}^{\text{cert}}) \tag{7.3}$$

and consists of a signature $\sigma_{\mathcal{P}}^{\text{cert}}$ which is issued by the operator on the PoS' combined public key $pk_{\mathcal{P}}$ and its attributes $a_{\mathcal{P}}$. A PoS obtains its certificate in the scope of CertifyPOS (cp. Section 7.2.3).

7.1.3 Local State of the Operator

The local state of the operator is a superset of what a PoS stores, because the operator can also act as a PoS. Likewise, the operator stores a public-private key pair $(pk_{\mathcal{P}}, sk_{\mathcal{P}})$ and a self-signed certificate $cert_{\mathcal{O}}$. The key pair is of the form

$$pk_{\mathcal{O}} := (pk_{\mathcal{O}}^{\text{fix}}, pk_{\mathcal{O}}^{\text{cert}}, pk_{\mathcal{O}}^{\text{upd}}, pk_{\mathcal{O}}^{\text{rc,sig}}, pk_{\mathcal{O}}^{\text{rc,enc}}) \quad sk_{\mathcal{O}} := (sk_{\mathcal{O}}^{\text{fix}}, sk_{\mathcal{O}}^{\text{cert}}, sk_{\mathcal{O}}^{\text{upd}}, sk_{\mathcal{O}}^{\text{rc,sig}}, sk_{\mathcal{O}}^{\text{rc,enc}}) \tag{7.4}$$

and the signature key pairs $(pk_{\mathcal{O}}^{\text{upd}}, sk_{\mathcal{O}}^{\text{upd}})$ and $(pk_{\mathcal{O}}^{\text{rc,sig}}, sk_{\mathcal{O}}^{\text{rc,sig}})$ serve the same purpose as in Section 7.1.2. On top, the signature key pair $(pk_{\mathcal{O}}^{\text{fix}}, sk_{\mathcal{O}}^{\text{fix}})$ is used to sign the fixed part of a wallet, the signature key pair $(pk_{\mathcal{O}}^{\text{cert}}, sk_{\mathcal{O}}^{\text{cert}})$ is used to issue certificates for PoSes and the encryption key pair $(pk_{\mathcal{O}}^{\text{rc,enc}}, sk_{\mathcal{O}}^{\text{rc,enc}})$ is used to collect encrypted recalculation tags from the PoSes.

The map $f_{bl_{\Phi_\lambda}}$ manages pairwise disjoint sets of fraud-detection IDs of blacklisted wallets. After a successful execution of IssueWallet the secret wallet ID λ is fixed. This also implies that the set $\{\varphi_{\lambda,x}\}$ of fraud-detection IDs which are used by the particular wallet are pre-determined but is of course unknown to the operator. Remember, the wallet ID λ serves as PRF seed (cp. Section 7.1.1). At the end of IssueWallet (cp. Section 4.3.1) the operator obtains a blacklisting tag ω_{bl} which allows the operator to recover the set $\{\varphi_{\lambda,x}\}$. The map $f_{bl_{\Phi_\lambda}}$ can be in one out of three possible states per ω_{bl}.

(1) "$f_{bl_{\Phi_\lambda}}(\omega_{\text{bl}})$ is undefined": The blacklisting tag ω_{bl} has not been generated, i.e. no wallet with this blacklisting tag has been issued.

(2) "$f_{bl_{\Phi_\lambda}}(\omega_{\text{bl}}) = \emptyset$": A wallet has been issued for the blacklisting tag ω_{bl}, but has not been blacklisted.

(3) "$f_{bl_{\Phi_\lambda}}(\omega_{\text{bl}}) = bl_{\Phi_\lambda} \neq \emptyset$": A wallet has been issued for the blacklisting tag ω_{bl} and blacklisted. The blacklist is bl_{Φ_λ}.

For an arbitrary, but fixed ω_{bl} the map $f_{bl_{\Phi_\lambda}}$ transits from state (1) to (2) at the end of IssueWallet (cp. Section 7.3.1) and from (2) to (3) at the end of BlacklistWallet (cp. Section 7.4.2). Note that $f_{bl_{\Phi_\lambda}}$ is pairwise disjoint only with overwhelming probability. Each of the sets $bl_{\Phi_\lambda} = \{\mathsf{PRF}(\lambda, 0), \ldots, \mathsf{PRF}(\lambda, x_{\text{bound}})\}$ has finite size $x_{\text{bound}} + 1$ and there are only polynomially many of them with uniformly drawn λ while the image of PRF is exponentially large.

7.1.4 Instantiation of Tags

As detailed out in Section 4.1.2, the main tasks IssueWallet, Disburse and Deposit generate various sorts of tags, namely blacklisting tags ω_{bl}, double-spending tags ω_{ds}, recalculation tags ω_{rc} and prove-participation tags ω_{pp}. These tags are used to periodically synchronize the local state of the parties and each sort of tags supports one of the utility tasks (cp. Section 4.1.2).

As the tags are not specific for a single task but link different tasks, this section gives an integrated explanation. As a common characteristic, three of these tags come as pairs with a hidden counterpart ψ_{bl}, ψ_{rc} and ψ_{pp}, resp.[2], which are not described in Section 4.1.2 as their implementation is specific to the realization π_{P5C}. The tags are output to the environment, passed around and thus part of the public interface, while their hidden counterparts are kept secret from the environment.

Blacklisting Tags

A blacklisting tag ω_{bl} is output to the operator at the end of IssueWallet and allows with the consent of the dispute resolver to recover the sequence of all fraud-detection IDs $bl_\Phi = ((\varphi_{\lambda,x}))_{x \in \{0,\ldots,x_{\text{bound}}\}}$ which are used by the wallet with the (secret) wallet ID λ. Further remember, that the wallet ID does not only uniquely identifies the wallet, but also serves as the seed for the Dodis-Yampolskiy (cp. Section 6.2.6 and [DY04]) PRF and determines the fraud-detection IDs by $\varphi_{\lambda,x} := \mathsf{PRF}(\lambda, x)$.

At first sight, the blacklisting feature could be implemented as a simple form of key-escrow mechanism. Ideally, the hidden blacklisting tag $\psi_{\text{bl}} := \lambda$ would be set equal to the wallet ID and the user would encrypt ψ_{bl} under the public key pk_{DR} of the dispute resolver as $\omega_{\text{bl}} \leftarrow \mathsf{Enc}(pk_{DR}, \psi_{\text{bl}})$ which is then sent to the operator for later use. However, two issues need to be considered:

(1) The wallet ID λ is jointly chosen by the user and the operator by a Blum Cointoss and thus consists of two shares λ', λ'' (cp. IssueWallet in Section 7.3.1). If only the user chose it, an adversary could tamper with recalculations and blacklisting, as well as with double-spending detection (e.g., by re-using the same wallet ID for different wallets).

[2] Conceptionally, there is also a hidden part for ω_{ds}, namely the DS mask u_1 (see later), but there is no need to store it and hence no separate symbol has been introduced although this causes a lack of symmetry.

(2) The wallet ID is part of the fixed commitment c_{fix} of the wallet (cp. Section 7.1.1).

Hence, the user has to prove to the operator that the encrypted value in ω_{bl} and the committed value in c_{fix} are equal and consistent to the Blum Cointoss. For practical reasons, we use Groth-Sahai NIZK proofs (cp. Section 6.2.1 and [GS08]) and structure-preserving, shrinking commitments (cp. Section 6.2.2 and [Abe+15]). In order to not quash practical efficiency due to a generic Cook reduction, we would need an encryption scheme whose message space equals the key space of the PRF (i.e., $\mathbb{Z}_p$) and which is compatible to the GS-NIZK proof system (i.e., is algebraic). Unfortunately, we are unaware of such an encryption scheme.[3]

Instead, we use a variant of a CCA-secure structure-preserving encryption scheme for vectors of G_1-elements which we adopted to our algebraic setting (cp. Section 6.2.4 and [Cam+11]). This makes it impossible to directly decrypt the original wallet ID $\lambda \in \mathbb{Z}_p$ and to recover λ from g_1^{λ} due to the hardness of the DLOG problem in G_1. Therefore, we apply the following workaround. Users split their share λ' into small chunks $\lambda'_0, \dots, \lambda'_{\ell-1} \in \{0, \dots, B-1\}$ such that $\lambda' = \sum_{i=0}^{\ell-1} \lambda'_i \cdot B^i$ for some base B. The base B is chosen in a way that it is feasible for the dispute resolver to recover λ'_i from $g_1^{\lambda'_i}$ by brute-force in a reasonable amount of time (e.g., $B = 2^{32}$). The user creates the hidden blacklisting tag as

$$\psi_{\text{bl}} \leftarrow \mathsf{ENC1.Enc}\big(pk_{\mathcal{DR}}, (\Lambda'_0, \dots, \Lambda'_{\ell-1}, \Lambda'', pk_{\mathcal{U}})\big) \qquad \text{with} \qquad \Lambda'_i := g_1^{\Lambda'_i} \tag{7.5}$$

and the operator complements it to the blacklisting tag as

$$\omega_{\text{bl}} := (\lambda'', \psi_{\text{bl}}) \tag{7.6}$$

The CCA-secure ciphertext ψ_{bl} includes the user's key $pk_{\mathcal{U}}$ to rule out malleability attacks. Otherwise, a malicious operator could potentially trick the dispute resolver into recovering the trapdoor for a different (innocent) user.

Double-Spending Tags

Our double-spending detection mechanism utilizes a well-known technique from the (offline) e-cash literature. The secret user key is hidden in the slope of a line in the plane. At every transaction, the operator challenges the user for a point on the line. The operator picks the DS challenge u_2 and the user replies with $t := u_2 \cdot sk_{\mathcal{U}} + u_1 \bmod \mathfrak{p}$. The concrete line is masked by the DS mask u_1 which encodes the line's ordinate and is secretly chosen by the user.

[3] Note that Paillier encryption works in a different algebraic setting and cannot easily be combined with Groth-Sahai proofs.

As long as each state of a wallet is only used once, each time a different DS mask u_1 and thus a different line is used and no information about $sk_{\mathcal{U}}$ is unveiled. In case of a double-spending, the same DS mask is used, the operator learns two points (u_2, t), (u_2', t') on the same line and can restore the user's secret key via $sk_{\mathcal{U}} := (t - t')/(u_2 - u_2') \bmod \mathfrak{p}$. In order to force the user to use the same DS mask u_1 in case of a double-spending, the DS mask for the next transaction is fixed as u_1^{next} in the previous transaction and put into the updatable commitment c_{upd} of the wallet (cf. Section 7.1.1).

The double-spending tag has the form

$$\omega_{\text{ds}} := (\varphi, t, u_2) \tag{7.7}$$

and also includes the fraud-detection ID φ to identify matching double-spending tags which have been created for the same wallet state. Moreover, the secret user key does not only allow to lookup the user's PID for the public key $pk_{\mathcal{U}} := g_1^{sk_{\mathcal{U}}}$, but also serves as a proof of guilt $\pi := sk_{\mathcal{U}}$ due to the hardness of the DLOG in G_1.

Recalculation Tags

The tasks Deposit and Disburse output recalculation tags that allow the operator to recalculate the true balance of a wallet given that the operator has recovered the blacklist $bl_{\Phi} = ((\varphi_{\lambda,x}))_{x \in \{0,\dots,x_{\text{bound}}\}}$ of fraud-detection IDs of the wallet before. The recalculation tag ω_{rc} and its hidden complement ψ_{rc} are simply constructed as

$$\psi_{\text{rc}} := (s, \varphi, p, pk_{\mathcal{P}}^{\text{rc}}, \sigma_{\text{rc}}) \tag{7.8}$$

$$\omega_{\text{rc}} \leftarrow \mathsf{ENC2.Enc}(pk_{\mathcal{O}}^{\text{rc,enc}}, \psi_{\text{rc}}) \tag{7.9}$$

The fraud-detection ID φ and price p are needed for the obvious reason that the operator needs to match φ with the set bl_{Φ} and to recalculate as balance as the sum of all prices. The serial number s is included to enforce uniqueness of the tags for formal reasons, if all other attributes are equal. This might happen if the same user commits double-spending at the same PoS and also obtains the same price. The signature σ_{rc} and the encryption realize an authenticated and confidential channel despite the fact that the framing protocol, i.e. the environment, is in charge to transport recalculation tags from the PoSes to the operator. The signature on the triple (s, φ, p) under the secret key $sk_{\mathcal{P}}^{\text{rc}}$ of the PoS rules out that the environment can inject fake recalculation tags in the name of an honest PoS. The encryption is required, because the price p might infringe upon a user's privacy and is not leaked by the ideal model as long as the user, the involved PoS and the operator are honest.

Prove-Participation Tags

At the end of the task Deposit a prove-participation tag ω_{pp} is output to the user and the PoS which allows the user to prove to have participated in this transaction. The recalculation tag ω_{pp} and its hidden complement ψ_{pp} are constructed as

$$\psi_{\text{pp}} := (pk_{\mathcal{P}}^{\text{pp}}, \sigma_{\text{pp}}, d_{pk_{\mathcal{U}}}) \tag{7.10}$$

$$\omega_{\text{pp}} := c_{pk_{\mathcal{U}}} \tag{7.11}$$

with $(c_{pk_{\mathcal{U}}}, d_{pk_{\mathcal{U}}}) \leftarrow \text{C2.Commit}(crs_{\text{com}}^{(2)}, sk_{\mathcal{U}})$ being a commitment on the user's key and $\sigma_{\text{pp}} \leftarrow \text{SIG.Sign}(sk_{\mathcal{P}}^{\text{pp}}, c_{pk_{\mathcal{U}}})$ a signature on the commitment that is valid under the public key of PoS which took part in the transaction. The principle idea is that the hiding property of the commitment, i.e. the "public" prove-participation tag ω_{pp} asserts anonymity. But when the suspected user is confronted with ω_{pp} again and summoned to prove its participation with a particular PoS, only the legitimate owner of ω_{pp} who has securely stored ψ_{pp} can unveil to the correct identity during the task ProveParticipation.

7.2 Setup Tasks

As in the system definition (cp. Section 4.2) all parties need to register themselves with a public key before they can participate in the system and PoSes needs to certified. In addition, the whole system needs to be setup once. The latter has no counterpart in the ideal model and is realized through the setup functionality $\mathcal{F}_{\text{CRS}}$.

7.2.1 System Setup

To setup the system once (see Fig. 7.2), the public parameter *crs* must be generated in a trustworthy way. The CRS *crs* consists of a description of the underlying algebraic framework *gp*, a splitting base B and the individual CRSes for the cryptographic building blocks. We assume that the CRS is implicitly available to all protocols and algorithms by means of $\mathcal{F}_{\text{CRS}}$.

7.2.2 Registrations

The tasks RegisterDR (cp. Figs. 7.3 and 7.4), RegisterOp (cp. Figs. 7.5 and 7.6), RegisterPOS (cp. Figs. 7.7 and 7.8) and RegisterUser (cp. Figs. 7.9 and 7.10) are realized in the obvious way. The respective core protocols run the key generation algorithms of the underlying building blocks and return a combined public-private key pair. After that the wrapper protocols register the public key at the bulletin board $\mathcal{F}_{\text{bb}}$.

$\mathsf{Setup}(1^n, B)$

$gp := (G_1, G_2, G_T, e, p, g_1, g_2) \leftarrow \mathsf{Setup}(1^n)$
$crs^{(1)}_{\mathsf{com}} \leftarrow \mathsf{C1.Setup}(gp)$
$crs^{(2)}_{\mathsf{com}} \leftarrow \mathsf{C2.Setup}(gp)$
$crs^{(3)}_{\mathsf{com}} \leftarrow \mathsf{C3.Setup}(gp)$
$crs^{(4)}_{\mathsf{com}} \leftarrow \mathsf{C4.Setup}(gp)$
$crs_{\mathsf{pok}} \leftarrow \mathsf{POK.Setup}(gp)$
$crs := (gp, B, crs^{(1)}_{\mathsf{com}}, crs^{(2)}_{\mathsf{com}}, crs^{(3)}_{\mathsf{com}}, crs^{(4)}_{\mathsf{com}}, crs_{\mathsf{pok}})$
return crs

Figure 7.2: System Setup Algorithm

UC-Protocol π_{P5C} (cont.) – Task RegisterDR

DR input: (register)

(1) If a key pair (pk_{DR}, sk_{DR}) has already been recorded, immediately output (registered) and halt.
(2) Obtain CRS *crs* from $\mathcal{F}_{\mathrm{CRS}}$.
(3) Run $(pk_{DR}, sk_{DR}) \leftarrow \mathsf{RegisterDR}(crs)$ (see Fig. 7.4).
(4) Record (pk_{DR}, sk_{DR}) internally and call $\mathcal{F}_{\mathrm{bb}}$ with input (register, pk_{DR}).

DR output: (registered)

Figure 7.3: The Protocol π_{P5C} (cont. from Fig. 7.1) – Task RegisterDR

$\mathsf{RegisterDR}(crs)$

parse $(gp, B, crs^{(1)}_{\mathsf{com}}, crs^{(2)}_{\mathsf{com}}, crs^{(3)}_{\mathsf{com}}, crs^{(4)}_{\mathsf{com}}, crs_{\mathsf{pok}}) := crs$
$(pk_{DR}, sk_{DR}) \leftarrow \mathsf{ENC.Gen}(gp)$
return (pk_{DR}, sk_{DR})

Figure 7.4: The Core Protocol for Task RegisterDR (used by Fig. 7.3)

UC-Protocol π_{P5C} (cont.) – Task RegisterOp

Operator input: (`register`, a_O)

(1) If a key pair (pk_O, sk_O) has already been recorded, immediately output (`registered`) and halt.
(2) Obtain CRS *crs* from $\mathcal{F}_{\text{CRS}}$.
(3) Run $(pk_O, sk_O, cert_O) \leftarrow \text{RegisterOp}(crs, a_O)$ (see Fig. 7.6).
(4) Record (pk_O, sk_O) and $(cert_O)$ internally and call $\mathcal{F}_{\text{bb}}$ with input (`register`, pk_O).

Operator output: (`registered`)

Figure 7.5: The Protocol π_{P5C} (cont. from Fig. 7.1) – Task RegisterOp

$\text{RegisterOp}(crs, a_O)$

$$
\begin{aligned}
&\text{parse } (gp, B, crs^{(1)}_{\text{com}}, crs^{(2)}_{\text{com}}, crs^{(3)}_{\text{com}}, crs^{(4)}_{\text{com}}, crs_{\text{pok}}) := crs\\
&(pk_O^{\text{fix}}, sk_O^{\text{fix}}) \leftarrow \text{SIG.Gen}(gp)\\
&(pk_O^{\text{cert}}, sk_O^{\text{cert}}) \leftarrow \text{SIG.Gen}(gp)\\
&(pk_O^{\text{upd}}, sk_O^{\text{upd}}) \leftarrow \text{SIG.Gen}(gp)\\
&(pk_O^{\text{rc,sig}}, sk_O^{\text{rc,sig}}) \leftarrow \text{SIG.Gen}(gp)\\
&(pk_O^{\text{rc,enc}}, sk_O^{\text{rc,enc}}) \leftarrow \text{ENC2.Gen}(gp)\\
&(pk_O, sk_O) := ((pk_O^{\text{fix}}, pk_O^{\text{cert}}, pk_O^{\text{upd}}, pk_O^{\text{rc,sig}}, pk_O^{\text{rc,enc}}), (sk_O^{\text{fix}}, sk_O^{\text{cert}}, sk_O^{\text{upd}}, sk_O^{\text{rc,sig}}, sk_O^{\text{rc,enc}}))\\
&\sigma_O^{\text{cert}} \leftarrow \text{SIG.Sign}(sk_O^{\text{cert}}, (pk_O^{\text{upd}}, a_O))\\
&cert_O := (pk_O^{\text{upd}}, a_O, \sigma_O^{\text{cert}})\\
&\text{return } (pk_O, sk_O, cert_O)
\end{aligned}
$$

Figure 7.6: The Core Protocol for Task RegisterOp (used by Fig. 7.5)

UC-Protocol π_{P5C} (cont.) – Task RegisterPOS

PoS input: (`register`)

(1) If a key pair $(pk_{\mathcal{P}}, sk_{\mathcal{P}})$ has already been recorded, immediately output (`registered`) and halt.
(2) Obtain CRS *crs* from $\mathcal{F}_{\text{CRS}}$.
(3) Run $(pk_{\mathcal{P}}, sk_{\mathcal{P}}) \leftarrow \text{RegisterPOS}(crs)$ (see Fig. 7.8).
(4) Record $(pk_{\mathcal{P}}, sk_{\mathcal{P}})$ internally and call $\mathcal{F}_{\text{bb}}$ with input (`register`, $pk_{\mathcal{P}}$).

PoS output: (`registered`)

Figure 7.7: The Protocol π_{P5C} (cont. from Fig. 7.1) – Task RegisterPOS

RegisterPOS(crs)
parse $(gp, B, crs^{(1)}_{\mathsf{com}}, crs^{(2)}_{\mathsf{com}}, crs^{(3)}_{\mathsf{com}}, crs^{(4)}_{\mathsf{com}}, crs_{\mathsf{pok}}) := crs$
$(pk^{\mathrm{upd}}_{\mathcal{P}}, sk^{\mathrm{upd}}_{\mathcal{P}}) \leftarrow \mathsf{SIG.Gen}(gp)$
$(pk^{\mathrm{rc}}_{\mathcal{P}}, sk^{\mathrm{rc}}_{\mathcal{P}}) \leftarrow \mathsf{SIG.Gen}(gp)$
$(pk^{\mathrm{pp}}_{\mathcal{P}}, sk^{\mathrm{pp}}_{\mathcal{P}}) \leftarrow \mathsf{SIG.Gen}(gp)$
$(pk_{\mathcal{P}}, sk_{\mathcal{P}}) := ((pk^{\mathrm{upd}}_{\mathcal{P}}, pk^{\mathrm{rc}}_{\mathcal{P}}, pk^{\mathrm{pp}}_{\mathcal{P}}), (sk^{\mathrm{upd}}_{\mathcal{P}}, sk^{\mathrm{rc}}_{\mathcal{P}}, sk^{\mathrm{pp}}_{\mathcal{P}}))$
return $(pk_{\mathcal{P}}, sk_{\mathcal{P}})$

Figure 7.8: The Core Protocol for Task RegisterPOS (used by Fig. 7.7)

UC-Protocol π_{P5C} (cont.) – Task RegisterUser

User input: `(register)`

(1) If a key pair $(pk_{\mathcal{U}}, sk_{\mathcal{U}})$ has already been recorded, immediately output `(registered)` and halt.
(2) Obtain CRS crs from $\mathcal{F}_{\mathrm{CRS}}$.
(3) Run $(pk_{\mathcal{U}}, sk_{\mathcal{U}}) \leftarrow \mathsf{RegisterUser}(crs)$ (see Fig. 7.10).
(4) Record $(pk_{\mathcal{U}}, sk_{\mathcal{U}})$ internally and call $\mathcal{F}_{\mathrm{bb}}$ with input $(\texttt{register}, pk_{\mathcal{U}})$.

User output: `(registered)`

Figure 7.9: The Protocol π_{P5C} (cont. from Fig. 7.1) – Task RegisterUser

RegisterUser(crs)
parse $(gp, B, crs^{(1)}_{\mathsf{com}}, crs^{(2)}_{\mathsf{com}}, crs^{(3)}_{\mathsf{com}}, crs^{(4)}_{\mathsf{com}}, crs_{\mathsf{pok}}) := crs$
$sk_{\mathcal{U}} \xleftarrow{R} \mathbb{Z}_p$
$pk_{\mathcal{U}} := g_1^{sk_{\mathcal{U}}}$
return $(pk_{\mathcal{U}}, sk_{\mathcal{U}})$

Figure 7.10: The Core Protocol for Task RegisterUser (used by Fig. 7.9)

The keys of the operator, a PoS and a user are described in Sections 7.1.1 to 7.1.3. The DR generates a key pair (pk_{DR}, sk_{DR}) for an IND-CCA secure encryption scheme. The key pk_{DR} is used to deposit the secret wallet ID and PRF key λ in encrypted form in the wallet-specific blacklisting tag ω_{bl} which allows to link this wallet's transactions in case of a dispute.

7.2.3 Point-of-Sale Certification

The task CertifyPOS (cp. Figs. 7.11 and 7.12) is executed between a PoS and the operator when a new PoS is deployed into the field. At the end of the task the PoS has obtained its certificate which is locally stored. It contains the PoS' public key $pk_{\mathcal{P}}$, its attributes $a_{\mathcal{P}}$ (which are chosen by the operator), and a signature on both, generated by the operator using $sk_{\mathcal{O}}^{cert}$.

Remember that it is advisable to encode some sort of limited time of validity into $a_{\mathcal{P}}$ to mitigate the impact of stolen or otherwise compromised PoS which may be unattendedly placed in the field (cp. Section 2.4). This implies that CertifyPOS has to be run repeatedly to refresh $cert_{\mathcal{P}}$ from time to time (cp. Section 4.2.2).

7.3 Main Tasks

This section describes the realization of main tasks IssueWallet, Deposit and Disburse. Although the tasks are presented in that order, the individual steps and messages of each task are not described in temporal order, but specific elements are explained in a semantic context across messages. We refer the reader to the figures for a temporal order of messages. Also, the principle structure of a wallet (cp. Section 7.1.1) and the tags should be known (cp. Section 7.1.4).

7.3.1 Wallet Issuing

This task IssueWallet (cp. Figs. 7.13 to 7.15) is executed between a user and the operator to create a new wallet with a fresh wallet ID λ and balance 0. It fulfills four objectives:

(1) Jointly computing a fresh and random serial number s for this transaction.

(2) Jointly computing a fresh and random wallet ID λ for the user that is only known to the user.

(3) Generating a blacklisting tag ω_{bl} that stores the wallet ID λ in a secret form.

(4) Assembling all components for a new wallet for the user.

For the first objective, both parties randomly choose shares of the serial number $s' \in G_1$ and $s'' \in G_1$, resp., which together form the serial number $s := s' \cdot s''$. To this end, the parties engage in a standard Blum coin toss in the messages 2–4.

Similarly, the parties run half of a Blum coin toss for the second objective in the messages 1 and 2. As the user starts and the coin toss is prematurely stopped after the second message, the wallet ID $\lambda := \lambda' + \lambda'' \in \mathbb{Z}_p$ is fixed and known by the user, but remains secret to the operator.

After the wallet ID λ has been pinned down, the user prepares the escrow of λ in the blacklisting tag for the third objective. The user deposits the split chunks $\{\Lambda'_i\}_{i\in\{0,\dots,\ell-1\}}$ of the user's share λ' in encrypted form in the hidden blacklisting tag ψ_{bl}, sends it to the operator in message 3, the operator augments it by the operator's share λ'' to form the complete blacklisting

UC-Protocol π_{P5C} (cont.) – Task CertifyPOS

PoS input: (`certify_pos`)

(1) At the PoS side:
  (a) Load the internally recorded $(pk_{\mathcal{P}}, sk_{\mathcal{P}})$.[⊥]
  (b) Receive $pk_{\mathcal{O}}$ from the bulletin-board $\mathcal{F}_{\mathrm{bb}}$ for PID $pid_{\mathcal{O}}$.[⊥]
  (c) Call $\mathcal{F}_{\mathrm{msg}}$ with (`establish-session`, `ident`, $pid_{\mathcal{O}}$, `certify_pos`).

(2) At the operator side side upon receiving (`establishing-session`, $ssid$, $pid_{\mathcal{P}}$, `certify_pos`) from $\mathcal{F}_{\mathrm{msg}}$:
  (a) Load the internally recorded $(pk_{\mathcal{O}}, sk_{\mathcal{O}})$.[⊥]
  (b) Receive $pk_{\mathcal{P}}$ from the bulletin-board $\mathcal{F}_{\mathrm{bb}}$ for PID $pid_{\mathcal{P}}$.[⊥]

Operator output: (`certifying_pos`, $pid_{\mathcal{P}}$)

Operator input: (`certifying_pos`, $a_{\mathcal{P}}$)

(3) At the operator side: Call $\mathcal{F}_{\mathrm{msg}}$ with (`accept`, $ssid$).

(4) At the PoS side: Receive (`accepted`, $ssid$) from $\mathcal{F}_{\mathrm{msg}}$.

(5) Both sides: Run the code of CertifyPOS between the PoS and the operator (see Fig. 7.12) using (`send`, $ssid, \dots$) of $\mathcal{F}_{\mathrm{msg}}$ for messaging:

$$((cert_{\mathcal{P}}), (\mathsf{OK})) \leftarrow \mathsf{CertifyPOS}\left\langle \mathcal{P}(pk_{\mathcal{O}}, pk_{\mathcal{P}}), \mathcal{O}(pk_{\mathcal{O}}, sk_{\mathcal{O}}, pk_{\mathcal{P}}, a_{\mathcal{P}}) \right\rangle .$$

(6) At the PoS side:
  (a) Parse $a_{\mathcal{P}}$ from $cert_{\mathcal{P}}$.
  (b) Record $cert_{\mathcal{P}}$ internally.
  (c) Call $\mathcal{F}_{\mathrm{msg}}$ with (`close`, $ssid$).

(7) At the operator side: Receive (`closed`, $ssid$) from $\mathcal{F}_{\mathrm{msg}}$.

PoS output: (`certified_pos`, $a_{\mathcal{P}}$)

Operator output: (`certified_pos`)

[⊥] If this does not exist, abort.

Figure 7.11: The Protocol π_{P5C} (cont. from Fig. 7.1) – Task CertifyPOS

$\mathcal{P}(pk_{\mathcal{O}}, pk_{\mathcal{P}})$		$\mathcal{O}(pk_{\mathcal{O}}, sk_{\mathcal{O}}, pk_{\mathcal{P}}, a_{\mathcal{P}})$
parse $(pk_{\mathcal{O}}^{\text{fix}}, pk_{\mathcal{O}}^{\text{cert}}, pk_{\mathcal{O}}^{\text{upd}}, pk_{\mathcal{O}}^{\text{rc,sig}}, pk_{\mathcal{O}}^{\text{rc,enc}}) := pk_{\mathcal{O}}$		parse $(pk_{\mathcal{O}}^{\text{fix}}, pk_{\mathcal{O}}^{\text{cert}}, pk_{\mathcal{O}}^{\text{upd}}, pk_{\mathcal{O}}^{\text{rc,sig}}, pk_{\mathcal{O}}^{\text{rc,enc}}) := pk_{\mathcal{O}}$
		parse $(sk_{\mathcal{O}}^{\text{fix}}, sk_{\mathcal{O}}^{\text{cert}}, sk_{\mathcal{O}}^{\text{upd}}, sk_{\mathcal{O}}^{\text{rc,sig}}, sk_{\mathcal{O}}^{\text{rc,enc}}) := sk_{\mathcal{O}}$
		$\sigma_{\mathcal{P}}^{\text{cert}} \leftarrow \text{SIG.Sign}(sk_{\mathcal{O}}^{\text{cert}}, (pk_{\mathcal{P}}, a_{\mathcal{P}}))$
		$cert_{\mathcal{P}} := (pk_{\mathcal{P}}, a_{\mathcal{P}}, \sigma_{\mathcal{P}}^{\text{cert}})$
	$\xleftarrow{cert_{\mathcal{P}}}$	
parse $(pk'_{\mathcal{P}}, a_{\mathcal{P}}, \sigma_{\mathcal{P}}^{\text{cert}}) := cert_{\mathcal{P}}$		
if $\text{SIG.Vfy}(pk_{\mathcal{O}}^{\text{cert}}, \sigma_{\mathcal{P}}^{\text{cert}}, (pk_{\mathcal{P}}, a_{\mathcal{P}})) = 0$		
return $\bot$		
return $(cert_{\mathcal{P}})$		return (OK)

Figure 7.12: The Core Protocol for Task CertifyPOS (used by Fig. 7.11)

tag ω_{bl} and locally stores $\omega_{\text{bl}} \mapsto \emptyset$ in $f_{bl_{\Phi_\lambda}}$ to mark the blacklisting tag as legitimately issued and not blacklisted. For a detailed explanation on ψ_{bl}, ω_{bl} see Section 7.1.4.

For the last objective, the user generates the fixed and updatable commitment c_{fix}, c_{upd}, resp., which are then signed by the operator (see messages 3–4). See Section 7.1.1 for a detailed description of the structure of a wallet. In order to show that these commitments are constructed correctly, the user uses P1 to compute a proof π for a statement *stmnt* from the language $L_{gp}^{(1)}$ defined by

$$L_{gp}^{(1)} := \left\{ \begin{pmatrix} pk_{\mathcal{U}} \\ pk_{DR} \\ \psi_{\text{bl}} \\ c_{\text{fix}} \\ c_{\text{upd}} \\ c'_{\text{wid}} \\ \Lambda'' \\ \lambda'' \end{pmatrix}^T \middle| \begin{array}{l} \exists\, \lambda, \lambda', \lambda'_0, \dots, \lambda'_{\ell-1}, r_1, r_2 \in \mathbb{Z}_p; \\ \Lambda, \Lambda', \Lambda'_0, \dots, \Lambda'_{\ell-1}, U_1^{\text{next}}, d_{\text{fix}}, d_{\text{upd}}, d'_{\text{wid}} \in G_1; \\ \text{C1.Open}(crs_{\text{com}}^{(1)}, (\Lambda, pk_{\mathcal{U}}), c_{\text{fix}}, d_{\text{fix}}) = 1 \\ \text{C1.Open}(crs_{\text{com}}^{(1)}, (\Lambda, 1, U_1^{\text{next}}, g_1), c_{\text{upd}}, d_{\text{upd}}) = 1 \\ \text{C3.Open}(crs_{\text{com}}^{(3)}, \Lambda', c'_{\text{wid}}, d'_{\text{wid}}) = 1 \\ \psi_{\text{bl}} = \text{ENC1.Enc}(pk_{DR}, (\Lambda'_0, \dots, \Lambda'_{\ell-1}, \Lambda'', pk_{\mathcal{U}}); r_1, r_2) \\ \lambda = \lambda' + \lambda'' \\ \Lambda = g_1^{\lambda}, \Lambda' = g_1^{\lambda'} \\ \lambda' = \sum_{i=0}^{\ell-1} \lambda'_i \cdot B^i \\ \forall i \in \{0, \dots, \ell-1\} : \\ \qquad \lambda'_i \in \{0, \dots, B-1\} \\ \qquad \Lambda'_i = g_1^{\lambda'_i} \end{array} \right\} \tag{7.12}$$

This proof system also asserts that the hidden blacklisting tag ψ_{bl} has been created correctly.

UC-Protocol π_{P5C} (cont.) – Task IssueWallet

User input: (issue_wallet)

(1) At the user side:

(a) Load the internally recorded $(pk_{\mathcal{U}}, sk_{\mathcal{U}})$.$^{\perp}$

(b) Receive pk_{O} from the bulletin-board $\mathcal{F}_{\text{bb}}$ for PID pid_{O}.$^{\perp}$

(c) Receive pk_{DR} from the bulletin-board $\mathcal{F}_{\text{bb}}$ for PID pid_{DR}.$^{\perp}$

(d) Call $\mathcal{F}_{\text{msg}}$ with (establish-session, ident, pid_{O}, issue_wallet).

(2) At the operator side upon receiving (establishing-session, $ssid$, $pid_{\mathcal{U}}$, issue_wallet) from $\mathcal{F}_{\text{msg}}$:

(a) Load the internally recorded (pk_{O}, sk_{O}).$^{\perp}$

(b) Load the internally recorded $cert_{O}$.$^{\perp}$

(c) Receive pk_{DR} from the bulletin-board $\mathcal{F}_{\text{bb}}$ for PID pid_{DR}.$^{\perp}$

(d) Receive $pk_{\mathcal{U}}$ from the bulletin-board $\mathcal{F}_{\text{bb}}$ for PID $pid_{\mathcal{U}}$.$^{\perp}$

Operator output: (issuing_wallet, $pid_{\mathcal{U}}$)

Operator input: (issuing_wallet, $a_{\mathcal{U}}$)

(3) At the operator side: Call $\mathcal{F}_{\text{msg}}$ with (accept, $ssid$).

(4) At the user side: Receive $\mathcal{F}_{\text{msg}}$ with (accepted, $ssid$).

(5) Both sides: Run the code of IssueWallet between the user and the operator (see Figs. 7.14 and 7.15) using (send, $ssid$, …) of $\mathcal{F}_{\text{msg}}$ for messaging:

$$((\tau), (s, \omega_{\text{bl}})) \leftarrow \mathsf{IssueWallet}\langle \mathcal{U}(pk_{DR}, pk_{\mathcal{U}}, sk_{\mathcal{U}}), O(pk_{DR}, sk_{O}, pk_{\mathcal{U}}, a_{\mathcal{U}}, cert_{O})\rangle .$$

(6) At the user side:

(a) Run the code of VerifyWallet$(pk_{O}, pk_{\mathcal{U}}, \tau)$ (see Fig. 7.30).

(b) If VerifyWallet returns 0, output $\perp$ and abort.

(c) Record τ internally.

(d) Parse s and $a_{\mathcal{U}}$ from τ.

(e) Call $\mathcal{F}_{\text{msg}}$ with (close, $ssid$).

(7) At the operator side upon receiving (closed, $ssid$) from $\mathcal{F}_{\text{msg}}$, append $\omega_{\text{bl}} \mapsto \emptyset$ to $f_{bl_{\Phi_\lambda}}$.

User output: (issued_wallet, s, $a_{\mathcal{U}}$)

Operator output: (issued_wallet, s, ω_{bl})

$^{\perp}$ If this does not exist, abort.

Figure 7.13: The Protocol π_{P5C} (cont. from Fig. 7.1) – Task IssueWallet

$\mathcal{U}(pk_{DR}, pk_{\mathcal{U}}, sk_{\mathcal{U}})$		$\mathcal{O}(pk_{DR}, sk_{\mathcal{O}}, pk_{\mathcal{U}}, a_{\mathcal{U}}, cert_{\mathcal{O}})$
		parse $(sk_{\mathcal{O}}^{\text{fix}}, sk_{\mathcal{O}}^{\text{cert}}, sk_{\mathcal{O}}^{\text{upd}}, sk_{\mathcal{O}}^{\text{rc,sig}}, sk_{\mathcal{O}}^{\text{rc,enc}}) := sk_{\mathcal{O}}$
$s' \xleftarrow{R} G_1$		$s'' \xleftarrow{R} G_1$
$\lambda'_i \xleftarrow{R} \{0, \dots, B-1\}$ for $i \in \{0, \dots, \ell-1\}$		
$\lambda' := \sum_{i=0}^{\ell-1} \lambda'_i \cdot B^i$		$\lambda'' \xleftarrow{R} \mathbb{Z}_p$
$(c'_{\text{wid}}, d'_{\text{wid}}) \leftarrow \text{C3.Commit}(crs_{\text{com}}^{(3)}, \lambda')$		$(c''_{\text{ser}}, d''_{\text{ser}}) \leftarrow \text{C4.Commit}(crs_{\text{com}}^{(4)}, s'')$
	$\xrightarrow{c'_{\text{wid}}}$	
	$\xleftarrow{cert_{\mathcal{O}}, a_{\mathcal{U}}, c''_{\text{ser}}, \lambda''}$	
parse $(pk_{\mathcal{O}}^{\text{upd}}, a_{\mathcal{O}}, \sigma_{\mathcal{O}}^{\text{cert}}) := cert_{\mathcal{O}}$		
if $\text{SIG.Vfy}(pk_{\mathcal{O}}^{\text{cert}}, \sigma_{\mathcal{O}}^{\text{cert}}, (pk_{\mathcal{O}}^{\text{upd}}, a_{\mathcal{O}})) = 0$		
return $\perp$		
$\lambda := \lambda' + \lambda''$		
$\Lambda := g_1^{\lambda}, \Lambda' := g_1^{\lambda'}, \Lambda'' := g_1^{\lambda''}$		$\Lambda'' := g_1^{\lambda''}$
$\Lambda'_i := g_1^{\lambda'_i}$ for $i \in \{0, \dots, \ell-1\}$		
$r_1, r_2 \xleftarrow{R} \mathbb{Z}_p$		
$\psi_{\text{bl}} \leftarrow \text{ENC1.Enc}(pk_{DR}, (\Lambda'_0, \dots, \Lambda'_{\ell-1}, \Lambda'', pk_{\mathcal{U}}); r_1, r_2)$		
$u_1^{\text{next}} \xleftarrow{R} \mathbb{Z}_p$		
$(c_{\text{fix}}, d_{\text{fix}}) \leftarrow \text{C1.Commit}(crs_{\text{com}}^{(1)}, (\lambda, sk_{\mathcal{U}}))$		
$(c_{\text{upd}}, d_{\text{upd}}) \leftarrow \text{C1.Commit}(crs_{\text{com}}^{(1)}, (\lambda, 0, u_1^{\text{next}}, 1))$		
$stmnt := (pk_{\mathcal{U}}, pk_{DR}, \psi_{\text{bl}}, c_{\text{fix}}, c_{\text{upd}}, c'_{\text{wid}}, \Lambda'', \lambda'')$		
$wit := (\lambda, \lambda', \lambda'_0, \dots, \lambda'_{\ell-1}, r_1, r_2, \Lambda, \Lambda', \Lambda'_0, \dots, \Lambda'_{\ell-1}, g_1^{u_1^{\text{next}}}, d_{\text{fix}}, d_{\text{upd}}, d'_{\text{wid}})$		
$\pi \leftarrow \text{P1.Prove}(crs_{\text{pok}}, stmnt, wit)$		
	$\xrightarrow{s', \psi_{\text{bl}}, c_{\text{fix}}, c_{\text{upd}}, \pi}$	

Figure 7.14: The Core Protocol for Task IssueWallet (used by Fig. 7.13)

$$\xrightarrow{s', \psi_{\text{bl}}, c_{\text{fix}}, c_{\text{upd}}, \pi}$$

$s := s' \cdot s''$

$stmnt := (pk_{\mathcal{U}}, pk_{\mathcal{DR}}, \psi_{\text{bl}},$
$\quad c_{\text{fix}}, c_{\text{upd}}, c'_{\text{wid}}, \Lambda'', \lambda'')$

if $\text{P1.Vfy}(crs_{\text{pok}}, stmnt, \pi) = 0$
$\quad$ return $\bot$

$\sigma_{\text{fix}} \leftarrow \text{SIG.Sign}(sk_{\mathcal{O}}^{\text{fix}}, (c_{\text{fix}}, a_{\mathcal{U}}))$

$\sigma_{\text{upd}} \leftarrow \text{SIG.Sign}(sk_{\mathcal{O}}^{\text{upd}}, (c_{\text{upd}}, s))$

$$\xleftarrow{s'', d''_{\text{ser}}, \sigma_{\text{fix}}, \sigma_{\text{upd}}}$$

if $\text{C4.Open}(crs_{\text{com}}^{(4)}, s'', c''_{\text{ser}}, d''_{\text{ser}}) = 0$
$\quad$ return $\bot$

$s := s' \cdot s''$

$\tau := (s, \text{PRF}(\lambda, 0), 1, \lambda, a_{\mathcal{U}}, c_{\text{upd}}, d_{\text{upd}}, \sigma_{\text{upd}},$
$\quad cert_{\mathcal{O}}, c_{\text{fix}}, d_{\text{fix}}, \sigma_{\text{fix}}, 0, u_1^{\text{next}})$

return (τ)

$\omega_{\text{bl}} := (\lambda'', \psi_{\text{bl}})$

return (s, ω_{bl})

Figure 7.15: The Core Protocol for Task IssueWallet (cont. from Fig. 7.14)

7.3.2 Deposition

The task Deposit (Figs. 7.16 to 7.20) is executed between an anonymous user and a PoS to deposit points on a wallet owned by the user. It serves the following objectives:

(1) Jointly computing a fresh and random serial number s for this transaction.

(2) Determine the price p to be deposited.

(3) Assembling all components for an updated wallet for the user.

(4) Generating (a) a double-spending tag ω_{ds}, (b) a recalculation tag ω_{rc} and (c) a prove-participation tag ω_{pp}.

As in Section 7.3.1 for IssueWallet the first objective is implemented by a standard Blum cointoss in the message 1–3.

To achieve the second objective, the task is interactive. After the user has send the attributes $a_{\mathcal{U}}, a_{\mathcal{P}}^{\text{prev}}$ which are required to determine the price p in message 2, those are output to the PoS. The PoS restarts the second part of Deposit with the price as input which is then sent back to the user in message 3.

UC-Protocol π_{P5C} (cont.) – Task Deposit, **Part 1**

User input: $(\texttt{deposit}, s^{\mathrm{prev}}, pid_{\mathcal{P}})$

(1) At the user side:

(a) Load the internally recorded $(pk_{\mathcal{U}}, sk_{\mathcal{U}})$.$^{\perp}$

(b) Receive $pk_{\mathcal{O}}$ from the bulletin-board $\mathcal{F}_{\mathrm{bb}}$ for PID $pid_{\mathcal{O}}$.$^{\perp}$

(c) Load the internally recorded token τ^{prev} for serial number s^{prev}.$^{\perp}$

(d) Call $\mathcal{F}_{\mathrm{msg}}$ with $(\texttt{establish-session}, \mathrm{anon}, pid_{\mathcal{P}}, \texttt{deposit})$.

(2) At the PoS side upon receiving $(\texttt{establishing-session}, ssid, \perp, \texttt{deposit})$ from $\mathcal{F}_{\mathrm{msg}}$:

(a) Load the internally recorded $(pk_{\mathcal{P}}, sk_{\mathcal{P}})$.$^{\perp}$

(b) Load the internally recorded $cert_{\mathcal{P}}$.$^{\perp}$

(c) Receive $pk_{\mathcal{O}}$ from the bulletin-board $\mathcal{F}_{\mathrm{bb}}$ for PID $pid_{\mathcal{O}}$.$^{\perp}$

PoS output: $(\texttt{depositing})$

PoS input: $(\texttt{depositing}, bl_{\Phi})$

(3) At the PoS side: Call $\mathcal{F}_{\mathrm{msg}}$ with $(\texttt{accept}, ssid)$.

(4) At the user side: Receive $(\texttt{accepted}, ssid)$ from $\mathcal{F}_{\mathrm{msg}}$.

(5) Both sides: Run the code of Deposit Part 1 between the user and the PoS (see Figs. 7.18 and 7.19) using $(\texttt{send}, ssid, \dots)$ of $\mathcal{F}_{\mathrm{msg}}$ for messaging:

$$\begin{pmatrix} \mathsf{OK}, \\ (s, a_{\mathcal{U}}, a_{\mathcal{P}}^{\mathrm{prev}}) \end{pmatrix} \leftarrow \mathsf{Deposit}_1 \left\langle \begin{matrix} \mathcal{U}(pk_{\mathcal{O}}, pk_{\mathcal{U}}, sk_{\mathcal{U}}, \tau^{\mathrm{prev}}), \\ \mathcal{P}(pk_{\mathcal{O}}, cert_{\mathcal{P}}, sk_{\mathcal{P}}, bl_{\Phi}) \end{matrix} \right\rangle$$

PoS output: $(\texttt{depositing}, s, a_{\mathcal{U}}, a_{\mathcal{P}}^{\mathrm{prev}})$

$^{\perp}$ If this does not exist, abort.

Figure 7.16: The Protocol π_{P5C} (cont. from Fig. 7.1) – Task Deposit, Part 1

For the third objective, the homomorphism of the commitment scheme is exploited. Also see Section 7.1.1 for a detailed description of the wallet. The user creates a re-randomized version c'_{upd} of the previous updatable commitment $c^{\mathrm{prev}}_{\mathrm{upd}}$. The commitment c'_{upd} contains the same values as $c^{\mathrm{prev}}_{\mathrm{upd}}$ except for a fresh DS mask u_1^{next} (see next paragraph) and is sent to the PoS in message 2. Re-randomization enables unlinkability. The PoS applies the homomorphic update c''_{upd} to c'_{upd} to deposit p points on the balance and to increase the transaction counter x by 1. The combination of serial number s and the modified updatable commitment c_{upd} is signed by the PoS with σ_{upd} and both are sent back to the user in message 3.

To generate the double-spending tag ω_{ds} for the current transaction, the PoS challenges the user with u_2 in the first message. In the second message, the user responds with the DS

UC-Protocol π_{P5C} (cont.) – Task Deposit, **Part 2**

PoS input: (depositing, p)

(6) Both sides: Run the code of Deposit Part 2 between the user and the PoS (see Fig. 7.20) using (send, $ssid, \dots$) of $\mathcal{F}_{\text{msg}}$ for messaging:

$$((\tau, \omega_{\text{pp}}, \psi_{\text{pp}}), (\omega_{\text{ds}}, \omega_{\text{rc}}, \omega_{\text{pp}})) \leftarrow \mathsf{Deposit}_2\langle \mathcal{U}(), \mathcal{P}(p)\rangle$$

(7) At the user side:

(a) Run the code of VerifyWallet($pk_{\mathcal{O}}, pk_{\mathcal{U}}, \tau$) (see Fig. 7.30).

(b) If VerifyWallet returns 0, output $\perp$ and abort.

(c) Append $\omega_{\text{pp}} \mapsto \psi_{\text{pp}}$ to f_{pp} and record τ internally.

(d) Parse s, $cert_{\mathcal{P}}$, p and b from τ.

(e) Parse $a_{\mathcal{P}}$ from $cert_{\mathcal{P}}$.

(f) Call $\mathcal{F}_{\text{msg}}$ with (close, $ssid$).

(8) At the PoS side: Receive (closed, $ssid$) from $\mathcal{F}_{\text{msg}}$.

User output: (deposited, $s, a_{\mathcal{P}}, p, b, \omega_{\text{pp}}$)

PoS output: (deposited, $\omega_{\text{ds}}, \omega_{\text{rc}}, \omega_{\text{pp}}$)

$\perp$ If this does not exist, abort.

Figure 7.17: The Protocol π_{P5C} (cont. from Fig. 7.1) – Task Deposit, Part 2

response $t := sk_{\mathcal{U}} \cdot u_2 + u_1 \bmod \mathfrak{p}$ and the current fraud-detection ID $\varphi := \mathsf{PRF}(\lambda, x)$ which has been calculated by the user in the beginning. This gives the PoS all information to construct the double-spending tag $\omega_{\text{ds}} := (\varphi, t, u_2)$. Note, that the currently used DS mask u_1 stems from the previous wallet state τ^{prev} as $u_1 = u_1^{\text{prev,next}}$. In preparation for the double-spending mechanism in the upcoming transaction, the user embeds a fresh DS mask u_1^{next} in the re-randomized version c'_{upd} of the current updatable commitment (see above).

The creation of the recalculation tag ω_{rc} is straightforward as the PoS has all necessary information at hand and can simply compile it. For details see Section 7.1.4.

For the prove-participation tag ω_{pp} and its hidden counterpart ψ_{pp} the user creates a commitment $(c_{pk_{\mathcal{U}}}, d_{pk_{\mathcal{U}}}) \leftarrow \mathsf{C2.Commit}(crs^{(2)}_{\text{com}}, sk_{\mathcal{U}})$ on the user's key and sends $c_{pk_{\mathcal{U}}}$ to the PoS in the second message. The PoS replies with a corresponding signature σ_{pp} in message 3. After that the user knows all components and can set the hidden prove-participation tag as $\psi_{\text{pp}} := (pk^{\text{pp}}_{\mathcal{P}}, \sigma_{\text{pp}}, d_{pk_{\mathcal{U}}})$ and the prove-participation tag as $\omega_{\text{pp}} := c_{pk_{\mathcal{U}}}$.

In order to show that everything has been computed honestly, the user sends a proof π as part of the second message. In particular, π shows that the user knows a signed wallet state

$\mathcal{U}(pk_{\mathcal{O}}, pk_{\mathcal{U}}, sk_{\mathcal{U}}, \tau^{\text{prev}})$		$\mathcal{P}(pk_{\mathcal{O}}, cert_{\mathcal{P}}, sk_{\mathcal{P}}, bl_{\Phi})$
parse $(pk_{\mathcal{O}}^{\text{fix}}, pk_{\mathcal{O}}^{\text{cert}}, pk_{\mathcal{O}}^{\text{upd}},$ $pk_{\mathcal{O}}^{\text{rc,sig}}, pk_{\mathcal{O}}^{\text{rc,enc}}) := pk_{\mathcal{O}}$		parse $(pk_{\mathcal{O}}^{\text{fix}}, pk_{\mathcal{O}}^{\text{cert}}, pk_{\mathcal{O}}^{\text{upd}},$ $pk_{\mathcal{O}}^{\text{rc,sig}}, pk_{\mathcal{O}}^{\text{rc,enc}}) := pk_{\mathcal{O}}$
parse $(s^{\text{prev}}, \varphi^{\text{prev}}, x, \lambda, a_{\mathcal{U}},$ $c_{\text{upd}}^{\text{prev}}, d_{\text{upd}}^{\text{prev}}, \sigma_{\text{upd}}^{\text{prev}}, cert_{\mathcal{P}}^{\text{prev}},$ $c_{\text{fix}}, d_{\text{fix}}, \sigma_{\text{fix}}, b^{\text{prev}}, u_1) := \tau^{\text{prev}}$		parse $(pk_{\mathcal{P}}, a_{\mathcal{P}}, \sigma_{\mathcal{P}}^{\text{cert}}) := cert_{\mathcal{P}}$ parse $(pk_{\mathcal{P}}^{\text{upd}}, pk_{\mathcal{P}}^{\text{rc}}, pk_{\mathcal{P}}^{\text{pp}}) := pk_{\mathcal{P}}$
parse $(pk_{\mathcal{P}}^{\text{prev}}, a_{\mathcal{P}}^{\text{prev}}, \sigma_{\mathcal{P}}^{\text{cert,prev}}) := cert_{\mathcal{P}}^{\text{prev}}$		parse $(sk_{\mathcal{P}}^{\text{upd}}, sk_{\mathcal{P}}^{\text{rc}}, sk_{\mathcal{P}}^{\text{pp}}) := sk_{\mathcal{P}}$
$\varphi := \mathsf{PRF}(\lambda, x)$		
$s' \xleftarrow{R} G_1$		$s'' \xleftarrow{R} G_1$
$u_1^{\text{next}} \xleftarrow{R} \mathbb{Z}_p$		$u_2 \xleftarrow{R} \mathbb{Z}_p$
$(c'_{\text{upd}}, d'_{\text{upd}}) \leftarrow \mathsf{C1.Commit}(crs_{\text{com}}^{(1)},$ $(\lambda, b^{\text{prev}}, u_1^{\text{next}}, x))$		$(c''_{\text{ser}}, d''_{\text{ser}}) \leftarrow \mathsf{C4.Commit}(crs_{\text{com}}^{(4)}, s'')$
	$\xleftarrow{u_2,\, c''_{\text{ser}},\, cert_{\mathcal{P}}}$	
parse $(pk_{\mathcal{P}}, a_{\mathcal{P}}, \sigma_{\mathcal{P}}^{\text{cert}}) := cert_{\mathcal{P}}$ if $\mathsf{SIG.Vfy}(pk_{\mathcal{O}}^{\text{cert}}, \sigma_{\mathcal{P}}^{\text{cert}}, (pk_{\mathcal{P}}, a_{\mathcal{P}})) = 0$ return $\perp$ parse$(pk_{\mathcal{P}}^{\text{upd}}, pk_{\mathcal{P}}^{\text{rc}}, pk_{\mathcal{P}}^{\text{pp}}) := pk_{\mathcal{P}}$ $t := u_2 sk_{\mathcal{U}} + u_1 \bmod p$ $(c_{pk_{\mathcal{U}}}, d_{pk_{\mathcal{U}}}) \leftarrow \mathsf{C2.Commit}(crs_{\text{com}}^{(2)}, sk_{\mathcal{U}})$ $stmnt := (pk_{\mathcal{O}}^{\text{fix}}, pk_{\mathcal{O}}^{\text{cert}}, \varphi, a_{\mathcal{U}}, a_{\mathcal{P}}^{\text{prev}},$ $c_{pk_{\mathcal{U}}}, c'_{\text{upd}}, t, u_2)$ $wit := (x, \lambda, sk_{\mathcal{U}}, u_1, s^{\text{prev}}, \varphi^{\text{prev}}, g_1^x, g_1^{\lambda},$ $pk_{\mathcal{U}}, g_1^{b^{\text{prev}}}, g_1^{u_1}, g_1^{u_1^{\text{next}}}, d_{pk_{\mathcal{U}}}, d_{\text{upd}}^{\text{prev}}, d'_{\text{upd}}, d_{\text{fix}},$ $pk_{\mathcal{P}}^{\text{prev}}, c_{\text{upd}}^{\text{prev}}, c_{\text{fix}}, \sigma_{\text{upd}}^{\text{prev}}, \sigma_{\mathcal{P}}^{\text{cert,prev}}, \sigma_{\text{fix}})$ $\pi \leftarrow \mathsf{P2.Prove}(crs_{\text{pok}}, stmnt, wit)$		
	$\xrightarrow{s', \pi, \varphi, a_{\mathcal{U}}, a_{\mathcal{P}}^{\text{prev}}, c_{pk_{\mathcal{U}}}, c'_{\text{upd}}, t}$	

Figure 7.18: The Core Protocol for Task Deposit, Part 1 (used by Fig. 7.16)

$\xrightarrow{s', \pi, \varphi, a_{\mathcal{U}}, a_{\mathcal{P}}^{\text{prev}}, c_{pk_{\mathcal{U}}}, c'_{\text{upd}}, t}$	
	$stmnt := (pk_{\mathcal{O}}^{\text{fix}}, pk_{\mathcal{O}}^{\text{cert}}, \varphi, a_{\mathcal{U}}, a_{\mathcal{P}}^{\text{prev}},$
	$\quad c_{pk_{\mathcal{U}}}, c'_{\text{upd}}, t, u_2)$
	if $\text{P2.Vfy}(crs_{\text{pok}}, stmnt, \pi) = 0$
	$\quad$ return $\bot$
	if $\varphi \in bl_{\Phi}$
	$\quad$ return `blacklisted_wallet`
	$s := s' \cdot s''$
return (OK)	return $(s, a_{\mathcal{U}}, a_{\mathcal{P}}^{\text{prev}})$

Figure 7.19: The Core Protocol for Task Deposit, Part 1 (cont., used by Fig. 7.16)

$\mathcal{U}()$	$\mathcal{P}(p)$
	$(c''_{\text{upd}}, d''_{\text{upd}}) \leftarrow \text{C1.Commit}(crs_{\text{com}}^{(1)},$
	$\quad (0, p, 0, 1))$
	$c_{\text{upd}} := c'_{\text{upd}} \cdot c''_{\text{upd}}$
	$\sigma_{\text{upd}} \leftarrow \text{SIG.Sign}(sk_{\mathcal{P}}^{\text{upd}}, (c_{\text{upd}}, s))$
	$\sigma_{\text{rc}} \leftarrow \text{SIG.Sign}(sk_{\mathcal{P}}^{\text{rc}}, (s, \varphi, g_1^{p}))$
	$\sigma_{\text{pp}} \leftarrow \text{SIG.Sign}(sk_{\mathcal{P}}^{\text{pp}}, c_{pk_{\mathcal{U}}})$
$\xleftarrow{s'', d''_{\text{ser}}, c_{\text{upd}}, d''_{\text{upd}}, \sigma_{\text{upd}}, p, \sigma_{\text{pp}}}$	
if $\text{C4.Open}(crs_{\text{com}}^{(4)}, s'', c''_{\text{ser}}, d''_{\text{ser}}) = 0$	
$\quad$ return $\bot$	
if $\text{SIG.Vfy}(pk_{\mathcal{P}}^{\text{pp}}, \sigma_{\text{pp}}, c_{pk_{\mathcal{U}}}) = 0$	
$\quad$ return $\bot$	
$s := s' \cdot s''$	
$d_{\text{upd}} := d'_{\text{upd}} \cdot d''_{\text{upd}}$	
$b := b^{\text{prev}} + p$	
$x^{\text{next}} := x + 1$	
$\tau := (s, \varphi, x^{\text{next}}, \lambda, a_{\mathcal{U}}, c_{\text{upd}}, d_{\text{upd}}, \sigma_{\text{upd}},$	$\omega_{\text{ds}} := (\varphi, t, u_2)$
$\quad cert_{\mathcal{P}}, c_{\text{fix}}, d_{\text{fix}}, \sigma_{\text{fix}}, b, u_1^{\text{next}})$	$\psi_{\text{rc}} := (s, \varphi, p, pk_{\mathcal{P}}^{\text{rc}}, \sigma_{\text{rc}})$
$\psi_{\text{pp}} := (pk_{\mathcal{P}}^{\text{pp}}, \sigma_{\text{pp}}, d_{pk_{\mathcal{U}}})$	$\omega_{\text{rc}} \leftarrow \text{ENC2.Enc}(pk_{\mathcal{O}}^{\text{rc,enc}}, \psi_{\text{rc}})$
$\omega_{\text{pp}} := c_{pk_{\mathcal{U}}}$	$\omega_{\text{pp}} := c_{pk_{\mathcal{U}}}$
return $(\tau, \omega_{\text{pp}}, \psi_{\text{pp}})$	return $(\omega_{\text{ds}}, \omega_{\text{rc}}, \omega_{\text{pp}})$

Figure 7.20: The Core Protocol for Task Deposit, Part 2 (used by Fig. 7.17)

involving commitments c_{fix} and $c_{\text{upd}}^{\text{prev}}$ such that $c_{\text{upd}}^{\text{prev}}$ and c'_{upd} are commitments on the same messages except for the DS mask, that the (hidden) signature on $c_{\text{upd}}^{\text{prev}}$ verifies under some (hidden) PoS key $pk_{\mathcal{P}}^{\text{prev}}$ certified by the operator, and that t, φ, and $c_{pk_{\mathcal{U}}}$ have been computed using the values contained in c_{fix} and $c_{\text{upd}}^{\text{prev}}$. Formally, the language $L_{gp}^{(2)}$ of the statement *stmnt* for the proof π is defined by

$$L_{gp}^{(2)} := \left\{ \begin{pmatrix} pk_{\mathcal{O}}^{\text{fix}} \\ pk_{\mathcal{O}}^{\text{cert}} \\ \varphi \\ a_{\mathcal{U}} \\ a_{\mathcal{P}}^{\text{prev}} \\ c_{pk_{\mathcal{U}}} \\ c'_{\text{upd}} \\ t \\ u_2 \end{pmatrix}^T \middle| \begin{array}{l} \exists\, x, \lambda, sk_{\mathcal{U}}, u_1 \in \mathbb{Z}_p; \\ s^{\text{prev}}, \varphi^{\text{prev}}, X, \Lambda, pk_{\mathcal{U}}, B^{\text{prev}}, U_1, U_1^{\text{next}}, d_{pk_{\mathcal{U}}}, d_{\text{upd}}^{\text{prev}}, d'_{\text{upd}}, d_{\text{fix}} \in G_1; \\ pk_{\mathcal{P}}^{\text{prev}} = (pk_{\mathcal{P}}^{\text{upd,prev}}, pk_{\mathcal{P}}^{\text{rc,prev}}) \in (G_1^3 \times G_2) \times (G_1^2 \times G_2^3) \\ c_{\text{upd}}^{\text{prev}}, c_{\text{fix}} \in G_2; \\ \sigma_{\text{upd}}^{\text{prev}}, \sigma_{\mathcal{P}}^{\text{cert,prev}}, \sigma_{\text{fix}} \in G_2^2 \times G_1 \;: \\ \mathsf{C1.Open}(crs_{\text{com}}^{(1)}, (\Lambda, pk_{\mathcal{U}}), c_{\text{fix}}, d_{\text{fix}}) = 1 \\ \mathsf{C2.Open}(crs_{\text{com}}^{(2)}, pk_{\mathcal{U}}, c_{pk_{\mathcal{U}}}, d_{pk_{\mathcal{U}}}) = 1 \\ \mathsf{C1.Open}(crs_{\text{com}}^{(1)}, (\Lambda, B^{\text{prev}}, U_1, X), c_{\text{upd}}^{\text{prev}}, d_{\text{upd}}^{\text{prev}}) = 1 \\ \mathsf{C1.Open}(crs_{\text{com}}^{(1)}, (\Lambda, B^{\text{prev}}, U_1^{\text{next}}, X), c'_{\text{upd}}, d'_{\text{upd}}) = 1 \\ \mathsf{SIG.Vfy}(pk_{\mathcal{O}}^{\text{fix}}, \sigma_{\text{fix}}, (c_{\text{fix}}, a_{\mathcal{U}})) = 1 \\ \mathsf{SIG.Vfy}(pk_{\mathcal{P}}^{\text{upd,prev}}, \sigma_{\text{upd}}^{\text{prev}}, (c_{\text{upd}}^{\text{prev}}, s^{\text{prev}})) = 1 \\ \mathsf{SIG.Vfy}(pk_{\mathcal{O}}^{\text{cert}}, \sigma_{\mathcal{P}}^{\text{cert,prev}}, (pk_{\mathcal{P}}^{\text{prev}}, a_{\mathcal{P}}^{\text{prev}})) = 1 \\ \varphi^{\text{prev}} = \mathsf{PRF}(\lambda, x-1),\; \varphi = \mathsf{PRF}(\lambda, x), \\ t = u_2 sk_{\mathcal{U}} + u_1 \\ pk_{\mathcal{U}} = g_1^{sk_{\mathcal{U}}},\; U_1 = g_1^{u_1},\; X = g_1^x,\; \Lambda = g_1^\lambda \end{array} \right\} \tag{7.13}$$

As a minor detail, the parties mutually exchange various "administrative" information which is check for validity. The PoS sends its certificate $cert_{\mathcal{P}}$ as part of the first message to show that it is a valid member of the system or the user aborts before responding to the DS challenge. Vice versa, the PoS aborts after the second message, if the user turns out to be blacklisted due to the fraud-detection ID φ being listed in bl_{Φ}.

7.3.3 Disbursement

The task Disburse (cp. Figs. 7.21 and 7.22) complements the task Deposit and is executed between a user and operator to disburse all points on a wallet which have been deposited before. As detailed out in the system definition (cp. Section 4.3.3) the given instantiation is tailored to the post-payment scenario from Section 2.3.3.

Unsurprisingly, the implementation of Disburse is very similar to Deposit and actually simpler: both parties are identified and thus certain checks of validity do not require a ZK

UC-Protocol π_{P5C} (cont.) – Task Disburse

User input: ($\mathtt{disburse}, s^{\text{prev}}$)

(1) At the user side:

(a) Load the internally recorded $(pk_{\mathcal{U}}, sk_{\mathcal{U}})$.$^{\perp}$

(b) Receive $pk_{\mathcal{O}}$ from the bulletin-board $\mathcal{F}_{\text{bb}}$ for PID $pid_{\mathcal{O}}$.$^{\perp}$

(c) Load the internally recorded token τ^{prev} for serial number s^{prev}.$^{\perp}$

(d) Call $\mathcal{F}_{\text{msg}}$ with ($\mathtt{establish\text{-}session}, \mathtt{ident}, pid_{\mathcal{O}}, \mathtt{disburse}$).

(2) At the operator side upon receiving ($\mathtt{establishing\text{-}session}, ssid, pid_{\mathcal{U}}, \mathtt{disburse}$) from $\mathcal{F}_{\text{msg}}$:

(a) Load the internally recorded $(pk_{\mathcal{O}}, sk_{\mathcal{O}})$.$^{\perp}$

(b) Receive $pk_{\mathcal{U}}$ from the bulletin-board $\mathcal{F}_{\text{bb}}$ for PID $pid_{\mathcal{U}}$.$^{\perp}$

Operator output: ($\mathtt{disbursing}, pid_{\mathcal{U}}$)

Operator input: ($\mathtt{disbursing}$)

(3) At the operator side: Call $\mathcal{F}_{\text{msg}}$ with ($\mathtt{accept}, ssid$).

(4) At the user side: Receive ($\mathtt{accepted}, ssid$) from $\mathcal{F}_{\text{msg}}$.

(5) Both sides: Run the code of Disburse between the user and the PoS (see Fig. 7.22) using ($\mathtt{send}, ssid, \ldots$) of $\mathcal{F}_{\text{msg}}$ for messaging:

$$\left(b^{\text{bill}}, (b^{\text{bill}}, \omega_{\text{ds}}, \omega_{\text{rc}})\right) \leftarrow \mathsf{Disburse}\left\langle \mathcal{U}(pk_{\mathcal{O}}, pk_{\mathcal{U}}, sk_{\mathcal{U}}, \tau^{\text{prev}}), \mathcal{O}(pk_{\mathcal{O}}, pk_{\mathcal{U}}) \right\rangle.$$

(6) At the user side: Call $\mathcal{F}_{\text{msg}}$ with ($\mathtt{close}, ssid$).

(7) At the operator side: Receive ($\mathtt{closed}, ssid$) from $\mathcal{F}_{\text{msg}}$.

User output: ($\mathtt{disbursed}, b^{\text{bill}}$)

Operator output: ($\mathtt{disbursed}, b^{\text{bill}}, \omega_{\text{ds}}, \omega_{\text{rc}}$)

$^{\perp}$ If this does not exist, abort.

Figure 7.21: The Protocol π_{P5C} (cont. from Fig. 7.1) – Task Disburse

proof, the price equals the previous balance and thus no additional input is required which allows the protocol to be non-interactive, no new serial number needs to negotiated as the wallet is destroyed and no prove-participation tag is necessary. Accordingly, the objectives of Disburse are a subset of the objectives of Deposit:

(1) Unveil the price $p := b^{\text{prev}}$ to the operator.

(2) Generating (a) a double-spending tag ω_{ds} and (b) a recalculation tag ω_{rc}.

We refer the reader to the previous section on Disburse for a description. Please note, that the second message still contains a ZK-proof π, because the updatable commitment c_{upd} which

$\mathcal{U}(pk_{\mathcal{O}}, pk_{\mathcal{U}}, sk_{\mathcal{U}}, \tau^{\text{prev}})$		$\mathcal{O}(pk_{\mathcal{O}}, pk_{\mathcal{U}})$
parse $(pk_{\mathcal{O}}^{\text{fix}}, pk_{\mathcal{O}}^{\text{cert}}, pk_{\mathcal{O}}^{\text{upd}}, pk_{\mathcal{O}}^{\text{rc,sig}}, pk_{\mathcal{O}}^{\text{rc,enc}}) := pk_{\mathcal{O}}$		parse $(pk_{\mathcal{O}}^{\text{fix}}, pk_{\mathcal{O}}^{\text{cert}}, pk_{\mathcal{O}}^{\text{upd}}, pk_{\mathcal{O}}^{\text{rc,sig}}, pk_{\mathcal{O}}^{\text{rc,enc}}) := pk_{\mathcal{O}}$
parse $(s^{\text{prev}}, \varphi^{\text{prev}}, x, \lambda, a_{\mathcal{U}}, c_{\text{upd}}^{\text{prev}}, d_{\text{upd}}^{\text{prev}}, \sigma_{\text{upd}}^{\text{prev}}, cert_{\mathcal{P}}^{\text{prev}}, c_{\text{fix}}, d_{\text{fix}}, \sigma_{\text{fix}}, b^{\text{prev}}, u_1) := \tau^{\text{prev}}$		
parse $(pk_{\mathcal{P}}^{\text{prev}}, a_{\mathcal{P}}^{\text{prev}}, \sigma_{\mathcal{P}}^{\text{cert,prev}}) := cert_{\mathcal{P}}^{\text{prev}}$		
$\varphi := \mathsf{PRF}(\lambda, x)$		
		$u_2 \xleftarrow{R} \mathbb{Z}_p$
	$\xleftarrow{\quad u_2 \quad}$	
$t := u_2 sk_{\mathcal{U}} + u_1 \bmod p$		
$stmnt := (pk_{\mathcal{U}}, pk_{\mathcal{O}}^{\text{fix}}, pk_{\mathcal{O}}^{\text{cert}}, \varphi, g_1^{b^{\text{prev}}}, t, u_2)$		
$wit := (x, \lambda, sk_{\mathcal{U}}, u_1, s^{\text{prev}}, \varphi^{\text{prev}}, g_1^x, g_1^\lambda, g_1^{u_1}, d_{\text{upd}}^{\text{prev}}, d_{\text{fix}}, pk_{\mathcal{P}}^{\text{prev}}, c_{\text{upd}}^{\text{prev}}, c_{\text{fix}}, \sigma_{\text{upd}}^{\text{prev}}, \sigma_{\mathcal{P}}^{\text{cert,prev}}, \sigma_{\text{fix}}, a_{\mathcal{U}}, a_{\mathcal{P}}^{\text{prev}})$		
$\pi \leftarrow \mathsf{P3.Prove}(crs_{\text{pok}}, stmnt, wit)$		
	$\xrightarrow{\quad \pi, \varphi, b^{\text{prev}}, t \quad}$	
		$stmnt := (pk_{\mathcal{U}}, pk_{\mathcal{O}}^{\text{fix}}, pk_{\mathcal{O}}^{\text{cert}}, \varphi, g_1^{b^{\text{prev}}}, t, u_2)$
		if $\mathsf{P3.Vfy}(crs_{\text{pok}}, stmnt, \pi) = 0$
		return $\bot$
	$\xleftarrow{\quad \mathsf{OK} \quad}$	
$b^{\text{bill}} := b^{\text{prev}}$		$b^{\text{bill}} := b^{\text{prev}}$
		$s \xleftarrow{R} G_1$
		$\sigma_{\text{rc}} \leftarrow \mathsf{SIG.Sign}(sk_{\mathcal{O}}^{\text{rc,sig}}, (s, \varphi, g_1^{-b^{\text{bill}}}))$
		$\omega_{\text{ds}} := (\varphi, t, u_2)$
		$\psi_{\text{rc}} := (s, \varphi, p, pk_{\mathcal{P}}^{\text{rc}}, \sigma_{\text{rc}})$
		$\omega_{\text{rc}} \leftarrow \mathsf{ENC2.Enc}(pk_{\mathcal{O}}^{\text{rc,enc}}, \psi_{\text{rc}})$
return (b^{bill})		return $(b^{\text{bill}}, \omega_{\text{ds}}, \omega_{\text{rc}})$

Figure 7.22: The Core Protocol for Task Disburse (used by Fig. 7.21)

contains the previous balance b^{prev} is only unveiled indirectly in order to assert unlinkability to the previous transaction. More precisely, P3 is used to compute a proof π for a statement *stmnt* from the language $L_{gp}^{(3)}$ defined by

$$L_{gp}^{(3)} := \left\{ \begin{pmatrix} pk_{\mathcal{U}} \\ pk_{\mathcal{O}}^{\text{fix}} \\ pk_{\mathcal{O}}^{\text{cert}} \\ \varphi \\ B^{\text{prev}} \\ t \\ u_2 \end{pmatrix}^T \middle| \begin{array}{l} \exists\, x, \lambda, sk_{\mathcal{U}}, u_1 \in \mathbb{Z}_p; \\ s^{\text{prev}}, \varphi^{\text{prev}}, X, \Lambda, U_1, d_{\text{upd}}^{\text{prev}}, d_{\text{fix}} \in G_1; \\ pk_{\mathcal{P}}^{\text{prev}} = (pk_{\mathcal{P}}^{\text{upd,prev}}, pk_{\mathcal{P}}^{\text{rc,prev}}) \in (G_1^3 \times G_2) \times (G_1^2 \times G_2^3) \\ c_{\text{upd}}^{\text{prev}}, c_{\text{fix}} \in G_2; \\ \sigma_{\text{upd}}^{\text{prev}}, \sigma_{\mathcal{P}}^{\text{cert,prev}}, \sigma_{\text{fix}} \in G_2^2 \times G_1; \\ a_{\mathcal{U}} \in G_2^j, a_{\mathcal{P}}^{\text{prev}} \in G_1^y : \\ \text{C1.Open}(crs_{\text{com}}^{(1)}, (\Lambda, pk_{\mathcal{U}}), c_{\text{fix}}, d_{\text{fix}}) = 1 \\ \text{C1.Open}(crs_{\text{com}}^{(1)}, (\Lambda, B^{\text{prev}}, U_1, X), c_{\text{upd}}^{\text{prev}}, d_{\text{upd}}^{\text{prev}}) = 1 \\ \text{SIG.Vfy}(pk_{\mathcal{O}}^{\text{fix}}, \sigma_{\text{fix}}, (c_{\text{fix}}, a_{\mathcal{U}})) = 1 \\ \text{SIG.Vfy}(pk_{\mathcal{P}}^{\text{upd,prev}}, \sigma_{\text{upd}}^{\text{prev}}, (c_{\text{upd}}^{\text{prev}}, s^{\text{prev}})) = 1 \\ \text{SIG.Vfy}(pk_{\mathcal{O}}^{\text{cert}}, \sigma_{\mathcal{P}}^{\text{cert,prev}}, (pk_{\mathcal{P}}^{\text{prev}}, a_{\mathcal{P}}^{\text{prev}})) = 1 \\ \varphi^{\text{prev}} = \text{PRF}(\lambda, x-1),\ \varphi = \text{PRF}(\lambda, x), \\ t = u_2 sk_{\mathcal{U}} + u_1 \\ pk_{\mathcal{U}} = g_1^{sk_{\mathcal{U}}},\ U_1 = g_1^{u_1},\ X = g_1^x,\ \Lambda = g_1^{\lambda} \end{array} \right\} \tag{7.14}$$

The proof is a simplified version of the one in the Deposit protocol. The balance b^{prev} and the public user key $pk_{\mathcal{U}}$ are now in the statement and not in the witness and nothing needs to be proven about c'_{upd} and $c_{pk_{\mathcal{U}}}$.

7.4 Utility Tasks

7.4.1 Double-Spending Detection and Guilt Verification

The double-spending tag ω_{ds} generated by the PoSes are periodically transmitted to the operator's database which is regularly checked for two double-spending tags $\omega_{\text{ds}} = (\varphi, t, u_2)$, $\omega'_{\text{ds}} = (\varphi', t', u'_2)$ which are associated to the same fraud-detection ID $\varphi = \varphi'$. If the database contains two such tags, the operator can use the task DetectDS (see Fig. 7.23) to extract the PID $pid_{\mathcal{U}}$ of the user to which these double-spending tags belong as well as a proof π that the user is guilty. For an explanation of the double-spending detection mechanism see Section 7.1.4. At the bottom line, two double-spending tags with the same fraud-detection ID denote two points on the same line whose slope is the secret key $sk_{\mathcal{U}}$ of a user. The secret key does not only establish the fraudster's identity but also serves as the proof of guilt. Any party can run the task VerifyGuilt (cp. Fig. 7.24) to check the validity of a pair $(pid_{\mathcal{U}}, \pi)$. The task is implemented

UC-Protocol π_{P5C} (cont.) – Task DetectDS

Operator input: (`detect_ds`, $\omega_{\text{ds}}, \omega'_{\text{ds}}$)

(1) Parse $(\varphi, t, u_2) := \omega_{\text{ds}}$ and $(\varphi', t', u'_2) := \omega'_{\text{ds}}$.
(2) If $\varphi \neq \varphi'$ or $u_2 = u'_2$, output $(pid_{\mathcal{U}} = \bot, \pi = \bot)$ to operator and terminate.
(3) $sk_{\mathcal{U}} := (t - t')/(u_2 - u'_2) \bmod \mathfrak{p}$.
(4) $pk_{\mathcal{U}} := g_1^{sk_{\mathcal{U}}}$.
(5) Receive $pid_{\mathcal{U}}$ from the bulletin-board $\mathcal{F}_{\text{bb}}$ for $pk_{\mathcal{U}}$; if $pid_{\mathcal{U}} = \bot$, set $\pi := \bot$, else $\pi := sk_{\mathcal{U}}$.

Operator output: (`detected_ds`, $pid_{\mathcal{U}}, \pi$)

Figure 7.23: The Protocol π_{P5C} (cont. from Fig. 7.1) – Task DetectDS

UC-Protocol π_{P5C} (cont.) – Task VerifyGuilt

Party input: (`verify_guilt`, $pid_{\mathcal{U}}, \pi$)

(1) Receive $pk_{\mathcal{U}}$ from the bulletin-board $\mathcal{F}_{\text{bb}}$ for PID $pid_{\mathcal{U}}$ or set $pk_{\mathcal{U}} := \bot$ if no $pid_{\mathcal{U}}$ is registered.
(2) If $g_1^{\pi} = pk_{\mathcal{U}}$, then *result* := OK, else *result* := NOK.

Party output: (`verified_guilt`, *result*)

Figure 7.24: The Protocol π_{P5C} (cont. from Fig. 7.1) – Task VerifyGuilt

as local algorithm as the check $g_1^{\pi} = pk_{\mathcal{U}}$ is all what is needed. For honest users who kept their secret key securely away protection against false accusation follows from the hardness of the DLOG.

7.4.2 Wallet Blacklisting

The task BlacklistWallet (cp. Figs. 7.25 and 7.26) executed between the dispute resolver and operator is used to recover the sequence bl_{Φ_λ} of fraud-detection IDs of a wallet and thereby allows blacklisting. The implementation is apparent as the blacklisting tag ω_{bl} is an encryption under the public key of the dispute resolver (cp. Section 7.1.4). Remember that we assume that the dispute resolver and operator agreed out-of-band what user is going to be blacklisted. After the dispute resolver has decrypted ω_{bl} it first checks, if the decrypted user key $pk_{\mathcal{U}}$ equals the expected key $pk'_{\mathcal{U}}$. Together with the CCA-security of the encryption scheme this rules out malleability attacks which might try to trick the dispute resolver to recover the fraud-detection IDs of different (possibly innocent) user than assumed. After that the dispute resolver

UC-Protocol π_{P5C} (cont.) – Task BlacklistWallet

Operator input: $(\texttt{blacklist\_wallet}, \omega_{\mathrm{bl}})$

(1) At the operator side:

(a) If $f_{bl_{\Phi_\lambda}}(\omega_{\mathrm{bl}})$ is undefined, output $(\texttt{blacklisted\_wallet}, \emptyset)$ to operator and halt.

(b) Call $\mathcal{F}_{\mathrm{msg}}$ with $(\texttt{establish-session}, \texttt{ident}, pid_{\mathcal{DR}}, \texttt{blacklist\_wallet})$.

(2) At the dispute resolver side: Receive $(\texttt{establishing-session}, ssid, pid_{\mathcal{O}}, \texttt{blacklist\_wallet})$ from $\mathcal{F}_{\mathrm{msg}}$.

Dispute resolver output: $(\texttt{blacklisting\_wallet})$

Dispute resolver input: $(\texttt{blacklisting\_wallet}, pid'_{\mathcal{U}})$

(3) At the dispute resolver side:

(a) Load the internally recorded $(pk_{\mathcal{DR}}, sk_{\mathcal{DR}})$.$^{\perp}$

(b) Receive $pk'_{\mathcal{U}}$ from the bulletin-board $\mathcal{F}_{\mathrm{bb}}$ for PID $pid'_{\mathcal{U}}$.$^{\perp}$

(c) Call $\mathcal{F}_{\mathrm{msg}}$ with $(\texttt{accept}, ssid)$.

(4) At the operator side: Receive $(\texttt{accepted}, ssid)$ from $\mathcal{F}_{\mathrm{msg}}$.

(5) Both sides: Run the code of BlacklistWallet between the dispute resolver and the operator (see Fig. 7.26) using $(\texttt{send}, ssid, \dots)$ of $\mathcal{F}_{\mathrm{msg}}$ for messaging:

$$\left((\texttt{OK}), (bl_{\Phi_\lambda})\right) \leftarrow \mathsf{BlacklistWallet}\left\langle \mathcal{DR}(pk_{\mathcal{DR}}, sk_{\mathcal{DR}}, pk'_{\mathcal{U}}), \mathcal{O}(\omega_{\mathrm{bl}})\right\rangle .$$

(6) At the operator side:

(a) Redefine $f_{bl_{\Phi_\lambda}}(\omega_{\mathrm{bl}}) := bl_{\Phi_\lambda}$.

(b) Call $\mathcal{F}_{\mathrm{msg}}$ with $(\texttt{close}, ssid)$.

(7) At the dispute resolver side: Receive $(\texttt{closed}, ssid)$ from $\mathcal{F}_{\mathrm{msg}}$.

Dispute resolver output: $(\texttt{blacklisted\_wallet})$

Operator output: $(\texttt{blacklisted\_wallet}, bl_{\Phi_\lambda})$

$^{\perp}$ If this does not exist, abort.

Figure 7.25: The Protocol π_{P5C} (cont. from Fig. 7.1) – Task BlacklistWallet

$DR(pk_{DR}, sk_{DR}, pk'_{\mathcal{U}})$		$O(\omega_{\text{bl}})$
	$\xleftarrow{\omega_{\text{bl}}}$	
$bl_{\Phi_\lambda} := \emptyset$ parse $(\lambda'', \psi_{\text{bl}}) := \omega_{\text{bl}}$ $(\Lambda'_0, \ldots, \Lambda'_{\ell-1}, \Lambda'', pk_{\mathcal{U}}) \leftarrow \mathsf{ENC1.Dec}(sk_{DR}, \psi_{\text{bl}})$ if decryption suceeds $\wedge\ \Lambda'' = g_1^{\lambda''} \wedge pk'_{\mathcal{U}} = pk_{\mathcal{U}}$ $\quad \lambda := \lambda'' + \sum_{i=0}^{\ell-1} \mathsf{DLOG}(\Lambda'_i) \cdot B^i$ $\quad bl_{\Phi_\lambda} := \{\mathsf{PRF}(\lambda, 0), \ldots, \mathsf{PRF}(\lambda, x_{\text{bound}})\}$		
	$\xrightarrow{bl_{\Phi_\lambda}}$	
return (OK)		return (bl_{Φ_λ})

Figure 7.26: The Core Protocol for Task BlacklistWallet (used by Fig. 7.25)

reconstructs the wallet ID λ from its chunks and evaluates the PRF $(x_{\text{bound}} + 1)$ times. Since each of the chunks λ'_i is small $(\lambda'_i < B)$, the dispute resolver can compute the discrete logarithms of $(\Lambda'_i$ in a reasonable amount of time. This algorithm is also not time-critical and is expected to be executed only a few times. At the end, the operator internally redefines $f_{bl_{\Phi_\lambda}}(\omega_{\text{bl}}) := bl_{\Phi_\lambda}$ with the receives blacklist bl_{Φ_λ} to mark the blacklisting tag ω_{bl} as blacklisted.

A tempting but insecure alternative Skipping ahead to the security proof, we would like to point out an alternative implementation. At first glance, it seems to be sufficient, if the dispute resolver decrypts the blacklisting tag ω_{bl}, only checks if the expected user key has been decrypted and then sends back the decrypted cleartext ψ_{bl} to the operator, but leaves the rest of the work to the operator. This seems tempting, because it minimizes the computational work for the trusted third party (the dispute resolver) and puts the operator is in charge of computing the DLOGs and evaluating the PRF. However, this shift of the work load let the security proof fail. The operator must not learn the (secret) wallet ID λ even for blacklisted users. The crux of the matter is that for honest users, who might also become blacklisted, the pseudo-random fraud-detection IDs are replaced by truly random numbers in the security proof as it is also the case in the ideal model to argue unlinkability. If the operator is corrupted, this would require to come up with a wallet ID λ that explains a sequence of truly random numbers, which have been output by previous transaction, as the image of the PRF. Hence, it is admissible that the dispute resolver sends an evaluated sequence of the PRF to the operator, but disclosure of the seed is unacceptable. Actually, for the same reason the security proof fails

UC-Protocol π_{P5C} (cont.) – Task RecalculateBalance

Operator input: (`recalculate_balance`, $bl_{\Phi}, \Omega_{\text{rc}}$)

(1) Load the internally recorded $(pk_{\mathcal{O}}, sk_{\mathcal{O}})$.$^{\perp}$

(2) Run $b^{\text{bill}} \leftarrow \text{RecalculateBalance}(pk_{\mathcal{O}}, sk_{\mathcal{O}}, bl_{\Phi_\lambda}, \Omega_{\text{rc}})$ (see Fig. 7.28).

Operator output: (`recalculated_balance`, b^{bill})

$^{\perp}$ If this does not exist, abort.

Figure 7.27: The Protocol π_{P5C} (cont. from Fig. 7.1) – Task RecalculateBalance

$\text{RecalculateBalance}(pk_{\mathcal{O}}, sk_{\mathcal{O}}, bl_{\Phi_\lambda}, \Omega_{\text{rc}})$

parse $(pk_{\mathcal{O}}^{\text{fix}}, pk_{\mathcal{O}}^{\text{cert}}, pk_{\mathcal{O}}^{\text{upd}}, pk_{\mathcal{O}}^{\text{rc,sig}}, pk_{\mathcal{O}}^{\text{rc,enc}}) := pk_{\mathcal{O}}$

parse $(sk_{\mathcal{O}}^{\text{fix}}, sk_{\mathcal{O}}^{\text{cert}}, sk_{\mathcal{O}}^{\text{upd}}, sk_{\mathcal{O}}^{\text{rc,sig}}, sk_{\mathcal{O}}^{\text{rc,enc}}) := sk_{\mathcal{O}}$

$\Psi_{\text{rc}} := \{\psi_{\text{rc}} \leftarrow \text{ENC2.Dec}(sk_{\mathcal{O}}^{\text{rc,enc}}, \omega_{\text{rc}}) \mid \omega_{\text{rc}} \in \Omega_{\text{rc}}\}$

$\Psi_{\text{rc}}^{\text{valid}} := \{(s, \varphi, p, pk_{\mathcal{P}}^{\text{rc}}, \sigma_{\text{rc}}) \in \psi_{\text{rc}} \mid \text{SIG.Vfy}(pk_{\mathcal{P}}^{\text{rc}}, \sigma_{\text{rc}}, (s, \varphi, g_1^p)) = 1\}$

$\Xi := \{(s, p) \mid \exists\, \psi_{\text{rc}} = (s, \varphi, p, \cdot, \cdot) \in \Psi_{\text{rc}}^{\text{valid}} \wedge \varphi \in bl_{\Phi}\}$

$b^{\text{bill}} := \sum_{(s,p)\in\Xi} p$

return (b^{bill})

Figure 7.28: The Core Protocol for Task RecalculateBalance (used by Fig. 7.27)

under adaptive corruption. Interestingly, the shift of work load from the dispute resolver to the operator which unveils the wallet ID λ to the operator and turns out to be formally insecure does not seem to allow for any "real-world attack".[4]

7.4.3 Balance Recalculation

The task RecalculateBalance (cp. Figs. 7.27 and 7.28) complements wallet blacklisting and allows to match the set of collected recalculation tag Ω_{rc} with the set of fraud-detection IDs bl_{Φ_λ} of a blacklisted wallet and thereby re-calculate the true balance of a wallet while taking parallel wallet states due to double-spending into account. The implementation is straightforward: The operator decrypts the recalculation tags, verifies their validity, i.e. drops those which are invalid, and uses the remaining set to sum over the prices of those tags whose fraud-detection ID is contained in bl_{Φ_λ}.

[4] At least, we could not come up with one.

As already discussed for the definition of the system RecalculateBalance only gives very weak guarantees (cp. Sections 4.4.3 and 5.4.2). However, here we would like to point out another detail that should trigger action in the "real world" out of the scope of the UC-model and thus cannot be appropriately described[5] by pseudo-code. The serial number s is assumed to uniquely identify a single transaction and only occur once. If the operator encounters the same serial number twice, this is a clear indicator that at least one PoS must be corrupted and RecalculateBalance should throw an exception. In practice, this event should lead to further investigations and actions. The operator should try to identify the corrupted PoS and exclude it from the network.

Please note, that a corrupted PoS might invent recalculation tags for the same serial number, validly sign them and send them to the operator. Those duplicates do not even need to belong to transactions that have taken place in the physical world.[6]

7.4.4 Prove of Participation

The task ProveParticipation (cp. Fig. 7.29) is used by users to prove to the violation enforcer that they participated in a specific Deposit transaction with a PoS. To this end, the violation enforcer has been triggered by the PoS to physically identify the offending user, e.g. by taking a photo. Remember, this task is probably only a required in specific scenarios such as post-payment scenarios in that users are not physically prevented from gaining whatever benefit the system offers without paying first (cp. Section 2.3.3). Moreover, due to physical limits it might be impossible to exactly identify a single user, but accidentally suspicious several users of which all but one are innocent. The structure of prove-participation tags is described in Section 7.1.4 and the implementation of ProveParticipation is straightforward. The presumingly guilty user is challenged on a set of prove-participation tags Ω_{pp} which are connected to the offending incident in a timely and spatial manner and which must be provided by the same PoS which triggered the physical identification. The suspected user then may pick one of the proposed tags and unveil it. The binding property of the commitment underlying ω_{pp} asserts that only the legitimate owner can do so successfully and also only for the associated transaction.

[5] Of course, there are options to extend the expressiveness of what can be described by pseudo-code. For example, introduce a new ideal functionality that provides a "handle" to the physical world and is used as a black-box. But this seems to be much of an overkill for a rather trivial issue.

[6] Note that part of the solution for the other issues is to also make the user sign the recalculation tags. This mitigates the problem, but does not entirely solve it. Still the environment could invent an user and corrupt it. The solution only prevents to create valid recalculation tags in cooperation with honest users.

UC-Protocol π_{P5C} (cont.) – Task ProveParticipation

Violation enforcer input: (prove_participation, $pid_{\mathcal{U}}, pid_{\mathcal{P}}, \Omega_{\text{pp}}$)

(1) At the violation enforcer side:
   (a) Receive $pk_{\mathcal{U}}$ and $pk_{\mathcal{P}}$ from the bulletin-board $\mathcal{F}_{\text{bb}}$ for PID $pid_{\mathcal{U}}$ and $pid_{\mathcal{P}}$.[⊥]
   (b) Parse $pk_{\mathcal{P}}^{\text{pp}}$ from $pk_{\mathcal{P}}$.
   (c) Call $\mathcal{F}_{\text{msg}}$ with input (establish-session, ident, $pid_{\mathcal{U}}$, prove_participation).
(2) At the user side upon receiving output (establishing-session, $ssid, pid_{VE}$, prove_participation) from $\mathcal{F}_{\text{msg}}$, call $\mathcal{F}_{\text{msg}}$ with input (accept, $ssid$).
(3) At the violation enforcer side upon receiving output (accepted, $ssid$) from $\mathcal{F}_{\text{msg}}$, call $\mathcal{F}_{\text{msg}}$ with input (send, $ssid, (pid_{\mathcal{P}}, \Omega_{\text{pp}})$).
(4) At the user side receive output (sent, $ssid, (pid_{\mathcal{P}}, \Omega_{\text{pp}})$) from $\mathcal{F}_{\text{msg}}$.

User output: (proving_participation, $pid_{\mathcal{P}}, \Omega_{\text{pp}}$)

User input: (proving_participation, ω_{pp})

(5) At the user side:
   (a) Set $\psi_{\text{pp}} := f_{\text{pp}}(\omega_{\text{pp}})$.[a]
   (b) Call $\mathcal{F}_{\text{msg}}$ with input (send, $ssid, (\omega_{\text{pp}}, \psi_{\text{pp}})$).
(6) At the violation enforcer side upon receiving output (sent, $ssid, (\omega_{\text{pp}}, \psi_{\text{pp}})$) from $\mathcal{F}_{\text{msg}}$ ...
   (a) Set $c_{pk_{\mathcal{U}}} := \omega_{\text{pp}}$.
   (b) Parse $(\cdot, \sigma_{\text{pp}}, d_{pk_{\mathcal{U}}}) := \psi_{\text{pp}}$.
   (c) If $\omega_{\text{pp}} \in \Omega_{\text{pp}}$ and $\text{C2.Open}(crs_{\text{com}}^{(2)}, pk_{\mathcal{U}}, c_{pk_{\mathcal{U}}}, d_{pk_{\mathcal{U}}}) = 1$ and $\text{SIG.Vfy}(pk_{\mathcal{P}}^{\text{pp}}, \sigma_{\text{pp}}, c_{pk_{\mathcal{U}}}) = 1$, then $result :=$ OK, else $result :=$ NOK.
   (d) Call $\mathcal{F}_{\text{msg}}$ with input (close, $ssid$).

User output: (proved_participation)

Violation enforcer output: (proved_participation, $result$)

[⊥] If this does not exist, abort.

[a] N.b., $\psi_{\text{pp}} = \bot$ may hold, if $f_{\text{pp}}(\omega_{\text{pp}})$ is undefined.

Figure 7.29: The Protocol π_{P5C} (cont. from Fig. 7.1) – Task ProveParticipation

VerifyWallet$(pk_{\mathcal{O}}, pk_{\mathcal{U}}, \tau)$

parse $(pk_{\mathcal{O}}^{\text{fix}}, pk_{\mathcal{O}}^{\text{cert}}, pk_{\mathcal{O}}^{\text{upd}}, pk_{\mathcal{O}}^{\text{rc,sig}}, pk_{\mathcal{O}}^{\text{rc,enc}}) := pk_{\mathcal{O}}$
parse $(s, \varphi, x^{\text{next}}, \lambda, a_{\mathcal{U}}, c_{\text{upd}}, d_{\text{upd}}, \sigma_{\text{upd}}, cert_{\mathcal{P}}, c_{\text{fix}}, d_{\text{fix}}, \sigma_{\text{fix}}, b, u_1^{\text{next}}) := \tau$
parse $(pk_{\mathcal{P}}, a_{\mathcal{P}}, \sigma_{\mathcal{P}}^{\text{cert}}) := cert_{\mathcal{P}}$
parse $(pk_{\mathcal{P}}^{\text{upd}}, pk_{\mathcal{P}}^{\text{rc}}) := pk_{\mathcal{P}}$
if
  C1.Open$(crs_{\text{com}}^{(1)}, (g_1^{\lambda}, pk_{\mathcal{U}}), c_{\text{fix}}, d_{\text{fix}}) = 0 \vee$
  SIG.Vfy$(pk_{\mathcal{O}}^{\text{fix}}, \sigma_{\text{fix}}, (c_{\text{fix}}, a_{\mathcal{U}})) = 0 \vee$
  C1.Open$(crs_{\text{com}}^{(1)}, (g_1^{\lambda}, g_1^{b}, g_1^{u_1^{\text{next}}}, g_1^{x^{\text{next}}}), c_{\text{upd}}, d_{\text{upd}}) = 0 \vee$
  SIG.Vfy$(pk_{\mathcal{P}}^{\text{upd}}, \sigma_{\text{upd}}, (c_{\text{upd}}, s)) = 0 \vee$
  SIG.Vfy$(pk_{\mathcal{O}}^{\text{cert}}, \sigma_{\mathcal{P}}^{\text{cert}}, (pk_{\mathcal{P}}, a_{\mathcal{P}})) = 0 \vee$
  PRF$(\lambda, x^{\text{next}} - 1) \neq \varphi$
then return 0
else return 1

Figure 7.30: Helper Algorithm VerifyWallet

7.4.5 Wallet Verification

The algorithm VerifyWallet (cp. Fig. 7.30) is not a task by itself, but only a helper algorithm that is used inside of IssueWallet and Deposit (cp. Figs. 7.13, 7.16 and 7.17). A user can verify with this algorithm that the wallet he stores at the end of a transaction is valid. In particular, the algorithm verifies that the commitments c_{fix} and c_{upd} are valid and contain the values they are supposed to contain, that σ_{fix} is a valid signature under $sk_{\mathcal{O}}^{\text{fix}}$ of c_{fix} and $a_{\mathcal{U}}$, that σ_{upd} is a valid signature under $sk_{\mathcal{P}}$ of c_{upd} and s, that the certificate $cert_{\mathcal{P}}$ containing $pk_{\mathcal{P}}$ is valid and that the fraud-detection ID φ was calculated using the correct values.

8 Security Theorem and Proof

In this chapter we show that π_{P5C} UC-realizes $\mathcal{F}_{\text{apc}}$ in the $(\mathcal{F}_{\text{CRS}}, \mathcal{F}_{\text{bb}})$-hybrid model for static corruption. More precisely, we show the following theorem:

Theorem 8.1 (Security Statement) *Assume that the SXDH-problem is hard for* $gp := (G_1, G_2, G_T, e, \mathfrak{p}, g_1, g_2)$*, the* x_{bound}*-DDHI problem is hard for* G_1*, the DLOG-problem is hard for* G_1 *and our building blocks (NIZK, commitment schemes, signature scheme, encryption schemes and PRF) are instantiated as described in Section 6.2. Then*

$$\pi_{\text{P5C}}^{\mathcal{F}_{\text{CRS}}, \mathcal{F}_{\text{bb}}, \mathcal{F}_{\text{msg}}} \geq_{\text{UC}} \mathcal{F}_{\text{apc}} \tag{8.1}$$

holds under static corruption of either

(1) a subset of users,

(2) all users and a subset of PoSes, operator and violation enforcer,

(3) a subset of PoSes, operator and violation enforcer, or

(4) all PoSes, operator and violation enforcer as well as a subset of users.

Proof Follows from Theorems 8.2 and 8.28. ■

Informally, this means the ideal model and our protocol are indistinguishable and therefore provide the same guarantees regarding security and privacy. Please note that the hardness of the DLOG-problem is already implied by the SXDH-assumption.

This chapter is organized as follows. In Section 8.1 we discuss the corruption model, especially the restrictions on the set of corrupted parties and why this limited corruption model seems not to be a severe restriction from a practical vantage point. In Section 8.2 we give a brief outline of the proof on a high level. The actual proof for Theorem 8.1 is given in two parts:

- In Section 8.3, Theorem 8.2 proves Theorem 8.1 for the corruption scenario (1) and (2). We call this case "Operator Security".
- In Section 8.4, Theorem 8.28 proves Theorem 8.1 for the corruption scenario (3) and (4). We call this case "User Security and Privacy".

Both sections follow the usual approach and prove the statement in a sequence of hybrids.

8.1 Adversarial Model

Firstly, we only consider security under static corruption. This is a technical necessity to enable the use of PRFs to generate fraud-detection IDs. With adaptive corruption the simulator would be required to come up with a consistent seed for the PRF that could explain the up to the point of corruption uniformly and randomly drawn fraud-detection IDs. We deem static corruption to provide a sufficient level of security as a statically corrupted party may always decide to interact honestly first and then deviate from the protocol later (cp. Definition 3.14 and the discussion thereafter). Adaptive corruption is tightly related to deniability which is not part of our desired properties. Instead, features like blacklisting, prove-of-participation and balance recalculation are quite contrary to deniability. Obviously, traceability of blacklisted users requires that users are indisputable bound to their past transactions.

Of course, there might be valid applications that do not require these features but demand deniability. In these cases, the tasks BlacklistWallet, RecalculateBalance and ProveParticipation could be removed from the system. This would allow to use a truly uniform random distribution instead of a PRF for the fraud-detection IDs and the encryption for the key escrow mechanism could be dropped, too. A close look at the security proof unveils that it holds under adaptive corruption after these modifications. In [Nag+17] the BBA+-scheme, which does not include these features, is shown to provide a security feature which is called *backward- and forward-privacy*. Although adaptive security and backward- and forward-privacy are not directly comparable due to formal reasons, the latter is even stronger than adaptive security on an informal level as it guarantees users to be unlinkable in future transactions even after a corruption.

Secondly, we separately consider operator security and user security which means that $\mathcal{Z}$ is only allowed to corrupt certain restricted sets of parties (cp. Theorem 8.1). For operator security either (1) a subset[1] of users or (2) all users and a subset of PoSes, operator and violation enforcer is allowed to be corrupted. For user security and privacy either (3) a subset of PoSes, operator and violation enforcer or (4) all of PoSes, operator and violation enforcer as well as a subset of users might be corrupted. It is best to picture the cases inversely: To prove operator security we consider a scenario in which at least some parties at the operator's side remain honest; to prove user security we consider a scenario in which at least some users remain honest. Please note that both scenarios also commonly cover the case in which all parties are corrupted. However, this extreme case is tedious as it is trivially simulatable.

One might believe that the combination of all cases above should already be sufficient to guarantee privacy, security and correctness under arbitrary corruption. For example, case (4)

[1] Note that "subset" also includes the empty or full set.

guarantees that privacy and correctness of accounting are still provided for honest users, even if all of the operator's side and some fellow users are corrupted. This ought to be the worst case from an honest user's perspective. Further note that the proof of indistinguishability quantifies over all environments $\mathcal{Z}$. This includes environments that—still in case (4)—first corrupt all the operator's side but then let some (formally corrupted) parties follow the protocol honestly.

From a technical point the crux are the ZK proofs which either can be extracted or simulated but not both in the same experiment for different transactions involving an honest user and a corrupted PoS in one transaction and vice versa a corrupted user and an honest PoS in another transaction. Note, that this problem vanishes in the cases (2) and (4), because in these cases all parties belonging to one side are completely corrupted and interactions with corrupted parties of the other side are trivially simulatable. This suggests as if the truly mixed case should fail due to some sort of malleability attack involving honest users at one side, a man-in-the-middle, who cobbles ZK proofs, and honest PoSes at the other side. One might expect to find an adversary who merges an ensemble of wallets in a way such that the resulting wallet states cannot be mapped in the ideal model. However, we were not able to construct such an adversary. Even more interestingly, as explained in Chapter 10 using a non-shrinking commitment scheme in exchange for less efficiency allows to waive extractable ZK proofs and thus enables a proof under arbitrary corruption. One would expect that this observation should help to "spot the weak point". All in all, it seems that the proof of indistinguishability (for our proposed, *efficient* implementation with shrinking commitments) under arbitrary corruption only fails due to a formal problem but does not allow for a "practical" attack in the real world.

8.2 Proof Outline

As mentioned above we separately prove operator security with respect to an environment $\mathcal{Z}^{\text{op-sec}}$ as well as user security and privacy with respect to an environment $\mathcal{Z}^{\text{user-sec}}$. Both proofs are conducted by explicitly specifying a simulator $\mathcal{S}^{\text{op-sec}}_{\pi_{\text{P5C}}}$ and $\mathcal{S}^{\text{user-sec}}_{\pi_{\text{P5C}}}$, resp., for the ideal experiments $\mathsf{EXEC}_{\pi_{\text{P5C}},\mathcal{S}^{\text{op-sec}}_{\pi_{\text{P5C}}},\mathcal{Z}^{\text{op-sec}}}(1^n)$, $\mathsf{EXEC}_{\pi_{\text{P5C}},\mathcal{S}^{\text{user-sec}}_{\pi_{\text{P5C}}},\mathcal{Z}^{\text{user-sec}}}(1^n)$, resp. For each scenario we define a sequence of hybrid experiments H_i together with simulators $\mathcal{S}_i$ and protocols π_i. Each hybrid is of the form

$$H_i := \mathsf{EXEC}_{\pi_i,\mathcal{S}_i,\mathcal{Z}}(1^n). \tag{8.2}$$

The first hybrid is identical to the real experiment and the last hybrid is identical to the ideal experiment. The general idea is that the protocol π_i for honest parties gradually declines from the real protocol $\pi_0 = \pi_{\text{P5C}}$ to a dummy protocol, which does nothing but relay in- and outputs. At the same time $\mathcal{S}_i$ progresses from a dummy adversary $\mathcal{S}_0 = \mathcal{D}$ to the final simulator, which can be split up into the ideal functionality $\mathcal{F}_{\text{apc}}$ and $\mathcal{S}^{\text{op-sec}}_{\pi_{\text{P5C}}}$ or $\mathcal{S}^{\text{user-sec}}_{\pi_{\text{P5C}}}$, resp. Instead of directly proving indistinguishability of the real and ideal experiment we can break the proof down into showing indistinguishability of each pair of consecutive hybrids. We achieve this by demonstrating that whenever $\mathcal{Z}^{\text{op-sec}}$ or $\mathcal{Z}^{\text{user-sec}}$, resp., can distinguish between two consecutive hybrids with non-negligible probability this yields an efficient adversary against one of the underlying cryptographic assumptions. The indistinguishability between the real and ideal experiment follows from the pairwise indistinguishable of consecutive hybrids.

The simulator for operator security $\mathcal{S}^{\text{op-sec}}_{\pi_{\text{P5C}}}$ and the simulator for user security $\mathcal{S}^{\text{user-sec}}_{\pi_{\text{P5C}}}$ have a good share of common code, because some combinations of corrupted parties occur within particular tasks for both settings. This is unsurprising if one considers that not much seems to lack for an arbitrary corruption setting. The shared code for the common part is presented in both simulators. Naturally, this causes redundancy, but this way each simulator is complete and we avoid a lot of confusing references. However, the hybrids H_i which transfer the real experiment into the ideal experiment are only presented once. They are only defined and proven for operator security (cp. Section 8.3) and re-used for user security (cp. Section 8.4). However, there are still segments within the sequence of hybrids that differ between operator security and user security.

For the proof of operator security (cp. Section 8.3) input privacy does not pose any problem. The user learns nearly everything about the operator as part of its prescribed output and thus simulation of mostly all messages is perfectly enabled. The crucial point is to prove that no user can deviate from the protocol and thereby cheat the operator. To this end, $\mathcal{S}^{\text{op-sec}}_{\pi_{\text{P5C}}}$ basically uses the extraction property of the zero-knowledge scheme to watch messages from the corrupted users for discrepancies.

Contrarily, the proof of user security (cp. Section 8.4) follows a different spirit. In this case, input privacy of the user is the crucial point. For these reasons, most hybrids replace messages from the user by information-theoretically "empty" messages that are independent from any user secret.

8.3 Proof of Operator Security

In this section we show the following theorem.

Theorem 8.2 (Operator Security) *Under the assumptions of Theorem 8.1*

$$\pi_{\text{P5C}}^{\mathcal{F}_{\text{CRS}},\mathcal{F}_{\text{bb}},\mathcal{F}_{\text{msg}}} \geq_{\text{UC}} \mathcal{F}_{\text{apc}} \tag{8.3}$$

holds under static corruption of

(1) *a subset of users, or*

(2) *all users and a subset of PoSes, operator and violation enforcer.*

The definition of the UC-simulator $\mathcal{S}^{\text{op-sec}}_{\pi_{\text{P5C}}}$ for Theorem 8.2 can be found in Figs. 8.2 to 8.18. Please note that while the real protocol π_{P5C} lives in the $(\mathcal{F}_{\text{CRS}}, \mathcal{F}_{\text{bb}}, \mathcal{F}_{\text{msg}})$-model the ideal functionality $\mathcal{F}_{\text{apc}}$ has no CRS. The CRS simulated by $\mathcal{S}^{\text{op-sec}}_{\pi_{\text{P5C}}}$, giving it a lever to extract the ZK proofs P1, P2, and P3 and to equivocate the commitments C2 and C4.

While the protocol executes, the simulator $\mathcal{S}^{\text{op-sec}}_{\pi_{\text{P5C}}}$ records certain information similar to what the parties or the ideal functionality internally record, namely the map of simulated prove-participation tags $\bar{f}_{\text{pp}}$, and the simulated transaction graph $\overline{TRDB}$. Basically, $\bar{f}_{\text{pp}}$ and $\overline{TRDB}$ correspond to f_{pp} and *TRDB* resp., but exist in the head of the simulator and are augmented by additional information. The simulator uses them as "lookup tables" to keep up a consistent simulation in later parts of the protocol. Obviously, this implies that information is stored redundantly: In the head of $\mathcal{S}^{\text{op-sec}}_{\pi_{\text{P5C}}}$ as $\bar{f}_{\text{pp}}$ and $\overline{TRDB}$ and inside the ideal functionality $\mathcal{F}_{\text{apc}}$ (in case of *TRDB*) or the environment (in case of f_{pp} for a corrupted user). A crucial part of the security proof is to show that these sets stay in sync.

Before starting with the security proof, we explain the *Simulated Transaction Graph* $\overline{TRDB}$. This *Simulated Transaction Graph* resembles the Ideal Transaction Graph (cp. Definition 5.1) but augments each node by the in- and out-commitments $(c^{\text{in}}_{\text{upd}}, c^{\text{in}}_{\text{fix}})$ and $(c^{\text{out}}_{\text{upd}}, c^{\text{out}}_{\text{fix}})$ from the real protocols. A *Simulated Transaction Entry* $\overline{trdb}$ has the form

$$\begin{aligned}\overline{trdb} = (&s^{\text{prev}}, s, \varphi, x, \lambda, pid_{\mathcal{U}}, pid_{\mathcal{P}}, p, b,\\ &U^{\text{next}}_1, \omega_{\text{ds}}, \omega_{\text{rc}}, \omega_{\text{pp}},\\ &c^{\text{in}}_{\text{fix}}, d^{\text{in}}_{\text{fix}}, m^{\text{in}}_{\text{fix}}, c^{\text{in}}_{\text{upd}}, d^{\text{in}}_{\text{upd}}, m^{\text{in}}_{\text{upd}},\\ &c^{\text{out}}_{\text{fix}}, d^{\text{out}}_{\text{fix}}, m^{\text{out}}_{\text{fix}}, c^{\text{out}}_{\text{upd}}, d^{\text{out}}_{\text{upd}}, m^{\text{out}}_{\text{upd}})\end{aligned} \tag{8.5}$$

with *c*, *d* and *m* with equal suffixes denoting a commitment, its decommitment information and the opening in the implicit message space (see Fig. 8.1). These commitments are the fixed and updatable part of the wallet before and after the transaction (cp. Chapter 7). At the beginning of a transaction in the scope of Deposit or Disburse the user loads his token τ^{prev} which contains two commitments c_{fix} and $c^{\text{prev}}_{\text{upd}}$, randomizes the commitments and at the end the user possesses

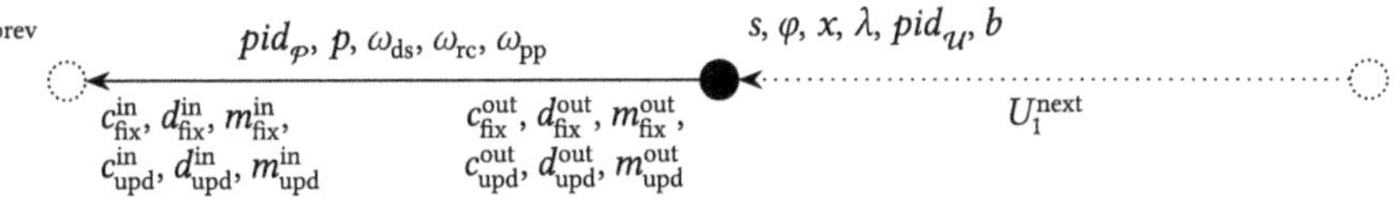

Figure 8.1: An entry $\overline{trdb} \in \overline{TRDB}$ visualized as an element of a directed graph

Simulator $\mathcal{S}^{\text{op-sec}}_{\pi_{\text{P5C}}}$

Setup: (1) Run a modified version of the algorithm $crs \leftarrow \text{Setup}(1^n)$ with

(a) $crs^{(2)}_{\text{com}} \leftarrow \text{C2.Setup}$ being replaced by $(crs^{(2)}_{\text{com}}, td_{\text{eqcom}}) \leftarrow \text{C2.SetupSim}$,

(b) $crs^{(4)}_{\text{com}} \leftarrow \text{C4.Setup}$ being replaced by $(crs^{(4)}_{\text{com}}, td_{\text{eqcom}}) \leftarrow \text{C4.SetupSim}$, and

(c) $crs_{\text{pok}} \leftarrow \text{POK.Setup}$ being replaced by $(crs_{\text{pok}}, td_{\text{epok}}) \leftarrow \text{POK.SetupExt}$.

(2) Record crs, td_{eqcom} and td_{epok}.

(3) Set $\overline{TRDB} := \emptyset$.

(4) Set $\bar{f}_{\text{keys}} : \mathcal{PID} \to \{0,1\}^*$ to the "empty" map.

(5) Set $\bar{f}_{\text{pp}} : \Omega_{\text{pp}} \to \Psi_{\text{pp}} \times \{0,1\}^*$ to the "empty" map.

The internal copy of $\mathcal{F}_{\text{msg}}$: $\mathcal{S}^{\text{op-sec}}_{\pi_{\text{P5C}}}$ runs an internal instance of $\mathcal{F}_{\text{msg}}$ in its head and proceeds as follows:

(1) Upon receiving input of the form (`establish-session`, ...), (`accept`, ...), (`send`, ...) or (`close`, ...) from $\mathcal{Z}^{\text{op-sec}}$ for $\mathcal{F}_{\text{msg}}$ in the name of a *corrupted* party, $\mathcal{S}^{\text{op-sec}}_{\pi_{\text{P5C}}}$ forwards this input to its internal instance of $\mathcal{F}_{\text{msg}}$ in the name of the same party.

(2) Upon receiving output of the form (`establishing-session`, ...), (`accepted`, ...), (`sent`, ...) or (`closed`, ...) from its internal instance of $\mathcal{F}_{\text{msg}}$ for a *corrupted* party, $\mathcal{S}^{\text{op-sec}}_{\pi_{\text{P5C}}}$ forwards this output to $\mathcal{Z}^{\text{op-sec}}$.

(3) Upon receiving leakage from its internal copy instance of $\mathcal{F}_{\text{msg}}$ for an adversary, $\mathcal{S}^{\text{op-sec}}_{\pi_{\text{P5C}}}$ forwards this leakage to $\mathcal{Z}^{\text{op-sec}}$ as the real dummy adversary would do.

(4) Upon receiving output of the form (`establishing-session`, ...), (`accepted`, ...), (`sent`, ...) or (`closed`, ...) from its internal instance of $\mathcal{F}_{\text{msg}}$ for an *honest* party, $\mathcal{S}^{\text{op-sec}}_{\pi_{\text{P5C}}}$ handles this output internally as desribed below in detail.

Figure 8.2: The Simulator for Operator Security

Simulator $\mathcal{S}^{\text{op-sec}}_{\pi_{\text{P5C}}}$

RegisterDR *(for honest dispute resolver):* Upon receiving leakage (`registering_dr`, pid_{DR}) from $\mathcal{F}_{\text{apc}}$ and if $\bar{f}_{\text{keys}}(pid_{DR})$ is undefined, run $(pk_{DR}, sk_{DR}) \leftarrow \text{RegisterDR}(crs)$, and append $pid_{DR} \mapsto (pk_{DR}, sk_{DR})$ to $\bar{f}_{\text{keys}}$.

RegisterOp *(for honest operator):* Upon receiving leakage (`registering_op`, $pid_{\mathcal{O}}, a_{\mathcal{O}}$) from $\mathcal{F}_{\text{apc}}$ and if $\bar{f}_{\text{keys}}(pid_{\mathcal{O}})$ is undefined, run $(pk_{\mathcal{O}}, sk_{\mathcal{O}}, cert_{\mathcal{O}}) \leftarrow \text{RegisterOp}(crs, a_{\mathcal{O}})$, and append $pid_{\mathcal{O}} \mapsto (pk_{\mathcal{O}}, sk_{\mathcal{O}}, cert_{\mathcal{O}})$ to $\bar{f}_{\text{keys}}$.

RegisterPOS *(for honest PoS):* Upon receiving leakage (`registering_pos`, $pid_{\mathcal{P}}$) from $\mathcal{F}_{\text{apc}}$ and if $\bar{f}_{\text{keys}}(pid_{\mathcal{P}})$ is undefined, run $(pk_{\mathcal{P}}, sk_{\mathcal{P}}) \leftarrow \text{RegisterPOS}(crs)$, and append $pid_{\mathcal{P}} \mapsto (pk_{\mathcal{P}}, sk_{\mathcal{P}}, \bot)$ to $\bar{f}_{\text{keys}}$.

RegisterPOS *(for corrupted PoS):* Upon receiving input (`register`, $pk_{\mathcal{P}}$) from $\mathcal{Z}^{\text{user-sec}}$ for $\mathcal{F}_{\text{bb}}$ in the name of $\mathcal{P}$ with PID $pid_{\mathcal{P}}$, and if $\bar{f}_{\text{keys}}(pid_{\mathcal{P}})$ is undefined, call $\mathcal{F}_{\text{apc}}$ with input (`register`) in the name of $\mathcal{P}$ with PID $pid_{\mathcal{P}}$, ignore the subsequent leak (`registering_pos`, $pid_{\mathcal{P}}$) from $\mathcal{F}_{\text{apc}}$ and append $pid_{\mathcal{P}} \mapsto (pk_{\mathcal{P}}, \bot, \bot)$ to $\bar{f}_{\text{keys}}$.[a]

RegisterUser *(for honest user):* Upon receiving leakage (`registering_user`, $pid_{\mathcal{U}}$) from $\mathcal{F}_{\text{apc}}$ and if $\bar{f}_{\text{keys}}(pid_{\mathcal{U}})$ is undefined, run $(pk_{\mathcal{U}}, sk_{\mathcal{U}}) \leftarrow \text{RegisterUser}(crs)$, and append $pid_{\mathcal{U}} \mapsto (pk_{\mathcal{U}}, sk_{\mathcal{U}})$ to $\bar{f}_{\text{keys}}$.

RegisterUser *(for corrupted user):* Upon receiving input (`register`, $pk_{\mathcal{U}}$) from $\mathcal{Z}^{\text{op-sec}}$ for $\mathcal{F}_{\text{bb}}$ in the name of $\mathcal{U}$ with PID $pid_{\mathcal{U}}$, and if $\bar{f}_{\text{keys}}(pid_{\mathcal{U}})$ is undefined, call $\mathcal{F}_{\text{apc}}$ with input (`register`) in the name of the same user, ignore the subsequent leak (`registering_user`, $pid_{\mathcal{U}}$) from $\mathcal{F}_{\text{apc}}$ and append $pid_{\mathcal{U}} \mapsto (pk_{\mathcal{U}}, \bot)$ to $\bar{f}_{\text{keys}}$.[b]

[a] Corrupted PoSes essentially have two options: They can either register "some" public key at the bulletin board or not. (N.b., the public key does not need to be honestly generated.) If they register their public keys, then they are regarded as registered from the perspective of the real protocols. Hence, the simulator must also register the PoSes with $\mathcal{F}_{\text{apc}}$, otherwise $\mathcal{F}_{\text{apc}}$ would subsequently abort, but the real protocols do not.

[b] Corrupted users essentially have two options: They can either register a public key at the bulletin board or not. (N.b., the public key does not need to be honestly generated.) If they register their public keys, then they are regarded as registered from the perspective of the real protocols. Hence, the simulator must also register the user with $\mathcal{F}_{\text{apc}}$, otherwise $\mathcal{F}_{\text{apc}}$ would subsequently abort, but the real protocols do not.

Figure 8.3: The Simulator for Operator Security (cont. from Fig. 8.2)

Simulator $\mathcal{S}^{\text{op-sec}}_{\pi_{\text{P5C}}}$

CertifyPOS *(for honest operator and honest PoS):* Upon receiving leakage ($\texttt{certifying\_pos}, pid_{\mathcal{P}}, a_{\mathcal{P}}$) from $\mathcal{F}_{\text{apc}}$ ...

(1) Set $(pk_{\mathcal{O}}, sk_{\mathcal{O}}, cert_{\mathcal{O}}) := \bar{f}_{\text{keys}}(pid_{\mathcal{O}})$ and $(pk_{\mathcal{P}}, sk_{\mathcal{P}}, cert^{\text{prev}}_{\mathcal{P}}) := \bar{f}_{\text{keys}}(pid_{\mathcal{P}})$.[a]

(2) Generate $cert_{\mathcal{P}} := (pk_{\mathcal{P}}, a_{\mathcal{P}}, \sigma^{\text{cert}}_{\mathcal{P}})$ with $\sigma^{\text{cert}}_{\mathcal{P}} \leftarrow \mathsf{SIG.Sign}(sk^{\text{cert}}_{\mathcal{O}}, (pk_{\mathcal{P}}, a_{\mathcal{P}}))$ faithfully.

(3) Re-define $\bar{f}_{\text{keys}}(pid_{\mathcal{P}}) := (pk_{\mathcal{P}}, sk_{\mathcal{P}}, cert_{\mathcal{P}})$ and let $\mathcal{F}_{\text{apc}}$ continue.

CertifyPOS *(for honest operator and corrupted PoS):* (1) Upon receiving output ($\texttt{establishing-session}, ssid, pid_{\mathcal{P}}, \texttt{certify\_pos}$) from $\mathcal{F}^{\text{sim}}_{\text{msg}}$ for $\mathcal{O}$, call $\mathcal{F}_{\text{apc}}$ with input ($\texttt{certify\_pos}$) in the name of $\mathcal{P}$ with $pid_{\mathcal{P}}$.

(2) Upon receiving leakage ($\texttt{certifying\_pos}, pid_{\mathcal{P}}, a_{\mathcal{P}}$) from $\mathcal{F}_{\text{apc}}$ ...

  (a) Set $(pk_{\mathcal{O}}, sk_{\mathcal{O}}, cert_{\mathcal{O}}) := \bar{f}_{\text{keys}}(pid_{\mathcal{O}})$ and $(pk_{\mathcal{P}}, \perp, cert^{\text{prev}}_{\mathcal{P}}) := \bar{f}_{\text{keys}}(pid_{\mathcal{P}})$.[b]

  (b) Call $\mathcal{F}^{\text{sim}}_{\text{msg}}$ with input ($\texttt{accept}, ssid$) in the name of $\mathcal{O}$.

(3) Upon being requested by $\mathcal{Z}^{\text{user-sec}}$ to provide the 1st message from $\mathcal{O}$ to $\mathcal{P}$ ...

  (a) Generate $cert_{\mathcal{P}} := (pk_{\mathcal{P}}, a_{\mathcal{P}}, \sigma^{\text{cert}}_{\mathcal{P}})$ with $\sigma^{\text{cert}}_{\mathcal{P}} \leftarrow \mathsf{SIG.Sign}(sk^{\text{cert}}_{\mathcal{O}}, (pk_{\mathcal{P}}, a_{\mathcal{P}}))$ faithfully.

  (b) Redefine $\bar{f}_{\text{keys}}(pid_{\mathcal{P}}) := (pk_{\mathcal{P}}, \perp, cert_{\mathcal{P}})$.

  (c) Call $\mathcal{F}^{\text{sim}}_{\text{msg}}$ with input ($\texttt{send}, ssid, cert_{\mathcal{P}}$) in the name of $\mathcal{O}$ for the 1st message from $\mathcal{O}$ to $\mathcal{P}$.

(4) Upon receiving output ($\texttt{closed}, ssid$) from $\mathcal{F}^{\text{sim}}_{\text{msg}}$ for $\mathcal{O}$, let $\mathcal{F}_{\text{apc}}$ deliver its output to $\mathcal{O}$.

(5) Upon receiving output ($\texttt{certified\_pos}, a_{\mathcal{P}}$) from $\mathcal{F}_{\text{apc}}$ for $\mathcal{P}$, do nothing.

[a] N.b.: These assignments exist. An honest operator or honest PoS, resp., must have called RegisterOp and RegisterPOS previously, otherwise $\mathcal{F}_{\text{apc}}$ would already have aborted.

[b] N.b.: These assignments exist. An honest operator must have called RegisterOp otherwise $\mathcal{F}_{\text{apc}}$ would already have aborted. The malicious PoS has either either registered its public key at the bulletin-board $\mathcal{F}_{\text{bb}}$ or not. If it had not registered at the bulletin-board, then the real protocol would have aborted at the operator's side. The ideal functionality $\mathcal{F}_{\text{apc}}$ would also have aborted and never leaked the message ($\texttt{certifying\_pos}, pid_{\mathcal{P}}, a_{\mathcal{P}}$) in the first place. Contrary, if PoS had registed at the bulletin-board, the real protocol does not abort. However, in this case $\mathcal{S}^{\text{user-sec}}_{\pi_{\text{P5C}}}$ would have (silently) defined $\bar{f}_{\text{keys}}(pid_{\mathcal{P}})$ and registered the PoS with $\mathcal{F}_{\text{apc}}$ and thus $\mathcal{F}_{\text{apc}}$ does not abort neither.

Figure 8.4: The Simulator for Operator Security (cont. from Fig. 8.2)

Simulator $\mathcal{S}^{\text{op-sec}}_{\pi_{\text{P5C}}}$ (cont.)

IssueWallet *(for honest operator and honest user):* Upon receiving leakage (`issuing_wallet`) from $\mathcal{F}_{\text{apc}}$ and being asked to provide ω_{bl} ...

(1) $\lambda'' \xleftarrow{R} \mathbb{Z}_p$.
(2) $\psi_{\text{bl}} \leftarrow \mathsf{ENC1.Enc}(pk_{DR}, (\overbrace{1, \dots, 1}^{\ell+2}))$.
(3) Set $\omega_{\text{bl}} := (\lambda'', \psi_{\text{bl}})$.
(4) Provide ω_{bl} to $\mathcal{F}_{\text{apc}}$.

Figure 8.5: The Simulator for Operator Security (cont. from Fig. 8.2)

two updated commitments $c_{\text{fix}}, c_{\text{upd}}$ which are stored in τ again. We call the initial commitments the *in*-commitments of the transaction and the resulting commitments the *out*-commitments.

Definition 8.3 (Simulated Transaction Graph (informal)) *The set* $\overline{TRDB} = \{\overline{trdb}_i\}$ *with* $\overline{trdb}_i$ *defined as in Eq.* (8.5) *is called the* Simulated Transaction Graph. *It inherits the graph structure of the Ideal Transaction Graph and augments each edge by additional labels, called the* in-commitments *and* out-commitments.

Two remarks are in order:

(1) Firstly, none of the (commitment, decommitment, message)-triples is neither completely received nor sent by the PoS or operator, respectively. The PoS receives a randomized version of the in-commitment and no decommitment at all. In the reverse direction, the PoS sends the out-commitment and a share of the decommitment. The complete triples only exist inside the user's token.

(2) Secondly, it is tempting but misleading to assume that $c^{\text{in}}_{\text{upd}} = c^{\text{prev}}_{\text{upd}}$ (or similar equations) hold. Note that we do not make any of these assumptions for the definition. Hence, we decided on a new notion and coined the term in-/out-commitments instead of re-using the term "previous commitment". Actually, these kinds of equalities are what we have to show.

The augmented information gives an alternative set of edges where two transactions $\overline{trdb}$ and $\overline{trdb}'$ are connected if $(c^{\text{out}}_{\text{upd}}, c^{\text{out}}_{\text{fix}})$ corresponds to $({c^{\text{in}}_{\text{upd}}}', {c^{\text{in}}_{\text{fix}}}')$.[2] The hybrids which are specific to operator security introduce additional "sanity checks" on this alternative graph structure: if the sanity check holds, both transaction graphs are still in sync and the simulator proceeds; if the

[2] N.b.: Commitments "correspond" if they are re-randomizations of each other, i.e. if they have the same message.

Simulator $\mathcal{S}^{\text{op-sec}}_{\pi_{\text{P5C}}}$ (cont.)

IssueWallet *(for honest operator and corrupted user)*: (1) Upon receiving output $(\texttt{establishing-session}, \mathit{ssid}, \mathit{pid}_{\mathcal{U}}, \texttt{issue\_wallet})$ from $\mathcal{F}^{\text{sim}}_{\text{msg}}$ for $\mathcal{O}$, call $\mathcal{F}_{\text{apc}}$ with input $(\texttt{issue\_wallet})$ in the name of $\mathcal{U}$ with $\mathit{pid}_{\mathcal{U}}$.

(2) Upon receiving leakage $(\texttt{issuing\_wallet}, s, a_{\mathcal{U}})$ from $\mathcal{F}_{\text{apc}}$ ...

(a) Set $(pk_{\mathcal{O}}, sk_{\mathcal{O}}, cert_{\mathcal{O}}) := \bar{f}_{\text{keys}}(pid_{\mathcal{O}})$ and $(pk_{\mathcal{DR}}, sk_{\mathcal{DR}}) := \bar{f}_{\text{keys}}(pid_{\mathcal{DR}})$.[a]

(b) Call $\mathcal{F}^{\text{sim}}_{\text{msg}}$ with input $(\texttt{accept}, \mathit{ssid})$ in the name of $\mathcal{O}$.

(3) Upon receiving output $(\texttt{sent}, \mathit{ssid}, c'_{\text{wid}})$ from $\mathcal{F}^{\text{sim}}_{\text{msg}}$ for $\mathcal{O}$ ...

(a) $(c''_{\text{ser}}, \bar{d}_{\text{ser}}) \leftarrow \text{C4.CommitSim}(crs^{(4)}_{\text{com}})$.

(b) $\lambda'' \xleftarrow{R} \mathbb{Z}_p$.

(c) Call $\mathcal{F}^{\text{sim}}_{\text{msg}}$ with input $(\texttt{send}, \mathit{ssid}, (cert_{\mathcal{O}}, a_{\mathcal{U}}, c''_{\text{ser}}, \lambda''))$ in the name of $\mathcal{O}$ for the 1st message from $\mathcal{O}$ to $\mathcal{U}$.

(4) Upon receiving output $(\texttt{sent}, \mathit{ssid}, (s', \psi_{\text{bl}}, c_{\text{fix}}, c_{\text{upd}}, \pi))$ from $\mathcal{F}^{\text{sim}}_{\text{msg}}$ for $\mathcal{O}$ ...

(a) $\mathit{stmnt} := (pk_{\mathcal{U}}, pk_{\mathcal{DR}}, \psi_{\text{bl}}, c_{\text{fix}}, c_{\text{upd}}, c'_{\text{wid}}, g_1^{\lambda''}, \lambda'')$.

(b) If $\text{P1.Vfy}(crs_{\text{pok}}, \mathit{stmnt}, \pi) = 0$, let $\mathcal{F}_{\text{apc}}$ abort.

(c) Extract $\mathit{Wit} = (\Lambda, \Lambda', \Lambda'_0, \dots, \Lambda'_{\ell-1}, \dots, U_1^{\text{next}}, d_{\text{fix}}, d_{\text{upd}}, d'_{\text{wid}}, SK_{\mathcal{U}}) \leftarrow \text{P1.Extract}(crs_{\text{pok}}, td_{\text{epok}}, \mathit{stmnt}, \pi)$.

(d) Assert that $(\mathit{stmnt}, \mathit{Wit})$ fullfills the projected equations from $L^{(1)}_{gp}$ and let $\mathcal{F}_{\text{apc}}$ continue, else give up simulation (event *E1*).

(5) Upon receiving leakage $(\texttt{issuing\_wallet})$ from $\mathcal{F}_{\text{apc}}$ and being asked to provide φ ...

(a) $\lambda := \lambda'' + \sum_{i=0}^{\ell-1} \text{DLOG}(\Lambda'_i) \cdot B^i$

(b) $\varphi := \text{PRF}(\lambda, x)$ with $x := 0$

(c) Provide φ to $\mathcal{F}_{\text{apc}}$.

[a] N.b.: These assignments exist. An honest operator or honest dispute resolver, resp., must have called RegisterOp and RegisterDR previously, otherwise $\mathcal{F}_{\text{apc}}$ would already have aborted.

Figure 8.6: The Simulator for Operator Security (cont. from Fig. 8.2)

Simulator $\mathcal{S}^{\text{op-sec}}_{\pi_{\text{P5C}}}$ (cont.)

IssueWallet *(for honest operator and corrupted user, continued):* (6) Upon receiving leakage (issuing_wallet) from $\mathcal{F}_{\text{apc}}$ and being asked to provide ω_{bl} ...

(a) Set $\omega_{\text{bl}} := (\lambda'', \psi_{\text{bl}})$.

(b) Provide ω_{bl} to $\mathcal{F}_{\text{apc}}$.

(7) Upon receiving output (issued_wallet, $s, a_{\mathcal{U}}$) from $\mathcal{F}_{\text{apc}}$ for $\mathcal{U}$ ...

(a) $s'' := s \cdot s'^{-1}$

(b) Equivoke $d''_{\text{ser}} \leftarrow \text{C4.Equivoke}(crs^{(4)}_{\text{com}}, td_{\text{eqcom}}, s'', c''_{\text{ser}}, \bar{d}_{\text{ser}})$.

(c) $\sigma_{\text{fix}} \leftarrow \text{SIG.Sign}(sk^{\text{fix}}_{\mathcal{O}}, (c_{\text{fix}}, a_{\mathcal{U}}))$

(d) $\sigma_{\text{upd}} \leftarrow \text{SIG.Sign}(sk^{\text{upd}}_{\mathcal{O}}, (c_{\text{upd}}, s))$

(e) Set $s^{\text{prev}} := \bot$, $p := 0$, $b := 0$, $c^{\text{in}}_{\text{fix}} := \bot$, $d^{\text{in}}_{\text{fix}} := \bot$, $m^{\text{in}}_{\text{fix}} := \bot$, $c^{\text{in}}_{\text{upd}} := \bot$, $d^{\text{in}}_{\text{upd}} := \bot$, $m^{\text{in}}_{\text{upd}} := \bot$, $c^{\text{out}}_{\text{fix}} := c_{\text{fix}}$, $d^{\text{out}}_{\text{fix}} := d_{\text{fix}}$, $m^{\text{out}}_{\text{fix}} := (\Lambda, pk_{\mathcal{U}})$, $c^{\text{out}}_{\text{upd}} := c_{\text{upd}}$, $d^{\text{out}}_{\text{upd}} := d_{\text{upd}}$, and $m^{\text{out}}_{\text{upd}} := (\Lambda, g_1^b, U_1^{\text{next}}, g_1^{x+1})$.

(f) Append $(s^{\text{prev}}, s, \varphi, x, \lambda, pid_{\mathcal{U}}, pid_{\mathcal{O}}, p, b, U_1^{\text{next}}, \omega_{\text{ds}}, \omega_{\text{rc}}, \omega_{\text{pp}}, c^{\text{in}}_{\text{fix}}, d^{\text{in}}_{\text{fix}}, m^{\text{in}}_{\text{fix}}, c^{\text{in}}_{\text{upd}}, d^{\text{in}}_{\text{upd}}, m^{\text{in}}_{\text{upd}}, c^{\text{out}}_{\text{fix}}, d^{\text{out}}_{\text{fix}}, m^{\text{out}}_{\text{fix}}, c^{\text{out}}_{\text{upd}}, d^{\text{out}}_{\text{upd}}, m^{\text{out}}_{\text{upd}})$ to $\overline{TRDB}$.

(g) Call $\mathcal{F}^{\text{sim}}_{\text{msg}}$ with input (sent, *ssid*, $(s'', d''_{\text{ser}}, \sigma_{\text{fix}}, \sigma_{\text{upd}})$) in the name of $\mathcal{O}$ for the 2nd message from $\mathcal{O}$ to $\mathcal{U}$.

(8) Upon receiving ouput (closed, *ssid*) from $\mathcal{F}^{\text{sim}}_{\text{msg}}$ for $\mathcal{O}$, let $\mathcal{F}_{\text{apc}}$ deliver its output to $\mathcal{O}$.

Figure 8.7: The Simulator for Operator Security (cont. from Fig. 8.2)

Simulator $\mathcal{S}^{\text{op-sec}}_{\pi_{\text{P5C}}}$ (cont.)

Deposit *(for honest PoS and honest user):* (1) Upon reveiving leakage (`depositing`, $pid_{\mathcal{U}}, \Omega^{\varphi}_{\text{ds}}$) from $\mathcal{F}_{\text{apc}}$, ...

(a) Set $(pk_{\mathcal{U}}, sk_{\mathcal{U}}) := \bar{f}_{\text{keys}}(pid_{\mathcal{U}})$.[a]

(b) Pick $u_2 \xleftarrow{R} \mathbb{Z}_p$.

(c) Check if $\exists\, \omega'_{\text{ds}} = (\varphi', t', u'_2) \in \Omega^{\varphi}_{\text{ds}}$, s.t. $\omega'_{\text{ds}} \neq \bot$ and $u'_2 \neq u_2$ hold.[b]

(d) If yes, $t := t' + sk_{\mathcal{U}}(u_2 - u'_2)$.

(e) Provide $\pi := sk_{\mathcal{U}}$ to $\mathcal{F}_{\text{apc}}$.

(2) Upon receiving leakage[c] (`depositing`, $s, \varphi, pid_{\mathcal{P}}$) from $\mathcal{F}_{\text{apc}}$ and being asked to provide $(\omega_{\text{ds}}, \omega_{\text{rc}}, \omega_{\text{pp}})$, ...

(a) Set $(pk_{\mathcal{O}}, \bot, \bot) := \bar{f}_{\text{keys}}(pid_{\mathcal{O}})$ and $(pk_{\mathcal{P}}, sk_{\mathcal{P}}, cert_{\mathcal{P}}) := \bar{f}_{\text{keys}}(pid_{\mathcal{P}})$.[d]

(b) Parse $pk^{\text{rc,enc}}_{\mathcal{O}}$ from $pk_{\mathcal{O}}$.

(c) Parse $pk^{\text{pp}}_{\mathcal{P}} / sk^{\text{pp}}_{\mathcal{P}}$ from $pk_{\mathcal{P}} / sk_{\mathcal{P}}$.

(d) If (t, u_2) is not yet defined, pick $(t, u_2) \xleftarrow{R} \mathbb{Z}^2_p$.[e]

(e) Set $\omega_{\text{ds}} := (\varphi, t, u_2)$.

(f) Set ψ_{rc} to an arbitrary value from the correct space.[f]

(g) Set $\omega_{\text{rc}} \leftarrow \mathsf{ENC2.Enc}(pk^{\text{rc,enc}}_{\mathcal{O}}, \psi_{\text{rc}})$.

(h) Run $(c_{pk_{\mathcal{U}}}, \bar{d}_{pk_{\mathcal{U}}}) \leftarrow \mathsf{C2.CommitSim}(crs^{(2)}_{\text{com}})$.

(i) Assign $\sigma_{\text{pp}} \leftarrow \mathsf{SIG.Sign}(sk^{\text{pp}}_{\mathcal{P}}, c_{pk_{\mathcal{U}}})$.

(j) Set $\omega_{\text{pp}} := c_{pk_{\mathcal{U}}}$ and $\psi_{\text{pp}} := (pk^{\text{pp}}_{\mathcal{P}}, \sigma_{\text{pp}}, \bar{d}_{pk_{\mathcal{U}}})$

(k) Define $\bar{f}_{\text{pp}}(\omega_{\text{pp}}) := (\psi_{\text{pp}}, g_1)$.

(l) Provide $(\omega_{\text{ds}}, \omega_{\text{rc}}, \omega_{\text{pp}})$ to $\mathcal{F}_{\text{apc}}$.

---

[a] N.b.: This assignment exists. An honest user must have called RegisterUser previously, otherwise $\mathcal{F}_{\text{apc}}$ would already have aborted.

[b] N.b., even if the user commits double-spending no "useful", previous double-spending tag may exist in $\Omega^{\varphi}_{\text{ds}}$, if the user only did so at corrupted PoSes that undermine double-spending detection.

[c] Here, we only consider an honest operator.

[d] N.b.: These assignments exist. The operator/PoS must have called RegisterOp/RegisterPOS previously, otherwise $\mathcal{F}_{\text{apc}}$ would already have aborted.

[e] Step 1d is only executed, if the user commits double-spending.

[f] The hidden recalculation tag is of the form $\psi_{\text{rc}} = (s, \varphi, p, pk^{\text{rc}}_{\mathcal{P}}, \sigma_{\text{rc}}) \in G_1 \times G_1 \times \mathbb{Z}_p \times (G_1^2 \times G_2^3) \times (G_2^2 \times G_1)$, e.g., $\psi_{\text{rc}} := (1, 1, 0, 1, 1, 1, 1, 1, 1, 1, 1)$ would be a good choice.

Figure 8.8: The Simulator for Operator Security (cont. from Fig. 8.2)

Simulator $\mathcal{S}^{\text{op-sec}}_{\pi_{\text{P5C}}}$ (cont.)

Deposit *(for honest PoS and corrupted user):*

(1) Upon receiving output $(\texttt{establishing-session}, \mathit{ssid}, \bot, \texttt{deposit})$ from $\mathcal{F}^{\text{sim}}_{\text{msg}}$ for $\mathcal{P}$ with $\mathit{pid}_{\mathcal{P}}$, ...

(a) Set $(\mathit{pk}_{\mathcal{O}}, \mathit{sk}_{\mathcal{O}}, \mathit{cert}_{\mathcal{O}}) := \bar{f}_{\text{keys}}(\mathit{pid}_{\mathcal{O}})$ and $(\mathit{pk}_{\mathcal{P}}, \mathit{sk}_{\mathcal{P}}, \mathit{cert}_{\mathcal{P}}) := \bar{f}_{\text{keys}}(\mathit{pid}_{\mathcal{P}})$; if these do not exist, let $\mathcal{F}^{\text{sim}}_{\text{msg}}$ abort.

(b) Parse $\mathit{pk}^{\text{pp}}_{\mathcal{P}}/\mathit{sk}^{\text{pp}}_{\mathcal{P}}$ from $\mathit{pk}_{\mathcal{P}}/\mathit{sk}_{\mathcal{P}}$ and $\mathit{pk}^{\text{rc,enc}}_{\mathcal{O}}$ from $\mathit{pk}_{\mathcal{O}}$.

(c) Call $\mathcal{F}^{\text{sim}}_{\text{msg}}$ with input $(\texttt{accept}, \mathit{ssid})$ in the name of $\mathcal{P}$ with $\mathit{pid}_{\mathcal{P}}$.

(2) Upon being requested by $\mathcal{Z}^{\text{op-sec}}$ to provide the 1st message from $\mathcal{P}$ to $\mathcal{U}$ ...

(a) Pick $u_2 \overset{R}{\leftarrow} \mathbb{Z}_p$.

(b) $(c''_{\text{ser}}, \bar{d}_{\text{ser}}) \leftarrow \mathsf{C4.CommitSim}(\mathit{crs}^{(4)}_{\text{com}})$.

(c) Call $\mathcal{F}^{\text{sim}}_{\text{msg}}$ with input $(\texttt{send}, \mathit{ssid}, (u_2, c''_{\text{ser}}, \mathit{cert}_{\mathcal{P}}))$ in the name of $\mathcal{P}$ for the 1st message from $\mathcal{P}$ to $\mathcal{U}$.

(3) Upon receiving output $(\texttt{sent}, \mathit{ssid}, (s', \pi, \varphi, a_{\mathcal{U}}, a^{\text{prev}}_{\mathcal{P}}, c_{\mathit{pk}_{\mathcal{U}}}, c'_{\text{upd}}, t))$ from $\mathcal{F}^{\text{sim}}_{\text{msg}}$ for $\mathcal{P}$ ...

(a) $\mathit{stmnt} := (\mathit{pk}^{\text{fix}}_{\mathcal{O}}, \mathit{pk}^{\text{cert}}_{\mathcal{O}}, \varphi, a_{\mathcal{U}}, a^{\text{prev}}_{\mathcal{P}}, c_{\mathit{pk}_{\mathcal{U}}}, c'_{\text{upd}}, t, u_2)$.

(b) If $\mathsf{P2.Vfy}(\mathit{crs}_{\text{pok}}, \mathit{stmnt}, \pi) = 0$, let $\mathcal{F}^{\text{sim}}_{\text{msg}}$ abort.

(c) Extract $\mathit{Wit} = (X, \Lambda, \mathit{pk}_{\mathcal{U}}, U_1, s^{\text{prev}}, \varphi^{\text{prev}}, X, \Lambda, \mathit{pk}_{\mathcal{U}}, B^{\text{prev}}, U_1, U^{\text{next}}_1, d_{\mathit{pk}_{\mathcal{U}}}, d^{\text{prev}}_{\text{upd}}, d'_{\text{upd}}, d_{\text{fix}}, \mathit{pk}^{\text{prev}}_{\mathcal{P}}, c^{\text{prev}}_{\text{upd}}, c_{\text{fix}}, \sigma^{\text{prev}}_{\text{upd}}, \sigma^{\text{cert,prev}}_{\mathcal{P}}, \sigma_{\text{fix}})$ $\leftarrow \mathsf{P2.Extract}(\mathit{crs}_{\text{pok}}, \mathit{td}_{\text{epok}}, \mathit{stmnt}, \pi)$.

(d) Assert that $(\mathit{stmnt}, \mathit{Wit})$ fulfills the projected equations from $L^{(2)}_{gp}$, else give up simulation (event *E1*).

(e) Lookup $\overline{\mathit{trdb}}^* := (s^{\text{prev},*}, s^*, \varphi^*, x^*, \lambda^*, \mathit{pid}^*_{\mathcal{U}}, \mathit{pid}^*_{\mathcal{O}}, p^*, b^*, U^*_1, \omega^{\text{prev},*}_{\text{ds}}, \omega^{\text{prev},*}_{\text{rc}}, \omega^{\text{prev},*}_{\text{pp}}, c^{\text{in}\,*}_{\text{fix}}, d^{\text{in}\,*}_{\text{fix}}, m^{\text{in}\,*}_{\text{fix}}, c^{\text{in}\,*}_{\text{upd}}, d^{\text{in}\,*}_{\text{upd}}, m^{\text{in}\,*}_{\text{upd}}, c^{\text{out}*}_{\text{fix}}, d^{\text{out}*}_{\text{fix}}, m^{\text{out}*}_{\text{fix}}, c^{\text{out}\,*}_{\text{upd}}, d^{\text{out}\,*}_{\text{upd}}, m^{\text{out}\,*}_{\text{upd}})$ with $s^* = s^{\text{prev}}$ being used as key; if no unique entry exists, give up simulation (event *E2*).

(f) Give up simulation if any of these conditions meet: $c^{\text{out}\,*}_{\text{upd}} \neq c^{\text{prev}}_{\text{upd}}$ (event *E3*), $\Lambda \neq g_1^{\lambda^*}$ (event *E4*), $c^{\text{out}*}_{\text{fix}} \neq c_{\text{fix}}$ (event *E5*), $\mathit{pk}_{\mathcal{U}} \neq \mathit{pk}^*_{\mathcal{U}}$ with $(\Lambda^*, \mathit{pk}^*_{\mathcal{U}}) := m^{\text{out}*}_{\text{fix}}$ (event *E6*), $B^{\text{prev}} \neq g_1^{b^*}$ (event *E7*), $X \neq g_1^{x^*+1}$ (event *E8*), or $U_1 \neq U^*_1$ (event *E9*).

(g) Set $\mathit{pid}_{\mathcal{U}} := \bar{f}^{-1}_{\text{keys}}(\mathit{pk}_{\mathcal{U}}, \cdot)$.[a]

(h) Call $\mathcal{F}_{\text{apc}}$ with input $(\texttt{deposit}, s^{\text{prev}}, \mathit{pid}_{\mathcal{P}})$ in the name of $\mathcal{U}$ with $\mathit{pid}_{\mathcal{U}}$.

[a] This assignment exist. Otherwise one of the previous tests would have already failed (cp. also proof).

Figure 8.9: The Simulator for Operator Security (cont. from Fig. 8.2)

Simulator $\mathcal{S}^{\text{op-sec}}_{\pi_{\text{P5C}}}$ (cont.)

Deposit *(for honest PoS and corrupted user, continued):* (4) Upon receiving leakage $(\texttt{depositing}, s, a_{\mathcal{U}})$ from $\mathcal{F}_{\text{apc}}$, let $\mathcal{F}_{\text{apc}}$ continue.

(5) Upon reveiving leakage $(\texttt{depositing}, pid_{\mathcal{U}}, \Omega^{\varphi}_{\text{ds}})$ from $\mathcal{F}_{\text{apc}}$ ...

(a) Check if $\exists\, \omega'_{\text{ds}} = (\varphi', t', u'_2) \in \Omega^{\varphi}_{\text{ds}}$, s.t. $u'_2 \neq u_2$ and $pk_{\mathcal{U}} = g_1^{sk_{\mathcal{U}}}$ for $sk_{\mathcal{U}} := (t - t') \cdot (u_2 - u'_2)^{-1} \bmod \mathfrak{p}$ holds.[a]

(b) If yes, re-define $\bar{f}_{\text{keys}}(pid_{\mathcal{U}}) := (pk_{\mathcal{U}}, sk_{\mathcal{U}})$.

(c) Provide $\pi := sk_{\mathcal{U}}$ to $\mathcal{F}_{\text{apc}}$.

(6) Upon receiving leakage $(\texttt{depositing})$ from $\mathcal{F}_{\text{apc}}$ and being asked to provide φ, return $\varphi := \mathsf{PRF}(\lambda^*, x)$ with $x := x^* + 1$ to $\mathcal{F}_{\text{apc}}$.[b]

(7) Upon receiving leakage $(\texttt{depositing}, s, \varphi)$ from $\mathcal{F}_{\text{apc}}$ and being asked to provide $(\omega_{\text{ds}}, \omega_{\text{rc}}, \omega_{\text{pp}})$, ...

(a) Set $\omega_{\text{ds}} := (\varphi, t, u_2)$.

(b) Set ψ_{rc} to an arbitrary value from the correct space.[c]

(c) Set $\omega_{\text{rc}} \leftarrow \mathsf{ENC2.Enc}(pk_{\mathcal{O}}^{\text{rc,enc}}, \psi_{\text{rc}})$.

(d) Assign $\sigma_{\text{pp}} \leftarrow \mathsf{SIG.Sign}(sk^{\text{pp}}_{\mathcal{P}}, c_{pk_{\mathcal{U}}})$.

(e) Set $\omega_{\text{pp}} := c_{pk_{\mathcal{U}}}$ and $\psi_{\text{pp}} := (pk^{\text{pp}}_{\mathcal{P}}, \sigma_{\text{pp}}, d_{pk_{\mathcal{U}}})$.

(f) Define $\bar{f}_{\text{pp}}(\omega_{\text{pp}}) := (\psi_{\text{pp}}, pk_{\mathcal{U}})$.

(g) Provide $(\omega_{\text{ds}}, \omega_{\text{rc}}, \omega_{\text{pp}})$ to $\mathcal{F}_{\text{apc}}$.

[a] N.b., even if the user commits double-spending no "useful", previous double-spending tag may exist in $\Omega^{\varphi}_{\text{ds}}$, if the user only did so at corrupted PoSes that undermine double-spending detection.

[b] N.b.: $\mathcal{F}_{\text{apc}}$ does not always ask for the next serial number. If the corrupted user re-uses an old token, then $\mathcal{F}_{\text{apc}}$ internally picks the next serial number which has already been determined in some earlier interaction. Hence, the $\mathcal{S}^{\text{op-sec}}_{\pi_{\text{P5C}}}$ only needs to provide the next serial number, if the chain of transactions is extended.

[c] The hidden recalculation tag is of the form $\psi_{\text{rc}} = (s, \varphi, p, pk^{\text{rc}}_{\mathcal{P}}, \sigma_{\text{rc}}) \in G_1 \times G_1 \times \mathbb{Z}_{\text{p}} \times (G_1^2 \times G_2^3) \times (G_2^2 \times G_1)$, e.g., $\psi_{\text{rc}} := (1, 1, 0, 1, 1, 1, 1, 1, 1, 1, 1)$ would be a good choice.

Figure 8.10: The Simulator for Operator Security (cont. from Fig. 8.2)

Simulator $\mathcal{S}^{\text{op-sec}}_{\pi_{\text{P5C}}}$ (cont.)

Deposit *(for honest PoS and corrupted user, continued):* (8) Upon receiving output $(\texttt{deposited}, s, a_{\mathcal{P}}, p, b, \omega_{\text{pp}})$ from $\mathcal{F}_{\text{apc}}$ for $\mathcal{U}$ ...

(a) Run $(c''_{\text{upd}}, d''_{\text{upd}}) \leftarrow \text{C1.Commit}(crs^{(1)}_{\text{com}}, (0, p, 0, 1))$, $c_{\text{upd}} := c'_{\text{upd}} \cdot c''_{\text{upd}}$, and $\sigma_{\text{upd}} \leftarrow \text{SIG.Sign}(sk^{\text{upd}}_{\mathcal{P}}, (c_{\text{upd}}, s))$ honestly as the real protocol would do.

(b) Set $s'' := s \cdot s'^{-1}$ and equivocate $d''_{\text{ser}} \leftarrow \text{C4.Equivoke}(crs^{(4)}_{\text{com}}, s'', c''_{\text{ser}}, \bar{d}_{\text{ser}})$.

(c) Set $c^{\text{in}}_{\text{fix}} := c_{\text{fix}}$, $d^{\text{in}}_{\text{fix}} := d_{\text{fix}}$, $m^{\text{in}}_{\text{fix}} := (\Lambda, pk_{\mathcal{U}})$, $c^{\text{in}}_{\text{upd}} := c^{\text{prev}}_{\text{upd}}$, $d^{\text{in}}_{\text{upd}} := d^{\text{prev}}_{\text{upd}}$, $m^{\text{in}}_{\text{upd}} := (\Lambda, B^{\text{prev}}, U_1, X)$, $c^{\text{out}}_{\text{fix}} := c_{\text{fix}}$, $d^{\text{out}}_{\text{fix}} := d'_{\text{fix}} \cdot d''_{\text{fix}}$, $m^{\text{out}}_{\text{fix}} := (\Lambda, pk_{\mathcal{U}})$, $c^{\text{out}}_{\text{upd}} := c_{\text{upd}}$, $d^{\text{out}}_{\text{upd}} := d'_{\text{upd}} \cdot d''_{\text{upd}}$, and $m^{\text{out}}_{\text{upd}} := (\Lambda, g^b_1, U^{\text{next}}_1, g^{x+1}_1)$.

(d) Append $(s^{\text{prev}}, s, \varphi, x, \lambda, pid_{\mathcal{U}}, pid_{\mathcal{P}}, p, b, U^{\text{next}}_1, \omega_{\text{ds}}, \omega_{\text{rc}}, \omega_{\text{pp}}, c^{\text{in}}_{\text{fix}}, d^{\text{in}}_{\text{fix}}, m^{\text{in}}_{\text{fix}}, c^{\text{in}}_{\text{upd}}, d^{\text{in}}_{\text{upd}}, m^{\text{in}}_{\text{upd}}, c^{\text{out}}_{\text{fix}}, d^{\text{out}}_{\text{fix}}, m^{\text{out}}_{\text{fix}}, c^{\text{out}}_{\text{upd}}, d^{\text{out}}_{\text{upd}}, m^{\text{out}}_{\text{upd}})$ to $\overline{TRDB}$.

(e) Call $\mathcal{F}^{\text{sim}}_{\text{msg}}$ with input $(\texttt{send}, ssid, (s'', d''_{\text{ser}}, c_{\text{upd}}, d''_{\text{upd}}, \sigma_{\text{upd}}, p, \sigma_{\text{pp}}))$ in the name of $\mathcal{P}$ for the 2nd message from $\mathcal{P}$ to $\mathcal{U}$.

(9) Upon receiving output $(\texttt{closed}, ssid)$ from $\mathcal{F}^{\text{sim}}_{\text{msg}}$ for $\mathcal{P}$, do nothing.

Figure 8.11: The Simulator for Operator Security (cont. from Fig. 8.2)

sanity check fails, the adversary has caused the transaction graphs to fall apart and the simulator immediately gives up the simulation. Each sanity check is related to the security of one of the building blocks or cryptographic assumptions. Together, these checks collectively assert that the alternative graph structure of the Simulated Transaction Graph coincides with the Ideal Transaction Graph and thus no efficient adversary can deviate from the Ideal Transaction Graph.

We proceed by giving concrete (incremental) definitions of all hybrids $H^{\text{op-sec}}_i$.

Hybrid $H^{\text{op-sec}}_0$ (The real experiment) The hybrid $H^{\text{op-sec}}_0$ is defined as

$$H^{\text{op-sec}}_0 := \text{EXEC}_{\pi^{\text{op-sec}}_0, \mathcal{S}^{\text{op-sec}}_0, \mathcal{Z}^{\text{op-sec}}}(1^n) \tag{8.6}$$

with $\mathcal{S}^{\text{op-sec}}_0 := \mathcal{D}$ being identical to the dummy adversary and $\pi^{\text{op-sec}}_0 := \pi_{\text{P5C}}$. Hence, $H^{\text{op-sec}}_0$ denotes the real experiment.

Hybrid $H^{\text{op-sec}}_1$ (Fake setup) In hybrid $H^{\text{op-sec}}_1$ we modify $\mathcal{S}^{\text{op-sec}}_1$ such that crs_{pok} is generated by SetupExt, and $crs^{(2)}_{\text{com}}$ as well as $crs^{(4)}_{\text{com}}$ are generated by SetupSim. $\mathcal{S}^{\text{op-sec}}_1$ initializes the simulated transaction graph $\overline{TRDB}$ and $\bar{f}_{\text{keys}}$ and $\bar{f}_{\text{pp}}$ as "empty" maps. Additionally, $\mathcal{S}^{\text{op-sec}}_1$ invokes an internal instance of $\mathcal{F}^{\text{sim}}_{\text{msg}}$ instead of the external instance $\mathcal{F}_{\text{msg}}$ and reroutes all

Simulator $\mathcal{S}^{\text{op-sec}}_{\pi_{\text{P5C}}}$ (cont.)

Disburse *(for honest operator and honest user):* (1) Upon reveiving leakage (`disbursing`, $pid_{\mathcal{U}}, \Omega^{\varphi}_{\text{ds}}$) from $\mathcal{F}_{\text{apc}}$, ...

(a) Set $(pk_{\mathcal{U}}, sk_{\mathcal{U}}) := \bar{f}_{\text{keys}}(pid_{\mathcal{U}})$.[a]

(b) Pick $u_2 \xleftarrow{R} \mathbb{Z}_p$.

(c) Check if $\exists\, \omega'_{\text{ds}} = (\varphi', t', u'_2) \in \Omega^{\varphi}_{\text{ds}}$, s.t. $\omega'_{\text{ds}} \neq \bot$ and $u'_2 \neq u_2$ hold.[b]

(d) If yes, $t := t' + sk_{\mathcal{U}}(u_2 - u'_2)$.

(e) Provide $\pi := sk_{\mathcal{U}}$ to $\mathcal{F}_{\text{apc}}$.

(2) Upon receiving leakage (`disbursing`, s, φ) from $\mathcal{F}_{\text{apc}}$ and being asked to provide $(\omega_{\text{ds}}, \omega_{\text{rc}})$, ...

(a) Set $(pk_{\mathcal{O}}, \bot, \bot) := \bar{f}_{\text{keys}}(pid_{\mathcal{O}})$ and parse $pk^{\text{rc,enc}}_{\mathcal{O}}$ from $pk_{\mathcal{O}}$.[c]

(b) If (t, u_2) is not yet defined, pick $(t, u_2) \xleftarrow{R} \mathbb{Z}^2_p$.[d]

(c) Set $\omega_{\text{ds}} := (\varphi, t, u_2)$.

(d) Set ψ_{rc} to an arbitrary value from the correct space.[e]

(e) Set $\omega_{\text{rc}} \leftarrow \text{ENC2.Enc}(pk^{\text{rc,enc}}_{\mathcal{O}}, \psi_{\text{rc}})$.

(f) Provide $(\omega_{\text{ds}}, \omega_{\text{rc}})$ to $\mathcal{F}_{\text{apc}}$.

---

[a] N.b.: This assignment exists. An honest user must have called RegisterUser previously, otherwise $\mathcal{F}_{\text{apc}}$ would already have aborted.

[b] N.b., even if the user commits double-spending no "useful", previous double-spending tag may exist in $\Omega^{\varphi}_{\text{ds}}$, if the user only did so at corrupted PoSes that undermine double-spending detection.

[c] N.b.: This assignment exists. The operator must have called RegisterOp previously, otherwise $\mathcal{F}_{\text{apc}}$ would already have aborted.

[d] Step 1d is only executed, if the user commits double-spending.

[e] The hidden recalculation tag is of the form $\psi_{\text{rc}} = (s, \varphi, p, pk^{\text{rc}}_{\mathcal{P}}, \sigma_{\text{rc}}) \in G_1 \times G_1 \times \mathbb{Z}_p \times (G_1^2 \times G_2^3) \times (G_2^2 \times G_1)$, e.g., $\psi_{\text{rc}} := (1, 1, 0, 1, 1, 1, 1, 1, 1, 1, 1)$ would be a good choice.

Figure 8.12: The Simulator for Operator Security (cont. from Fig. 8.2)

Simulator $\mathcal{S}^{\text{op-sec}}_{\pi_{\text{P5C}}}$ (cont.)

Disburse *(for honest operator and corrupted user):* (1) Upon receiving output (establishing-session, $ssid, pid_{\mathcal{U}}$, disburse) from $\mathcal{F}^{\text{sim}}_{\text{msg}}$ for O with pid_O, ...

(a) Set $(pk_O, sk_O, cert_O) := \bar{f}_{\text{keys}}(pid_O)$ and $(pk_{\mathcal{U}}, \cdot) := \bar{f}_{\text{keys}}(pid_{\mathcal{U}})$; if these do not exist, let $\mathcal{F}^{\text{sim}}_{\text{msg}}$ abort.

(b) Parse and $pk^{\text{rc,enc}}_O$ from pk_O.

(c) Call $\mathcal{F}^{\text{sim}}_{\text{msg}}$ with input (accept, $ssid$) in the name of O with pid_O.

(2) Upon being requested by $\mathcal{Z}^{\text{op-sec}}$ to provide the 1st message from O to $\mathcal{U}$ ...

(a) Pick $u_2 \xleftarrow{R} \mathbb{Z}_p$.

(b) Call $\mathcal{F}^{\text{sim}}_{\text{msg}}$ with input (send, $ssid, u_2$) in the name of O for the 1st message from O to $\mathcal{U}$.

(3) Upon receiving output (sent, $ssid, (\pi, \varphi, b^{\text{prev}}, t)$) from $\mathcal{F}^{\text{sim}}_{\text{msg}}$ for O ...

(a) $stmnt := (pk_{\mathcal{U}}, pk^{\text{fix}}_O, pk^{\text{cert}}_O, \varphi, g_1^{b^{\text{prev}}}, t, u_2)$.

(b) If P3.Vfy$(crs_{\text{pok}}, stmnt, \pi) = 0$, let $\mathcal{F}_{\text{apc}}$ abort.

(c) Extract $Wit = (X, \Lambda, pk_{\mathcal{U}}, U_1, s^{\text{prev}}, \varphi^{\text{prev}}, X, \Lambda, U_1, d^{\text{prev}}_{\text{upd}}, d_{\text{fix}}, pk^{\text{prev}}_{\mathcal{P}}, c^{\text{prev}}_{\text{upd}}, c_{\text{fix}}, \sigma^{\text{prev}}_{\text{upd}}, \sigma^{\text{cert,prev}}_{\mathcal{P}}, \sigma_{\text{fix}}, a_{\mathcal{U}}, a^{\text{prev}}_{\mathcal{P}}) \leftarrow$ P3.Extract$(crs_{\text{pok}}, td_{\text{epok}}, stmnt, \pi)$.

(d) Assert that $(stmnt, Wit)$ fullfills the projected equations from $L^{(3)}_{gp}$, else give up simulation (event *E1*)

(e) Lookup $\overline{trdb}^* := (s^{\text{prev},*}, s^*, \varphi^*, x^*, \lambda^*, pid^*_{\mathcal{U}}, pid^*_O, p^*, b^*, U^*_1, \omega^{\text{prev},*}_{\text{ds}}, \omega^{\text{prev},*}_{\text{rc}}, \omega^{\text{prev},*}_{\text{pp}}, {c^{\text{in}}_{\text{fix}}}^*, {d^{\text{in}}_{\text{fix}}}^*, {m^{\text{in}}_{\text{fix}}}^*, {c^{\text{in}}_{\text{upd}}}^*, {d^{\text{in}}_{\text{upd}}}^*, {m^{\text{in}}_{\text{upd}}}^*, {c^{\text{out}}_{\text{fix}}}^*, {d^{\text{out}}_{\text{fix}}}^*, {m^{\text{out}}_{\text{fix}}}^*, {c^{\text{out}}_{\text{upd}}}^*, {d^{\text{out}}_{\text{upd}}}^*, {m^{\text{out}}_{\text{upd}}}^*)$ with $s^* = s^{\text{prev}}$ being used as key; if no unique entry exists, give up simulation (event *E2*).

(f) Give up simulation if any of these conditions meet: ${c^{\text{out}}_{\text{upd}}}^* \neq c^{\text{prev}}_{\text{upd}}$ (event *E3*), $\Lambda \neq g_1^{\lambda^*}$ (event *E4*), ${c^{\text{out}}_{\text{fix}}}^* \neq c_{\text{fix}}$ (event *E5*), $pk_{\mathcal{U}} \neq pk^*_{\mathcal{U}}$ with $(\Lambda^*, pk^*_{\mathcal{U}}) := {m^{\text{out}}_{\text{fix}}}^*$ (event *E6*), $B^{\text{prev}} \neq g_1^{b^*}$ (event *E7*), $X \neq g_1^{x^*+1}$ (event *E8*), or $U_1 \neq U^*_1$ (event *E9*).

(g) Call $\mathcal{F}_{\text{apc}}$ with input (disburse, s^{prev}) in the name of $\mathcal{U}$ with $pid_{\mathcal{U}}$.

Figure 8.13: The Simulator for Operator Security (cont. from Fig. 8.2)

Simulator $\mathcal{S}^{\text{op-sec}}_{\pi_{\text{P5C}}}$ (cont.)

Disburse *(for honest operator and corrupted user, continued):* (4) Upon reveiving leakage (disbursing, $pid_{\mathcal{U}}, \Omega^{\varphi}_{\text{ds}}$) from $\mathcal{F}_{\text{apc}}$ ...

(a) Check if $\exists\, \omega'_{\text{ds}} = (\varphi', t', u'_2) \in \Omega^{\varphi}_{\text{ds}}$, s.t. $u'_2 \neq u_2$ and $pk_{\mathcal{U}} = g_1^{sk_{\mathcal{U}}}$ for $sk_{\mathcal{U}} := (t - t') \cdot (u_2 - u'_2)^{-1} \bmod \mathfrak{p}$ holds.[a]
(b) If yes, re-define $\bar{f}_{\text{keys}}(pid_{\mathcal{U}}) := (pk_{\mathcal{U}}, sk_{\mathcal{U}})$.
(c) Provide $\pi := sk_{\mathcal{U}}$ to $\mathcal{F}_{\text{apc}}$.

(5) Upon receiving leakage (disbursing) from $\mathcal{F}_{\text{apc}}$ and being asked to provide φ, return $\varphi := \mathsf{PRF}(\lambda^*, x)$ with $x := x^* + 1$ to $\mathcal{F}_{\text{apc}}$.[b]

(6) Upon receiving leakage (disbursing, s, φ) from $\mathcal{F}_{\text{apc}}$ and being asked to provide $(\omega_{\text{ds}}, \omega_{\text{rc}})$, ...
(a) Set $\omega_{\text{ds}} := (\varphi, t, u_2)$.
(b) Set ψ_{rc} to an arbitrary value from the correct space.[c]
(c) Set $\omega_{\text{rc}} \leftarrow \mathsf{ENC2.Enc}(pk_{\mathcal{O}}^{\text{rc,enc}}, \psi_{\text{rc}})$.
(d) Provide $(\omega_{\text{ds}}, \omega_{\text{rc}})$ to $\mathcal{F}_{\text{apc}}$.

(7) Upon receiving output (disbursed, b^{bill}) from $\mathcal{F}_{\text{apc}}$ for $\mathcal{U}$ ...
(a) Set $c^{\text{in}}_{\text{fix}} := c_{\text{fix}}$, $d^{\text{in}}_{\text{fix}} := d_{\text{fix}}$, $m^{\text{in}}_{\text{fix}} := (\Lambda, pk_{\mathcal{U}})$, $c^{\text{in}}_{\text{upd}} := c^{\text{prev}}_{\text{upd}}$, $d^{\text{in}}_{\text{upd}} := d^{\text{prev}}_{\text{upd}}$, $m^{\text{in}}_{\text{upd}} := (\Lambda, B^{\text{prev}}, U_1, X)$, $c^{\text{out}}_{\text{fix}} := \bot$, $d^{\text{out}}_{\text{fix}} := \bot$, $m^{\text{out}}_{\text{fix}} := \bot$, $c^{\text{out}}_{\text{upd}} := \bot$, $d^{\text{out}}_{\text{upd}} := \bot$, and $m^{\text{out}}_{\text{upd}} := \bot$.
(b) Append $(s^{\text{prev}}, s, \varphi, x, \lambda, pid_{\mathcal{U}}, pid_{\mathcal{P}}, p, b, U_1^{\text{next}}, \omega_{\text{ds}}, \omega_{\text{rc}}, \omega_{\text{pp}}, c^{\text{in}}_{\text{fix}}, d^{\text{in}}_{\text{fix}}, m^{\text{in}}_{\text{fix}}, c^{\text{in}}_{\text{upd}}, d^{\text{in}}_{\text{upd}}, m^{\text{in}}_{\text{upd}}, c^{\text{out}}_{\text{fix}}, d^{\text{out}}_{\text{fix}}, m^{\text{out}}_{\text{fix}}, c^{\text{out}}_{\text{upd}}, d^{\text{out}}_{\text{upd}}, m^{\text{out}}_{\text{upd}})$ to $\overline{TRDB}$.
(c) Call $\mathcal{F}^{\text{sim}}_{\text{msg}}$ with input (send, $ssid$, OK) in the name of $\mathcal{O}$ for the 2nd message from $\mathcal{O}$ to $\mathcal{U}$.

(8) Upon receiving output (closed, $ssid$) from $\mathcal{F}^{\text{sim}}_{\text{msg}}$ for $\mathcal{O}$, do nothing.

[a] N.b., even if the user commits double-spending no "useful", previous double-spending tag may exist in $\Omega^{\varphi}_{\text{ds}}$, if the user only did so at corrupted PoSes that undermine double-spending detection.
[b] N.b.: $\mathcal{F}_{\text{apc}}$ does not always ask for the next serial number. If the corrupted user re-uses an old token, then $\mathcal{F}_{\text{apc}}$ internally picks the next serial number which has already been determined in some earlier interaction. Hence, the $\mathcal{S}^{\text{op-sec}}_{\pi_{\text{P5C}}}$ only needs to provide the next serial number, if the chain of transactions is extended.
[c] The hidden recalculation tag is of the form $\psi_{\text{rc}} = (s, \varphi, p, pk^{\text{rc}}_{\mathcal{P}}, \sigma_{\text{rc}}) \in G_1 \times G_1 \times \mathbb{Z}_{\mathfrak{p}} \times (G_1^2 \times G_2^3) \times (G_2^2 \times G_1)$, e.g., $\psi_{\text{rc}} := (1,1,0,1,1,1,1,1,1,1,1)$ would be a good choice.

Figure 8.14: The Simulator for Operator Security (cont. from Fig. 8.2)

Simulator $\mathcal{S}^{\text{op-sec}}_{\pi_{\text{P5C}}}$ (cont.)

DetectDS *(for honest operator):* (1) Upon receiving leakage ($\texttt{detecting\_ds}, \omega_{\text{ds}}, \omega'_{\text{ds}}$) from $\mathcal{F}_{\text{apc}}$ and being asked to provide $(pid_{\mathcal{U}}, \pi, result)$, ...

(a) Parse $(\varphi, t, u_2) := \omega_{\text{ds}}$ and $(\varphi', t', u'_2) := \omega'_{\text{ds}}$.

(b) If $\varphi = \varphi'$ and $u_2 \neq u'_2$:

(i) Set $sk_{\mathcal{U}} := (t - t')/(u_2 - u'_2) \bmod \mathfrak{p}$.

(ii) Set $pk_{\mathcal{U}} := g_1^{sk_{\mathcal{U}}}$.

Else, set $(pk_{\mathcal{U}}, sk_{\mathcal{U}}) := (\bot, \bot)$.

(c) Set $pid_{\mathcal{U}} := \bar{f}^{-1}_{\text{keys}}(pk_{\mathcal{U}}, \cdot)$; if $\bar{f}^{-1}_{\text{keys}}$ is not defined for $pk_{\mathcal{U}}$, set $pid_{\mathcal{U}} := \bot$.

(d) If $pid_{\mathcal{U}} \neq \bot$, then set $(\pi, result) := (sk_{\mathcal{U}}, \mathsf{OK})$, else set $(\pi, result) := (\bot, \mathsf{NOK})$.

(e) Provide $(pid_{\mathcal{U}}, \pi, result)$ to $\mathcal{F}_{\text{apc}}$.

(2) Upon receiving leakage ($\texttt{detecting\_ds}, pid_{\mathcal{U}}$) from $\mathcal{F}_{\text{apc}}$ and being asked to provide π, ...

(a) Set $(pk_{\mathcal{U}}, sk_{\mathcal{U}}) := \bar{f}_{\text{keys}}(pid_{\mathcal{U}})$.[a]

(b) Provide $\pi := sk_{\mathcal{U}}$ to $\mathcal{F}_{\text{apc}}$.

VerifyGuilt *(for honest party):* Upon receiving leakage ($\texttt{verifying\_guilt}, pid_{\mathcal{U}}, \pi$) from $\mathcal{F}_{\text{apc}}$ and being asked to provide *result* ...

(1) Set $(pk_{\mathcal{U}}, \cdot) := \bar{f}_{\text{keys}}(pid_{\mathcal{U}})$.

(2) If $g_1^{\pi} = pk_{\mathcal{U}}$, then provide $result := \mathsf{OK}$, else $result := \mathsf{NOK}$ to $\mathcal{F}_{\text{apc}}$.

[a] This assignment exist. ($\texttt{detecting\_ds}, pid_{\mathcal{U}}$) is only leaked, if the user truly committed double-spending. In this case Step 5 in Fig. 8.9 and Step 4 in Fig. 8.13 have been called previously. In all other cases the honest user and therefore $\mathcal{S}^{\text{op-sec}}_{\pi_{\text{P5C}}}$ knows $sk_{\mathcal{U}}$ anyway.

Figure 8.15: The Simulator for Operator Security (cont. from Fig. 8.2)

Simulator $\mathcal{S}^{\text{op-sec}}_{\pi_{\text{P5C}}}$ (cont.)

BlacklistWallet *(for honest operator):* Upon receiving leakage (`blacklisting_wallet`, λ, x) from $\mathcal{F}_{\text{apc}}$ and being asked to provide φ, provide $\varphi := \mathsf{PRF}(\lambda, x)$ to $\mathcal{F}_{\text{apc}}$.

RecalculateBalance *(for honest operator):* Upon receiving leakage (`recalculating_balance`, bl_Φ, $\Omega^{\text{fake}}_{\text{rc}}$) from $\mathcal{F}_{\text{apc}}$ and being asked to provide p^{deviate} ...

(1) $\Psi^{\text{fake}}_{\text{rc}} := \{\psi_{\text{rc}} \leftarrow \mathsf{ENC2.Dec}(sk^{\text{rc,enc}}_{\mathcal{O}}, \omega_{\text{rc}}) \mid \omega_{\text{rc}} \in \Omega^{\text{fake}}_{\text{rc}}\}$
(2) $\Psi^{\text{fake,valid}}_{\text{rc}} := \{(s, \varphi, p, pk^{\text{rc}}_{\mathcal{P}}, \sigma_{\text{rc}}) \in \psi_{\text{rc}} \mid \mathsf{SIG.Vfy}(pk^{\text{rc}}_{\mathcal{P}}, \sigma_{\text{rc}}, (s, \varphi, g_1^p)) = 1\}$
(3) $\Xi := \{(s, p) \mid \exists\, \psi_{\text{rc}} = (s, \varphi, p, \cdot, \cdot) \in \Psi^{\text{fake,valid}}_{\text{rc}} \wedge \varphi \in bl_\Phi\}$
(4) Provide $p^{\text{deviate}} := \sum_{(s,p)\in\Xi} p$ to $\mathcal{F}_{\text{apc}}$.

Figure 8.16: The Simulator for Operator Security (cont. from Fig. 8.2)

input/output accordingly. All calls to the bulletin-board $\mathcal{F}_{\text{bb}}$ are handled internally by $\mathcal{S}^{\text{op-sec}}_1$ using the map $\bar{f}_{\text{keys}}$.

Hybrid $H^{\text{op-sec}}_2$ (Simulate honest keys) Hybrid $H^{\text{op-sec}}_2$ replaces the code in the tasks RegisterDR, RegisterOp, RegisterPOS and RegisterUser of the protocol $\pi^{\text{op-sec}}_2$ such that the simulator $\mathcal{S}^{\text{op-sec}}_2$ is asked for the keys instead. Also, if corrupted PoSes or users try to register a (maliciously) generated public key at the bulletin-board $\mathcal{F}_{\text{bb}}$, then $\mathcal{S}^{\text{op-sec}}_2$ calls RegisterPOS or RegisterUser, resp., in order to simultaneously register the parties for $\mathcal{F}_{\text{apc}}$. $\mathcal{S}^{\text{op-sec}}_2$ defines $\bar{f}_{\text{keys}}$ appropriately. This equals the method in which the keys are generated in the ideal experiment.

Hybrid $H^{\text{op-sec}}_3$ (Simulate PoS' certificate) In hybrid $H^{\text{op-sec}}_3$ the task CertifyPOS is modified. The protocol $\pi^{\text{op-sec}}_3$ is modified such that the simulator $\mathcal{S}^{\text{op-sec}}_3$ receives the message (`certifying_pos`, $pid_{\mathcal{P}}$, $a_{\mathcal{P}}$), creates the certificate $cert_{\mathcal{P}}$ including the signature $\sigma^{\text{cert}}_{\mathcal{P}}$ and records it. Whenever the honest operator or honest PoSes running $\pi^{\text{op-sec}}_3$ would send $cert_{\mathcal{P}}$ (or $\sigma^{\text{cert}}_{\mathcal{P}}$) as part of their messages in the scope of IssueWallet or Deposit, they omit $cert_{\mathcal{P}}$. Instead, the simulator $\mathcal{S}^{\text{op-sec}}_3$ injects $cert_{\mathcal{P}}$ into the messages.

Hybrid $H^{\text{op-sec}}_4$ (Simulate wallet signatures and wallet update information) Hybrid $H^{\text{op-sec}}_4$ replaces the code in the tasks IssueWallet and Deposit of the protocol $\pi^{\text{op-sec}}_4$ such that the operator/PoS do not create signatures, but the simulator $\mathcal{S}^{\text{op-sec}}_4$ creates the signatures σ_{fix}, σ_{upd} and σ_{pp} resp. and injects them into the messages instead.

Moreover, in Deposit in case of a corrupted user the PoS running $\pi^{\text{op-sec}}_4$ does not send c_{upd} and d''_{upd} in its final message, but outputs the price p to simulator $\mathcal{S}^{\text{op-sec}}_4$ as $\mathcal{F}_{\text{apc}}$ would do. Simulator $\mathcal{S}^{\text{op-sec}}_4$ creates c_{upd} and d''_{upd} honestly and injects them into the message.

Simulator $\mathcal{S}^{\text{op-sec}}_{\pi_{\text{P5C}}}$ (cont.)

ProveParticipation *(for honest user and honest violation enforcer):* (nothing to do, note that $\mathcal{F}_{\text{apc}}$ only leaks, if user or violation enforcer is corrupted)

ProveParticipation *(for corrupted user and honest violation enforcer):* (1) Upon receiving output (proving_participation, $pid_{\mathcal{P}}, \Omega_{\text{pp}}$) from $\mathcal{F}_{\text{apc}}$ for $\mathcal{U}$ with $pid_{\mathcal{U}}$, call $\mathcal{F}^{\text{sim}}_{\text{msg}}$ with input (establish-session, ident, $pid_{\mathcal{U}}$, prove_participation) in the name of *VE*.

(2) Upon receiving output (accepted, *ssid*) from $\mathcal{F}^{\text{sim}}_{\text{msg}}$ for *VE*, call $\mathcal{F}^{\text{sim}}_{\text{msg}}$ with input (send, *ssid*, $(pid_{\mathcal{P}}, \Omega_{\text{pp}})$) in the name of *VE*.

(3) Upon receiving output (sent, *ssid*, $(\omega_{\text{pp}}, \psi_{\text{pp}})$) from $\mathcal{F}^{\text{sim}}_{\text{msg}}$ for *VE*, ...

(a) Set $(pk_{\mathcal{U}}, \cdot) := \bar{f}_{\text{keys}}(pid_{\mathcal{U}})$ and $(pk_{\mathcal{P}}, \cdot, \cdot) := \bar{f}_{\text{keys}}(pid_{\mathcal{P}})$.[a]

(b) Parse $pk^{\text{pp}}_{\mathcal{P}}$ from $pk_{\mathcal{P}}$.

(c) Set $(\psi^*_{\text{pp}}, pk^*_{\mathcal{U}}) := \bar{f}_{\text{pp}}(\omega_{\text{pp}})$.

(d) Set $c_{pk_{\mathcal{U}}} := \omega_{\text{pp}}$.

(e) Parse $(\cdot, \sigma_{\text{pp}}, d_{pk_{\mathcal{U}}}) := \psi_{\text{pp}}$ and $(\cdot, \sigma^*_{\text{pp}}, d^*_{pk_{\mathcal{U}}}) := \psi^*_{\text{pp}}$.[b]

(f) If $\psi_{\text{pp}} = \bot$ or $\mathsf{SIG.Vfy}(pk^{\text{pp}}_{\mathcal{P}}, \sigma_{\text{pp}}, c_{pk_{\mathcal{U}}}) = 0$ or $\mathsf{C2.Open}(crs^{(2)}_{\text{com}}, pk_{\mathcal{U}}, c_{pk_{\mathcal{U}}}, d_{pk_{\mathcal{U}}}) = 0$, call $\mathcal{F}_{\text{apc}}$ with input (proving_participation, $\bot$) in the name of $\mathcal{U}$.

(g) If $\psi^*_{\text{pp}} = \bot$, i.e., ω_{pp} has not legitimately issued, and $pid_{\mathcal{P}} \notin \mathcal{PID}_{\text{corr}}$, give up simulation with event *E10*.

(h) If $\mathsf{C2.Open}(crs^{(2)}_{\text{com}}, pk_{\mathcal{U}}, c_{pk_{\mathcal{U}}}, d_{pk_{\mathcal{U}}}) = 1$ and $pk_{\mathcal{U}} \neq pk^*_{\mathcal{U}} \neq \bot$, give up simulation with event *E11*.

(i) Call $\mathcal{F}_{\text{apc}}$ with input (proving_participation, ω_{pp}) in the name of $\mathcal{U}$.[c]

(4) Upon receiving leakage (proving_participation) from $\mathcal{F}_{\text{apc}}$ and being asked to provide *result*,[d] provide *result* = OK to $\mathcal{F}_{\text{apc}}$.

(5) Upon receiving output (proved_participation) from $\mathcal{F}_{\text{apc}}$ for $\mathcal{U}$, call $\mathcal{F}^{\text{sim}}_{\text{msg}}$ with input (close, *ssid*) in the name of *VE*.

[a] These assignment exists, otherwise $\mathcal{F}_{\text{apc}}$ would already have aborted previously.

[b] If $\bar{f}_{\text{pp}}(\omega_{\text{pp}})$ is undefined, we stipulate $\psi^*_{\text{pp}} = \bot$ and set $\sigma^*_{\text{pp}} = d^*_{pk_{\mathcal{U}}} = \bot$.

[c] $\psi^*_{\text{pp}} = \bot$ holds, if and only if ω_{pp} is made up by the environment. In this case and if the PoS is corrupted, too, Step 4 will be executed.

[d] N.b., $\mathcal{F}_{\text{apc}}$ only leaks this, if ω_{pp} has not legitimately been issued and the PoS with $pid_{\mathcal{P}}$ is corrupted, too.

Figure 8.17: The Simulator for Operator Security (cont. from Fig. 8.2)

Simulator $\mathcal{S}^{\text{op-sec}}_{\pi_{\text{P5C}}}$ (cont.)

ProveParticipation *(for honest user and corrupted violation enforcer):* (1) Upon receiving output (`establishing-session`, $ssid, pid_{VE}$, `prove_participation`) from $\mathcal{F}^{\text{sim}}_{\text{msg}}$ for $\mathcal{U}$ with $pid_{\mathcal{U}}$, call $\mathcal{F}^{\text{sim}}_{\text{msg}}$ with input (`accept`, $ssid$) in the name of $\mathcal{U}$.

(2) Upon receiving output (`sent`, $ssid, pid_{\mathcal{P}}, \Omega_{\text{pp}}$) from $\mathcal{F}^{\text{sim}}_{\text{msg}}$ for $\mathcal{U}$, call $\mathcal{F}_{\text{apc}}$ with input (`prove_participation`, $pid_{\mathcal{U}}, pid_{\mathcal{P}}, \Omega_{\text{pp}}$) in the name of VE.

(3) Upon receiving leakage (`proving_participation`, ω_{pp}) from $\mathcal{F}_{\text{apc}}$, let $\mathcal{F}_{\text{apc}}$ continue.

(4) Upon receiving output (`proved_participation`, $result$) from $\mathcal{F}_{\text{apc}}$ for VE, ...

 (a) If $result = \mathsf{NOK}$, set $\psi_{\text{pp}} := \bot$, else

  (i) Set $(pk_{\mathcal{U}}, \cdot) := \bar{f}_{\text{keys}}(pid_{\mathcal{U}})$.

  (ii) Set $(\psi_{\text{pp}}, \cdot) := \bar{f}_{\text{pp}}(\omega_{\text{pp}})$.[a]

  (iii) Set $c_{pk_{\mathcal{U}}} := \omega_{\text{pp}}$ and parse $(pk^{\text{pp}}_{\mathcal{P}}, \sigma_{\text{pp}}, \bar{d}_{pk_{\mathcal{U}}}) := \psi_{\text{pp}}$.

  (iv) $d_{pk_{\mathcal{U}}} \leftarrow \text{C2.Equivoke}(crs^{(2)}_{\text{com}}, pk_{\mathcal{U}}, c_{pk_{\mathcal{U}}}, \bar{d}_{pk_{\mathcal{U}}})$.

  (v) Redefine $\psi_{\text{pp}} := (pk^{\text{pp}}_{\mathcal{P}}, \sigma_{\text{pp}}, d_{pk_{\mathcal{U}}})$ and $\bar{f}_{\text{pp}}(\omega_{\text{pp}}) := (\psi_{\text{pp}}, pk_{\mathcal{U}})$.

 (b) Call $\mathcal{F}^{\text{sim}}_{\text{msg}}$ with input (`send`, $ssid, (\omega_{\text{pp}}, \psi_{\text{pp}})$) in the name of $\mathcal{U}$.

(5) Upon receiving output (`closed`, $ssid$) from $\mathcal{F}^{\text{sim}}_{\text{msg}}$ for $\mathcal{U}$, let $\mathcal{F}_{\text{apc}}$ delivers its output to $\mathcal{U}$.

[a] This exists as otherwise $\mathcal{F}_{\text{apc}}$ would have returned $result = \mathsf{NOK}$.

Figure 8.18: The Simulator for Operator Security (cont. from Fig. 8.2)

Hybrid $H_5^{\text{op-sec}}$ (Simulate serial number) $H_5^{\text{op-sec}}$ modifies the tasks of IssueWallet and Deposit in case of a corrupted user. The code of $\pi_5^{\text{op-sec}}$ for the operator/PoS is modified such that it does not send c''_{ser} in the scope of IssueWallet or Deposit. Instead $\mathcal{S}_5^{\text{op-sec}}$ runs $(c''_{\text{ser}}, \bar{d}_{\text{ser}}) \leftarrow \text{C4.CommitSim}(crs_{\text{com}}^{(4)})$ and injects c''_{ser} into the message. Moreover, $\pi_5^{\text{op-sec}}$ for the operator/PoS is modified such that it uniformly and independently picks $s \overset{R}{\leftarrow} \mathbb{Z}_p$ and passes s to $\mathcal{S}_5^{\text{op-sec}}$ as part of the final message. $\mathcal{S}_5^{\text{op-sec}}$ calculates $s'' := s \cdot (s')^{-1}$, executes $d''_{\text{ser}} \leftarrow \text{C4.Equivoke}(crs_{\text{com}}^{(4)}, td_{\text{eqcom}}, s'', c''_{\text{ser}}, \bar{d}_{\text{ser}})$ and injects s'' together with d''_{ser} into the messages from operator/PoS to the user.

Hybrid $H_6^{\text{op-sec}}$ (Recover wallet ID and scrutinize equations) When $\mathcal{S}_6^{\text{op-sec}}$ receives a NIZK proof π in the scope of IssueWallet, Deposit and Disburse, it extracts the witness and recovers $\lambda := \lambda'' + \sum_{i=0}^{\ell-1} \text{DLOG}(\Lambda_i') \cdot B^i$.

Moreover, the verification of the proof is moved from $\pi_6^{\text{op-sec}}$ for the honest operator/PoS to the simulator. If the verification fails, $\mathcal{S}_6^{\text{op-sec}}$ aborts as the operator/PoS running the real protocol would do.

Additionally, $\mathcal{S}_6^{\text{op-sec}}$ checks if the pair of the statement and the extracted witness fulfills the languages $L_{gp}^{(1)}$, $L_{gp}^{(2)}$, and $L_{gp}^{(3)}$ resp. If not, $\mathcal{S}_6^{\text{op-sec}}$ give up the simulation with failure event (*E1*).

Hybrid $H_7^{\text{op-sec}}$ (Record Tags) $H_7^{\text{op-sec}}$ replaces the code protocol $\pi_7^{\text{op-sec}}$ of the tasks IssueWallet, Deposit and Disburse such that the various tags are not exclusively created by the parties' code but with support from $\mathcal{S}_7^{\text{op-sec}}$ and then recorded by $\mathcal{S}_7^{\text{op-sec}}$. More precisely, these are

$$\omega_{\text{bl}} := (\lambda'', \psi_{\text{bl}}) \qquad \omega_{\text{ds}} := (\varphi, t, u_2) \tag{8.7}$$

$$\omega_{\text{rc}} \leftarrow \text{ENC2.Enc}(pk_{\mathcal{O}}^{\text{rc,enc}}, \psi_{\text{rc}}) \qquad \omega_{\text{pp}} := c_{pk_{\mathcal{U}}} \tag{8.8}$$

To this end, $\pi_7^{\text{op-sec}}$ and $\mathcal{S}_7^{\text{op-sec}}$ are changed in detail as follows.

For the blacklisting tag ω_{bl}: In the scope of IssueWallet the honest operator does not pick the share λ'' of the wallet ID and sends it, but lets $\mathcal{S}_7^{\text{op-sec}}$ pick λ'' and inject it into the message. When the honest or corrupted user sends[3] ψ_{bl}, $\mathcal{S}_7^{\text{op-sec}}$ removes it from the message and the code of operator is modified such that operator does not expect to receive ψ_{bl}. Instead, the operator asks $\mathcal{S}_7^{\text{op-sec}}$ to provide the final ω_{bl} which is then output by operator. Also, $\mathcal{S}_7^{\text{op-sec}}$ records $f_{\Omega_{\text{bl}}}(\lambda) := \omega_{\text{bl}}$ as $\mathcal{F}_{\text{apc}}$ would do.[4]

[3] N.b.: $\mathcal{S}_7^{\text{op-sec}}$ controls $\mathcal{F}_{\text{msg}}^{\text{sim}}$ and therefore also sees the message of an honest user that runs $\pi_7^{\text{op-sec}}$.

[4] $\mathcal{S}_7^{\text{op-sec}}$ knows λ due to hybrid $H_6^{\text{op-sec}}$.

For the double-spending tag ω_{ds}: In the scope of Deposit/Disburse the honest PoS/operator does not pick the DS challenge u_2 and sends it, but lets $\mathcal{S}_7^{\text{op-sec}}$ pick u_2 and inject it into the message. When the honest or corrupted user sends the DS response t, $\mathcal{S}_7^{\text{op-sec}}$ removes it from the message and the code of PoS/operator is modified such that they do not expect to receive t. Instead, they ask $\mathcal{S}_7^{\text{op-sec}}$ to provide the final ω_{ds} which is then output by operator. Also, the code for honest users is modified such that it explicitly leaks s, φ to $\mathcal{S}_7^{\text{op-sec}}$. This equals the behavior of $\mathcal{F}_{\text{apc}}$.

For the recalculation tag ω_{rc}: In the scope of Deposit/Disburse the code $\pi_7^{\text{op-sec}}$ of the honest PoS/operator is modified such that they ask $\mathcal{S}_7^{\text{op-sec}}$ for the final ω_{rc} which is then output by PoS/operator. To this end they provisionally leak the honestly created ω'_{rc} to $\mathcal{S}_7^{\text{op-sec}}$ which replies with $\omega_{\text{rc}} := \omega'_{\text{rc}}$. Also, the honest PoS additionally leaks p in the scope of Deposit, if the operator is corrupted.[5]

For the prove-participation tag ω_{pp}: When the honest or corrupted user sends $c_{pk_{\mathcal{U}}}$ in the scope of Deposit, $\mathcal{S}_7^{\text{op-sec}}$ removes it from the message and the code of the honest PoS is modified such that it does not expect to receive $c_{pk_{\mathcal{U}}}$. Instead, PoS asks $\mathcal{S}_7^{\text{op-sec}}$ to provide the final ω_{pp} which is then output by PoS. Also, the code of PoS is modified such that it does send σ_{pp} back to user, as it cannot sign $c_{pk_{\mathcal{U}}}$ anymore. Instead, the $\pi_7^{\text{op-sec}}$ leaks $pid_{\mathcal{P}}$ to $\mathcal{S}_7^{\text{op-sec}}$ which then runs $\sigma_{\text{pp}} \leftarrow \mathsf{SIG.Sign}(sk_{\mathcal{P}}^{\text{pp}}, c_{pk_{\mathcal{U}}})$ as the PoS would do and injects σ_{pp} into the response from the PoS to the user. Please note, that $\mathcal{S}_7^{\text{op-sec}}$ knows the secret key $sk_{\mathcal{P}}^{\text{pp}}$ as the PoS is honest. Moreover, the code of the honest user is modified such that it asks $\mathcal{S}_7^{\text{op-sec}}$ for the final ω_{pp} which is then output by user. To this end, the code $\pi_7^{\text{op-sec}}$ for honest users is modified such that they provisionally leak the honestly created $(\omega'_{\text{pp}}, \psi'_{\text{pp}})$ to $\mathcal{S}_7^{\text{op-sec}}$ which replies with $\omega_{\text{pp}} := \omega'_{\text{pp}}$ and defines $\bar{f}_{\text{pp}}(\omega'_{\text{pp}}) := (\psi'_{\text{pp}}, pk_{\mathcal{U}})$.

In summary, these modifications leak (s, φ) (for ω_{ds}-tags), $pid_{\mathcal{P}}$ (for ω_{pp}-tags) and—in case of a corrupted operator in Deposit—also p (for ω_{rc}-tags). This equals the behavior of the final $\mathcal{F}_{\text{apc}}$ (cp. Fig. 4.11, Step 10 and Fig. 4.12, Step 7). On top, $\pi_7^{\text{op-sec}}$ *provisionally* leaks ω'_{rc} and ω'_{pp} which are still honestly created by $\pi_7^{\text{op-sec}}$ and simply mirrored back by $\mathcal{S}_7^{\text{op-sec}}$ as ω_{rc} and ω_{pp}, resp. This over-leakage is reverted in hybrids $H_{26}^{\text{op-sec}}$ and $H_{27}^{\text{op-sec}}$.

Hybrid $H_8^{\text{op-sec}}$ (Create simulated transaction graph and lookup tables) When $\mathcal{S}_8^{\text{op-sec}}$ receives a NIZK proof π in the scope of IssueWallet, Deposit and Disburse, it uses the extracted witness from hybrid $H_6^{\text{op-sec}}$ to assemble all parts of $\overline{trdb}$ and appends $\overline{trdb}$ to $\overline{TRDB}$. This also includes $\omega_{\text{bl}}, \omega_{\text{ds}}, \omega_{\text{rc}}$ and ω_{pp} created in the hybrid $H_7^{\text{op-sec}}$.

[5] N.b., for operator security the operator is always honest, i.e. the latter case never holds. However, we explicitly consider this case here, as this allows us to reuse this hybrid as hybrid H_7 to prove user security.

When a new entry $\overline{trdb}$ is assembled in the scope of the tasks Deposit or Disburse, $\mathcal{S}_{8}^{\text{op-sec}}$ compiles the set $\Omega_{\text{ds}}^{\varphi} := \{\omega_{\text{ds}}^{\varphi} \mid (\dots, \varphi, \dots, \omega_{\text{ds}}^{\varphi}, \dots) \in \overline{TRDB}\}$ as $\mathcal{F}_{\text{apc}}$ would do. If there exist matching double-spending tags $\omega_{\text{ds}}, \omega'_{\text{ds}} \in \Omega_{\text{ds}}^{\varphi}$, then set $f_{\pi}(pid_{\mathcal{U}}, \pi) := \text{OK}$ with $\pi := sk_{\mathcal{U}}$ to record this incident of double-spending as $\mathcal{S}_{\pi_{\text{P5C}}}^{\text{op-sec}}$ would do. If $pid_{\mathcal{U}} \in \mathcal{PID}_{\text{corr}}$ reconstruct $sk_{\mathcal{U}}$ as $\mathcal{S}_{\pi_{\text{P5C}}}^{\text{op-sec}}$ would do first and redefine $\bar{f}_{\text{keys}}(pid_{\mathcal{U}}) := (pk_{\mathcal{U}}, sk_{\mathcal{U}})$ (cp. Step 5 in Fig. 8.9 and Step 4 in Fig. 8.13).

Hybrid $H_{9}^{\text{op-sec}}$ (Check predecessor) In the scope of Deposit or Disburse, the simulator $\mathcal{S}_{9}^{\text{op-sec}}$ looks up the predecessor entry with s^{prev} being used as the unique key. If this fails, $\mathcal{S}_{9}^{\text{op-sec}}$ gives up the simulation with event *E2*.

Hybrid $H_{10}^{\text{op-sec}}$ (Check updatable part of wallet) The simulator $\mathcal{S}_{10}^{\text{op-sec}}$ additionally checks for $c_{\text{upd}}^{\text{out}*} \neq c_{\text{upd}}^{\text{prev}}$ and gives up the simulation with event *E3*, if the check succeeds.

Hybrid $H_{11}^{\text{op-sec}}$ (Check wallet ID) The simulator $\mathcal{S}_{11}^{\text{op-sec}}$ additionally checks for $\Lambda \neq g_1^{\lambda^*}$ and gives up the simulation with event *E4*, if the check succeeds.

Hybrid $H_{12}^{\text{op-sec}}$ (Check fixed part of wallet) The simulator $\mathcal{S}_{12}^{\text{op-sec}}$ additionally checks for $c_{\text{fix}}^{\text{out}*} \neq c_{\text{fix}}$ and gives up the simulation with event *E5*, if the check succeeds.

Hybrid $H_{13}^{\text{op-sec}}$ (Check user ID) The simulator $\mathcal{S}_{13}^{\text{op-sec}}$ parses $(\Lambda^*, pk_{\mathcal{U}}^*) := m_{\text{fix}}^{\text{out}*}$ and checks for $pk_{\mathcal{U}} \neq pk_{\mathcal{U}}^*$. If the check succeeds, it gives up the simulation with event *E6*.

Hybrid $H_{14}^{\text{op-sec}}$ (Check balance) The simulator $\mathcal{S}_{14}^{\text{op-sec}}$ additionally checks for $B^{\text{prev}} \neq g_1^{b^*}$ and gives up the simulation with event *E7*, if the check succeeds.

Hybrid $H_{15}^{\text{op-sec}}$ (Check transaction counter) The simulator $\mathcal{S}_{15}^{\text{op-sec}}$ additionally checks for $X \neq g_1^{x^*+1}$ and gives up the simulation with event *E8*, if the check succeeds.

Hybrid $H_{16}^{\text{op-sec}}$ (Check DS mask) The simulator $\mathcal{S}_{16}^{\text{op-sec}}$ additionally checks for $U_1 \neq U_1^*$ and gives up the simulation with event *E9*, if the check succeeds.

Hybrid $H_{17}^{\text{op-sec}}$ (Utilize lookup tables for DetectDS) This hybrid modifies the code $\pi_{17}^{\text{op-sec}}$ for $\mathcal{O}$ in the task DetectDS. In the task DetectDS the honest $\mathcal{O}$ becomes a dummy party, too, which simply forwards its inputs ω_{ds} and ω'_{ds}. The code is moved to the simulator and $\mathcal{S}_{17}^{\text{op-sec}}$ uses its "lookup table" $\overline{TRDB}$ the same way as the $\mathcal{F}_{\text{apc}}$ and the final simulator $\mathcal{S}_{\pi_{\text{P5C}}}^{\text{op-sec}}$ does. More precisely, for legitimately issued, distinct and matching double-spending tags, $\mathcal{S}_{17}^{\text{op-sec}}$ looks up $(pk_{\mathcal{U}}, sk_{\mathcal{U}}) := \bar{f}_{\text{keys}}(pid_{\mathcal{U}})$, returns $\pi := sk_{\mathcal{U}}$ and records $f_{\pi}(pid_{\mathcal{U}}, \pi) := \text{OK}$.

Hybrid $H_{18}^{\text{op-sec}}$ (Utilize lookup tables for VerifyGuilt) This hybrid modifies the code $\pi_{18}^{\text{op-sec}}$ for parties in the task VerifyGuilt. The honest party does not locally run the algorithm itself, but simply forwards its input to the simulator (as the dummy party would do) and $\mathcal{S}_{18}^{\text{op-sec}}$ queries $f_\pi(pid_\mathcal{U}, \pi)$ as $\mathcal{F}_{\text{apc}}$ would do or proceeds as $\mathcal{S}_{\pi_{\text{P5C}}}^{\text{op-sec}}$, if $f_\pi(pid_\mathcal{U}, \pi)$ has not yet been defined.

Hybrid $H_{19}^{\text{op-sec}}$ (Utilize lookup tables for BlacklistWallet, forego decryption of blacklisting tags) The dispute resolver DR becomes a dummy party and simply sends it input $(\texttt{blacklist\_wallet}, pid'_\mathcal{U})$ to the simulator $\mathcal{S}_{19}^{\text{op-sec}}$ in order to signal its consent to blacklist the user. The simulator $\mathcal{S}_{19}^{\text{op-sec}}$ utilizes the Simulated Transaction Graph $\overline{TRDB}$ as well as $f_{\Omega_{\text{bl}}}$ and runs the code as the ideal functionality $\mathcal{F}_{\text{apc}}$ would do eventually. Especially, $\mathcal{S}_{19}^{\text{op-sec}}$ does not decrypt ω_{bl}, but uses the recorded $f_{\Omega_{\text{bl}}}^{-1}(\omega_{\text{bl}})$ from hybrid $H_7^{\text{op-sec}}$ to determine the original λ.[6]

Hybrid $H_{20}^{\text{op-sec}}$ (Utilize lookup tables for RecalculateBalance, forego decryption of recalculation tags) This hybrid utilizes $\overline{TRDB}$ to link legitimately issued recalculation tags to their origin.

When the task RecalculateBalance is invoked, $\mathcal{S}_{20}^{\text{op-sec}}$ partitions the set of recalculation tags Ω_{rc} into two set $\Omega_{\text{rc}}^{\text{genuine}}$ and $\Omega_{\text{rc}}^{\text{fake}}$ the same way as $\mathcal{F}_{\text{apc}}$ would do (cp. Figs. 4.16 and 8.16). Recalculation tags $\omega_{\text{rc}} \in \Omega_{\text{rc}}^{\text{genuine}}$ are not decrypted, but $\mathcal{S}_{20}^{\text{op-sec}}$ queries $\overline{TRDB}$ to create a set $\Xi^{\text{genuine}} := \{(s, p)\}$. Recalculation tags $\omega_{\text{rc}} \in \Omega_{\text{rc}}^{\text{fake}}$ are still decrypted, their signature is checked for validity and $\Xi^{\text{fake}} := \{(s, p)\}$ is compiled from the decrypted values. Then the balance is calculated as $b^{\text{bill}} := \sum_{(s,p)\in\Xi^{\text{genuine}}} p + \sum_{(s,p)\in\Xi^{\text{fake}}} p$.

This behavior equals the joint behavior of $\mathcal{F}_{\text{apc}}$ and the final simulator $\mathcal{S}_{\pi_{\text{P5C}}}^{\text{op-sec}}$ (cp. Figs. 4.16 and 8.16).

Hybrid $H_{21}^{\text{op-sec}}$ (Utilize lookup tables for ProveParticipation, check signature) This hybrid utilizes $\bar{f}_{\text{pp}}$ to assert that prove-participation tags are honestly signed. This sanity check is a preparatory step for the eventual switch from the real code to the ideal code in hybrid $H_{23}^{\text{op-sec}}$ by ruling out that a corrupted user forges signatures.

More precisely the following changes are applied by $H_{21}^{\text{op-sec}}$ in the scope of ProveParticipation for an honest violation enforcer interacting with a corrupted user:

The party VE becomes a dummy party and simply forwards the input $pid_\mathcal{P}$ and set of prove-participation tags Ω_{pp} to $\mathcal{S}_{21}^{\text{op-sec}}$. The simulator interacting with $\mathcal{Z}^{\text{op-sec}}$ still runs the real code (as a real VE would do), but utilizes its map $\bar{f}_{\text{pp}}$ to add the following check. When $\mathcal{Z}^{\text{op-sec}}$ (playing the corrupted user) sends ω_{pp} and $pid_\mathcal{P}$ is honest, the simulator tries to look up its

[6] The operator is honest and the real code would abort for a ω_{bl} that has not legitimately been issued. Hence, $f_{\Omega_{\text{bl}}}^{-1}(\omega_{\text{bl}})$ is always defined.

original complement $(\psi^*_{\text{pp}}, pk^*_{\mathcal{U}}) := \bar{f}_{\text{pp}}(\omega_{\text{pp}})$. If this does not exist, i.e., if $\psi^*_{\text{pp}} = \bot$, but $\mathcal{Z}^{\text{op-sec}}$ has provided a valid signature, then the simulator gives up the simulation with event *E10*.

Hybrid $H^{\text{op-sec}}_{22}$ (Utilize lookup tables for ProveParticipation, check user ID) Similar to $H^{\text{op-sec}}_{21}$ this hybrid introduces another sanity check in the scope of ProveParticipation in case of a corrupted user and an honest violation enforcer:

If an original complement $(\psi^*_{\text{pp}}, pk^*_{\mathcal{U}}) := \bar{f}_{\text{pp}}(\omega_{\text{pp}})$ for ω_{pp} exists but the environment $\mathcal{Z}^{\text{op-sec}}$ unveils the commitment $c_{pk_{\mathcal{U}}} = \omega_{\text{pp}}$ to a different $pk_{\mathcal{U}}$ than it has originally been issued, the simulator gives up with event *E11*.

Otherwise it still runs the real code for ProveParticipation.

Hybrid $H^{\text{op-sec}}_{23}$ (Utilize lookup tables for ProveParticipation, forego unveil of prove-participation tags) This hybrid utilizes $\overline{TRDB}$ and $\bar{f}_{\text{pp}}$ to link legitimately issued prove-participation tags to their origin. More precisely, the following changes are applied by $H^{\text{op-sec}}_{23}$ in the scope of ProveParticipation:

For a corrupted user and honest violation enforcer: This hybrid completes the changes introduced by hybrids $H^{\text{op-sec}}_{21}$ and $H^{\text{op-sec}}_{22}$. When $\mathcal{Z}^{\text{op-sec}}$ sends $\omega_{\text{pp}}, \psi_{\text{pp}}$ in the name of the corrupted user, the simulator first checks if the commitment unveils correctly and if the signature is valid. If anything is inconsistent, the simulator runs the code of the ideal functionality with input $\omega_{\text{pp}} := \bot$. Also, if the sanity checks of both previous hybrids pass, then the code of the ideal functionality is executed with the provided ω_{pp} as its input. If the ideal code asks for a result bit (because ω_{pp} is unknown and the PoS is corrupted), the simulator returns *result* = OK. This equals the joint behavior of the final simulator $\mathcal{S}^{\text{op-sec}}$ (cp. Fig. 8.17) and $\mathcal{F}_{\text{apc}}$ (cp. Fig. 4.17).

For an honest user and corrupted violation enforcer: The code of the honest users is modified such that they do not send $(\omega_{\text{pp}}, \psi_{\text{pp}})$ but only ω_{pp}. Also, the users do not internally test, if ω_{pp} is one of their own prove-participation tags, but simply forward them as a dummy party would do. $\mathcal{S}^{\text{op-sec}}_{23}$ uses $\overline{TRDB}$ to link ω_{pp} to its original transaction and thereby determines the result. If the result is positive, $\mathcal{S}^{\text{op-sec}}_{23}$ looks up the corresponding ψ_{pp} in $\bar{f}_{\text{pp}}$ and simulates the message $(\omega_{\text{pp}}, \psi_{\text{pp}})$. Note, ψ_{pp} are not yet equivocated (as the final simulator would do), but $\mathcal{S}^{\text{op-sec}}_{23}$ sends the original ψ_{pp} that have been recorded in hybrid $H^{\text{op-sec}}_{7}$.

Hybrid $H^{\text{op-sec}}_{24}$ (Fake blacklisting tags for honest users) The code $\pi^{\text{op-sec}}_{24}$ for honest users in the scope of IssueWallet is modified such that they do not send ω_{bl}. Instead, $\mathcal{S}^{\text{op-sec}}_{24}$ returns $\omega_{\text{bl}} := (\lambda'', \psi_{\text{bl}})$ with $\psi_{\text{bl}} \leftarrow \text{ENC1.Enc}(pk_{\mathcal{DR}}, (1, \dots, 1))$, when $\mathcal{O}$ asks for a ω_{bl} (cp. hybrid $H^{\text{op-sec}}_{7}$).

Hybrid $H_{25}^{\text{op-sec}}$ (Fake double-spending tags for honest users) The code $\pi_{25}^{\text{op-sec}}$ for honest users in the scope of Deposit and Disburse is modified such that they do not send a real DS response t. When the operator asks for double-spending tag (cp. hybrid $H_7^{\text{op-sec}}$), the simulator $\mathcal{S}_{25}^{\text{op-sec}}$ proceeds as follows. $\mathcal{S}_{25}^{\text{op-sec}}$ compiles the set $\Omega_{\text{ds}}^{\varphi} := \{\omega_{\text{ds}}^{\varphi} \mid (\dots, \varphi, \dots, \omega_{\text{ds}}^{\varphi}, \dots) \in \overline{TRDB}\}$. (N.b., this already happens for *corrupted* users in hybrid $H_8^{\text{op-sec}}$ to recover their secret key). If no $(\varphi, t', u_2') \in \Omega_{\text{ds}}^{\varphi}$ has been recorded previously, $\mathcal{S}_{25}^{\text{op-sec}}$ picks $t \xleftarrow{R} \mathbb{Z}_p$ randomly. Otherwise $\mathcal{S}_{25}^{\text{op-sec}}$ sets $t := t' + sk_{\mathcal{U}}(u_2 - u_2')$. This equals the behavior of the final simulator $\mathcal{S}_{\pi_{\text{P5C}}}^{\text{op-sec}}$.

Hybrid $H_{26}^{\text{op-sec}}$ (Fake recalculation tags for honest users) The code $\pi_{26}^{\text{op-sec}}$ for honest operator/PoS in the scope of Deposit and Disburse abandons the over-leakage of ω_{rc}' that has provisionally been introduced by hybrid $H_7^{\text{op-sec}}$. When they ask for ω_{rc} the simulator does not simply reflect $\omega_{\text{rc}} := \omega_{\text{rc}}'$, but instead creates ω_{rc} on its own. The simulator does so in two different ways, depending on the corruption status of the operator.

If the operator is corrupted,[7] the simulator creates $\psi_{\text{rc}} := (s, \varphi, p, pk_{\mathcal{P}}^{\text{rc}}, \sigma_{\text{rc}})$ with $\sigma_{\text{rc}} \leftarrow \mathsf{SIG.Sign}(sk_{\mathcal{P}}^{\text{rc}}, (s, \varphi, g_1^p))$ faithfully and provides a true encryption $\omega_{\text{rc}} \leftarrow \mathsf{ENC2.Enc}(pk_{\mathcal{O}}^{\text{rc,enc}}, \psi_{\text{rc}})$. We stress that $\mathcal{S}_{26}^{\text{op-sec}}$ knows all relevant information s, φ, $pid_{\mathcal{P}}$ and p due to the leakage introduced by hybrid $H_7^{\text{op-sec}}$.

If the operator is honest, $\mathcal{S}_{26}^{\text{op-sec}}$ provides an encryption $\omega_{\text{rc}} \leftarrow \mathsf{ENC2.Enc}(pk_{\mathcal{O}}^{\text{rc,enc}}, \psi_{\text{rc}})$ for an arbitrary ψ_{rc} from the correct space.

Hybrid $H_{27}^{\text{op-sec}}$ (Fake prove-participation tags for honest users) The hybrid $H_{27}^{\text{op-sec}}$ modifies Deposit and ProveParticipation.

In Deposit the honest users do not leak $(\omega_{\text{pp}}, \psi_{\text{pp}})$ anymore. This leakage has provisionally been introduced by hybrid $H_7^{\text{op-sec}}$. Instead, $\mathcal{S}_{27}^{\text{op-sec}}$ simulates the commitment as $(c_{pk_{\mathcal{U}}}, \bar{d}_{pk_{\mathcal{U}}}) \leftarrow \mathsf{C2.CommitSim}(crs_{\text{com}}^{(2)})$ and runs $\sigma_{\text{pp}} \leftarrow \mathsf{SIG.Sign}(sk_{\mathcal{P}}^{\text{pp}}, c_{pk_{\mathcal{U}}})$. $\mathcal{S}_{27}^{\text{op-sec}}$ sets $\omega_{\text{pp}} := c_{pk_{\mathcal{U}}}$ and $\psi_{\text{pp}} := (pk_{\mathcal{P}}^{\text{pp}}, \sigma_{\text{pp}}, \bar{d}_{pk_{\mathcal{U}}})$, returns ω_{pp} and defines $\bar{f}_{\text{pp}}(\omega_{\text{pp}}) := (\psi_{\text{pp}}, g_1)$.

Moreover, the code for ProveParticipation in case of an honest user and a corrupted violation enforcer is adapted (cp. hybrid $H_{23}^{\text{op-sec}}$). After $\mathcal{S}_{27}^{\text{op-sec}}$ has looked up the corresponding $\psi_{\text{pp}}, g_1) := \bar{f}_{\text{pp}}(\omega_{\text{pp}})$, but before sending ψ_{pp} to $\mathcal{Z}^{\text{op-sec}}$ playing the corrupted VE, $\mathcal{S}_{27}^{\text{op-sec}}$ parses $(pk_{\mathcal{P}}^{\text{pp}}, \sigma_{\text{pp}}, \bar{d}_{pk_{\mathcal{U}}}) := \psi_{\text{pp}})$, equivocates the decommitment $d_{pk_{\mathcal{U}}} \leftarrow \mathsf{C2.Equivoke}(crs_{\text{com}}^{(2)}, pk_{\mathcal{U}}, c_{pk_{\mathcal{U}}}, \bar{d}_{pk_{\mathcal{U}}})$, redefines $\psi_{\text{pp}} := (pk_{\mathcal{P}}^{\text{pp}}, \sigma_{\text{pp}}, d_{pk_{\mathcal{U}}})$ and then sends ψ_{pp}.

Again, this equals the behavior of the final simulator $\mathcal{S}_{\pi_{\text{P5C}}}^{\text{op-sec}}$.

For the proof of Theorem 8.2 we show the indistinguishability of subsequent hybrids by a series of hybrids. The hybrids $H_2^{\text{op-sec}}$ to $H_4^{\text{op-sec}}$, $H_7^{\text{op-sec}}$ and $H_8^{\text{op-sec}}$ are rather trivial and thus Lemma 8.5 handles various hybrids at once.

[7] N.b., for operator security the operator is always honest, i.e. this case never holds. However, we explicitly consider this case here, as this allows us to reuse this hybrid as hybrid H_{17} to prove user security.

Lemma 8.4 (Indistinguishability between $H_0^{\text{op-sec}}$ and $H_1^{\text{op-sec}}$) *Under the assumptions of Theorem 8.2, $H_0^{\text{op-sec}} \stackrel{c}{\equiv} H_1^{\text{op-sec}}$ holds.*

Proof This hop solely changes how the *crs* is created during the setup phase. This is indistinguishable for crs_{pok}, and $crs_{\text{com}}^{(4)}$ (see the extractability property of Definition 6.9 and the equivocality property of Definition 6.11, resp., condition (a) each). ■

Lemma 8.5 (Indistinguishability between their respective predecessors and $H_2^{\text{op-sec}}$, $H_3^{\text{op-sec}}$, $H_4^{\text{op-sec}}$, $H_7^{\text{op-sec}}$, $H_8^{\text{op-sec}}$, resp.) *Under the assumptions of Theorem 8.2, $H_1^{\text{op-sec}} \stackrel{c}{\equiv} H_2^{\text{op-sec}} \stackrel{c}{\equiv} H_3^{\text{op-sec}} \stackrel{c}{\equiv} H_4^{\text{op-sec}}$, and $H_6^{\text{op-sec}} \stackrel{c}{\equiv} H_7^{\text{op-sec}} \stackrel{c}{\equiv} H_8^{\text{op-sec}}$ hold.*

Proof The hops are all indistinguishable as they do not change anything in the view of $\mathcal{Z}^{\text{op-sec}}$. Please note, that $\mathcal{Z}^{\text{op-sec}}$ only sees the in-/output of honest parties and these hops only syntactically change what parts of the code are executed by the parties or by the simulator. With each hop the parties degrade more to a dummy party while at the same time more functionality is put into the simulator. ■

Lemma 8.6 (Indistinguishability between $H_4^{\text{op-sec}}$ and $H_5^{\text{op-sec}}$) *Under the assumptions of Theorem 8.2, $H_4^{\text{op-sec}} \stackrel{c}{\equiv} H_5^{\text{op-sec}}$ holds.*

Proof This hop is indistinguishable as the equivocated decommitment information is perfectly indistinguishable from a decommitment that has originally been created with the correct message (cp. Definition 6.11, Item (3)). ■

So far, none of hops between two consecutive hybrids changes anything from the environment's perspective: either the hops are only syntactical or the modification is perfectly indistinguishable. Hence, no reduction argument is required. In the contrary, each of the upcoming security proofs roughly follows the same lines of argument. If the environment $\mathcal{Z}^{\text{op-sec}}$ can efficiently distinguish between two consecutive hybrids, then we can construct an efficient adversary $\mathcal{B}$ against one of the underlying cryptographic building blocks. To this end, $\mathcal{B}$ plays the adversary against a particular security property in the outer game and internally executes the UC-experiment in its head while mimicking the role of the simulator. It is important to note that although $\mathcal{B}$ emulates the environment internally, it only has *black-box access* to it. In other words, although everything happens inside "the head of $\mathcal{B}$" it cannot somehow magically extract $\mathcal{Z}^{\text{op-sec}}$'s attack strategy.

Lemma 8.7 (Indistinguishability between $H_5^{\text{op-sec}}$ and $H_6^{\text{op-sec}}$) *Under the assumptions of Theorem 8.2, $H_5^{\text{op-sec}} \stackrel{c}{\equiv} H_6^{\text{op-sec}}$ holds.*

PROOF First note that the only effective change between $H_5^{\text{op-sec}}$ and $H_6^{\text{op-sec}}$ are the additional checks that abort the simulation with event *E1*, if the extracted witnesses are invalid. Again, the other modifications are purely syntactical. To proof indistinguishability between $H_5^{\text{op-sec}}$ and $H_6^{\text{op-sec}}$ we split this hop into three sub-hybrids. Each sub-hybrid introduces the check for one of the languages $L_{gp}^{(1)}$, $L_{gp}^{(2)}$ and $L_{gp}^{(3)}$, resp. In the following only the sub-hybrid for the language $L_{gp}^{(1)}$ is considered, the indistinguishability of the remaining two is proved analogously. Further note, that the view of $\mathcal{Z}^{\text{op-sec}}$ is perfectly indistinguishable, if the simulation does not abort.

Assume there is an environment $\mathcal{Z}^{\text{op-sec}}$ that trigger the event *E1* in the first sub-hybrid with non-negligible advantage. This immediately yields an efficient adversary $\mathcal{B}$ against the extraction property of the NIZK scheme. Internally, $\mathcal{B}$ runs $\mathcal{Z}^{\text{op-sec}}$ in its head plays the role of the simulator and all honest parties. Externally, $\mathcal{B}$ plays the adversary in Definition 6.9, Item (3b). If the event *E1* occurs internally, $\mathcal{B}$ outputs the corresponding pair $(stmnt, \pi)$. In the second and third sub-hybrid $\mathcal{B}$ internally extracts the witness for the previous sub-hybrid using the extraction trapdoor td_{epok} which $\mathcal{B}$ obtains as part of its input. ∎

Remark 8.8 *We observe that Lemma 8.7 implies that the equations*

$$\mathsf{C1.Open}(crs_{\text{com}}^{(1)}, m, c_{\text{fix}}, d_{\text{fix}}) = 1 \quad \textit{with} \quad m = (\Lambda, pk_{\mathcal{U}}) \tag{8.9}$$

$$\mathsf{C1.Open}(crs_{\text{com}}^{(1)}, m, c_{\text{upd}}, d_{\text{upd}}) = 1 \quad \textit{with} \quad m = (\Lambda, 1, U_1^{\text{next}}, g_1) \tag{8.10}$$

$$\mathsf{C1.Open}(crs_{\text{com}}^{(1)}, m, c_{\text{upd}}^{\text{prev}}, d_{\text{upd}}^{\text{prev}}) = 1 \quad \textit{with} \quad m = (\Lambda, B^{\text{prev}}, U_1, X) \tag{8.11}$$

$$\mathsf{C1.Open}(crs_{\text{com}}^{(1)}, m, c'_{\text{upd}}, d'_{\text{upd}}) = 1 \quad \textit{with} \quad m = (\Lambda, B^{\text{prev}}, U_1^{\text{next}}, X) \tag{8.12}$$

$$\mathsf{C3.Open}(crs_{\text{com}}^{(3)}, \Lambda', c'_{\text{wid}}, d'_{\text{wid}}) = 1 \tag{8.13}$$

$$\mathsf{C2.Open}(crs_{\text{com}}^{(2)}, pk_{\mathcal{U}}, c_{pk_{\mathcal{U}}}, d_{pk_{\mathcal{U}}}) = 1 \tag{8.14}$$

and

$$\mathsf{SIG.Vfy}(pk_{\mathcal{O}}^{\text{fix}}, \sigma_{\text{fix}}, m) = 1 \quad \textit{with} \quad m = (c_{\text{fix}}, a_{\mathcal{U}}) \tag{8.15}$$

$$\mathsf{SIG.Vfy}(pk_{\mathcal{P}}^{\text{upd,prev}}, \sigma_{\text{upd}}^{\text{prev}}, m) = 1 \quad \textit{with} \quad m = (c_{\text{upd}}^{\text{prev}}, s^{\text{prev}}) \tag{8.16}$$

$$\mathsf{SIG.Vfy}(pk_{\mathcal{O}}^{\text{cert}}, \sigma_{\mathcal{P}}^{\text{cert,prev}}, m) = 1 \quad \textit{with} \quad m = (pk_{\mathcal{P}}^{\text{prev}}, a_{\mathcal{P}}^{\text{prev}}) \tag{8.17}$$

$$\tag{8.18}$$

resp., hold and that all variables can efficiently be extracted. Remember, that F_{gp} acts as the identity function on group elements. Likewise, the equation

$$T = pk_{\mathcal{U}}^{u_2} \cdot U_1 \quad \textit{with} \quad T = g_1^t \tag{8.19}$$

holds. Note, that the $\mathbb{Z}_p$-elements t and u_2 cannot be extracted, but are known and part of the statement. Moreover, given the extracted chunks of the wallet ID $\Lambda'_0, \dots, \Lambda'_{\ell-1}$ the unique wallet ID λ can be reconstructed. The projection F_{gp} becomes injective if the pre-image is restricted to $\mathbb{Z}_p$ and the inverse, i.e. DLOG, can be efficiently computed as $\lambda'_0, \dots, \lambda'_{\ell-1}$ are sufficiently "small".

Up to this point, we already know that $H_0^{\text{op-sec}} \overset{c}{\equiv} H_8^{\text{op-sec}}$ holds. Except for two small changes (from $H_4^{\text{op-sec}}$ to $H_5^{\text{op-sec}}$ and from $H_5^{\text{op-sec}}$ to $H_6^{\text{op-sec}}$) all hops are only syntactical.

The remaining subsequent hybrids can roughly be divided into two groups. The hybrids from $H_9^{\text{op-sec}}$ to $H_{16}^{\text{op-sec}}$ cover modifications that affect corrupted users while $H_{17}^{\text{op-sec}}$ to $H_{27}^{\text{op-sec}}$ cover modifications that affect honest users.

The hybrids we deal with first, i.e., hybrids $H_9^{\text{op-sec}}$ to $H_{16}^{\text{op-sec}}$, only add more sanity checks but do not change any messages. However, only $\overline{TRDB}$ and these sanity checks enable a reduction to cryptographic assumptions and thus are vital to prove operator security. Intuitively, these sanity checks assert that a malicious user cannot make the simulated transaction database and the ideal transaction database fell apart without immediately being noticed or the malicious user has successfully broken a cryptographic assumption. To this end, two additional lemmas about the structure of $\overline{TRDB}$ are necessary. These lemmas are in the same spirit as Lemmas 5.2 and 5.3. Intuitively, the commitments c_{fix}, c_{upd} induce a graph structure onto $\overline{TRDB}$ comparable to the wallet ID λ and serial number s.

Lemma 8.9 (Forest Structure of the Simulated Transaction Graph)

(1) *Every $\overline{trdb} = (s^{\text{prev}}, s, \dots) \in \overline{TRDB}$ is uniquely identified by s with overwhelming probability.*

(2) *The Simulated Transaction Graph $\overline{TRDB}$ is a forest with edges defined by (s^{prev}, s).*

Proof (1) A new entry is only inserted in the scope of IssueWallet, Deposit or Disburse. Proof by Induction: The statement is correct for the empty $\overline{TRDB}$. For each insertion, the simulator $\mathcal{S}_8^{\text{op-sec}}$ (and every following simulator) draws s uniformly and independently. The chance to pick a serial number that has already been used is negligible.

(2) As the serial number s of the new node is randomly chosen, no existing node can point to the new node as its predecessor and thus no cycle is closed with overwhelming probability. ∎

Lemma 8.10 (Indistinguishability between $H_8^{\text{op-sec}}$ and $H_9^{\text{op-sec}}$) *Under the assumptions of Theorem 8.2, $H_8^{\text{op-sec}} \overset{c}{\equiv} H_9^{\text{op-sec}}$ holds.*

Proof Assume there is an environment $\mathcal{Z}^{\text{op-sec}}$ that trigger the event *E2* with non-negligible advantage. This immediately yields an efficient adversary $\mathcal{B}$ against the EUF-CMA security of

SIG. We only need to deal with the case that s^* does not exist. If it exists, Lemma 8.9, Item (1) implies its uniqueness. We need to distinguish two cases. On an abstract level these cases correspond to the following scenarios: Either the previous PoS exists. Then the signature $\sigma_{\text{upd}}^{\text{prev}}$ on $(c_{\text{upd}}^{\text{prev}}, s^{\text{prev}})$ is a forgery. Or alternatively, the allegedly previous PoS does not exits but has been imagined by the user. Then $(c_{\text{upd}}^{\text{prev}}, s^{\text{prev}})$ may have an honest, valid signature (because the user feigned the PoS), but the certificate $cert_{\mathcal{P}}^{\text{prev}}$ for the fake PoS constitutes a forgery. Please note, that the simulator always records an entry $\overline{trdb}$ when it legitimately issues a signature σ_{upd} and vice versa.

(1) *A record* $pid_{\mathcal{P}}^{\text{prev}} \mapsto (pk_{\mathcal{P}}^{\text{prev}}, sk_{\mathcal{P}}^{\text{prev}})$ *has been recorded:* In other words, $(c_{\text{upd}}^{\text{prev}}, s^{\text{prev}})$ has never been legitimately issued by the allegedly previous PoS.[8] We construct an efficient adversary $\mathcal{B}$ against the EUF-CMA security of SIG. Internally, $\mathcal{B}$ runs $\mathcal{Z}^{\text{op-sec}}$ in its head and plays the role of the simulator and all honest parties. Externally, $\mathcal{B}$ plays the EUF-CMA security experiment with a challenger C and a signing oracle $O^{\text{SIG}}_{pk_{\mathcal{P}}^{\text{upd,prev}}, sk_{\mathcal{P}}^{\text{upd,prev}}}$. $\mathcal{B}$ needs to guess for which $pid_{\mathcal{P}}^{\text{prev}}$ the event $(E2)$ eventually occurs. When the PoS with $pid_{\mathcal{P}}^{\text{prev}}$ registers itself, and $\mathcal{B}$ playing $\mathcal{S}_9^{\text{op-sec}}$ needs to internally provide $pk_{\mathcal{P}}^{\text{prev}} = (pk_{\mathcal{P}}^{\text{upd,prev}}, pk_{\mathcal{P}}^{\text{rc,prev}})$ it embeds the external challenge public key as $pk_{\mathcal{P}}^{\text{upd,prev}}$. Whenever $\mathcal{B}$ playing the role of $\mathcal{S}_9^{\text{op-sec}}$ needs to issue a signature with respect to $pk_{\mathcal{P}}^{\text{upd,prev}}$, it uses its external EUF-CMA oracle $O^{\text{SIG}}_{pk_{\mathcal{P}}^{\text{upd,prev}}, sk_{\mathcal{P}}^{\text{upd,prev}}}$. When the event $(E2)$ occurs, $\mathcal{B}$ extracts $(c_{\text{upd}}^{\text{prev}}, s^{\text{prev}})$ and $\sigma_{\text{upd}}^{\text{prev}}$ from the proof and outputs the forgery. N.b., $(c_{\text{upd}}^{\text{prev}}, s^{\text{prev}})$ has never been signed with respect to $pk_{\mathcal{P}}^{\text{upd,prev}}$ by assumption.

(2) *A record* $pid_{\mathcal{P}}^{\text{prev}} \mapsto (pk_{\mathcal{P}}^{\text{prev}}, sk_{\mathcal{P}}^{\text{prev}}, cert_{\mathcal{P}})$ *has not been recorded:* We construct an efficient adversary $\mathcal{B}$ against the EUF-CMA security of SIG along the same lines as above. Internally, $\mathcal{B}$ runs $\mathcal{Z}^{\text{op-sec}}$ in its head and plays the role of the simulator and all honest parties. Externally, $\mathcal{B}$ plays the EUF-CMA security experiment with a challenger C and a signing oracle $O^{\text{SIG}}_{pk_{\mathcal{O}}^{\text{cert}}, sk_{\mathcal{O}}^{\text{cert}}}$. When the adversary $\mathcal{B}$ has to internally provide $pk_{\mathcal{O}} = (pk_{\mathcal{O}}^{\text{cert}}, pk_{\mathcal{O}}^{\text{upd}}, pk_{\mathcal{O}}^{\text{fix}}, pk_{\mathcal{O}}^{\text{rc,sig}}, pk_{\mathcal{O}}^{\text{rc,enc}})$ playing the role of $\mathcal{S}_9^{\text{op-sec}}$ in the scope of RegisterOp, $\mathcal{B}$ embeds the external challenge public key as $pk_{\mathcal{O}}^{\text{cert}}$. Whenever $\mathcal{B}$ playing the role of $\mathcal{S}_9^{\text{op-sec}}$ in the scope of CertifyPOS Certification needs to issue signatures with respect to $pk_{\mathcal{O}}^{\text{cert}}$, it uses its external EUF-CMA oracle $O^{\text{SIG}}_{pk_{\mathcal{O}}^{\text{cert}}, sk_{\mathcal{O}}^{\text{cert}}}$. When the event $(E2)$ occurs, $\mathcal{B}$ extracts $cert_{\mathcal{P}}^{\text{prev}} = (pk_{\mathcal{P}}, a_{\mathcal{P}}, \sigma_{\mathcal{P}}^{\text{cert}})$ from the proof and outputs $(pk_{\mathcal{P}}, a_{\mathcal{P}})$ together with $\sigma_{\mathcal{P}}^{\text{cert}}$ as the forgery. N.b.: $(pk_{\mathcal{P}}, a_{\mathcal{P}})$ has never been signed by the operator

[8] N.b.: PoS may also denote the operator, if the transaction at hand happens to be the first after a IssueWallet and thus s^* has been signed by the operator playing the role an PoS. For brevity, we only consider PoSes here.

with respect to $pk_{\mathcal{O}}^{\text{cert}}$ as otherwise a mapping $pid_{\mathcal{P}}^{\text{prev}} \mapsto (pk_{\mathcal{P}}^{\text{prev}}, sk_{\mathcal{P}}^{\text{prev}}, cert_{\mathcal{P}})$ would have been recorded.

The forgeries are indeed valid due to Remark 8.8. ∎

Remark 8.11 *Without Lemma 8.10 it is unclear in Lemma 8.9, Item (2) if the denoted predecessor of edge (s^{prev}, s) actually exists. The simulator extracts the serial number s^{prev} of the predecessor from the proof and puts this serial number into the newly added $\overline{trdb}$. With this in mind Lemma 8.9, Item (2) would have to be interpreted such that an edge (s^{prev}, s) is ignored, if the predecessor did not exist. Nonetheless, $\overline{TRDB}$ is still a forest and Lemma 8.9, Item (2) remains correct. Anyway, this oddity is ruled out by Lemma 8.10.*

Lemma 8.12 (Indistinguishability between $H_9^{\text{op-sec}}$ and $H_{10}^{\text{op-sec}}$) *Under the assumptions of Theorem 8.2, $H_9^{\text{op-sec}} \overset{c}{\equiv} H_{10}^{\text{op-sec}}$ holds.*

Proof Assume there is an environment $\mathcal{Z}^{\text{op-sec}}$ that trigger the event *E3* with non-negligible advantage. This immediately yields an efficient adversary $\mathcal{B}$ against the EUF-CMA security of SIG by the same argument as in the proof of Lemma 8.10 as $(c_{\text{upd}}^{\text{prev}}, s^{\text{prev}})$ are jointly signed by the same signature σ_{upd}. ∎

Lemma 8.13 (Indistinguishability between $H_{10}^{\text{op-sec}}$ and $H_{11}^{\text{op-sec}}$) *Under the assumptions of Theorem 8.2, $H_{10}^{\text{op-sec}} \overset{c}{\equiv} H_{11}^{\text{op-sec}}$ holds.*

Proof Assume there is an environment $\mathcal{Z}^{\text{op-sec}}$ that trigger the event *E4* with non-negligible advantage. We construct an efficient adversary $\mathcal{B}$ against the binding property of C1. Internally, $\mathcal{B}$ runs $\mathcal{Z}^{\text{op-sec}}$ in its head and plays the role of the simulator and all honest parties. Externally, $\mathcal{B}$ plays the role of the adversary as defined by Definition 6.11, Item (2). When the event (*E3*) occurs, $\mathcal{B}$ sets

$$m_{\text{upd}}^{\text{prev}} := (\Lambda, B^{\text{prev}}, U_1, X) \tag{8.20}$$

from the extracted witness and obtains

$$m_{\text{upd}}^{\text{out}\,*} = (\Lambda^*, B^*, U_1^*, X^*) \tag{8.21}$$

from $\overline{TRDB}$. $\mathcal{B}$ outputs $(c_{\text{upd}}^{\text{out}\,*}, m_{\text{upd}}^{\text{prev}}, d_{\text{upd}}^{\text{prev}}, m_{\text{upd}}^{\text{out}\,*}, d_{\text{upd}}^{\text{out}\,*})$ to the external game. By assumption $\Lambda \neq \Lambda^*$ holds and Remark 8.8 asserts that both openings are valid. ∎

Lemma 8.14 (Tree-wise Uniqueness of the Wallet Identifier) *The wallet ID λ maps one-to-one and onto a connected component (i.e., tree) of the Simulated Transaction Graph.*

Proof Same argument as in the proof of Lemma 5.3. ∎

Lemma 8.15 (Indistinguishability between $H_{11}^{\text{op-sec}}$ and $H_{12}^{\text{op-sec}}$) *Under the assumptions of Theorem 8.2, $H_{11}^{\text{op-sec}} \stackrel{c}{\equiv} H_{12}^{\text{op-sec}}$ holds.*

Proof We introduce a sub-hybrid that splits between two cases why event *E5* is triggered: (1) $c_{\text{fix}}^{\text{out}^*} \neq c_{\text{fix}}$ and c_{fix} is not recorded in any $\overline{trdb} \in \overline{TRDB}$. (2) $c_{\text{fix}}^{\text{out}^*} \neq c_{\text{fix}}$ and c_{fix} is recorded in some record $\overline{trdb}^{\ddagger} \in \overline{TRDB}$. An environment $\mathcal{Z}^{\text{op-sec}}$ that can differentiate between $H_{11}^{\text{op-sec}}$ and the sub-hybrid yields an efficient adversary $\mathcal{B}$ against the EUF-CMA security of SIG. An environment $\mathcal{Z}^{\text{op-sec}}$ that can differentiate between the sub-hybrid and $H_{12}^{\text{op-sec}}$ yields an efficient adversary $\mathcal{B}$ against the binding property of C1.

(1) We construct an efficient adversary $\mathcal{B}$ against the EUF-CMA security of SIG. Internally, $\mathcal{B}$ runs $\mathcal{Z}^{\text{op-sec}}$ in its head, and plays the role of the simulator and all honest parties. Externally, $\mathcal{B}$ plays the EUF-CMA security experiment with a challenger C and a signing oracle $O^{\text{SIG}}_{pk_{\mathcal{O}}^{\text{fix}}, sk_{\mathcal{O}}^{\text{fix}}}$. When $\mathcal{B}$ must internally provide $pk_{\mathcal{O}} = (pk_{\mathcal{O}}^{\text{cert}}, pk_{\mathcal{O}}^{\text{upd}}, pk_{\mathcal{O}}^{\text{fix}}, pk_{\mathcal{O}}^{\text{rc,sig}}, pk_{\mathcal{O}}^{\text{rc,enc}})$ playing the role of $\mathcal{S}_{12}^{\text{op-sec}}$ in the scope of RegisterOp, $\mathcal{B}$ embeds the external challenge public key as $pk_{\mathcal{O}}^{\text{fix}}$. Whenever $\mathcal{B}$ playing the role of $\mathcal{S}_{12}^{\text{op-sec}}$ needs to issue signatures with respect to $pk_{\mathcal{O}}^{\text{fix}}$, it uses its external EUF-CMA oracle $O^{\text{SIG}}_{pk_{\mathcal{O}}^{\text{fix}}, sk_{\mathcal{O}}^{\text{fix}}}$. When the event (*E5*) occurs, $\mathcal{B}$ extracts c_{fix} and σ_{fix} from the proof and outputs the forgery.

(2) We construct an efficient adversary $\mathcal{B}$ against the binding property of C1. Internally, $\mathcal{B}$ runs $\mathcal{Z}^{\text{op-sec}}$ in its head and plays the role of the simulator and all honest parties. Externally, $\mathcal{B}$ plays the role of the adversary as defined by Definition 6.11, Item (2). As (*E5*) has not been raised earlier, $c_{\text{fix}}^{\text{out}(i)} = c_{\text{fix}}^{\text{out}^*} \neq c_{\text{fix}}$ holds for all $c_{\text{fix}}^{\text{out}(i)}$ in the same tree. Consequently, $\overline{trdb}^{\ddagger}$ with $c_{\text{fix}}^{\text{out}\ddagger} = c_{\text{fix}}$ is part of a different tree in $\overline{TRDB}$ and thus $\Lambda^{\ddagger} \neq \Lambda^* = \Lambda$ follows by Lemma 8.14. $\mathcal{B}$ sets

$$m_{\text{fix}} := (\Lambda, pk_{\mathcal{U}}) \tag{8.22}$$

from the extracted witness and obtains

$$m_{\text{fix}}^{\text{out}\ddagger} = (\Lambda^{\ddagger}, pk_{\mathcal{U}}^{\ddagger}) \tag{8.23}$$

from $\overline{TRDB}$. $\mathcal{B}$ outputs $(c_{\text{fix}}, m_{\text{fix}}, d_{\text{fix}}, m_{\text{fix}}^{\text{out}\ddagger}, d_{\text{fix}}^{\text{out}\ddagger})$ to the external game.

Remark 8.8 asserts that the forgery in (1) and both openings in (2) are indeed valid. ∎

Lemma 8.16 (Indistinguishability between $H_{12}^{\text{op-sec}}, H_{13}^{\text{op-sec}}, H_{14}^{\text{op-sec}}, H_{15}^{\text{op-sec}}$ and $H_{16}^{\text{op-sec}}$) *Under the assumptions of Theorem 8.2, $H_{12}^{\text{op-sec}} \stackrel{c}{\equiv} H_{13}^{\text{op-sec}} \stackrel{c}{\equiv} H_{14}^{\text{op-sec}} \stackrel{c}{\equiv} H_{15}^{\text{op-sec}} \stackrel{c}{\equiv} H_{16}^{\text{op-sec}}$ holds.*

Proof If an environment $\mathcal{Z}^{\text{op-sec}}$ can distinguish between any of the hops from $H_{12}^{\text{op-sec}}$ to $H_{16}^{\text{op-sec}}$ this yields an efficient adversary against the binding property of C1. As usual, $\mathcal{B}$ runs $\mathcal{Z}^{\text{op-sec}}$ in its head and internally plays the role of the simulator and all honest parties. Externally, $\mathcal{B}$ plays the role of the adversary as defined by Definition 6.11, Item (2). If event (*E7*) or (*E8*) occurs, $\mathcal{B}$ sets

$$m_{\text{upd}}^{\text{prev}} = (\Lambda, B^{\text{prev}}, U_1, g_1 X) \tag{8.24}$$

from the extracted witness and obtains

$$m_{\text{upd}}^{\text{out}\,*} := (\Lambda^*, B^*, U_1^*, X^*) \tag{8.25}$$

from $\overline{TRDB}$. $\mathcal{B}$ outputs $(c_{\text{upd}}, m_{\text{upd}}^{\text{prev}}, d_{\text{upd}}^{\text{prev}}, m_{\text{upd}}^{\text{out}\,*}, d_{\text{upd}}^{\text{out}\,*})$ to the external game. If the event (*E6*) is triggered, $\mathcal{B}$ proceeds analogous but for the fixed part of wallet c_{fix}. ■

Again, we interrupt the line of argument to summarize what we have so far. We know that $H_0^{\text{op-sec}} \overset{c}{\equiv} H_{16}^{\text{op-sec}}$ holds. From a high-level perspective, most of the previous hybrids ensured that corrupted users cannot fool the operator (or PoSes) within tasks that expand the transaction database, i.e. essentially within the main tasks IssueWallet, Deposit and Disburse.

The remaining hybrids from $H_{17}^{\text{op-sec}}$ to $H_{27}^{\text{op-sec}}$ largely considers modifications to the utility tasks with honest users being of special concern. The final simulator $\mathcal{S}^{\text{op-sec}}$ needs to provide various tags (ω_{ds}, ω_{bl}, ω_{rc} and ω_{pp}) to $\mathcal{F}_{\text{apc}}$ that are output by the main tasks and later re-used in the utility tasks. Until now, i.e. up to simulator $\mathcal{S}_{16}^{\text{op-sec}}$, real messages sent by users have been used to compile and record real tags (cp. hybrid $H_7^{\text{op-sec}}$). These have been played back when necessary. While little needs to be changed for corrupted users, the final simulator $\mathcal{S}^{\text{op-sec}}$ must provide these tags for honest users without having access to any messages. $H_{17}^{\text{op-sec}}$ to $H_{27}^{\text{op-sec}}$ introduce the necessary modifications.

Lemma 8.17 (Indistinguishability between $H_{16}^{\text{op-sec}}$ and $H_{17}^{\text{op-sec}}$) *Under the assumptions of Theorem 8.2, $H_{16}^{\text{op-sec}} \overset{c}{\equiv} H_{17}^{\text{op-sec}}$ holds.*

Proof We need to distinguish the same cases as in $\mathcal{S}^{\text{op-sec}}$.

If $\mathcal{Z}^{\text{op-sec}}$ calls DetectDS with two double-spending tags $\omega_{\text{ds}} = (\varphi, t, u_2)$, $\omega'_{\text{ds}} = (\varphi', t', u'_2)$ that do not stem from the system, do not match or are otherwise unusable, the hop is perfectly indistinguishable, because $\mathcal{S}_{17}^{\text{op-sec}}$ simply runs the same algorithm as the honest operator in the real game. At the bottom line, both calculate $sk_{\mathcal{U}} := (t - t')/(u_2 - u'_2) \bmod \mathfrak{p}$ and return the result. We stress that in both experiments—the real protocol and the ideal functionality—there is no guarantee that the returned $sk_{\mathcal{U}}$ is even a valid secret key. This follows the garbage-in-garbage-out principle.

We now consider genuine double-spending tags that have been output by the system before and match each other, i.e., they are distinct and have a common fraud-detection ID φ. In this case $\mathcal{S}_{17}^{\text{op-sec}}$ does not recover $sk_{\mathcal{U}}$ from the double-spending tags by calculation, but looks up the secret key $sk_{\mathcal{U}}^*$ that has been recorded in $\bar{f}_{\text{keys}}$ for $pid_{\mathcal{U}}$ and returns $\pi := sk_{\mathcal{U}}^*$ as a proof of guilt. The only way how $\mathcal{Z}^{\text{op-sec}}$ could possibly distinguish between $H_{16}^{\text{op-sec}}$ and $H_{17}^{\text{op-sec}}$ is that $sk_{\mathcal{U}} \neq sk_{\mathcal{U}}^*$ holds which entails $pk_{\mathcal{U}} \neq g_1^{sk_{\mathcal{U}}}$ or $pk_{\mathcal{U}} \neq g_1^{sk_{\mathcal{U}}^*}$. Intuitively, this attack means the environment has been able to let a user commit double-spending such that the generated double-spending tags do not allow to calculate a valid proof of guilt.

If the user is honest, the user's key has been generated by $\mathcal{S}_{17}^{\text{op-sec}}$ and recorded in $\bar{f}_{\text{keys}}$ ab initio. In particular, $pk_{\mathcal{U}} = g_1^{sk_{\mathcal{U}}^*}$ holds and the honest user always correctly answers the double-spending challenge. Simple math shows that $sk_{\mathcal{U}} := (t - t')/(u_2 - u_2') = ((u_2 sk_{\mathcal{U}}^* + u_1) - (u_2' sk_{\mathcal{U}}^* + u_1))/(u_2 - u_2') = sk_{\mathcal{U}}^*$ follows.

If the user is corrupted, the user's secret key is generated by the environment. In this case, $sk_{\mathcal{U}}^*$ is recovered by $\mathcal{S}_{17}^{\text{op-sec}}$ in the scope of Deposit or Disburse and recorded in $\bar{f}_{\text{keys}}$ due to the change in hybrid $H_8^{\text{op-sec}}$. $\mathcal{S}_8^{\text{op-sec}}$ uses the same equation during Deposit/Disburse to recover $sk_{\mathcal{U}}^*$ as the honest operator uses in DetectDS to recover $sk_{\mathcal{U}}$ in the real game. In other words, the recovery of the secret key is only brought forward from a belated double-spending detection in the real experiment to the point of time when the double-spending actually occurs in the simulated experiment. As the same equation is used, $sk_{\mathcal{U}}^* = sk_{\mathcal{U}}$ follows trivially, if the recovery has succeeded.

It remains to show, that $sk_{\mathcal{U}}^*$ is always successfully recovered, i.e. that the test $pk_{\mathcal{U}} = g_1^{sk_{\mathcal{U}}^*}$ (cp. Step 5 in Fig. 8.9 and Step 4 in Fig. 8.13) succeeds. In short, this holds due to the soundness of the NIZK and the binding property of C1. Otherwise hybrid $H_6^{\text{op-sec}}$ or hybrid $H_{16}^{\text{op-sec}}$ would already have aborted with event *E1* or *E9*, resp. More precisely, using Remark 8.8 we conclude that the two equations $T = pk_{\mathcal{U}}^{u_2} \cdot U_1$ and $T' = pk_{\mathcal{U}}^{u_2'} \cdot U_1$ with extracted $pk_{\mathcal{U}}$, T, T' and U_1 hold. Moreover, $T = g_1^t$, $T' = g_1^{t'}$ hold and t, t' as well as u_2, u_2' are known as part of the statement. By equating we obtain $T \cdot pk_{\mathcal{U}}^{-u_2} = T' \cdot pk_{\mathcal{U}}^{-u_2'}$ which yields $pk_{\mathcal{U}} = (TT'^{-1})^{1/(u_2 - u_2')} = g_1^{(t-t')/(u_2-u_2')} = g_1^{sk_{\mathcal{U}}^*}$. ■

Lemma 8.18 (Indistinguishability between $H_{17}^{\text{op-sec}}$ and $H_{18}^{\text{op-sec}}$) *Under the assumptions of Theorem 8.2, $H_{17}^{\text{op-sec}} \stackrel{c}{\equiv} H_{18}^{\text{op-sec}}$ holds.*

Proof VerifyGuilt is a local algorithm and does not send any messages. Hence, $\mathcal{Z}^{\text{op-sec}}$ can distinguish between $H_{17}^{\text{op-sec}}$ and $H_{18}^{\text{op-sec}}$, if and only if VerifyGuilt returns a different result bit for the same input.

First note, that $\mathcal{S}_{18}^{\text{op-sec}}$ still falls back to the real algorithm, if $\mathcal{Z}^{\text{op-sec}}$ calls VerifyGuilt with an input $(pid_{\mathcal{U}}, \pi)$ for a corrupted user and a π which is made-up by $\mathcal{Z}^{\text{op-sec}}$, i.e., if the internal map f_π of simulator $\mathcal{S}_{18}^{\text{op-sec}}$ is undefined (cp. Step 2 in Fig. 4.14). In this case $H_{18}^{\text{op-sec}}$ is perfectly indistinguishable from $H_{17}^{\text{op-sec}}$. In other words, $\mathcal{Z}^{\text{op-sec}}$ has to call VerifyGuilt for an honest user $pid_{\mathcal{U}}$ or for a genuine proof of guilt π, in order to trigger a distinguishing result bit, if at all.

Also note, that the real code and the ideal functionality are both deterministic. W.l.o.g. it therefore suffices to consider first-time invocations of VerifyGuilt for a particular input $(pid_{\mathcal{U}}, \pi)$. Under this restriction $f_\pi(pid_{\mathcal{U}}, \pi)$ is only defined, if it has been set in the scope of Deposit or Disburse (cp. Step 5 in Fig. 8.9 and Step 4 in Fig. 8.13) or in the scope of DetectDS (cp. Fig. 4.13). The necessary modifications have been introduced by hybrids $H_8^{\text{op-sec}}$ and $H_{17}^{\text{op-sec}}$, resp. However, we can ignore that $f_\pi(pid_{\mathcal{U}}, \pi)$ is solely defined, because VerifyGuilt is invoked a second time (cp. Step 4 in Fig. 4.14).

We discuss both cases for a different outcome separately.

VerifyGuilt$(pid_{\mathcal{U}}, \pi)$ *returns* NOK *in* $H_{17}^{\text{op-sec}}$ *(real code) but* OK *in* $H_{18}^{\text{op-sec}}$ *(ideal functionality):*
VerifyGuilt$(pid_{\mathcal{U}}, \pi)$ only returns OK in $H_{18}^{\text{op-sec}}$, if $f_\pi(pid_{\mathcal{U}}, \pi) = \text{OK}$ has been defined by Deposit, Disburse or DetectDS. In all three cases, the simulator provides a proof of guilt $\pi := sk_{\mathcal{U}}$ with $(pk_{\mathcal{U}}, sk_{\mathcal{U}}) := \bar{f}_{\text{keys}}(pid_{\mathcal{U}})$. We already know from the assertions made in the proof of Lemma 8.17 that $pk_{\mathcal{U}} = g_1^{sk_{\mathcal{U}}}$ holds for those key pairs recorded in $\bar{f}_{\text{keys}}$. However, if $pk_{\mathcal{U}} = g_1^{sk_{\mathcal{U}}}$ holds, then the real code of VerifyGuilt in $H_{17}^{\text{op-sec}}$ returns OK (cp. Fig. 7.24) which contradicts the initial assumption. We conclude, this case can never occur.

VerifyGuilt$(pid_{\mathcal{U}}, \pi)$ *returns* OK *in* $H_{17}^{\text{op-sec}}$ *(real code) but* NOK *in* $H_{18}^{\text{op-sec}}$ *(ideal functionality):*
As VerifyGuilt running the real code returns OK, $pk_{\mathcal{U}} = g_1^{\pi}$ holds. As VerifyGuilt in $H_{18}^{\text{op-sec}}$ returns NOK, we conclude that $f_\pi(pid_{\mathcal{U}}, \pi)$ is undefined and using the introductory remarks this implies that the user with $pid_{\mathcal{U}}$ is honest. (Remember: For an undefined $f_\pi(pid_{\mathcal{U}}, \pi)$ and a corrupted user, $H_{18}^{\text{op-sec}}$ falls back to the real code.) If $f_\pi(pid_{\mathcal{U}}, \pi)$ was defined in $H_{18}^{\text{op-sec}}$, then it had to be defined as OK, because we excluded repeated invocations of VerifyGuilt and Deposit or Disburse only define f_π in positive cases. The latter immediately contradicts, that VerifyGuilt returns NOK in $H_{18}^{\text{op-sec}}$. The same observation also yields that the user under consideration does not commit double-spending or otherwise the simulator would have defined $f_\pi(pid_{\mathcal{U}}, \pi) = \text{OK}$ in the scope of Deposit or Disburse.

In summary, VerifyGuilt$(pid_{\mathcal{U}}, \pi)$ returns OK in $H_{17}^{\text{op-sec}}$ but NOK in $H_{18}^{\text{op-sec}}$ if and only if there is an environment $\mathcal{Z}^{\text{op-sec}}$ that comes up with a correct proof of guilt $\pi = sk_{\mathcal{U}}$ for a *honest* user without letting this user commit double-spending. This immediately yields an efficient adversary $\mathcal{B}$ against the DLOG assumption.

Externally, $\mathcal{B}$ gets a group element $g \in G_1$ as its input. Internally, $\mathcal{B}$ runs $\mathcal{Z}^{\text{op-sec}}$ in its head and plays the role of the simulator and all honest parties. $\mathcal{B}$ guesses the honest user for that $\mathcal{Z}^{\text{op-sec}}$ eventually calls the distinguishing VerifyGuilt. When $\mathcal{B}$ has to internally provide $pk_{\mathcal{U}}$ in the scope of RegisterUser, it uses $pk_{\mathcal{U}} = g$. Note, that $\mathcal{B}$ does not need to know $sk_{\mathcal{U}}$ for a successful simulation. As the user is honest, all PoS and operator are honest, too.[9] Hence, for this particular user no messages need to be simulated. When $\mathcal{Z}^{\text{op-sec}}$ calls VerifyGuilt with a correct $\pi := sk_{\mathcal{U}}$, $\mathcal{B}$ outputs $sk_{\mathcal{U}}$ as the DLOG. ■

Lemma 8.19 (Indistinguishability between $H_{18}^{\text{op-sec}}$ and $H_{19}^{\text{op-sec}}$) *Under the assumptions of Theorem 8.2, $H_{18}^{\text{op-sec}} \stackrel{c}{\equiv} H_{19}^{\text{op-sec}}$ holds.*

Proof This hop is perfectly indistinguishable from the environment's perspective as the modifications made by hybrid $H_{19}^{\text{op-sec}}$ do not change the output. Note that operator and dispute resolver are both honest. Due to the correctness of ENC1 the ciphertext ω_{bl} determines a unique message (for a fix key pair pk_{DR}, sk_{DR}). Hence, the originally recorded wallet ID $\lambda := f_{\Omega_{\text{bl}}}^{-1}(\omega_{\text{bl}})$ equals the one that ω_{bl} decrypts to. ■

Lemma 8.20 (Indistinguishability between $H_{19}^{\text{op-sec}}$ and $H_{20}^{\text{op-sec}}$) *Under the assumptions of Theorem 8.2, $H_{19}^{\text{op-sec}} \stackrel{c}{\equiv} H_{20}^{\text{op-sec}}$ holds.*

Proof The task RecalculateBalance is an algorithm that locally executed by the operator and the operator is honest. The hop is perfectly indistinguishable from the environment's perspective as the modifications made by hybrid $H_{20}^{\text{op-sec}}$ do not change the output using the same argument as for the previous hop. The set of recalculation tags $\Omega_{\text{rc}} = \Omega_{\text{rc}}^{\text{genuine}} \uplus \Omega_{\text{rc}}^{\text{fake}}$ is partitioned into two disjoint subsets. Due to the correctness of ENC2 looking up the original recorded cleartext $\psi_{\text{rc}}^{\text{genuine}}$ for a $\omega_{\text{rc}}^{\text{genuine}} \in \Omega_{\text{rc}}^{\text{genuine}}$ yields the same result as actual decryption. The treatment of $\Omega_{\text{rc}}^{\text{fake}}$ is not changed at all. ■

Lemma 8.21 (Indistinguishability between $H_{20}^{\text{op-sec}}$ and $H_{21}^{\text{op-sec}}$) *Under the assumptions of Theorem 8.2, $H_{20}^{\text{op-sec}} \stackrel{c}{\equiv} H_{21}^{\text{op-sec}}$ holds.*

Proof Assume there is an environment $\mathcal{Z}^{\text{op-sec}}$ that triggers event *E10* with non-negligible probability. This immediately yields an efficient adversary $\mathcal{B}$ against the EUF-CMA security of SIG. Internally, $\mathcal{B}$ runs $\mathcal{Z}^{\text{op-sec}}$ in its head and plays the role of the simulator and all honest parties. Externally, $\mathcal{B}$ plays the EUF-CMA security game with a challenger C and a signing

[9] This is a consequence of the considered corruption model. In the case of operator security, corrupted PoSes are only admissible, if all users are corrupted.

oracle $O^{\mathsf{SIG}}_{pk^{\mathrm{pp}}_{\mathcal{P}}, sk^{\mathrm{pp}}_{\mathcal{P}}}$. $\mathcal{B}$ needs to guess the honest PoS with $pid_{\mathcal{P}}$ for which the environment $\mathcal{Z}^{\text{op-sec}}$ eventually forges a signature while it plays a corrupted user who tries to prove its participation in a transaction with this particular PoS towards an honest violation enforcer. When the PoS with $pid_{\mathcal{P}}$ registers itself in the scope of RegisterPOS and $\mathcal{B}$ playing $\mathcal{S}^{\text{op-sec}}_{21}$ needs to provide $pk_{\mathcal{P}} = (pk^{\mathrm{upd}}_{\mathcal{P}}, pk^{\mathrm{rc}}_{\mathcal{P}}, pk^{\mathrm{pp}}_{\mathcal{P}})$ it embeds the external challenge public key as $pk^{\mathrm{pp}}_{\mathcal{P}}$. Whenever $\mathcal{B}$ playing the role of $\mathcal{S}^{\text{op-sec}}_{21}$ needs to issue a signature with respect to $pk^{\mathrm{pp}}_{\mathcal{P}}$, it uses its external EUF-CMA oracle $O^{\mathsf{SIG}}_{pk^{\mathrm{pp}}_{\mathcal{P}}, sk^{\mathrm{pp}}_{\mathcal{P}}}$. When the event *E10* occurs, $\mathcal{B}$ extracts $c_{pk_{\mathcal{U}}}$ from ω_{pp} and σ_{pp} from ψ_{pp} and outputs the forgery. N.b., the $c_{pk_{\mathcal{U}}}$ has never been signed with respect to $pk^{\mathrm{pp}}_{\mathcal{P}}$ by assumption as otherwise $\bar{f}_{\mathrm{pp}}$ would have been defined for the pair $\omega_{\mathrm{pp}}, \psi_{\mathrm{pp}}$ and the event *E10* would not have been triggered. ∎

Lemma 8.22 (Indistinguishability between $H^{\text{op-sec}}_{21}$ and $H^{\text{op-sec}}_{22}$) *Under the assumptions of Theorem 8.2, $H^{\text{op-sec}}_{21} \stackrel{c}{\equiv} H^{\text{op-sec}}_{22}$ holds.*

Proof Assume there is an environment $\mathcal{Z}^{\text{op-sec}}$ that triggers event *E11* with non-negligible probability. This immediately yields an efficient adversary $\mathcal{B}$ against the binding property of C2. Internally, $\mathcal{B}$ runs $\mathcal{Z}^{\text{op-sec}}$ in its head and plays the role of the simulator and all honest parties. When the event *E11* occurs, $\mathcal{B}$ extracts $c_{pk_{\mathcal{U}}}$ from ω_{pp}, gathers the current public key $pk_{\mathcal{U}}$ of the user it currently interacts with and the provided decommitment $d_{pk_{\mathcal{U}}}$, looks up the original public key $pk^{*}_{\mathcal{U}}$ and original decommitment $d^{*}_{pk_{\mathcal{U}}}$ that have been recorded by f_{pp} and outputs $(c_{pk_{\mathcal{U}}}, d_{pk_{\mathcal{U}}}, pk_{\mathcal{U}})$ and $(c_{pk_{\mathcal{U}}}, d^{*}_{pk_{\mathcal{U}}}, pk^{*}_{\mathcal{U}})$. Note, $pk_{\mathcal{U}} \neq pk^{*}_{\mathcal{U}}$ holds and both openings are valid by assumption. ∎

Lemma 8.23 (Indistinguishability between $H^{\text{op-sec}}_{22}$ and $H^{\text{op-sec}}_{23}$) *Under the assumptions of Theorem 8.2, $H^{\text{op-sec}}_{22} \stackrel{c}{\equiv} H^{\text{op-sec}}_{23}$ holds.*

Proof At the bottom line this hop only changes what part of code is executed by which entity, i.e. the hop is perfectly indistinguishable from the perspective of $\mathcal{Z}^{\text{op-sec}}$.

This is obvious in the case of an honest user and a corrupted violation enforcer. Honest users always send the true decommitment information that originally belongs to their prove-participation tag and they only do so for prove-participation tags that are their own ones. This is exactly what the simulator does on behalf of the dummy user.

In case of a corrupted user and an honest violation enforcer the only way for $\mathcal{Z}^{\text{op-sec}}$ to distinguish between $H^{\text{op-sec}}_{22}$ and $H^{\text{op-sec}}_{23}$ is to make the honest violation enforcer output a different result bit. In summary, this is impossible due to the sanity checks that have been introduced in $H^{\text{op-sec}}_{21}$ and $H^{\text{op-sec}}_{22}$. The detailed argument considers the branches of the program flow individually. If the signature is invalid, i.e. $\mathsf{SIG.Vfy}(pk^{\mathrm{pp}}_{\mathcal{P}}, \sigma_{\mathrm{pp}}, c_{pk_{\mathcal{U}}}) = 0$ holds, or the decommitment fails, i.e. $\mathsf{C2.Open}(crs^{(2)}_{\mathrm{com}}, pk_{\mathcal{U}}, c_{pk_{\mathcal{U}}}, d_{pk_{\mathcal{U}}}) = 0$ holds, the simulator calls the ideal functionality with input $\omega_{\mathrm{pp}} = \bot$ (cp. Step 3f in Fig. 8.17) and the ideal functionality always outputs *result* = NOK to *VE*. The real code also returns *result* = NOK under the same condition. We now consider the case that the simulator runs the ideal code with an input $\omega_{\mathrm{pp}} \neq \bot$. Step 3i in Fig. 8.17 is only reached, if the conditions of Steps 3f to 3h failed all. Formally, this means

$$\begin{aligned}\neg\Big(& \big(\psi_{\mathrm{pp}} = \bot \vee \mathsf{Vfy}(pk_{\mathcal{P}}^{\mathrm{pp}}, \sigma_{\mathrm{pp}}, c_{pk_{\mathcal{U}}}) = 0 \vee \mathsf{Open}(crs_{\mathrm{com}}^{(2)}, pk_{\mathcal{U}}, c_{pk_{\mathcal{U}}}, d_{pk_{\mathcal{U}}}) = 0\big) \\ & \vee \big(\psi_{\mathrm{pp}}^{*} = \bot \wedge pid_{\mathcal{P}} \notin \mathcal{PID}_{\mathrm{corr}}\big) \\ & \vee \big(\mathsf{Open}(crs_{\mathrm{com}}^{(2)}, pk_{\mathcal{U}}, c_{pk_{\mathcal{U}}}, d_{pk_{\mathcal{U}}}) = 1 \wedge pk_{\mathcal{U}} \neq pk_{\mathcal{U}}^{*}\big)\Big)\end{aligned} \tag{8.27}$$

holds. After simplification (note that some parts cancel out due to inverse conditions on Open)

$$\begin{aligned}& \psi_{\mathrm{pp}} \neq \bot \wedge \mathsf{Vfy}(pk_{\mathcal{P}}^{\mathrm{pp}}, \sigma_{\mathrm{pp}}, c_{pk_{\mathcal{U}}}) = 1 \wedge \mathsf{Open}(crs_{\mathrm{com}}^{(2)}, pk_{\mathcal{U}}, c_{pk_{\mathcal{U}}}, d_{pk_{\mathcal{U}}}) = 1 \\ & \wedge pk_{\mathcal{U}} = pk_{\mathcal{U}}^{*} \wedge (\psi_{\mathrm{pp}}^{*} \neq \bot \vee pid_{\mathcal{P}} \in \mathcal{PID}_{\mathrm{corr}})\end{aligned} \tag{8.29}$$

remains. We further note, that $pk_{\mathcal{U}} = pk_{\mathcal{U}}^{*}$ implies $\omega_{\mathrm{pp}}^{*} \neq \bot$, or inversely stated, if ω_{pp}^{*} was invalid, then $pk_{\mathcal{U}}^{*}$ would be undefined, too. Hence, the last predicate inside the or-bracket is irrelevant and can be dropped. Also, we exploit that $pk_{\mathcal{U}} = pk_{\mathcal{U}}^{*}$ can equivalently be substituted by $pid_{\mathcal{U}} = pid_{\mathcal{U}}^{*}$ and we finally obtain

$$\begin{aligned}& \psi_{\mathrm{pp}} \neq \bot \wedge \mathsf{Vfy}(pk_{\mathcal{P}}^{\mathrm{pp}}, \sigma_{\mathrm{pp}}, c_{pk_{\mathcal{U}}}) = 1 \wedge \mathsf{Open}(crs_{\mathrm{com}}^{(2)}, pk_{\mathcal{U}}, c_{pk_{\mathcal{U}}}, d_{pk_{\mathcal{U}}}) = 1 \\ & \wedge \psi_{\mathrm{pp}}^{*} \neq \bot \wedge pid_{\mathcal{U}} = pid_{\mathcal{U}}^{*}\end{aligned} \tag{8.31}$$

The first line of this expression is exactly the condition under that the real code returns *result* = OK, the last line is the condition under that the ideal functionality returns OK. ■

Lemma 8.24 (Indistinguishability between $H_{23}^{\text{op-sec}}$ and $H_{24}^{\text{op-sec}}$) *Under the assumptions of Theorem 8.2, $H_{23}^{\text{op-sec}} \stackrel{c}{\equiv} H_{24}^{\text{op-sec}}$ holds.*

Proof In this hop all encryptions ψ_{bl} of wallet IDs λ are replaced by encryptions of a 1-vector for all honest users. This does not change the output of an honest operator, as $H_{19}^{\text{op-sec}}$ has eliminated their decryption.

We further split this hop into a sequence of sub-hybrids, with each sub-hybrid replacing a single encryption in reverse order of appearance. Assume $\mathcal{Z}^{\text{op-sec}}$ can distinguish between $H_{23}^{\text{op-sec}}$ and $H_{24}^{\text{op-sec}}$ with non-negligible advantage. This yields an efficient adversary $\mathcal{B}$ against the IND-CCA security of the encryption scheme ENC1. Internally, $\mathcal{B}$ runs $\mathcal{Z}^{\text{op-sec}}$ and plays the role of all parties and the simulator for $\mathcal{Z}^{\text{op-sec}}$. Externally, $\mathcal{B}$ plays the IND-CCA security game with a challenger C and a decryption oracle $O_{pk_{\mathcal{DR}}, sk_{\mathcal{DR}}}^{\mathsf{ENC1}}$. When $\mathcal{B}$—playing the role of the simulator—needs to provide the public key in the scope of RegisterDR, it embeds the challenge key pk_{DR}. $\mathcal{B}$ needs to guess the index of the sub-hybrid that causes a non-negligible difference, i.e., $\mathcal{B}$ needs to guess which (user) wallet causes distinguishability. For the first $(i-1)$ invocations of IssueWallet, $\mathcal{B}$ encrypts the true seed, in the ith invocation $\mathcal{B}$ embeds the external challenge and $\mathcal{B}$ encrypts a 1-vector for the remaining invocations of IssueWallet. If $\mathcal{Z}^{\text{op-sec}}$ invokes the task BlacklistWallet between O and VE and $\mathcal{B}$ needs to restore the wallet ID, the following two cases may occur: (1) The presented blacklisting tag ω_{bl} is genuine. In this case $\mathcal{B}$ uses the lookup table $f_{\Omega_{\text{bl}}}^{-1}$ that has been edified in $H_7^{\text{op-sec}}$ to recover the original wallet ID λ and thereby the correct set of fraud-detection IDs (cp. hybrid $H_{19}^{\text{op-sec}}$). (2) The presented blacklisting tag ω_{bl} is a fake. In this case $\mathcal{B}$ uses its decryption oracle $O^{\text{ENC1}}_{pk_{DR}, sk_{DR}}$ to restore the wallet ID λ and to create a set of fraud-detection IDs. $\mathcal{B}$ outputs whatever $\mathcal{Z}^{\text{op-sec}}$ outputs. ∎

Lemma 8.25 (Indistinguishability between $H_{24}^{\text{op-sec}}$ and $H_{25}^{\text{op-sec}}$) *Under the assumptions of Theorem 8.2, $H_{24}^{\text{op-sec}} \stackrel{c}{\equiv} H_{25}^{\text{op-sec}}$ holds.*

Proof This hop is perfectly indistinguishable. As long as no double-spending occurs, the user chooses a fresh u_1 in every transaction and thus a single point (u_2, t) is information-theoretically independent from $sk_{\mathcal{U}}$. ∎

Lemma 8.26 (Indistinguishability between $H_{25}^{\text{op-sec}}$ and $H_{26}^{\text{op-sec}}$) *Under the assumptions of Theorem 8.2, $H_{25}^{\text{op-sec}} \stackrel{c}{\equiv} H_{26}^{\text{op-sec}}$ holds.*

Proof This hop only replaces the encryption of recalculation tags, if the operator is honest. If the operator is corrupted, the hop only changes what part of the code are executed by which entity and the hop is perfectly indistinguishable.

If there is an environment $\mathcal{Z}^{\text{op-sec}}$ that can efficiently distinguish with non-negligible advantage this yields an adversary $\mathcal{B}$ against the IND-CCA security of ENC2. The proof is analogous to the proof of Lemma 8.24, but for the operator instead of the violation enforcer and blacklisting tags replaced by recalculation tags.

Externally, $\mathcal{B}$ plays the IND-CCA security game with a challenger C and a decryption oracle $O^{\text{ENC2}}_{pk_O^{\text{rc,enc}}, sk_O^{\text{rc,enc}}}$. When $\mathcal{B}$—playing the role of the simulator—needs to provide the public key $pk_O = (pk_O^{\text{cert}}, pk_O^{\text{upd}}, pk_O^{\text{fix}}, pk_O^{\text{rc,sig}}, pk_O^{\text{rc,enc}})$ in the scope of RegisterOp, it embeds the challenge key $pk_O^{\text{rc,enc}}$. $\mathcal{B}$ needs to guess the index of the sub-hybrid that causes a non-negligible difference, i.e., $\mathcal{B}$ needs to guess which recalculation tag causes distinguishability. For the first $(i-1)$ invocations of Deposit and Disburse, $\mathcal{B}$ encrypts a true recalculation tag, in the ith invocation $\mathcal{B}$ embeds the external challenge and $\mathcal{B}$ encrypts an arbitrary, but fixed value for the remaining invocations of Deposit and Disburse. If $\mathcal{Z}^{\text{op-sec}}$ invokes the task RecalculateBalance for O, the following two cases may occur: (1) The presented recalculation tag ω_{bl} is genuine. In this case

$\mathcal{B}$ uses the simulated transaction database $\overline{TRDB}$ that has been edified in $H_7^{\text{op-sec}}$ to recover the original values $(s, \varphi, pid_{\mathcal{P}}, p)$ (cp. hybrid $H_{20}^{\text{op-sec}}$). (2) The presented recalculation tag ω_{bl} is a fake. In this case $\mathcal{B}$ uses its decryption oracle $O^{\text{ENC2}}_{pk_{\mathcal{O}}^{\text{rc,enc}}, sk_{\mathcal{O}}^{\text{rc,enc}}}$ to restore the necessary values. $\mathcal{B}$ outputs whatever $\mathcal{Z}^{\text{op-sec}}$ outputs. ∎

Lemma 8.27 (Indistinguishability between $H_{26}^{\text{op-sec}}$ and $H_{27}^{\text{op-sec}}$) *Under the assumptions of Theorem 8.2, $H_{26}^{\text{op-sec}} \stackrel{c}{\equiv} H_{27}^{\text{op-sec}}$ holds.*

Proof In this hop the simulator $\mathcal{S}_{27}^{\text{op-sec}}$ sends simulated commitments $c_{pk_{\mathcal{U}}}$ as prove-participation tags ω_{pp} for honest user. In case the violation enforcer is corrupted, simulator $\mathcal{S}_{27}^{\text{op-sec}}$ equivocates these commitments to the correct $pk_{\mathcal{U}}$ on demand, when $\mathcal{Z}^{\text{op-sec}}$ calls ProveParticipation for an honest user and an affected ω_{pp}. If $\mathcal{Z}^{\text{op-sec}}$ has a non-negligible advantage to distinguish between $H_{26}^{\text{op-sec}}$ and $H_{27}^{\text{op-sec}}$, then an efficient adversary $\mathcal{B}$ can be constructed against the hiding property and equivocality of C2. Again, this proof proceeds in a series of sub-hybrids with each sub-hybrid replacing a single $c_{pk_{\mathcal{U}}}$ by a simulated commitment. ∎

Taking all the aforementioned statements together, Theorem 8.2 from the beginning of this section follows. For the sake of formal completeness, we recall it again.

Theorem 8.2 (Operator Security) *Under the assumptions of Theorem 8.1*

$$\pi_{\text{P5C}}^{\mathcal{F}_{\text{CRS}}, \mathcal{F}_{\text{bb}}, \mathcal{F}_{\text{msg}}} \geq_{\text{UC}} \mathcal{F}_{\text{apc}} \tag{8.3}$$

holds under static corruption of

(1) a subset of users, or

(2) all users and a subset of PoSes, operator and violation enforcer.

Proof A direct consequence of Lemmas 8.4 to 8.27. ∎

8.4 Proof of User Security and Privacy

In this section we show the remaining half of Theorem 8.1 by proofing the the following theorem.

Theorem 8.28 (User Security and Privacy) *Under the assumptions of Theorem 8.1*

$$\pi_{\text{P5C}}^{\mathcal{F}_{\text{CRS}}, \mathcal{F}_{\text{bb}}, \mathcal{F}_{\text{msg}}} \geq_{\text{UC}} \mathcal{F}_{\text{apc}} \tag{8.32}$$

holds under static corruption of

Simulator $\mathcal{S}^{\text{user-sec}}_{\pi_{\text{P5C}}}$

Setup: (1) Run a modified version of the algorithm $crs \leftarrow \text{Setup}(1^n)$ with

(a) $crs^{(2)}_{\text{com}} \leftarrow \text{C2.Setup}$ being replaced by $(crs^{(2)}_{\text{com}}, td_{\text{eqcom}}) \leftarrow \text{C2.SetupSim}$,

(b) $crs^{(4)}_{\text{com}} \leftarrow \text{C4.Setup}$ being replaced by $(crs^{(4)}_{\text{com}}, td_{\text{extcom}}) \leftarrow \text{C4.SetupExt}$, and

(c) $crs_{\text{pok}} \leftarrow \text{POK.Setup}$ being replaced by $(crs_{\text{pok}}, td_{\text{spok}}) \leftarrow \text{POK.SetupSim}$.

(2) Record crs, td_{eqcom}, td_{extcom}, and td_{spok}.

(3) Set $\bar{f}_{\text{keys}} : \mathcal{PID} \rightarrow \{0,1\}^*$ to the "empty" map.

(4) Set $\bar{f}_{\text{pp}} : \Omega_{\text{pp}} \rightarrow \Psi_{\text{pp}} \times \{0,1\}^*$ to the "empty" map.

The internal copy of $\mathcal{F}_{\text{msg}}$: $\mathcal{S}^{\text{user-sec}}_{\pi_{\text{P5C}}}$ runs an internal instance of $\mathcal{F}_{\text{msg}}$ in its head and proceeds as follows:

(1) Upon receiving input of the form (`establish-session`, ...), (`accept`, ...), (`send`, ...) or (`close`, ...) from $\mathcal{Z}^{\text{user-sec}}$ for $\mathcal{F}_{\text{msg}}$ in the name of a *corrupted* party, $\mathcal{S}^{\text{user-sec}}_{\pi_{\text{P5C}}}$ forwards this input to its internal instance of $\mathcal{F}_{\text{msg}}$ in the name of the same party.

(2) Upon receiving output of the form (`establishing-session`, ...), (`accepted`, ...), (`sent`, ...) or (`closed`, ...) from its internal instance of $\mathcal{F}_{\text{msg}}$ for a *corrupted* party, $\mathcal{S}^{\text{user-sec}}_{\pi_{\text{P5C}}}$ forwards this output to $\mathcal{Z}^{\text{user-sec}}$.

(3) Upon receiving leakage from its internal copy instance of $\mathcal{F}_{\text{msg}}$ for an adversary, $\mathcal{S}^{\text{user-sec}}_{\pi_{\text{P5C}}}$ forwards this leakage to $\mathcal{Z}^{\text{user-sec}}$ as the real dummy adversary would do.

(4) Upon receiving output of the form (`establishing-session`, ...), (`accepted`, ...), (`sent`, ...) or (`closed`, ...) from its internal instance of $\mathcal{F}_{\text{msg}}$ for an *honest* party, $\mathcal{S}^{\text{user-sec}}_{\pi_{\text{P5C}}}$ handles this output internally as desribed below in detail.

Figure 8.19: The Simulator for User Security and Privacy

(1) a subset of PoSes, operator and violation enforcer, or

(2) all PoSes, operator and violation enforcer as well as a subset of users.

The definition of the UC-simulator $\mathcal{S}^{\text{user-sec}}_{\pi_{\text{P5C}}}$ for Theorem 8.28 can be found in Figs. 8.19 to 8.34. Please note that while the real protocol π_{P5C} lives in the $(\mathcal{F}_{\text{CRS}}, \mathcal{F}_{\text{bb}}, \mathcal{F}_{\text{msg}})$-model, the ideal functionality $\mathcal{F}_{\text{apc}}$ has no CRS. The CRS is simulated, providing $\mathcal{S}^{\text{user-sec}}_{\pi_{\text{P5C}}}$ with a lever to simulate the ZK proofs P1, P2, and P3, to equivocate C2, and to extract C4.

As before, we define a sequence of hybrid experiments $H^{\text{user-sec}}_i$ together with simulators $\mathcal{S}^{\text{user-sec}}_i$ and protocols $\pi^{\text{user-sec}}_i$ such that the first hybrid H_0 is identical to the real experiment and the last protocol π_{18} is identical to the ideal experiment. The general proof strategy is

Simulator $\mathcal{S}^{\text{user-sec}}_{\pi_{\text{P5C}}}$

RegisterDR *(for honest dispute resolver):* Upon receiving leakage ($\texttt{registering\_dr}, pid_{DR}$) from $\mathcal{F}_{\text{apc}}$ and if $\bar{f}_{\text{keys}}(pid_{DR})$ is undefined, run $(pk_{DR}, sk_{DR}) \leftarrow \text{RegisterDR}(crs)$, and append $pid_{DR} \mapsto (pk_{DR}, sk_{DR})$ to $\bar{f}_{\text{keys}}$.

RegisterOp *(for honest operator):* Upon receiving leakage ($\texttt{registering\_op}, pid_{O}, a_{O}$) from $\mathcal{F}_{\text{apc}}$ and if $\bar{f}_{\text{keys}}(pid_{O})$ is undefined, run $(pk_{O}, sk_{O}, cert_{O}) \leftarrow \text{RegisterOp}(crs, a_{O})$, and append $pid_{O} \mapsto (pk_{O}, sk_{O}, cert_{O})$ to $\bar{f}_{\text{keys}}$.

RegisterOp *(for corrupted operator):* Upon receiving input ($\texttt{register}, pk_{O}$) from $\mathcal{Z}^{\text{user-sec}}$ for $\mathcal{F}_{\text{bb}}$ in the name of O with PID pid_{O}, and if $\bar{f}_{\text{keys}}(pid_{O})$ is undefined, call $\mathcal{F}_{\text{apc}}$ with input ($\texttt{register}$) in the name of O with PID pid_{O}, ignore the subsequent leak ($\texttt{registering\_op}, pid_{O}$) from $\mathcal{F}_{\text{apc}}$ and append $pid_{O} \mapsto (pk_{O}, \bot, \bot)$ to $\bar{f}_{\text{keys}}$.[a]

RegisterPOS *(for honest PoS):* Upon receiving leakage ($\texttt{registering\_pos}, pid_{\mathcal{P}}$) from $\mathcal{F}_{\text{apc}}$ and if $\bar{f}_{\text{keys}}(pid_{\mathcal{P}})$ is undefined, run $(pk_{\mathcal{P}}, sk_{\mathcal{P}}) \leftarrow \text{RegisterPOS}(crs)$, and append $pid_{\mathcal{P}} \mapsto (pk_{\mathcal{P}}, sk_{\mathcal{P}}, \bot)$ to $\bar{f}_{\text{keys}}$.

RegisterPOS *(for corrupted PoS):* Upon receiving input ($\texttt{register}, pk_{\mathcal{P}}$) from $\mathcal{Z}^{\text{user-sec}}$ for $\mathcal{F}_{\text{bb}}$ in the name of $\mathcal{P}$ with PID $pid_{\mathcal{P}}$, and if $\bar{f}_{\text{keys}}(pid_{\mathcal{P}})$ is undefined, call $\mathcal{F}_{\text{apc}}$ with input ($\texttt{register}$) in the name of $\mathcal{P}$ with PID $pid_{\mathcal{P}}$, ignore the subsequent leak ($\texttt{registering\_pos}, pid_{\mathcal{P}}$) from $\mathcal{F}_{\text{apc}}$ and append $pid_{\mathcal{P}} \mapsto (pk_{\mathcal{P}}, \bot, \bot)$ to $\bar{f}_{\text{keys}}$.[b]

RegisterUser *(for honest user):* Upon receiving leakage ($\texttt{registering\_user}, pid_{\mathcal{U}}$) from $\mathcal{F}_{\text{apc}}$ and if $\bar{f}_{\text{keys}}(pid_{\mathcal{U}})$ is undefined, run $(pk_{\mathcal{U}}, sk_{\mathcal{U}}) \leftarrow \text{RegisterUser}(crs)$, and append $pid_{\mathcal{U}} \mapsto (pk_{\mathcal{U}}, sk_{\mathcal{U}})$ to $\bar{f}_{\text{keys}}$.

[a] A corrupted operator essentially has two options: It can either register "some" public key at the bulletin board or not. (N.b., the public key does not need to be honestly generated.) If it registers its public key, then it is regarded as registered from the perspective of the real protocols. Hence, the simulator must also register the operator with $\mathcal{F}_{\text{apc}}$, otherwise $\mathcal{F}_{\text{apc}}$ would subsequently abort, but the real protocols do not.

[b] Corrupted PoSes essentially have two options: They can either register "some" public key at the bulletin board or not. (N.b., the public key does not need to be honestly generated.) If they register their public keys, then they are regarded as registered from the perspective of the real protocols. Hence, the simulator must also register the PoSes with $\mathcal{F}_{\text{apc}}$, otherwise $\mathcal{F}_{\text{apc}}$ would subsequently abort, but the real protocols do not.

Figure 8.20: The Simulator for User Security and Privacy (cont. from Fig. 8.19)

Simulator $\mathcal{S}^{\text{user-sec}}_{\pi_{\text{P5C}}}$

CertifyPOS *(for honest operator and honest PoS):* Upon receiving leakage (`certifying_pos`, $pid_{\mathcal{P}}, a_{\mathcal{P}}$) from $\mathcal{F}_{\text{apc}}$ ...

(1) Set $(pk_{\mathcal{O}}, sk_{\mathcal{O}}, cert_{\mathcal{O}}) := \bar{f}_{\text{keys}}(pid_{\mathcal{O}})$ and $(pk_{\mathcal{P}}, sk_{\mathcal{P}}, cert^{\text{prev}}_{\mathcal{P}}) := \bar{f}_{\text{keys}}(pid_{\mathcal{P}})$.[a]

(2) Generate $cert_{\mathcal{P}} := (pk_{\mathcal{P}}, a_{\mathcal{P}}, \sigma^{\text{cert}}_{\mathcal{P}})$ with $\sigma^{\text{cert}}_{\mathcal{P}} \leftarrow \text{SIG.Sign}(sk^{\text{cert}}_{\mathcal{O}}, (pk_{\mathcal{P}}, a_{\mathcal{P}}))$ faithfully.

(3) Re-define $\bar{f}_{\text{keys}}(pid_{\mathcal{P}}) := (pk_{\mathcal{P}}, sk_{\mathcal{P}}, cert_{\mathcal{P}})$ and let $\mathcal{F}_{\text{apc}}$ continue.

CertifyPOS *(for honest operator and corrupted PoS):* (1) Upon receiving output (`establishing-session`, $ssid, pid_{\mathcal{P}}$, `certify_pos`) from $\mathcal{F}^{\text{sim}}_{\text{msg}}$ for $\mathcal{O}$, call $\mathcal{F}_{\text{apc}}$ with input (`certify_pos`) in the name of $\mathcal{P}$ with $pid_{\mathcal{P}}$.

(2) Upon receiving leakage (`certifying_pos`, $pid_{\mathcal{P}}, a_{\mathcal{P}}$) from $\mathcal{F}_{\text{apc}}$ ...

  (a) Set $(pk_{\mathcal{O}}, sk_{\mathcal{O}}, cert_{\mathcal{O}}) := \bar{f}_{\text{keys}}(pid_{\mathcal{O}})$ and $(pk_{\mathcal{P}}, \perp, cert^{\text{prev}}_{\mathcal{P}}) := \bar{f}_{\text{keys}}(pid_{\mathcal{P}})$.[b]

  (b) Call $\mathcal{F}^{\text{sim}}_{\text{msg}}$ with input (`accept`, $ssid$) in the name of $\mathcal{O}$.

(3) Upon being requested by $\mathcal{Z}^{\text{user-sec}}$ to provide the 1st message from $\mathcal{O}$ to $\mathcal{P}$ ...

  (a) Generate $cert_{\mathcal{P}} := (pk_{\mathcal{P}}, a_{\mathcal{P}}, \sigma^{\text{cert}}_{\mathcal{P}})$ with $\sigma^{\text{cert}}_{\mathcal{P}} \leftarrow \text{SIG.Sign}(sk^{\text{cert}}_{\mathcal{O}}, (pk_{\mathcal{P}}, a_{\mathcal{P}}))$ faithfully.

  (b) Redefine $\bar{f}_{\text{keys}}(pid_{\mathcal{P}}) := (pk_{\mathcal{P}}, \perp, cert_{\mathcal{P}})$.

  (c) Call $\mathcal{F}^{\text{sim}}_{\text{msg}}$ with input (`send`, $ssid$, $cert_{\mathcal{P}}$) in the name of $\mathcal{O}$ for the 1st message from $\mathcal{O}$ to $\mathcal{P}$.

(4) Upon receiving output (`closed`, $ssid$) from $\mathcal{F}^{\text{sim}}_{\text{msg}}$ for $\mathcal{O}$, let $\mathcal{F}_{\text{apc}}$ deliver its output to $\mathcal{O}$.

(5) Upon receiving output (`certified_pos`, $a_{\mathcal{P}}$) from $\mathcal{F}_{\text{apc}}$ for $\mathcal{P}$, do nothing.

[a] N.b.: These assignments exist. An honest operator or honest PoS, resp., must have called RegisterOp and RegisterPOS previously, otherwise $\mathcal{F}_{\text{apc}}$ would already have aborted.

[b] N.b.: These assignments exist. An honest operator must have called RegisterOp otherwise $\mathcal{F}_{\text{apc}}$ would already have aborted. The malicious PoS has either either registered its public key at the bulletin-board $\mathcal{F}_{\text{bb}}$ or not. If it had not registered at the bulletin-board, then the real protocol would have aborted at the operator's side. The ideal functionality $\mathcal{F}_{\text{apc}}$ would also have aborted and never leaked the message (`certifying_pos`, $pid_{\mathcal{P}}, a_{\mathcal{P}}$) in the first place. Contrary, if PoS had registed at the bulletin-board, the real protocol does not abort. However, in this case $\mathcal{S}^{\text{user-sec}}_{\pi_{\text{P5C}}}$ would have (silently) defined $\bar{f}_{\text{keys}}(pid_{\mathcal{P}})$ and registered the PoS with $\mathcal{F}_{\text{apc}}$ and thus $\mathcal{F}_{\text{apc}}$ does not abort neither.

Figure 8.21: The Simulator for User Security and Privacy (cont. from Fig. 8.19)

Simulator $\mathcal{S}^{\text{user-sec}}_{\pi_{\text{P5C}}}$

CertifyPOS *(for corrupted operator and honest PoS):* (1) Upon receiving output ($\texttt{certifying\_pos}, pid_{\mathcal{P}}$) from $\mathcal{F}_{\text{apc}}$ for $\mathcal{O}$, call $\mathcal{F}^{\text{sim}}_{\text{msg}}$ with input ($\texttt{establish-session}, \texttt{ident}, pid_{\mathcal{O}}, \texttt{certify\_pos}$) in the name of $\mathcal{P}$ with $pid_{\mathcal{P}}$.

(2) Upon receiving output ($\texttt{accepted}, ssid$) from $\mathcal{F}^{\text{sim}}_{\text{msg}}$ for $\mathcal{P}$, do nothing.

(3) Upon receiving output ($\texttt{sent}, ssid, cert_{\mathcal{P}}$) from $\mathcal{F}^{\text{sim}}_{\text{msg}}$ for $\mathcal{P}$, ...

(a) Set $(pk_{\mathcal{O}}, \bot, \bot) := \bar{f}_{\text{keys}}(pid_{\mathcal{O}})$ and $(pk_{\mathcal{P}}, sk_{\mathcal{P}}, cert^{\text{prev}}_{\mathcal{P}}) := \bar{f}_{\text{keys}}(pid_{\mathcal{P}})$[a]

(b) Parse $a_{\mathcal{P}}$ and $\sigma^{\text{cert}}_{\mathcal{P}}$ from $cert_{\mathcal{P}}$.

(c) Parse $pk^{\text{cert}}_{\mathcal{O}}$ from $pk_{\mathcal{O}}$.

(d) If $\mathsf{SIG.Vfy}(pk^{\text{cert}}_{\mathcal{O}}, \sigma^{\text{cert}}_{\mathcal{P}}, (pk_{\mathcal{P}}, a_{\mathcal{P}})) = 0$, set $a_{\mathcal{P}} := \bot$ and $cert_{\mathcal{P}} := \bot$.

(e) Redefine $\bar{f}_{\text{keys}}(pid_{\mathcal{P}}) := (pk_{\mathcal{P}}, sk_{\mathcal{P}}, cert_{\mathcal{P}})$.

(f) Call $\mathcal{F}_{\text{apc}}$ with input ($\texttt{certifying\_pos}, a_{\mathcal{P}}$) in the name of $\mathcal{O}$ and ignore the subsequent leak ($\texttt{certifying\_pos}, pid_{\mathcal{P}}, \bot$) from $\mathcal{F}_{\text{apc}}$.

(4) Upon receiving output ($\texttt{certified\_pos}$) from $\mathcal{F}_{\text{apc}}$ for $\mathcal{O}$, call $\mathcal{F}^{\text{sim}}_{\text{msg}}$ with input ($\texttt{close}, ssid$) in the name of $\mathcal{P}$.

CertifyPOS *(for corrupted operator and corrupted PoS):* (nothing to do as $\mathcal{Z}^{\text{user-sec}}$ plays both parties)

[a] See previous footnote with inverse roles.

Figure 8.22: The Simulator for User Security and Privacy (cont. from Fig. 8.19)

Simulator $\mathcal{S}^{\text{user-sec}}_{\pi_{\text{P5C}}}$ (cont.)

IssueWallet *(for honest operator and honest user):* (1) Upon receiving leakage ($\texttt{issuing\_wallet}$) from $\mathcal{F}_{\text{apc}}$ and being asked to provide ω_{bl} ...

(a) $\lambda'' \stackrel{R}{\leftarrow} \mathbb{Z}_p$.

(b) $\psi_{\text{bl}} \leftarrow \mathsf{ENC1.Enc}(pk_{\mathcal{DR}}, (\overbrace{1, \ldots, 1}^{\ell+2}))$.

(c) Set $\omega_{\text{bl}} := (\lambda'', \psi_{\text{bl}})$.

(d) Provide ω_{bl} to $\mathcal{F}_{\text{apc}}$.

Figure 8.23: The Simulator for User Security and Privacy (cont. from Fig. 8.19)

Simulator $\mathcal{S}^{\text{user-sec}}_{\pi_{\text{P5C}}}$ (cont.)

IssueWallet *(for corrupted operator and honest user):* (1) Upon receiving output $(\texttt{issuing\_wallet}, pid_{\mathcal{U}})$ from $\mathcal{F}_{\text{apc}}$ for $\mathcal{O}$, call $\mathcal{F}^{\text{sim}}_{\text{msg}}$ with input $(\texttt{establish-session}, \texttt{ident}, pid_{\mathcal{O}}, \texttt{issue\_wallet})$ in the name of $\mathcal{U}$ with $pid_{\mathcal{U}}$.

(2) Upon receiving output $(\texttt{accepted}, ssid)$ from $\mathcal{F}^{\text{sim}}_{\text{msg}}$ for $\mathcal{U}$, ...

  (a) Set $(pk_{\mathcal{U}}, sk_{\mathcal{U}}) := \bar{f}_{\text{keys}}(pid_{\mathcal{U}})$ and $(pk_{DR}, sk_{DR}) := \bar{f}_{\text{keys}}(pid_{DR})$.[a]

  (b) $(c'_{\text{wid}}, d'_{\text{wid}}) \leftarrow \mathsf{C3.Commit}(crs^{(3)}_{\text{com}}, 0)$.

  (c) Call $\mathcal{F}^{\text{sim}}_{\text{msg}}$ with input $(\texttt{send}, ssid, c'_{\text{wid}})$ in the name of $\mathcal{U}$ for the 1st message from $\mathcal{U}$ to $\mathcal{O}$.

(3) Upon receiving output $(\texttt{sent}, ssid, (cert_{\mathcal{O}}, a_{\mathcal{U}}, c''_{\text{ser}}, \lambda''))$ from $\mathcal{F}^{\text{sim}}_{\text{msg}}$ for $\mathcal{U}$, ...

  (a) Parse $(pk^{\text{upd}}_{\mathcal{O}}, a_{\mathcal{O}}, \sigma^{\text{cert}}_{\mathcal{O}}) := cert_{\mathcal{O}}$.

  (b) If $\mathsf{SIG.Vfy}(pk^{\text{cert}}_{\mathcal{O}}, \sigma^{\text{cert}}_{\mathcal{O}}, (pk^{\text{upd}}_{\mathcal{O}}, a_{\mathcal{O}})) = 0$ abort.

  (c) $\Lambda'' := g_1^{\lambda''}$

  (d) $s'' \leftarrow \mathsf{C4.Extract}(crs^{(4)}_{\text{com}}, td_{\text{extcom}}, c''_{\text{ser}})$.

  (e) Call $\mathcal{F}_{\text{apc}}$ with input $(\texttt{issue\_wallet}, a_{\mathcal{U}})$ in the name of $\mathcal{O}$ with $pid_{\mathcal{O}}$.

(4) Upon receiving leakage $(\texttt{issuing\_wallet}, s, a_{\mathcal{U}})$ from $\mathcal{F}_{\text{apc}}$ ...

  (a) $s' := s \cdot s''^{-1}$.

  (b) $\psi_{\text{bl}} \leftarrow \mathsf{ENC1.Enc}(pk_{DR}, (\overbrace{1, \dots, 1}^{\ell+2}))$.

  (c) $(c_{\text{fix}}, d_{\text{fix}}) \leftarrow \mathsf{C1.Commit}(crs^{(1)}_{\text{com}}, (0, 0))$.

  (d) $(c_{\text{upd}}, d_{\text{upd}}) \leftarrow \mathsf{C1.Commit}(crs^{(1)}_{\text{com}}, (0, 0, 0, 0))$.

  (e) $stmnt := (pk_{\mathcal{U}}, pk_{DR}, \psi_{\text{bl}}, c_{\text{fix}}, c_{\text{upd}}, c'_{\text{wid}}, \Lambda'', \lambda'')$.

  (f) $\pi \leftarrow \mathsf{P1.ProveSim}(crs_{\text{pok}}, td_{\text{spok}}, stmnt)$.

  (g) Call $\mathcal{F}^{\text{sim}}_{\text{msg}}$ with input $(\texttt{send}, ssid, (s', \psi_{\text{bl}}, c_{\text{fix}}, c_{\text{upd}}, \pi))$ in the name of $\mathcal{U}$ for the 2nd message from $\mathcal{U}$ to $\mathcal{O}$.

(5) Upon receiving output $(\texttt{sent}, ssid, (s'', d''_{\text{ser}}, \sigma_{\text{fix}}, \sigma_{\text{upd}}))$ from $\mathcal{F}^{\text{sim}}_{\text{msg}}$ for $\mathcal{U}$, let $\mathcal{F}_{\text{apc}}$ continue.

[a] N.b.: These assignments exist. An honest user or honest dispute resolver, resp., must have called RegisterUser and RegisterDR previously, otherwise $\mathcal{F}_{\text{apc}}$ would already have aborted.

Figure 8.24: The Simulator for User Security and Privacy (cont. from Fig. 8.19)

Simulator $\mathcal{S}_{\pi_{\text{P5C}}}^{\text{user-sec}}$ (cont.)

IssueWallet *(for corrupted operator and honest user, continued):* (6) Upon receiving leakage (issuing_wallet) from $\mathcal{F}_{\text{apc}}$ and being asked to provide ω_{bl} ...

(a) Set $\omega_{\text{bl}} := (\lambda'', \psi_{\text{bl}})$.
(b) Provide ω_{bl} to $\mathcal{F}_{\text{apc}}$.

(7) Upon receiving output (issued_wallet, s, ω_{bl}) from $\mathcal{F}_{\text{apc}}$ for O ...

(a) If $\text{C4.Open}(crs^{(4)}_{\text{com}}, s'', c''_{\text{ser}}, d''_{\text{ser}}) = 0$, let $\mathcal{F}_{\text{apc}}$ abort.
(b) Create real token τ faithfully.
(c) If $\text{VerifyWallet}(pk_{\mathcal{O}}, pk_{\mathcal{U}}, \tau) = 0$, let $\mathcal{F}_{\text{apc}}$ abort.
(d) Let $\mathcal{F}_{\text{apc}}$ deliver its output to $\mathcal{U}$.

Figure 8.25: The Simulator for User Security and Privacy (cont. from Fig. 8.19)

explained in Section 8.2 and is the same as in Section 8.3. We stress that some of the hybrids are nearly identical to those in Section 8.3. We proceed by giving concrete definitions of all hybrids $H_i^{\text{user-sec}}$.

Hybrid $H_0^{\text{user-sec}}$ (The real experiment) The hybrid $H_0^{\text{user-sec}}$ is defined as

$$H_0^{\text{user-sec}} := \text{EXEC}_{\pi_0^{\text{user-sec}}, \mathcal{S}_0^{\text{user-sec}}, \mathcal{Z}^{\text{user-sec}}}(1^n) \tag{8.33}$$

with $\mathcal{S}_0^{\text{user-sec}} := \mathcal{D}$ being identical to the dummy adversary and $\pi_0^{\text{user-sec}} := \pi_{\text{P5C}}$. Hence, $H_0^{\text{user-sec}}$ denotes the real experiment.

Hybrid $H_1^{\text{user-sec}}$ (Fake setup) In hybrid $H_1^{\text{user-sec}}$ we modify $\mathcal{S}_1^{\text{user-sec}}$ such that crs_{pok} is generated by SetupSim, $crs^{(2)}_{\text{com}}$ is generated by C2.SetupSim and $crs^{(4)}_{\text{com}}$ is generated by C4.SetupExt. $\mathcal{S}_1^{\text{user-sec}}$ initializes $\bar{f}_{\text{keys}}$ and $\bar{f}_{\text{pp}}$ as "empty" maps. Additionally, $\mathcal{S}_1^{\text{user-sec}}$ invokes an internal instance of $\mathcal{F}_{\text{msg}}^{\text{sim}}$ instead of the external instance $\mathcal{F}_{\text{msg}}$ and reroutes all input/output accordingly. All calls to the bulletin-board $\mathcal{F}_{\text{bb}}$ are handled internally by $\mathcal{S}_1^{\text{user-sec}}$ using the map $\bar{f}_{\text{keys}}$.

Hybrid $H_2^{\text{user-sec}}$ (Simulate honest keys) Hybrid $H_2^{\text{user-sec}}$ replaces the code in the tasks RegisterDR, RegisterOp, RegisterPOS and RegisterUser of the protocol $\pi_2^{\text{user-sec}}$ such that the simulator $\mathcal{S}_2^{\text{user-sec}}$ is asked for the keys instead. Also, if corrupted PoSes or users try to register a (maliciously) generated public key at the bulletin-board $\mathcal{F}_{\text{bb}}$, then $\mathcal{S}_2^{\text{user-sec}}$ calls RegisterPOS or RegisterUser, resp., in order to simultaneously register the parties for $\mathcal{F}_{\text{apc}}$. $\mathcal{S}_2^{\text{user-sec}}$ defines $\bar{f}_{\text{keys}}$ appropriately. This equals the method in which the keys are generated in the ideal experiment.

Simulator $\mathcal{S}^{\text{user-sec}}_{\pi_{\text{P5C}}}$ (cont.)

Deposit *(for honest PoS and honest user):* (1) Upon reveiving leakage (`depositing`, $pid_{\mathcal{U}}, \Omega^{\varphi}_{\text{ds}}$) from $\mathcal{F}_{\text{apc}}$, ...

(a) Set $(pk_{\mathcal{U}}, sk_{\mathcal{U}}) := \bar{f}_{\text{keys}}(pid_{\mathcal{U}})$.[a]

(b) Pick $u_2 \overset{\text{R}}{\leftarrow} \mathbb{Z}_{\text{p}}$.

(c) Check if $\exists\, \omega'_{\text{ds}} = (\varphi', t', u'_2) \in \Omega^{\varphi}_{\text{ds}}$, s.t. $\omega'_{\text{ds}} \neq \bot$ and $u'_2 \neq u_2$ hold.[b]

(d) If yes, $t := t' + sk_{\mathcal{U}}(u_2 - u'_2)$.

(e) Provide $\pi := sk_{\mathcal{U}}$ to $\mathcal{F}_{\text{apc}}$.

(2) Upon receiving leakage (`depositing`, $s, \varphi, pid_{\mathcal{P}}$) or (`depositing`, $s, \varphi, pid_{\mathcal{P}}, p$) from $\mathcal{F}_{\text{apc}}$ and being asked to provide $(\omega_{\text{ds}}, \omega_{\text{rc}}, \omega_{\text{pp}})$, ...

(a) Set $(pk_{\mathcal{O}}, \bot, \bot) := \bar{f}_{\text{keys}}(pid_{\mathcal{O}})$.[c]

(b) Parse $pk^{\text{rc,enc}}_{\mathcal{O}}$ from $pk_{\mathcal{O}}$.

(c) Parse $pk^{\text{rc}}_{\mathcal{P}}/sk^{\text{rc}}_{\mathcal{P}}$ and $pk^{\text{pp}}_{\mathcal{P}}/sk^{\text{pp}}_{\mathcal{P}}$ from $pk_{\mathcal{P}}/sk_{\mathcal{P}}$.

(d) If (t, u_2) is not yet defined, pick $(t, u_2) \overset{\text{R}}{\leftarrow} \mathbb{Z}^2_{\text{p}}$.[d]

(e) Set $\omega_{\text{ds}} := (\varphi, t, u_2)$.

(f) If p has not been leaked (i.e., operator is honest):

(i) Set ψ_{rc} to an arbitrary value from the correct space.[e]

Else (i.e., operator is corrupted):

(i) Set $\sigma_{\text{rc}} \leftarrow \mathsf{SIG.Sign}(sk^{\text{rc}}_{\mathcal{P}}, (s, \varphi, g_1^{p}))$.

(ii) Set $\psi_{\text{rc}} := (s, \varphi, p, pk^{\text{rc}}_{\mathcal{P}}, \sigma_{\text{rc}})$.

(g) Set $\omega_{\text{rc}} \leftarrow \mathsf{ENC2.Enc}(pk^{\text{rc,enc}}_{\mathcal{O}}, \psi_{\text{rc}})$.

(h) Run $(c_{pk_{\mathcal{U}}}, \bar{d}_{pk_{\mathcal{U}}}) \leftarrow \mathsf{C2.CommitSim}(crs^{(2)}_{\text{com}})$.

(i) Assign $\sigma_{\text{pp}} \leftarrow \mathsf{SIG.Sign}(sk^{\text{pp}}_{\mathcal{P}}, c_{pk_{\mathcal{U}}})$.

(j) Set $\omega_{\text{pp}} := c_{pk_{\mathcal{U}}}$ and $\psi_{\text{pp}} := (pk^{\text{pp}}_{\mathcal{P}}, \sigma_{\text{pp}}, \bar{d}_{pk_{\mathcal{U}}})$

(k) Define $\bar{f}_{\text{pp}}(\omega_{\text{pp}}) := (\psi_{\text{pp}}, g_1)$.

(l) Provide $(\omega_{\text{ds}}, \omega_{\text{rc}}, \omega_{\text{pp}})$ to $\mathcal{F}_{\text{apc}}$.

[a] N.b.: This assignment exists. An honest user must have called RegisterUser previously, otherwise $\mathcal{F}_{\text{apc}}$ would already have aborted.

[b] N.b., even if the user commits double-spending no "useful", previous double-spending tag may exist in $\Omega^{\varphi}_{\text{ds}}$, if the user only did so at corrupted PoSes that undermine double-spending detection.

[c] N.b.: These assignments exist. The operator/PoS must have called RegisterOp/RegisterPOS previously, otherwise $\mathcal{F}_{\text{apc}}$ would already have aborted.

[d] Step 1d is only executed, if the user commits double-spending.

[e] The hidden recalculation tag is of the form $\psi_{\text{rc}} = (s, \varphi, p, pk^{\text{rc}}_{\mathcal{P}}, \sigma_{\text{rc}}) \in G_1 \times G_1 \times \mathbb{Z}_p \times (G_1^2 \times G_2^3) \times (G_2^2 \times G_1)$, e.g., $\psi_{\text{rc}} := (1, 1, 0, 1, 1, 1, 1, 1, 1, 1, 1)$ would be a good choice.

Figure 8.26: The Simulator for User Security and Privacy (cont. from Fig. 8.19)

Simulator $\mathcal{S}^{\text{user-sec}}_{\pi_{\text{P5C}}}$ (cont.)

Deposit *(for corrupted PoS and honest user):* (1) Upon receiving output (depositing) from $\mathcal{F}_{\text{apc}}$ for $\mathcal{P}$, call $\mathcal{F}^{\text{sim}}_{\text{msg}}$ with input (establish-session, anon, $pid_{\mathcal{P}}$, deposit) in the name of some imaginary user $\mathcal{U}$ with a randomly chosen $pid^{\text{fake}}_{\mathcal{U}}$.

(2) Upon receiving output (accepted, $ssid$) from $\mathcal{F}^{\text{sim}}_{\text{msg}}$ for $\mathcal{U}$, do nothing.

(3) Upon receiving output (sent, $ssid$, $(u_2, c''_{\text{ser}}, cert_{\mathcal{P}})$) from $\mathcal{F}^{\text{sim}}_{\text{msg}}$ for $\mathcal{U}$, ...

   (a) Set $(pk_{\mathcal{O}}, \cdot, \cdot) := \bar{f}_{\text{keys}}(pid_{\mathcal{O}})$.[a]

   (b) Parse $(pk_{\mathcal{P}}, a_{\mathcal{P}}, \sigma^{\text{cert}}_{\mathcal{P}}) := cert_{\mathcal{P}}$.

   (c) Parse $pk^{\text{upd}}_{\mathcal{P}}$ and $pk^{\text{pp}}_{\mathcal{P}}$ from $pk_{\mathcal{P}}$.

   (d) If $\mathsf{SIG.Vfy}(pk^{\text{cert}}_{\mathcal{O}}, \sigma^{\text{cert}}_{\mathcal{P}}, (pk_{\mathcal{P}}, a_{\mathcal{P}})) = 0$, let $\mathcal{F}_{\text{apc}}$ and $\mathcal{F}^{\text{sim}}_{\text{msg}}$ abort.

   (e) $s'' \leftarrow \mathsf{C4.Extract}(crs^{(4)}_{\text{com}}, c''_{\text{ser}})$.

   (f) Call $\mathcal{F}_{\text{apc}}$ with input (deposit, $\emptyset$)[b] in the name of $\mathcal{P}$ with $pid_{\mathcal{P}}$.

(4) Upon receiving leakage (depositing, s, $a_{\mathcal{U}}$) from $\mathcal{F}_{\text{apc}}$, let $\mathcal{F}_{\text{apc}}$ continue.

(5) Upon reveiving leakage (depositing, $pid_{\mathcal{U}}$, $\Omega^{\varphi}_{\text{ds}}$) from $\mathcal{F}_{\text{apc}}$, ...

   (a) Set $(pk_{\mathcal{U}}, sk_{\mathcal{U}}) := \bar{f}_{\text{keys}}(pid_{\mathcal{U}})$.[c]

   (b) Check if $\exists\, \omega'_{\text{ds}} = (\varphi', t', u'_2) \in \Omega^{\varphi}_{\text{ds}}$, s.t. $\omega'_{\text{ds}} \neq \bot$ and $u'_2 \neq u_2$ hold.[d]

   (c) If yes, $t := t' + sk_{\mathcal{U}}(u_2 - u'_2)$.

   (d) Provide $\pi := sk_{\mathcal{U}}$ to $\mathcal{F}_{\text{apc}}$.

[a] N.b.: This assignment exists. An operator must have called RegisterOp previously, otherwise $\mathcal{F}_{\text{apc}}$ would already have aborted.

[b] Use empty set as blacklist.

[c] N.b.: This assignment exists. An honest user must have called RegisterUser previously, otherwise $\mathcal{F}_{\text{apc}}$ would already have aborted.

[d] N.b., even if the user commits double-spending no "useful", previous double-spending tag may exist in $\Omega^{\varphi}_{\text{ds}}$, if the user only did so at corrupted PoSes that undermine double-spending detection.

Figure 8.27: The Simulator for User Security and Privacy (cont. from Fig. 8.19)

Simulator $\mathcal{S}^{\text{user-sec}}_{\pi_{\text{P5C}}}$ (cont.)

Deposit *(for corrupted PoS and honest user, continued):* (6) Upon receiving output $(\texttt{depositing}, s, a_{\mathcal{U}}, a_{\mathcal{P}}^{\text{prev}})$ from $\mathcal{F}_{\text{apc}}$ for $\mathcal{P}$ ...

(a) $s' := s \cdot s''^{-1}$.

(b) Run $(c_{pk_{\mathcal{U}}}, \bar{d}_{pk_{\mathcal{U}}}) \leftarrow \text{C2.CommitSim}(crs_{\text{com}}^{(2)})$.

(c) $(c'_{\text{upd}}, d'_{\text{upd}}) \leftarrow \text{C1.Commit}(crs_{\text{com}}^{(1)}, (0, 0, 0, 0))$.

(d) If t is not yet defined, pick $t \overset{R}{\leftarrow} \mathbb{Z}_p$.[a]

(e) $stmnt := (pk_{\mathcal{O}}, pk_{\mathcal{O}}^{\text{cert}}, \varphi, a_{\mathcal{U}}, a_{\mathcal{P}}^{\text{prev}}, c_{pk_{\mathcal{U}}}, c'_{\text{upd}}, t, u_2)$.

(f) $\pi \leftarrow \text{P2.ProveSim}(crs_{\text{pok}}, td_{\text{spok}}, stmnt)$.

(g) Call $\mathcal{F}_{\text{msg}}^{\text{sim}}$ with input $(\text{send}, ssid, (s', \pi, \varphi, a_{\mathcal{U}}, a_{\mathcal{P}}^{\text{prev}}, c_{pk_{\mathcal{U}}}, c'_{\text{upd}}, t))$ in the name of $\mathcal{U}$.

(7) Upon receiving output $(\texttt{sent}, ssid, (s'', d''_{\text{ser}}, c_{\text{upd}}, d''_{\text{upd}}, \sigma_{\text{upd}}, p, \sigma_{\text{pp}})$ from $\mathcal{F}_{\text{msg}}^{\text{sim}}$ for $\mathcal{U}$, ...

(a) $d_{\text{upd}} := d'_{\text{upd}} \cdot d''_{\text{upd}}$.

(b) If $\text{C1.Open}(crs_{\text{com}}^{(1)}, (1, g_1^p, 1, g_1), c_{\text{upd}}, d_{\text{upd}}) = 0$ let $\mathcal{F}_{\text{apc}}$ abort.

(c) If $\text{SIG.Vfy}(pk_{\mathcal{P}}^{\text{upd}}, \sigma_{\text{upd}}, (c_{\text{upd}}, s)) = 0$, let $\mathcal{F}_{\text{apc}}$ abort.

(d) If $\text{SIG.Vfy}(pk_{\mathcal{P}}^{\text{pp}}, \sigma_{\text{pp}}, c_{pk_{\mathcal{U}}}) = 0$, let $\mathcal{F}_{\text{apc}}$ abort.

(e) Call $\mathcal{F}_{\text{apc}}$ with input $(\texttt{depositing}, p)$ in the name of $\mathcal{P}$.

(8) Upon receiving leakage $(\texttt{depositing}, s, \varphi, pid_{\mathcal{P}})$ or $(\texttt{depositing}, s, \varphi, pid_{\mathcal{P}}, p)$ from $\mathcal{F}_{\text{apc}}$ and being asked to provide $(\omega_{\text{ds}}, \omega_{\text{rc}}, \omega_{\text{pp}})$, ...

(a) Set $\omega_{\text{ds}} := (\varphi, t, u_2)$.

(b) Set ψ_{rc} to an arbitrary value from the correct space.[b]

(c) Set $\omega_{\text{rc}} \leftarrow \text{ENC2.Enc}(pk_{\mathcal{O}}^{\text{rc,enc}}, \psi_{\text{rc}})$.

(d) Set $\omega_{\text{pp}} := c_{pk_{\mathcal{U}}}$ and $\psi_{\text{pp}} := (pk_{\mathcal{P}}^{\text{pp}}, \sigma_{\text{pp}}, \bar{d}_{pk_{\mathcal{U}}})$.

(e) Define $\bar{f}_{\text{pp}}(\omega_{\text{pp}}) := (\psi_{\text{pp}}, g_1)$.

(f) Provide $(\omega_{\text{ds}}, \omega_{\text{rc}}, \omega_{\text{pp}})$ to $\mathcal{F}_{\text{apc}}$.

(9) Upon receiving output $(\texttt{deposited}, \omega_{\text{ds}}, \omega_{\text{rc}}, \omega_{\text{pp}})$ from $\mathcal{F}_{\text{apc}}$ for $\mathcal{P}$, let $\mathcal{F}_{\text{apc}}$ deliver its output to $\mathcal{U}$.

[a] Step 5c is only executed, if the user commits double-spending.

[b] The hidden recalculation tag is of the form $\psi_{\text{rc}} = (s, \varphi, p, pk_{\mathcal{P}}^{\text{rc}}, \sigma_{\text{rc}}) \in G_1 \times G_1 \times \mathbb{Z}_p \times (G_1^2 \times G_2^3) \times (G_2^2 \times G_1)$, e.g., $\psi_{\text{rc}} := (1, 1, 0, 1, 1, 1, 1, 1, 1, 1, 1)$ would be a good choice.

Figure 8.28: The Simulator for User Security and Privacy (cont. from Fig. 8.19)

Simulator $\mathcal{S}^{\text{user-sec}}_{\pi_{\text{P5C}}}$ (cont.)

Disburse *(for honest operator and honest user):* (1) Upon reveiving leakage $(\texttt{disbursing}, pid_{\mathcal{U}}, \Omega^{\varphi}_{\text{ds}})$ from $\mathcal{F}_{\text{apc}}$, ...

(a) Set $(pk_{\mathcal{U}}, sk_{\mathcal{U}}) := \bar{f}_{\text{keys}}(pid_{\mathcal{U}})$.[a]

(b) Pick $u_2 \overset{\text{R}}{\leftarrow} \mathbb{Z}_{\text{p}}$.

(c) Check if $\exists\, \omega'_{\text{ds}} = (\varphi', t', u'_2) \in \Omega^{\varphi}_{\text{ds}}$, s.t. $\omega'_{\text{ds}} \neq \bot$ and $u'_2 \neq u_2$ hold.[b]

(d) If yes, $t := t' + sk_{\mathcal{U}}(u_2 - u'_2)$.

(e) Provide $\pi := sk_{\mathcal{U}}$ to $\mathcal{F}_{\text{apc}}$.

(2) Upon receiving leakage $(\texttt{disbursing}, s, \varphi)$ from $\mathcal{F}_{\text{apc}}$ and being asked to provide $(\omega_{\text{ds}}, \omega_{\text{rc}})$, ...

(a) Set $(pk_{\mathcal{O}}, \bot, \bot) := \bar{f}_{\text{keys}}(pid_{\mathcal{O}})$ and parse $pk^{\text{rc,enc}}_{\mathcal{O}}$ from $pk_{\mathcal{O}}$.[c]

(b) If (t, u_2) is not yet defined, pick $(t, u_2) \overset{\text{R}}{\leftarrow} \mathbb{Z}^2_{\text{p}}$.[d]

(c) Set $\omega_{\text{ds}} := (\varphi, t, u_2)$.

(d) Set ψ_{rc} to an arbitrary value from the correct space.[e]

(e) Set $\omega_{\text{rc}} \leftarrow \mathsf{ENC2.Enc}(pk^{\text{rc,enc}}_{\mathcal{O}}, \psi_{\text{rc}})$.

(f) Provide $(\omega_{\text{ds}}, \omega_{\text{rc}})$ to $\mathcal{F}_{\text{apc}}$.

[a] N.b.: This assignment exists. An honest user must have called RegisterUser previously, otherwise $\mathcal{F}_{\text{apc}}$ would already have aborted.

[b] N.b., even if the user commits double-spending no "useful", previous double-spending tag may exist in $\Omega^{\varphi}_{\text{ds}}$, if the user only did so at corrupted PoSes that undermine double-spending detection.

[c] N.b.: This assignment exists. The operator must have called RegisterOp previously, otherwise $\mathcal{F}_{\text{apc}}$ would already have aborted.

[d] Step 1d is only executed, if the user commits double-spending.

[e] The hidden recalculation tag is of the form $\psi_{\text{rc}} = (s, \varphi, p, pk^{\text{rc}}_{\varphi}, \sigma_{\text{rc}}) \in G_1 \times G_1 \times \mathbb{Z}_{\text{p}} \times (G_1^2 \times G_2^3) \times (G_2^2 \times G_1)$, e.g., $\psi_{\text{rc}} := (1, 1, 0, 1, 1, 1, 1, 1, 1, 1, 1)$ would be a good choice.

Figure 8.29: The Simulator for User Security and Privacy (cont. from Fig. 8.19)

Simulator $\mathcal{S}^{\text{user-sec}}_{\pi_{\text{P5C}}}$ (cont.)

Disburse *(for corrupted operator and honest user):* (1) Upon receiving output (disbursing, $pid_{\mathcal{U}}$) from $\mathcal{F}_{\text{apc}}$ for $\mathcal{O}$, ...

(a) Set $(pk_{\mathcal{O}}, \bot, \bot) := \bar{f}_{\text{keys}}(pid_{\mathcal{O}})$.[a]

(b) Call $\mathcal{F}^{\text{sim}}_{\text{msg}}$ with input (establish-session, ident, $pid_{\mathcal{O}}$, deposit) in the name of $\mathcal{U}$ with $pid_{\mathcal{U}}$.

(2) Upon receiving output (accepted, $ssid$) from $\mathcal{F}^{\text{sim}}_{\text{msg}}$ for $\mathcal{U}$, do nothing.

(3) Upon receiving output (sent, $ssid, u_2$) from $\mathcal{F}^{\text{sim}}_{\text{msg}}$ for $\mathcal{U}$, call $\mathcal{F}_{\text{apc}}$ with input (disbursing) in the name of $\mathcal{O}$.

(4) Upon reveiving leakage (disbursing, $pid_{\mathcal{U}}, \Omega^{\varphi}_{\text{ds}}$) from $\mathcal{F}_{\text{apc}}$, ...

(a) Set $(pk_{\mathcal{U}}, sk_{\mathcal{U}}) := \bar{f}_{\text{keys}}(pid_{\mathcal{U}})$.[b]

(b) Check if $\exists\, \omega'_{\text{ds}} = (\varphi', t', u'_2) \in \Omega^{\varphi}_{\text{ds}}$, s.t. $\omega'_{\text{ds}} \neq \bot$ and $u'_2 \neq u_2$ hold.[c]

(c) If yes, $t := t' + sk_{\mathcal{U}}(u_2 - u'_2)$.

(d) Provide $\pi := sk_{\mathcal{U}}$ to $\mathcal{F}_{\text{apc}}$.

(5) Upon receiving leakage (disbursing, s, φ) from $\mathcal{F}_{\text{apc}}$ and being asked to provide $(\omega_{\text{ds}}, \omega_{\text{rc}})$, ...

(a) If t is not yet defined, pick $t \xleftarrow{R} \mathbb{Z}_p$.[d]

(b) Set $\omega_{\text{ds}} := (\varphi, t, u_2)$.

(c) Set ψ_{rc} to an arbitrary value from the correct space.[e]

(d) Set $\omega_{\text{rc}} \leftarrow \mathsf{ENC2.Enc}(pk^{\text{rc,enc}}_{\mathcal{O}}, \psi_{\text{rc}})$.

(e) Provide $(\omega_{\text{ds}}, \omega_{\text{rc}})$ to $\mathcal{F}_{\text{apc}}$.

(6) Upon receiving output (disbursed, $b^{\text{bill}}, \omega_{\text{ds}}, \omega_{\text{rc}}$) from $\mathcal{F}_{\text{apc}}$ for $\mathcal{O}$ ...

(a) $stmnt := (pk_{\mathcal{U}}, pk^{\text{fix}}_{\mathcal{O}}, pk^{\text{cert}}_{\mathcal{O}}, \varphi, g_1^{b^{\text{bill}}}, t, u_2)$.

(b) $\pi \leftarrow \mathsf{P3.ProveSim}(crs_{\text{pok}}, td_{\text{spok}}, stmnt)$.

(c) Call $\mathcal{F}^{\text{sim}}_{\text{msg}}$ with input (send, $ssid, (\pi, \varphi, b^{\text{bill}}, t)$) in the name of $\mathcal{U}$.

(7) Upon receiving output (sent, $ssid$, OK) from $\mathcal{F}^{\text{sim}}_{\text{msg}}$ for $\mathcal{U}$, let $\mathcal{F}_{\text{apc}}$ deliver its output to $\mathcal{U}$.

---

[a] N.b.: These assignments exist. The operator, must have called RegisterOp previously, otherwise $\mathcal{F}_{\text{apc}}$ would already have aborted.

[b] N.b.: This assignment exists. An honest user must have called RegisterUser previously, otherwise $\mathcal{F}_{\text{apc}}$ would already have aborted.

[c] N.b., even if the user commits double-spending no "useful", previous double-spending tag may exist in $\Omega^{\varphi}_{\text{ds}}$, if the user only did so at corrupted PoSes that undermine double-spending detection.

[d] Step 4c is only executed, if the user commits double-spending.

[e] The hidden recalculation tag is of the form $\psi_{\text{rc}} = (s, \varphi, p, pk^{\text{rc}}_{\varphi}, \sigma_{\text{rc}}) \in G_1 \times G_1 \times \mathbb{Z}_p \times (G_1^2 \times G_2^3) \times (G_2^2 \times G_1)$, e.g., $\psi_{\text{rc}} := (1, 1, 0, 1, 1, 1, 1, 1, 1, 1, 1)$ would be a good choice.

Figure 8.30: The Simulator for User Security and Privacy (cont. from Fig. 8.19)

Simulator $\mathcal{S}^{\text{user-sec}}_{\pi_{\text{P5C}}}$ (cont.)

DetectDS *(for honest operator):* (1) Upon receiving leakage $(\texttt{detecting\_ds}, \omega_{\text{ds}}, \omega'_{\text{ds}})$ from $\mathcal{F}_{\text{apc}}$ and being asked to provide $(pid_{\mathcal{U}}, \pi, result)$, ...

(a) Parse $(\varphi, t, u_2) := \omega_{\text{ds}}$ and $(\varphi', t', u'_2) := \omega'_{\text{ds}}$.

(b) If $\varphi = \varphi'$ and $u_2 \neq u'_2$:

(i) Set $sk_{\mathcal{U}} := (t - t')/(u_2 - u'_2) \bmod \mathfrak{p}$.

(ii) Set $pk_{\mathcal{U}} := g_1^{sk_{\mathcal{U}}}$.

Else, set $(pk_{\mathcal{U}}, sk_{\mathcal{U}}) := (\bot, \bot)$.

(c) Set $pid_{\mathcal{U}} := \bar{f}^{-1}_{\text{keys}}(pk_{\mathcal{U}}, \cdot)$; if $\bar{f}^{-1}_{\text{keys}}$ is not defined for $pk_{\mathcal{U}}$, set $pid_{\mathcal{U}} := \bot$.

(d) If $pid_{\mathcal{U}} \neq \bot$, then set $(\pi, result) := (sk_{\mathcal{U}}, \texttt{OK})$, else set $(\pi, result) := (\bot, \texttt{NOK})$.

(e) Provide $(pid_{\mathcal{U}}, \pi, result)$ to $\mathcal{F}_{\text{apc}}$.

(2) Upon receiving leakage $(\texttt{detecting\_ds}, pid_{\mathcal{U}})$ from $\mathcal{F}_{\text{apc}}$ and being asked to provide π, ...

(a) Set $(pk_{\mathcal{U}}, sk_{\mathcal{U}}) := \bar{f}_{\text{keys}}(pid_{\mathcal{U}})$.[a]

(b) Provide $\pi := sk_{\mathcal{U}}$ to $\mathcal{F}_{\text{apc}}$.

VerifyGuilt *(for honest party):* Upon receiving leakage $(\texttt{verifying\_guilt}, pid_{\mathcal{U}}, \pi)$ from $\mathcal{F}_{\text{apc}}$ and being asked to provide *result* ...

(1) Set $(pk_{\mathcal{U}}, \cdot) := \bar{f}_{\text{keys}}(pid_{\mathcal{U}})$.

(2) If $g_1^{\pi} = pk_{\mathcal{U}}$, then provide $result := \texttt{OK}$, else $result := \texttt{NOK}$ to $\mathcal{F}_{\text{apc}}$.

[a] This assignment exist. $(\texttt{detecting\_ds}, pid_{\mathcal{U}})$ is only leaked, if the user truly committed double-spending. In this case Step 5 in Fig. 8.27 and Step 4 in Fig. 8.30 have been called previously. In all other cases the honest user and therefore $\mathcal{S}^{\text{user-sec}}_{\pi_{\text{P5C}}}$ knows $sk_{\mathcal{U}}$ anyway.

Figure 8.31: The Simulator for User Security and Privacy (cont. from Fig. 8.19)

Simulator $\mathcal{S}^{\text{user-sec}}_{\pi_{\text{P5C}}}$ (cont.)

BlacklistWallet *(for honest operator):* Upon receiving leakage (`blacklisting_wallet`, λ, x) from $\mathcal{F}_{\text{apc}}$ and being asked to provide φ, provide $\varphi := \mathsf{PRF}(\lambda, x)$ to $\mathcal{F}_{\text{apc}}$.

BlacklistWallet *(for corrupted operator):* (1) Upon receiving output (`establishing-session`, *ssid*, $pid_{\mathcal{O}}$, `blacklist_wallet`) from $\mathcal{F}_{\text{msg}}$ for *DR*, ...

(a) Set $(pk_{DR}, sk_{DR}) := \bar{f}_{\text{keys}}(pid_{DR})$; if $\bar{f}_{\text{keys}}(pid_{DR})$ is undefined, let $\mathcal{F}_{\text{msg}}$ abort.

(b) Call $\mathcal{F}_{\text{msg}}$ with input (`accept`, *ssid*).

(2) Upon receiving output (`sent`, ω_{bl}) from $\mathcal{F}_{\text{msg}}$ for *DR*, ...

(a) Parse $(\lambda'', \psi_{\text{bl}}) := \omega_{\text{bl}}$.

(b) Assign $(\Lambda'_0, \ldots, \Lambda'_{\ell-1}, \Lambda'', pk_{\mathcal{U}}) \leftarrow \mathsf{ENC1.Dec}(sk_{DR}, \psi_{\text{bl}})$.

(c) If decryption fails, call $\mathcal{F}_{\text{msg}}$ with input (`send`, *ssid*, $\emptyset$) in the name of *DR* for the message from *DR* to *O* and halt.

(d) If $\Lambda'_0 = \cdots = \Lambda'_{\ell-1} = \Lambda'' = pk_{\mathcal{U}} = 1$ or $\Lambda'' \neq g_1^{\lambda''}$ holds[a]:

(i) Set $(pid_{\mathcal{U}}, \lambda) := (\bot, \bot)$.

Else:

(i) Set $\lambda := \lambda'' + \sum_{i=0}^{\ell-1} \mathsf{DLOG}(\Lambda'_i) \cdot B^i$.

(ii) Set $pid_{\mathcal{U}} := \bar{f}^{(-1)}_{\text{keys}}(pk_{\mathcal{U}}, \cdot)$; if $\bar{f}^{(-1)}_{\text{keys}}(pk_{\mathcal{U}}, \cdot)$ is undefined, set $(pid_{\mathcal{U}}, \lambda) := (\bot, \bot)$.

(e) Call $\mathcal{F}_{\text{apc}}$ with input (`blacklist_wallet`, ω_{bl}).

(3) Upon receiving leakage `blacklisting_wallet` from $\mathcal{F}_{\text{apc}}$ and being asked to provide $(pid_{\mathcal{U}}, \lambda)$, provide $(pid_{\mathcal{U}}, \lambda)$ to $\mathcal{F}_{\text{apc}}$.[b]

(4) Upon receiving leakage (`blacklisting_wallet`, λ, x) from $\mathcal{F}_{\text{apc}}$ and being asked to provide φ, provide $\varphi := \mathsf{PRF}(\lambda, x)$ to $\mathcal{F}_{\text{apc}}$.

(5) Upon receving output (`blacklisted_wallet`, bl_{Φ_λ}) from $\mathcal{F}_{\text{apc}}$ for *O*, call $\mathcal{F}_{\text{msg}}$ with input (`send`, *ssid*, bl_{Φ_λ}) in the name of *DR* for the message from *DR* to *O*.

(6) Upon receiving output (`closed`, *ssid*) from $\mathcal{F}_{\text{msg}}$ for *DR*, let $\mathcal{F}_{\text{apc}}$ delivers its output to *DR*.

[a] This might hold, if ω_{bl} is a simulated blacklisting tag for an honest user (cp. Step 1b in Fig. 8.23 or Step 4b in Fig. 8.24).

[b] N.b.: $\mathcal{F}_{\text{apc}}$ asks for alternative $pid_{\mathcal{U}}, \lambda$, if and only if ω_{bl} has not been recorded internally. I.e., for a simulated, but legitemately issued ω_{bl}, which encrypts a "useless" 1-vector, $\mathcal{S}^{\text{user-sec}}_{\pi_{\text{P5C}}}$ is not compelled to provide $(pid_{\mathcal{U}}, \lambda)$.

Figure 8.32: The Simulator for User Security and Privacy (cont. from Fig. 8.19)

Simulator $\mathcal{S}^{\text{user-sec}}_{\pi_{\text{P5C}}}$ (cont.)

RecalculateBalance *(only for honest operator[a]):* Upon receiving leakage (`recalculating_balance`, $bl_{\Phi}, \Omega^{\text{fake}}_{\text{rc}}$) from $\mathcal{F}_{\text{apc}}$ and being asked to provide p^{deviate} ...

(1) $\Psi^{\text{fake}}_{\text{rc}} := \{\psi_{\text{rc}} \leftarrow \text{ENC2.Dec}(sk^{\text{rc,enc}}_{\mathcal{O}}, \omega_{\text{rc}}) \mid \omega_{\text{rc}} \in \Omega^{\text{fake}}_{\text{rc}}\}$

(2) $\Psi^{\text{fake,valid}}_{\text{rc}} := \{(s, \varphi, p, pk^{\text{rc}}_{\mathcal{P}}, \sigma_{\text{rc}}) \in \psi_{\text{rc}} \mid \text{SIG.Vfy}(pk^{\text{rc}}_{\mathcal{P}}, \sigma_{\text{rc}}, (s, \varphi, g_1^p)) = 1\}$

(3) $\Xi := \{(s, p) \mid \exists\, \psi_{\text{rc}} = (s, \varphi, p, \cdot, \cdot) \in \Psi^{\text{fake,valid}}_{\text{rc}} \wedge \varphi \in bl_{\Phi}\}$

(4) Provide $p^{\text{deviate}} := \sum_{(s,p)\in\Xi} p$ to $\mathcal{F}_{\text{apc}}$.

[a] This a local algorithm and hence there is nothing to simulate for a corrupted operator

Figure 8.33: The Simulator for User Security and Privacy (cont. from Fig. 8.19)

Note, the modifications of hybrid $H_2^{\text{user-sec}}$ are identical to hybrid $H_2^{\text{op-sec}}$.

Hybrid $H_3^{\text{user-sec}}$ (Simulate PoS' certificate) In hybrid $H_3^{\text{user-sec}}$ the task CertifyPOS is modified. For an honest operator or an honest PoS the code of $\pi_3^{\text{user-sec}}$ is replaced by the code of a dummy party. The simulator $\mathcal{S}_3^{\text{user-sec}}$ behaves in this case as the final simulator $\mathcal{S}^{\text{user-sec}}_{\pi_{\text{P5C}}}$ would. More precisely, if both parties are honest, protocol $\pi_3^{\text{user-sec}}$ is modified such that the simulator $\mathcal{S}_3^{\text{user-sec}}$ receives the message (`certifying_pos`, $pid_{\mathcal{P}}, a_{\mathcal{P}}$) and creates the certificate $cert_{\mathcal{P}}$. If the PoS is corrupted, but the operator honest, the certificate $cert_{\mathcal{P}}$ is also created by simulator $\mathcal{S}_3^{\text{user-sec}}$. If the PoS is honest, but the operator corrupted, simulator $\mathcal{S}_3^{\text{user-sec}}$ receives $cert_{\mathcal{P}}$ as part of the message from the operator. In either case, simulator $\mathcal{S}_3^{\text{user-sec}}$ learns $cert_{\mathcal{P}}$ and internally records it in $\bar{f}_{\text{keys}}$. Whenever the honest operator or honest PoSes running $\pi_3^{\text{user-sec}}$ would send $cert_{\mathcal{P}}$ (or $\sigma^{\text{cert}}_{\mathcal{P}}$) as part of their messages in the scope of IssueWallet or Deposit, they omit $cert_{\mathcal{P}}$. Instead, the simulator $\mathcal{S}_3^{\text{user-sec}}$ injects $cert_{\mathcal{P}}$ into the messages.

Note, except for the additional case that the PoS is honest and the operator corrupted, the modifications of hybrid $H_3^{\text{user-sec}}$ are identical to hybrid $H_3^{\text{op-sec}}$.

Hybrid $H_4^{\text{user-sec}}$ (Extract serial number) $H_4^{\text{user-sec}}$ modifies the tasks of IssueWallet and Deposit in case of a corrupted operator/PoS. The code of $\pi_4^{\text{user-sec}}$ for the user is modified such that it does not send s' but randomly picks s and sends it to $\mathcal{S}_4^{\text{user-sec}}$. Then $\mathcal{S}_4^{\text{user-sec}}$ extracts $s'' \leftarrow \text{C4.Extract}(crs^{(4)}_{\text{com}}, c''_{\text{ser}})$, calculates $s' := s \cdot (s'')^{-1}$ and inserts s' into the message from the user to the operator or PoS respectively.

Hybrid $H_5^{\text{user-sec}}$ (Simulate ZK-proofs) This hybrid modifies $\pi_5^{\text{user-sec}}$ such that the honest users do not send any proofs. Instead, the simulator $\mathcal{S}_5^{\text{user-sec}}$ appends simulated proofs to the messages from the user to the operator or PoSes without knowing the witness.

Simulator $\mathcal{S}^{\text{user-sec}}_{\pi_{\text{P5C}}}$ (cont.)

ProveParticipation *(for honest user and honest violation enforcer):* (nothing to do, note that $\mathcal{F}_{\text{apc}}$ only leaks, if user or violation enforcer is corrupted)

ProveParticipation *(for honest user and corrupted violation enforcer):*

(1) Upon receiving output (establishing-session, $ssid, pid_{VE}$, prove_participation) from $\mathcal{F}^{\text{sim}}_{\text{msg}}$ for $\mathcal{U}$ with $pid_{\mathcal{U}}$, call $\mathcal{F}^{\text{sim}}_{\text{msg}}$ with input (accept, $ssid$) in the name of $\mathcal{U}$.

(2) Upon receiving output (sent, $ssid, pid_{\mathcal{P}}, \Omega_{\text{pp}}$) from $\mathcal{F}^{\text{sim}}_{\text{msg}}$ for $\mathcal{U}$, call $\mathcal{F}_{\text{apc}}$ with input (prove_participation, $pid_{\mathcal{U}}, pid_{\mathcal{P}}, \Omega_{\text{pp}}$) in the name of VE.

(3) Upon receiving leakage (proving_participation, ω_{pp}) from $\mathcal{F}_{\text{apc}}$, let $\mathcal{F}_{\text{apc}}$ continue.

(4) Upon receiving output (proved_participation, $result$) from $\mathcal{F}_{\text{apc}}$ for VE, ...

   (a) If $result = \mathsf{NOK}$, set $\psi_{\text{pp}} := \bot$, else

      (i) Set $(pk_{\mathcal{U}}, \cdot) := \bar{f}_{\text{keys}}(pid_{\mathcal{U}})$.

      (ii) Set $(\psi_{\text{pp}}, \cdot) := \bar{f}_{\text{pp}}(\omega_{\text{pp}})$.[a]

      (iii) Set $c_{pk_{\mathcal{U}}} := \omega_{\text{pp}}$ and parse $(pk^{\text{pp}}_{\mathcal{P}}, \sigma_{\text{pp}}, \bar{d}_{pk_{\mathcal{U}}}) := \psi_{\text{pp}}$.

      (iv) $d_{pk_{\mathcal{U}}} \leftarrow \text{C2.Equivoke}(crs^{(2)}_{\text{com}}, pk_{\mathcal{U}}, c_{pk_{\mathcal{U}}}, \bar{d}_{pk_{\mathcal{U}}})$.

      (v) Redefine $\psi_{\text{pp}} := (pk^{\text{pp}}_{\mathcal{P}}, \sigma_{\text{pp}}, d_{pk_{\mathcal{U}}})$ and $\bar{f}_{\text{pp}}(\omega_{\text{pp}}) := (\psi_{\text{pp}}, pk_{\mathcal{U}})$.

   (b) Call $\mathcal{F}^{\text{sim}}_{\text{msg}}$ with input (send, $ssid, (\omega_{\text{pp}}, \psi_{\text{pp}})$) in the name of $\mathcal{U}$.

(5) Upon receiving output (closed, $ssid$) from $\mathcal{F}^{\text{sim}}_{\text{msg}}$ for $\mathcal{U}$, let $\mathcal{F}_{\text{apc}}$ delivers its output to $\mathcal{U}$.

[a] This exists as otherwise $\mathcal{F}_{\text{apc}}$ would have returned $result = \mathsf{NOK}$.

Figure 8.34: The Simulator for User Security and Privacy (cont. from Fig. 8.19)

Hybrid $H_6^{\text{user-sec}}$ (Fake commitments for wallet ID and wallet components) Hybrid $H_6^{\text{user-sec}}$ modifies $\pi_6^{\text{user-sec}}$ such that honest users do not send the commitments c'_{wid}, c_{fix} and c_{upd} in the IssueWallet and c'_{upd} in the Deposit task. Instead, $\mathcal{S}_6^{\text{user-sec}}$ injects suitable commitments to vectors of zeros. This equals the behavior of the final simulator $\mathcal{S}_{\pi_{\text{P5C}}}^{\text{user-sec}}$.

Hybrid $H_7^{\text{user-sec}}$ (Record Tags) $H_7^{\text{user-sec}}$ replaces the code protocol $\pi_7^{\text{user-sec}}$ of the tasks IssueWallet, Deposit and Disburse such that the various tags are not exclusively created by the parties' code but with support from $\mathcal{S}_7^{\text{user-sec}}$ and then recorded by $\mathcal{S}_7^{\text{user-sec}}$. More precisely, these are

$$\omega_{\text{bl}} := (\lambda'', \psi_{\text{bl}}) \qquad \omega_{\text{ds}} := (\varphi, t, u_2) \tag{8.34}$$

$$\omega_{\text{rc}} \leftarrow \mathsf{ENC2.Enc}(pk_{\mathcal{O}}^{\text{rc,enc}}, \psi_{\text{rc}}) \qquad \omega_{\text{pp}} := c_{pk_{\mathcal{U}}} \tag{8.35}$$

To this end, $\pi_7^{\text{user-sec}}$ and $\mathcal{S}_7^{\text{user-sec}}$ are changed in detail as follows.

For the blacklisting tag ω_{bl}: In the scope of IssueWallet the code of honest user is modified such that it does not expect to receive the operator's share λ'' of the wallet ID. Instead, the wallet ID λ is uniformly picked by $\mathcal{S}_7^{\text{user-sec}}$ as $\mathcal{F}_{\text{apc}}$ would do and λ is provisionally provided to the user. Moreover, the honest user does not sent ψ_{bl}, but $\mathcal{S}_7^{\text{user-sec}}$ sets $\lambda' := \lambda \cdot \lambda''^{-1}$, creates the hidden part ψ_{bl} the same way as an honest user would do and sends it to the operator. Also, $\mathcal{S}_7^{\text{user-sec}}$ records $f_{\Omega_{\text{bl}}}(\lambda) := \omega_{\text{bl}}$ as $\mathcal{F}_{\text{apc}}$ would do.

For the double-spending tag ω_{ds}: The code for honest users is modified such that it explicitly leaks s, φ to $\mathcal{S}_7^{\text{user-sec}}$. Also, they do not expect to receive the DS challenge u_2 nor reply with a DS response t. Instead, $\mathcal{S}_7^{\text{user-sec}}$ intercepts u_2 when it is sent by the operator/PoS and manages a set $\Omega_{\text{ds}}^{\varphi}$ for each φ in the following way. If $\Omega_{\text{ds}}^{\varphi}$ is still empty, $\mathcal{S}_7^{\text{user-sec}}$ picks a random DS mask u_1, calculates $t = u_2 \cdot sk_{\mathcal{U}} + u_1$, adds $\omega_{\text{ds}} := (\varphi, t, u_2)$ to $\Omega_{\text{ds}}^{\varphi}$ and replies with t to the operator/PoS.[10] If $\Omega_{\text{ds}}^{\varphi}$ in not empty, $\mathcal{S}_7^{\text{user-sec}}$ picks an arbitrary $(\varphi, t', u_2') \in \Omega_{\text{ds}}^{\varphi}$, calculates $t := t' + sk_{\mathcal{U}}(u_2 - u_2')$, and then proceeds the same way (cp. Step 1d in Fig. 8.26, Step 5c in Fig. 8.26, Step 1d in Fig. 8.29, and Step 4c in Fig. 8.30).

For the recalculation tag ω_{rc}: In the scope of Deposit/Disburse the code $\pi_7^{\text{user-sec}}$ of the honest PoS/operator is modified such that they ask $\mathcal{S}_7^{\text{user-sec}}$ for the final ω_{rc} which is then output by PoS/operator. To this end they provisionally leak the honestly created ω'_{rc} to $\mathcal{S}_7^{\text{user-sec}}$ which replies with $\omega_{\text{rc}} := \omega'_{\text{rc}}$. Also, the honest PoS additionally leaks p in the scope of Deposit, if the operator is corrupted.

10 Note, that $\mathcal{S}_7^{\text{user-sec}}$ knows $sk_{\mathcal{U}}$ as the user is honest.

For the prove-participation tag ω_{pp}: The code of the honest users is modified such that they ask $\mathcal{S}_7^{\text{user-sec}}$ for the final ω_{pp} which is then output by the users. The honest user does not send $c_{pk_{\mathcal{U}}}$ anymore nor expects to receive σ_{pp}. Instead, $\mathcal{S}_7^{\text{user-sec}}$ creates $c_{pk_{\mathcal{U}}}, d_{pk_{\mathcal{U}}}$ itself[11] and injects $c_{pk_{\mathcal{U}}}$ into the message from the user to the PoS. When the PoS replies with σ_{pp}, $\mathcal{S}_7^{\text{user-sec}}$ compiles $(\omega_{\mathrm{pp}}, \psi_{\mathrm{pp}}) := (c_{pk_{\mathcal{U}}}, (pk_{\mathcal{P}}^{\mathrm{pp}}, \sigma_{\mathrm{pp}}, d_{pk_{\mathcal{U}}}))$, internally records $\bar{f}_{\mathrm{pp}}(\omega_{\mathrm{pp}}) := (\psi_{\mathrm{pp}}, pk_{\mathcal{U}})$ and provides ω_{pp} to the user. Moreover, when the honest user sends $(\omega_{\mathrm{pp}}, \psi_{\mathrm{pp}})$ in the scope of ProveParticipation, the honest user only sends ω_{pp} and $\mathcal{S}_7^{\text{user-sec}}$ injects ψ_{pp} using $\bar{f}_{\mathrm{pp}}$.

In summary, these modifications leak (s, φ) (for ω_{ds}-tags) and—in case of a corrupted operator in Deposit—also p (for ω_{rc}-tags). This equals the behavior of the final $\mathcal{F}_{\mathrm{apc}}$ (cp. Fig. 4.11, Step 10 and Fig. 4.12, Step 7).

On top, $\pi_7^{\text{user-sec}}$ *provisionally* leaks ω_{rc}' which is still honestly created by $\pi_7^{\text{user-sec}}$ and simply mirrored back by $\mathcal{S}_7^{\text{user-sec}}$ as ω_{rc}. This over-leakage is reverted in hybrid $H_{17}^{\text{user-sec}}$. Also, $\mathcal{S}_7^{\text{user-sec}}$ exploits the user's identity to create ω_{pp} honestly, which the final simulator cannot do. This is repaired in hybrid $H_{18}^{\text{user-sec}}$.

Hybrid $H_8^{\text{user-sec}}$ (Decoupling the PRF) This hybrid introduces a new incorruptible entity $\mathcal{F}_{\varphi\text{-rand}}$ into the experiment that is only accessible by honest users and the simulator through subroutine input/output tapes.[12] $\mathcal{F}_{\varphi\text{-rand}}$ provides the following functionality: Internally, $\mathcal{F}_{\varphi\text{-rand}}$ manages a partial map f_Φ, mapping pairs of wallet IDs λ and counters x to fraud-detection IDs. Whenever an as yet undefined value $f_\Phi(\lambda, x)$ is required, $\mathcal{F}_{\varphi\text{-rand}}$ defines $f_\Phi(\lambda, x) := \mathsf{PRF}(\lambda, x)$. If an honest user or the simulator requests a fraud-detection ID φ for (λ, x), $\mathcal{F}_{\varphi\text{-rand}}$ returns $f_\Phi(\lambda, x)$.

Hybrid $H_9^{\text{user-sec}}$ (Create lookup table for double spending) When $\mathcal{S}_9^{\text{user-sec}}$ compiles the set $\Omega_{\mathrm{ds}}^{\varphi}$ within the scope of Deposit or Disburse (cp. hybrid $H_7^{\text{user-sec}}$) and there exist matching double-spending tags $\omega_{\mathrm{ds}}, \omega_{\mathrm{ds}}' \in \Omega_{\mathrm{ds}}^{\varphi}$, then set $f_\pi(pid_{\mathcal{U}}, \pi) := \mathsf{OK}$ with $\pi := sk_{\mathcal{U}}$ to record this incident of double-spending as $\mathcal{S}_{\pi_{\mathrm{P5C}}}^{\text{user-sec}}$ would do.

Hybrid $H_{10}^{\text{user-sec}}$ (Utilize lookup tables for VerifyGuilt) In case the calling party is honest, this hybrid is the same as hybrid $H_{18}^{\text{op-sec}}$. Otherwise this hybrid does not change anything.

Hybrid $H_{11}^{\text{user-sec}}$ (Utilize lookup tables for BlacklistWallet, forego decryption of blacklisting tags) The dispute resolver *DR* becomes a dummy party and simply sends it input

11 Note, that $\mathcal{S}_7^{\text{user-sec}}$ because it simulates $\mathcal{F}_{\mathrm{msg}}$ internally and thus knows the identity of the user.

12 I.e., communication is confidential, reliable and trustworthy. One might think of this entity as a preliminary version of the eventual ideal functionality.

(`blacklist_wallet`, $pid'_{\mathcal{U}}$) to the simulator $\mathcal{S}_{11}^{\text{user-sec}}$ in order to signal its consent to blacklist the user. The simulator $\mathcal{S}_{11}^{\text{user-sec}}$ utilizes $f_{\Omega_{\text{bl}}}$ from hybrid $H_7^{\text{user-sec}}$ and runs the joint code as the ideal functionality $\mathcal{F}_{\text{apc}}$ and $\mathcal{S}_{\pi_{\text{P5C}}}^{\text{user-sec}}$ would do eventually. Especially, $\mathcal{S}_{11}^{\text{user-sec}}$ checks $f_{\Omega_{\text{bl}}}^{-1}(\omega_{\text{bl}})$ to decide whether ω_{bl} is a genuine or a fake tag. If $\lambda := f_{\Omega_{\text{bl}}}^{-1}(\omega_{\text{bl}})$ is defined and hence denotes a genuine tag, simulator $\mathcal{S}_{11}^{\text{user-sec}}$ does not decrypt ω_{bl}, but used the recorded wallet ID λ and $\mathcal{F}_{\varphi\text{-rand}}$ to create the blacklist bl_{Φ_λ}. If $\lambda := f_{\Omega_{\text{bl}}}^{-1}(\omega_{\text{bl}})$ is undefined and hence denotes a fake tag, simulator $\mathcal{S}_{11}^{\text{user-sec}}$ decrypts ω_{bl} as the real dispute resolver would do. If the decrypted user ID $pid_{\mathcal{U}}$ denotes a corrupted user, simulator $\mathcal{S}_{11}^{\text{user-sec}}$ creates a blacklist bl_{Φ_λ} using the real code. Especially simulator $\mathcal{S}_{11}^{\text{user-sec}}$ does not call $\mathcal{F}_{\varphi\text{-rand}}$, but directly uses the PRF to obtain a list of fraud-detection IDs $bl_{\Phi_\lambda} := \{\varphi_{\lambda,0}, \dots, \varphi_{\lambda,x_{\text{bound}}}\}$ for the decrypted wallet ID λ. If the decrypted user ID $pid_{\mathcal{U}}$ denotes an honest user, simulator $\mathcal{S}_{11}^{\text{user-sec}}$ creates a blacklist bl_{Φ_λ} uses $\mathcal{F}_{\varphi\text{-rand}}$.

Hybrid $H_{12}^{\text{user-sec}}$ (Utilize lookup tables for RecalculateBalance, forego decryption of recalculation tags) When the task RecalculateBalance is invoked, $\mathcal{S}_{12}^{\text{user-sec}}$ partitions the set of recalculation tags Ω_{rc} into two set $\Omega_{\text{rc}}^{\text{genuine}}$ and $\Omega_{\text{rc}}^{\text{fake}}$ the same way as $\mathcal{F}_{\text{apc}}$ would do. Recalculation tags $\omega_{\text{rc}} \in \Omega_{\text{rc}}^{\text{genuine}}$ are not decrypted, but $\mathcal{S}_{12}^{\text{user-sec}}$ uses the serial number and price of the original transaction to create a set $\Xi^{\text{genuine}} := \{(s, p)\}$. Recalculation tags $\omega_{\text{rc}} \in \Omega_{\text{rc}}^{\text{fake}}$ are still decrypted, their signature is checked for validity and $\Xi^{\text{fake}} := \{(s, p)\}$ is compiled from the decrypted values. Then the balance is calculated as $b^{\text{bill}} := \sum_{(s,p)\in\Xi^{\text{genuine}}} p + \sum_{(s,p)\in\Xi^{\text{fake}}} p$.
This behavior equals the joint behavior of $\mathcal{F}_{\text{apc}}$ and the final simulator $\mathcal{S}_{\pi_{\text{P5C}}}^{\text{op-sec}}$ (cp. Figs. 4.16 and 8.33).

The modifications of hybrid $H_{12}^{\text{user-sec}}$ are identical to those of hybrid $H_{20}^{\text{op-sec}}$.

Hybrid $H_{13}^{\text{user-sec}}$ (Utilize lookup tables for ProveParticipation, forego unveil of prove-participation tags) This hybrid utilizes $\bar{f}_{\text{pp}}$ to link legitimately issued prove-participation tags to their origin. The code of the honest users is modified such that they do not send $(\omega_{\text{pp}}, \psi_{\text{pp}})$ but only ω_{pp}. Also, the users do not internally test, if ω_{pp} is one of their own prove-participation tags, but simply forward them as a dummy party would do. If the result is positive, $\mathcal{S}_{13}^{\text{user-sec}}$ looks up the corresponding ψ_{pp} in $\bar{f}_{\text{pp}}$ and simulates the message $(\omega_{\text{pp}}, \psi_{\text{pp}})$. Note, ψ_{pp} are not yet equivocated (as the final simulator would do), but $\mathcal{S}_{13}^{\text{user-sec}}$ sends the original ψ_{pp} that have been recorded in hybrid $H_7^{\text{user-sec}}$.

Note that hybrid $H_{13}^{\text{user-sec}}$ is a simplified variant of hybrid $H_{23}^{\text{op-sec}}$. In hybrid $H_{13}^{\text{user-sec}}$, only honest users interacting with a corrupted violation enforcer need to be considered. If the user was corrupted, the violation enforcer would have to be corrupted, too, as required by Theorem 8.28.

Hybrid $H_{14}^{\text{user-sec}}$ (Fake blacklisting tags for honest users) The code $\pi_{14}^{\text{user-sec}}$ for honest users in the scope of IssueWallet is modified such that they do not send ω_{bl}. Instead, $\mathcal{S}_{14}^{\text{user-sec}}$

returns $\omega_{\mathrm{bl}} := (\lambda'', \psi_{\mathrm{bl}})$ with $\psi_{\mathrm{bl}} \leftarrow \mathsf{ENC1.Enc}(pk_{DR}, (1, \ldots, 1))$, when O asks for a ω_{bl} (cp. hybrid $H_7^{\text{user-sec}}$).

Hybrid $H_{15}^{\text{user-sec}}$ (Use truly random fraud-detection IDs) Hybrid $H_{15}^{\text{user-sec}}$ replaces the PRF inside $\mathcal{F}_{\varphi\text{-rand}}$ by truly random values. Whenever an as yet undefined value $f_\Phi(\lambda, x)$ is required, $\mathcal{F}_{\varphi\text{-rand}}$ independently and uniformly draws a fresh random fraud-detection ID φ and sets $f_\Phi(\lambda, x) := \varphi$.

Hybrid $H_{16}^{\text{user-sec}}$ (Fake double-spending tags for honest users) The code $\pi_{16}^{\text{user-sec}}$ for honest users in the scope of Deposit and Disburse is modified such that they do not send a real DS response t. When the operator asks for double-spending tag (cp. hybrid $H_7^{\text{user-sec}}$), the simulator $\mathcal{S}_{16}^{\text{user-sec}}$ proceeds as follows. If no $(\varphi, t', u_2') \in \Omega_{\mathrm{ds}}^{\varphi}$ has been recorded previously, $\mathcal{S}_{16}^{\text{user-sec}}$ picks $t \stackrel{R}{\leftarrow} \mathbb{Z}_p$ randomly. This equals the behavior of the final simulator $\mathcal{S}_{\pi_{\mathrm{P5C}}}^{\text{user-sec}}$.

Note, the modifications of this hybrid are identical to hybrid $H_{25}^{\text{op-sec}}$.

Hybrid $H_{17}^{\text{user-sec}}$ (Fake recalculation tags for honest users) The code $\pi_{17}^{\text{user-sec}}$ for honest operator/PoS in the scope of Deposit and Disburse abandons the over-leakage of ω_{rc}' that has provisionally been introduced by hybrid $H_7^{\text{user-sec}}$. When they ask for ω_{rc} the simulator does not simply reflect $\omega_{\mathrm{rc}} := \omega_{\mathrm{rc}}'$, but instead creates ω_{rc} on its own. The simulator does so in two different ways, depending on the corruption status of the operator.

If the operator is corrupted,[13] the simulator creates $\psi_{\mathrm{rc}} := (s, \varphi, p, pk_{\mathcal{P}}^{\mathrm{rc}}, \sigma_{\mathrm{rc}})$ with $\sigma_{\mathrm{rc}} \leftarrow \mathsf{SIG.Sign}(sk_{\mathcal{P}}^{\mathrm{rc}}, (s, \varphi, g_1^p))$ faithfully and provides a true encryption $\omega_{\mathrm{rc}} \leftarrow \mathsf{ENC2.Enc}(pk_O^{\mathrm{rc,enc}}, \psi_{\mathrm{rc}})$. We stress that $\mathcal{S}_{17}^{\text{user-sec}}$ knows all relevant information s, φ, $pid_{\mathcal{P}}$ and p due to the leakage introduced by hybrid $H_7^{\text{user-sec}}$.

If the operator is honest, $\mathcal{S}_{17}^{\text{user-sec}}$ provides an encryption $\omega_{\mathrm{rc}} \leftarrow \mathsf{ENC2.Enc}(pk_O^{\mathrm{rc,enc}}, \psi_{\mathrm{rc}})$ for an arbitrary ψ_{rc} from the correct space.

Note, the modifications of this hybrid are identical to hybrid $H_{26}^{\text{op-sec}}$.

Hybrid $H_{18}^{\text{user-sec}}$ (Fake prove-participation tags for honest users) The hybrid $H_{18}^{\text{user-sec}}$ modifies Deposit and ProveParticipation.

In Deposit the simulator $\mathcal{S}_{18}^{\text{user-sec}}$ does not use the user's identity to create $(\omega_{\mathrm{pp}}, \psi_{\mathrm{pp}})$. Instead, $\mathcal{S}_{18}^{\text{user-sec}}$ simulates the commitment as $(c_{pk_{\mathcal{U}}}, \bar{d}_{pk_{\mathcal{U}}}) \leftarrow \mathsf{C2.CommitSim}(crs_{\mathrm{com}}^{(2)})$. $\mathcal{S}_{18}^{\text{user-sec}}$ sets $\omega_{\mathrm{pp}} := c_{pk_{\mathcal{U}}}$ and $\psi_{\mathrm{pp}} := (pk_{\mathcal{P}}^{\mathrm{pp}}, \sigma_{\mathrm{pp}}, \bar{d}_{pk_{\mathcal{U}}})$, returns ω_{pp} and defines $\bar{f}_{\mathrm{pp}}(\omega_{\mathrm{pp}}) := (\psi_{\mathrm{pp}}, g_1)$.

Moreover, the code for ProveParticipation in case of an honest user and a corrupted violation enforcer is adapted (cp. hybrid $H_{13}^{\text{user-sec}}$). After $\mathcal{S}_{18}^{\text{user-sec}}$ has looked up the corresponding

[13] N.b., for operator security the operator is always honest, i.e. this case never holds. However, we explicitly consider this case here, as this allows us to reuse this hybrid as hybrid $H_{17}^{\text{user-sec}}$ to prove user security.

$\psi_{\text{pp}}, g_1) := \bar{f}_{\text{pp}}(\omega_{\text{pp}})$, but before sending ψ_{pp} to $\mathcal{Z}^{\text{op-sec}}$ playing the corrupted *VE*, $\mathcal{S}_{18}^{\text{user-sec}}$ parses $(pk_{\mathcal{P}}^{\text{pp}}, \sigma_{\text{pp}}, \bar{d}_{pk_{\mathcal{U}}}) := \psi_{\text{pp}})$, equivocates the decommitment $d_{pk_{\mathcal{U}}} \leftarrow \text{C2.Equivoke}(crs_{\text{com}}^{(2)}, pk_{\mathcal{U}}, c_{pk_{\mathcal{U}}}, \bar{d}_{pk_{\mathcal{U}}})$, redefines $\psi_{\text{pp}} := (pk_{\mathcal{P}}^{\text{pp}}, \sigma_{\text{pp}}, d_{pk_{\mathcal{U}}})$ and then sends ψ_{pp}.

Again, this equals the behavior of the final simulator $\mathcal{S}_{\pi_{\text{P5C}}}^{\text{op-sec}}$.

As before, the proof of Theorem 8.28 is shown by the pairwise indistinguishability of subsequent hybrids. Most of the proofs have already been shown in a similar vein in Section 8.3. In those cases, the proofs are either only sketched or the reader is referred to the corresponding proof in the previous section.

Lemma 8.29 (Indistinguishability between $H_0^{\text{user-sec}}$ to $H_4^{\text{user-sec}}$, $H_6^{\text{user-sec}}$ to $H_{10}^{\text{user-sec}}$, $H_{11}^{\text{user-sec}}$ to $H_{14}^{\text{user-sec}}$, as well as $H_{15}^{\text{user-sec}}$ to $H_{18}^{\text{user-sec}}$, resp.) *Under the assumptions of Theorem 8.28, $H_0^{\text{user-sec}} \overset{c}{\equiv} \dots \overset{c}{\equiv} H_4^{\text{user-sec}}$, $H_6^{\text{user-sec}} \overset{c}{\equiv} \dots \overset{c}{\equiv} H_{10}^{\text{user-sec}}$, $H_{11}^{\text{user-sec}} \overset{c}{\equiv} \dots \overset{c}{\equiv} H_{14}^{\text{user-sec}}$, and $H_{15}^{\text{user-sec}} \overset{c}{\equiv} \dots \overset{c}{\equiv} H_{18}^{\text{user-sec}}$, resp. holds.*

Proof The indistinguishability $H_0^{\text{user-sec}} \overset{c}{\equiv} H_1^{\text{user-sec}}$ is proven similar to the proof of Lemma 8.4. However, with respect to the CRS of the NIZK scheme the composable zero-knowledge property of Definition 6.9 has to be used.

The modifications within the sequence of hybrids $H_1^{\text{user-sec}} \overset{c}{\equiv} H_2^{\text{user-sec}} \overset{c}{\equiv} H_3^{\text{user-sec}}$ and $H_6^{\text{user-sec}} \overset{c}{\equiv} H_7^{\text{user-sec}} \overset{c}{\equiv} H_8^{\text{user-sec}} \overset{c}{\equiv} H_9^{\text{user-sec}}$ are only syntactical. Therefore, the same argument as for Lemma 8.5 applies. Note, the tentative functionality $\mathcal{F}_{\varphi\text{-rand}}$ which is inserted by the hop from $H_7^{\text{user-sec}}$ to $H_8^{\text{user-sec}}$ is inaccessible by $\mathcal{Z}^{\text{user-sec}}$ and still uses the real PRF to generate fraud-detection IDs.

The hop from $H_3^{\text{user-sec}}$ to $H_4^{\text{user-sec}}$ does not change anything from the perspective of $\mathcal{Z}^{\text{user-sec}}$ as C4 is perfectly F_{gp}-extractable (cp. Definition 6.11, Item (4)).

The hop from $H_9^{\text{user-sec}}$ to $H_{10}^{\text{user-sec}}$ is identical to the hop from hybrid $H_{17}^{\text{op-sec}}$ to $H_{18}^{\text{op-sec}}$. See proof of Lemma 8.18.

The chain of indistinguishable hybrids $H_{11}^{\text{user-sec}} \overset{c}{\equiv} H_{12}^{\text{user-sec}} \overset{c}{\equiv} H_{13}^{\text{user-sec}} \overset{c}{\equiv} H_{14}^{\text{user-sec}}$ corresponds to $H_{19}^{\text{op-sec}} \overset{c}{\equiv} H_{20}^{\text{op-sec}} \overset{c}{\equiv} H_{23}^{\text{op-sec}} \overset{c}{\equiv} H_{24}^{\text{op-sec}}$. See Lemmas 8.20, 8.23 and 8.24 for the proofs. Note that for the hop from $H_{12}^{\text{user-sec}}$ to $H_{13}^{\text{user-sec}}$ only the case of honest users needs to be considered in Lemma 8.23. If the user was corrupted, the violation enforcer would have to be corrupted, too, due to the restrictions imposed by Theorem 8.28.

The sequence $H_{15}^{\text{user-sec}} \overset{c}{\equiv} H_{16}^{\text{user-sec}} \overset{c}{\equiv} H_{17}^{\text{user-sec}} \overset{c}{\equiv} H_{18}^{\text{user-sec}}$ is identical to $H_{24}^{\text{op-sec}} \overset{c}{\equiv} H_{25}^{\text{op-sec}} \overset{c}{\equiv} H_{26}^{\text{op-sec}} \overset{c}{\equiv} H_{27}^{\text{op-sec}}$ and proven by Lemmas 8.25 to 8.27. ∎

Lemma 8.30 (Indistinguishability between $H_4^{\text{user-sec}}$ and $H_5^{\text{user-sec}}$) *Under the assumptions of Theorem 8.28, $H_4^{\text{user-sec}} \overset{c}{\equiv} H_5^{\text{user-sec}}$ holds.*

Proof This hop replaces the real proofs by simulated proofs. To show indistinguishability despite this change, we actually have to consider a sequence of sub-hybrids—one for each of the different ZK proof systems P1, P2 and P3. In the first sub-hybrid all proofs for P1 are replaced by simulated proofs, in the second sub-hybrid all proofs for P2 are replaced and finally all proofs for P3. Assume there exists $\mathcal{Z}^{\text{user-sec}}$ that notices a difference between $H_4^{\text{user-sec}}$ and the first sub-hybrid. Then we can construct an adversary $\mathcal{B}$ that has a non-negligible advantage $\mathsf{Adv}^{\text{pok-zk}}_{\mathsf{POK},\mathcal{B}}(n)$. Internally, $\mathcal{B}$ runs $\mathcal{Z}^{\text{user-sec}}$ and plays the protocol and simulator for $\mathcal{Z}^{\text{user-sec}}$. All calls of the simulator to P1.Prove are forwarded by $\mathcal{B}$ to its own oracle in the external challenge game which is either P1.Prove or P1.ProveSim. $\mathcal{B}$ outputs whatever $\mathcal{Z}^{\text{user-sec}}$ outputs. The second and third sub-hybrid follow the same line, but this time $\mathcal{B}$ internally needs to generate simulated proofs for the proof system that has already been replaced in the previous sub-hybrid. As $\mathcal{B}$ gets the simulation trapdoor as part of its input in the external challenge game, $\mathcal{B}$ can do so. ■

Lemma 8.31 (Indistinguishability between $H_5^{\text{user-sec}}$ and $H_6^{\text{user-sec}}$) *Under the assumptions of Theorem 8.28, $H_5^{\text{user-sec}} \stackrel{c}{\equiv} H_6^{\text{user-sec}}$ holds.*

Proof In this hop the commitments c'_{wid}, c_{fix}, c_{upd} and c'_{upd} are replaced with commitments to zero-messages for every honest user. Again, the hop from $H_5^{\text{user-sec}}$ to $H_6^{\text{user-sec}}$ is further split into a sequence of sub-hybrids with each sub-hybrid replacing a single commitment in reverse order of appearance. Assume $\mathcal{Z}^{\text{user-sec}}$ can distinguish between $H_5^{\text{user-sec}}$ and $H_6^{\text{user-sec}}$ with non-negligible advantage. This yields an efficient adversary $\mathcal{B}$ against the hiding property of C1. Please note that none of the commitments are ever opened, hence in each sub-hybrid only a single message is replaced. Internally, $\mathcal{B}$ runs $\mathcal{Z}^{\text{user-sec}}$ and plays the role of all parties and the simulator for $\mathcal{Z}^{\text{user-sec}}$. Externally, $\mathcal{B}$ plays the hiding game. First, $\mathcal{B}$ guesses the index i of the sub-hybrid which lets $\mathcal{Z}^{\text{user-sec}}$ distinguish. For the first $(i-1)$ commitments, $\mathcal{B}$ commits to the true message. For the ith commitment, $\mathcal{B}$ sends the actual message and an all-zero message to the external challenger. $\mathcal{B}$ embeds the external challenge commitment (either to the actual message or the all-zero message) as the ith commitment. All remaining commitments are replaced by commitments to zeros. $\mathcal{B}$ outputs whatever $\mathcal{Z}^{\text{user-sec}}$ outputs. ■

Lemma 8.32 (Indistinguishability between $H_{10}^{\text{user-sec}}$ and $H_{11}^{\text{user-sec}}$) *Under the assumptions of Theorem 8.28, $H_{10}^{\text{user-sec}} \stackrel{c}{\equiv} H_{11}^{\text{user-sec}}$ holds.*

Proof This hop is perfectly indistinguishable from the environment's perspective as the modifications made by hybrid $H_{11}^{\text{user-sec}}$ do not change the output. Note that the dispute resolver is always honest. At the bottom line, identicalness of the outputs follows from the correctness of ENC1. If the operator is honest, too, the argument from Lemma 8.19 applies. If the operator is corrupted, the operator might send a blacklisting tag ω_{bl} which is not genuine. In this case, ω_{bl} is still decrypted as the real dispute resolver would do. Note that $\mathcal{F}_{\varphi\text{-rand}}$ still uses the PRF internally, hence the resulting blacklist is perfectly indistinguishable from the previous hop, no matter whether the user under consideration is corrupted or not. ∎

Lemma 8.33 (Indistinguishability between $H_{14}^{\text{user-sec}}$ and $H_{15}^{\text{user-sec}}$) *Under the assumptions of Theorem 8.28, $H_{14}^{\text{user-sec}} \stackrel{c}{\equiv} H_{15}^{\text{user-sec}}$ holds.*

Proof In this hop the pseudo-random fraud-detection IDs for honest users are replaced by uniformly drawn random IDs. Again, we proceed by introducing a sequence of sub-hybrids. In each sub-hybrid the fraud-detection IDs for one particular wallet ID λ are replaced. If $\mathcal{Z}^{\text{user-sec}}$ can distinguish between two of the sub-hybrids, this immediately yields an efficient adversary against the pseudo-random game as defined in Definition 6.17. Internally, $\mathcal{B}$ runs $\mathcal{Z}^{\text{user-sec}}$ and plays the protocol and simulator for $\mathcal{Z}^{\text{user-sec}}$. Externally, $\mathcal{B}$ interacts with an oracle that is either a true random function $R(\cdot)$ or a pseudo-random function $\mathsf{PRF}(\hat{\lambda}, \cdot)$ for an unknown seed $\hat{\lambda}$. Whenever $\mathcal{B}$ playing $\mathcal{F}_{\varphi\text{-rand}}$ internally needs to draw a fraud-detection ID for the particular wallet λ, $\mathcal{B}$ uses its external oracle. $\mathcal{B}$ outputs whatever $\mathcal{Z}^{\text{user-sec}}$ outputs. Please note, this argument crucially uses the fact that $\mathcal{Z}^{\text{user-sec}}$ is information-theoretically independent of λ. The blacklisting tags ψ_{bl} have already been replaced by encryptions of 1-vectors in the previous hybrid $H_{14}^{\text{user-sec}}$. This enables the external challenger to pick any seed $\hat{\lambda}$. ∎

Again, we conclude this section by gathering the results and repeating the initial theorem.

Theorem 8.28 (User Security and Privacy) *Under the assumptions of Theorem 8.1*

$$\pi_{\text{P5C}}^{\mathcal{F}_{\text{CRS}}, \mathcal{F}_{\text{bb}}, \mathcal{F}_{\text{msg}}} \geq_{\text{UC}} \mathcal{F}_{\text{apc}} \tag{8.32}$$

holds under static corruption of

(1) *a subset of PoSes, operator and violation enforcer, or*

(2) *all PoSes, operator and violation enforcer as well as a subset of users.*

Proof A direct consequence of Lemmas 8.29 to 8.33. ∎

9 Performance Evaluation

In order to evaluate the practicality of P5C, we reconsider the performance figures from [Nag+17; Nag+20]. Please note, that in neither case the exact protocol as presented here is implemented. In [Nag+17] BBA+ lacks many of the functional improvements, especially the blacklisting mechanism. Therefore, no costly range proofs to escrow the secret wallet ID are necessary during IssueWallet. Moreover, BBA+ does not support user/PoS attributes. Hence, the message sizes and zero-knowledge proofs are smaller. In [Nag+20] a scheme which includes all functional features has been implemented and thus it is very close to the scheme presented in this thesis. Still, the belated fixes which have been introduced by this thesis are missing. However, the fixes have not changed the computationally costly zero-knowledge proofs and thus should only have little impact on the performance figures.

In summary, the following implementation figures have to be taken with a pinch of salt.

9.1 Hardware

As to the hardware, the users, the PoSes and the remaining parties, mostly the operator but also the dispute resolver and violation enforcer have to be considered separately. For the latter group it is reasonable to assume that they may use typical PC hardware, or—if it was necessary—reasonably powerful workstation/server hardware. In [Nag+17; Nag+20] the runtime of the operator (also known as toll service provider in [Nag+20]) is measured on a standard laptop featuring an i7-6600U processor for simplicity. In contrast, users and PoSes are typically equipped with hardware which only offers lower computational powers, because it has to be mobile, is deployed in the field or embedded into another system.

For BBA+ [Nag+17] the authors consider a pre-payment system or customer loyalty program. Hence users are assumed to be individuals who use their smartphones to manage their wallets. In [Nag+17] the user side has been implemented on a OnePlus 3 smartphone. It features a Snapdragon 820 Quad-Core processor (2 × 2.15 GHz & 2 × 1.6 GHz), 6 GB RAM and runs Android OS v7.1.1 (Nougat).

For the feature-complete scheme in the ETC setting [Nag+20] the user side correspond to vehicles. The user side has been measured on an evaluation board that features an i.MX6 Dual-Core processor running at 800 MHz with 1 GB DDR3 RAM and 4 GB eMMC Flash. The processor runs an embedded Linux, is ARM Cortex-A9 based (32-bit), and also exists in a more powerful Quad-Core variant. The same processor is used in real vehicles as part of the Savari MobiWAVE-1000 on-board unit [Sav17]. For the PoS hardware, which corresponds to toll gantries, we take the ECONOLITE Connected Vehicle Coprocessor Module as a reference system, which was specifically designed to enable third-party-developed or processor-intensive applications [ECO18] and measured on comparable hardware.

9.2 Parameter Choice and Instantiation of Setup Assumptions

As for the bilinear group setting, we use the Barreto-Naehrig curves Fp254BNb and Fp254n2BNb [BN06; Kaw+16] and the optimal Ate pairing since this choice results in the shortest execution times [Moo+15]. This yields a security level of about 100 bit [BD17].

In [Nag+20] the scheme is evaluated for two sizes of attribute vectors: $|a_{\mathcal{U}}| = |a_{\mathcal{P}}| = 1$ and $|a_{\mathcal{U}}| = |a_{\mathcal{P}}| = 4$. With curves of 254-bit order, each vector component can encode up to 253 bits of arbitrary information. In practice, it should be possible to encode multiple attributes into one such component.

The secure messaging functionality of $\mathcal{F}_{\text{msg}}$ to securely exchange protocol messages has been realized by the IND-CCA-secure encryption scheme from [CKS08] in combination with AES-CBC and HMAC-SHA256. The remaining two setup assumptions $\mathcal{F}_{\text{CRS}}$ and $\mathcal{F}_{\text{bb}}$ have not been implemented as independent components, but hard-coded. This is reasonable for the CRS which becomes a fixed system parameter after it has been generated trustworthily and standardized once. Using a static list of keys for $\mathcal{F}_{\text{bb}}$ is viable for a testbed, but has obviously to be replaced by a key registration service in reality. Please note, that the latter has no impact on the runtime measurements which are considered here. The remaining building blocks have been instantiated as in Section 6.2.

9.3 Tool Chain, Libraries and Optimizations

The scheme is implemented C++17 using the RELIC toolkit v.0.4.1, an open source cryptography and arithmetic library written in C, with support for pairing-friendly elliptic curves [AG16]. We developed our own library for Groth-Sahai NIZK proofs [EG14; GS08] and employed the method in [CCs08] to realize the range proofs. In order to utilize the capabilities of our hardware, the user side algorithms were optimized for two CPU cores. We also optimized the computations performed by the operator/PoS, taking advantage of the four CPU cores and the batching techniques for Groth-Sahai verification by Herold et al. [Her+17].

Protocol	$\lvert a_{\mathcal{U}}\rvert = \lvert a_{\mathcal{P}}\rvert = 1$				$\lvert a_{\mathcal{U}}\rvert = \lvert a_{\mathcal{P}}\rvert = 4$			
	t_{user} [ms]	$t_{\text{op/pos}}$ [ms]	n_{user} [byte]	$n_{\text{op/pos}}$ [byte]	t_{user} [ms]	$t_{\text{op/pos}}$ [ms]	n_{user} [byte]	$n_{\text{op/pos}}$ [byte]
IssueWallet	27 064	8 490	87 951	944	27 183	8 545	88 107	1 152
Deposit								
– Offline (pre-/post-processing)	2 749	–	–	–	2 750	–	–	–
– Online	348	475	8 128	976	456	5256	8 336	1 088
– Online (cached certificate)	41	475	8 128	976	40	526	8 336	1 088

Runtime t is averaged over 1 000 executions. Transmitted data n is rounded up to full bytes.

Table 9.1: Performance results of [Nag+20]

9.4 Implementation Results

In this thesis we only reconsider the most important results and concentrate on the main tasks which include the expensive NIZKs. Table 9.1 shows the results of our measurements for the feature-complete scheme in the ETC setting in terms of execution time and transmitted data.

The performance of the task IssueWallet is dominated by the key escrow mechanism which requires to split the secret wallet ID into a B-ary representation and proof its correctness. This has a major impact on the zero-knowledge proof both in terms of runtime and size. This is also reflected by the fact that the number of attributes has only a slight effect. At first glance, a runtime of roughly 35 seconds appears impractical. However, the task is not time-critical and only needs to be executed once per wallet.

Also, the task Deposit is dictated by the zero-knowledge proof. Without any further optimizations the task would require (2 749 + 348 =) 3 097 ms at the user side and 475 ms at the PoS side or 3 572 ms in total. Clearly, this is too long for practical use. Fortunately, all parts of the expensive NIZK proof which are independent of the challenge value u_2 can be precomputed. This includes all but one equation of the zero-knowledge language. Also assembling the updated wallet after the last message has been exchanged can be moved to a post-processing phase. This way the computation time at the user side can be reduced to 348 ms between the first and the last message. When caching valid PoS certificates, the runtime can be further reduced to approximately 40 ms. The computation time at the PoS is dominated by the verification of the NIZK and thus cannot be outsourced. In summary, all computations in the online phase of Deposit can be performed in about 515 ms.

Protocol	t_{user} [ms]	$t_{\text{op/pos}}$ [ms]	n_{user} [byte]	$n_{\text{op/pos}}$ [byte]
IssueWallet	129	89	672	352
Deposit				
– Offline (pre-/post-processing)	285	—	—	—
– Online	76	436	4 576	464
Disburse				
– Offline (pre-/post-processing)	268	—	—	—
– Online	76	430	4 544	464
Disburse (with range proofs)				
– Offline (pre-/post-processing)	271	—	—	—
– Online	623	853	13 920	448

Table 9.2: Performance results of [Nag+17]

Table 9.2 shows the performance results of BBA+ from [Her+17]. First note, that BBA+ [Nag+17] has no support for user attribute vectors and also does not use PoS certificates. This means the results needs to be contrasted with the results for one attribute and cached certificates in Table 9.1.

The task IssueWallet is faster by magnitudes, because BBA+ has no blacklisting mechanism and thus does not need to perform a costly range proof to escrow the wallet ID. This is reflected in runtime and message size. The combined runtime for the user and operator is 218 ms vs. 35 s and the combined message size is 1 kB vs. 89 kB.

The performance of the online phase of Disburse for BBA+ [Her+17] is approximately in the same scale as for the ETC system in [Nag+20]. The computation time is 76 ms vs. 41 ms at the user side and 436 ms vs. 475 ms at the PoS side. The differences at the user is due to the use of different hardware, i.e. a smartphone vs. an OBU evaluation board. The amount of transfer data in [Her+17] is approximately half of the amount in [Nag+20]. Remember, that [Her+17] is missing some features. Hence, no prove-participation tag is sent and the NIZK is smaller, because fraud-detection IDs are not images of a PRF but randomly drawn and the NIZK lacks the attribute vectors of the user and the previous PoS.

Also, Herold et al. show performance results for a different variant of the task Disburse. In our running prime example, Disburse simply unveils the current balance of the wallet. This also matches the scenario in [Nag+20]. In this case the performance of Disburse is approximately the same as for Deposit. Alternatively, Disburse may use range proofs to show that the wallet contains sufficient funds. Typically, pre-payment scenarios benefit from the higher privacy and are discussed in Section 2.3.2. In this case, the runtime increases by a factor of eight at the user side and nearly doubles at the PoS side. Also, the amount of data which is sent by the user increases by a factor of three.

9.4.1 Storage Requirements

The storage requirements are of no concern with respect to today's hardware. The wallet itself consumes 1 kB of memory and is fixed in size. During Deposit, the user and the PoS collect data in order to, e.g., prevent double-spending or to prove participation in a protocol run. In Deposit, the user has to store 137 bytes of transaction information and (optionally) 268 bytes to cache the PoS certificate for later re-use. Assuming that users perform 10000 transactions in one billing period, they have to store 1.37 MB of transaction information and, even if all visited PoSes were different, 2.68 MB of cached certificates.

A PoS has to store 246 bytes of transaction information after each run of Deposit for the double-spending tags, prove-participation tags and recalculation tags. All this information is eventually aggregated at the operator's database. Even for large scale deployments with hundreds of millions of transactions per month, the resulting database would only consume a few gigabytes.

9.4.2 Computing DLOGs

To blacklist a user, the dispute resolver has to compute a number of discrete logarithms to recover the wallet ID λ. With our choice of parameters, λ is split into 32-bit values, thus resulting in the computation of eight 32-bit DLOGs. While DLOGs of this size can be brute-forced naively, the technique of Bernstein et al. [BL12] can be used to speed up this process. Using their algorithm, computing a discrete logarithm in an interval of order 2^{32} takes around 1.5 seconds on a single core of a standard desktop using a 55 kB table of precomputed elements. These precomputations need to be done only *once* by the dispute resolver when setting up the system and take one hour on a desktop computer. Thus, the required DLOGs can be computed in reasonable time by the dispute resolver.

10 Summary, Open Problems and Future Work

The final chapter of this thesis serves two purposes. First some improvements of the definition of $\mathcal{F}_{\text{apc}}$ and the scheme π_{P5C} are discussed. Section 10.1 deals with smaller improvements. These improvements are rather straight-forward and have been discovered during the writing of this thesis, but have not found their way into the final version. Section 10.2 discusses what has to be changed to enable simulation-based security not only under restricted sets but also under arbitrary corruption of the parties. This change comes at the cost of less efficiency. Finally, Section 10.3 concludes the thesis and give some pointers to future work beyond the rather simple improvements which already has been discussed.

10.1 Minor Improvements

The following three minor improvements are not expected to cause any problems or provide any new insights. The first one only affects a seemingly inconsequential design decision that has been (badly) determined in a very early stage and pervades the whole system. Hence, it has turned out not to be fixable without much labor in exchange for very little benefit. The other two improvements have been unveiled when the synchronization of the transaction tags has been formalized explicitly.

10.1.1 Wallet Handles

The first improvement removes the serial number s from all input/output in all tasks. Instead, a newly introduced *wallet handle*—which must not be confused with the (secret) wallet ID λ—is used where needed. The serial number is given as output to the user only to enable several wallets per user and to provide the user with an option to denote which wallet should be used in a particular task. But the serial number is actually too much. It does not only denote a wallet but a whole wallet state and thus also empowers formally honest users to commit double-spending. This leads to the awkward distinction between honest and well-behaving users on the one hand side and honest but misbehaving users on the other hand side.

Although outputting the (secret) wallet ID λ to the user seems to be what is wanted, this does not work out, because it would allow the environment to evaluate the PRF and check for real fraud-detection IDs vs. ideal fraud-detection IDs. At the bottom line, this is the same problem as in the formalization of symmetric encryption in UC. There, the (secret) encryption key must not be output to the environment, as the environment could distinguish encrypted messages from random simulations, but still an option to select which key shall be used is required. The solution is to introduce wallet handles which are truly random numbers and map one-to-one and onto the underlying wallet ID, but are information-theoretically independent of the fraud-detection IDs. More precisely, at the end of IssueWallet the user (and only the user, not the operator) obtains a wallet handle that is internally drawn by $\mathcal{F}_{\text{apc}}$ and mapped to the wallet ID. The user re-inputs the wallet handle into Deposit and Disburse. Internally, $\mathcal{F}_{\text{apc}}$ looks up the latest state of the corresponding wallet. This way honest users are also unable to commit double-spending. Still double-spending is possible, but the user must be formally corrupted first. For the latter, $\mathcal{F}_{\text{apc}}$ asks the adversary to provide the serial number of an alternative wallet state, if the user is corrupted. Hence, the distinction between well-behaving and misbehaving (honest) users can be dropped.

The introduction of wallet handles allows to get rid of some inelegant leakage. In IssueWallet and Deposit the $\mathcal{F}_{\text{apc}}$ explicitly leaks the serial number s to the adversary. Although this is not a serious problem, because s is a random number, the only reason for the leakage is to enable the simulation of a Blum cointoss which is consistent to the later output. If the serial number is not output, the Blum cointoss can be simulated blindly. This also applies to some other tasks.

All in all, this modification would lead to a cleaner, more concise and more "semantical" interface. However, the change is not only a cosmetic one. The observation of the previous paragraph with respect to the Blum cointoss is also a key element for the extension to full-fledged security under arbitrary corruption (cp. Section 10.2).

10.1.2 Recalculation Tags

The next improvement affects the recalculation tags ω_{rc}. As stated in Sections 4.4.3 and 7.4.3 only very little guarantees are provided. The operator must rely on the PoSes that they provide correct and complete sets of recalculation tags. Although, the hidden recalculation tag $\psi_{\text{rc}} := (s, \varphi, p, pk_{\mathcal{P}}^{\text{rc}}, \sigma_{\text{rc}})$ is signed by the PoS this does not ensure that the signed price p is actually the same price as used in the transaction. Also, corrupted PoSes can create additional recalculation tags or drop them.

As an intermediate step, the hidden recalculation tag ψ_{rc} could be sent to the user. This way, the PoS is deterred from dropping a recalculation tag, because the user owns a copy which is validly signed by the PoS. The corrupted PoS can still put a different price into its copy of the recalculation tag, but the user can check this and immediately file a claim out-of-band. This intermediate step would likely increase the security level in a "practical" sense, but cannot be formally captured by the model and a corrupted PoS can still inject additional recalculation tags.

A more comprehensive solution would also make the user sign the recalculation tag. This way, the PoS cannot unilaterally alter the price later and also not create fake tags. However, this solution comes with two obstacles.

A straightforward signature $\sigma_{\mathcal{U}}^{\mathrm{rc}}$ by the user contradicts the user's privacy in Deposit as the PoS somehow needs to check its validity. Instead, the user is equipped with a signing key pair $(pk_{\mathcal{U}}^{\mathrm{rc}}, sk_{\mathcal{U}}^{\mathrm{rc}})$ whose public part $pk_{\mathcal{U}}^{\mathrm{rc}}$ needs to be certified, i.e. signed by the operator, similar to what is done in CertifyPOS for PoSes. This could either be part of IssueWallet or an independent task. Under the assumption that the signing scheme has the non-standard, but quite natural security property that a pure signature $\sigma_{\mathcal{U}}^{\mathrm{rc}}$ does not unveil anything about the public key $pk_{\mathcal{U}}^{\mathrm{rc}}$ under which it is valid, the following approach is possible. The user signs the recalculation tag and sends the signature $\sigma_{\mathcal{U}}^{\mathrm{rc}}$ together with a NIZK proof π^{rc} that the signature is valid under an (anonymous) user key which again is validly signed by the operator. Then the hidden recalculation tag is extended to $\psi_{\mathrm{rc}} := (s, \varphi, p, pk_{\mathcal{P}}^{\mathrm{rc}}, \pi^{\mathrm{rc}}, \sigma_{\mathcal{P}}^{\mathrm{rc}}, \sigma_{\mathcal{U}}^{\mathrm{rc}})$ with $\sigma_{\mathcal{P}}^{\mathrm{rc}} = \sigma_{\mathrm{rc}}$ denoting the PoS signature as before. Please note, that this is very closely related to the concepts of group or ring signatures. If the signature scheme unveils the public key for which it is valid, then the signature $\sigma_{\mathcal{U}}^{\mathrm{rc}}$ can additionally be encapsulated in a commitment. We stress that it does not suffice, if the participating PoS is convinced that the user has signed the recalculation tag, but the operator who collects all recalculation tags later, needs to be convinced, too.

Unfortunately, this comprehensive solution does not only increase the computational complexity of Deposit but also requires an additional round of communication. The user can only create $\sigma_{\mathcal{U}}^{\mathrm{rc}}$ after the price p has been learned. At the current state, Deposit sends p as part of the last (i.e. third) message from the PoS to the user (cp. Fig. 7.20). This message also sends the updatable commitment c_{upd} and the associated signature σ_{upd}. These components must remain in the last message, as otherwise a malicious user could run away with a new wallet before Deposit is completed. Hence, it is not admissible to only add one additional message in which the user sends $(\pi^{\mathrm{rc}}, \sigma_{\mathcal{U}}^{\mathrm{rc}})$ at the end, but instead the currently third message becomes the fifth message, the price p is pushed forward to a newly added third message and the user sends $(\pi^{\mathrm{rc}}, \sigma_{\mathcal{U}}^{\mathrm{rc}})$ in the newly added forth message.

Finally, the task RecalculateBalance needs to be extended into a two-party task involving the user. The user and the operator both input their set of recalculation tags and both sets are united. This way, neither side can drop a recalculation tag. For the case that the user does not agree to participate, RecalculateBalance can still be run by the operator alone using the empty set $\emptyset$ for the user's input.

Skipping ahead, the merger of the improved recalculation tag with the improved prove-participation tag (cp. next section) into a joint *receipt tag* seems appealing, because both share overlapping information and thereby modeling a true digital counterpart of a physical invoice. However, this is only syntactical embellishment.

10.1.3 Prove-Participation Tags

The prove-participation tags exhibit a practical problem that is very similar to the afore discussed recalculation tags. The PoS which has triggered the violation enforcer to physically identify a user is the same PoS which also provides a set of prove-participation tag Ω_{pp} to the violation enforcer. This allows a PoS to intentionally embezzle the relevant prove-participation tags which are connected to the incident and thereby disable the user to refute the accusation (cp. Sections 4.4.4 and 7.4.4). Note, that the hidden prove-participation tag $\psi_{\mathrm{pp}} := (pk_{\mathcal{P}}^{\mathrm{pp}}, \sigma_{\mathrm{pp}}, d_{pk_{\mathcal{U}}})$ already contains a signature on the prove-participation tag $\omega_{\mathrm{pp}} := c_{pk_{\mathcal{U}}}$ by the PoS. At least, this allows users to prove that they have participated in *some* transaction with the accusing PoS, but it does not prove that this has been the specific transaction under investigation.

In a former approach the serial number s has been part of ψ_{pp}, but s is as random as the commitment value $c_{pk_{\mathcal{U}}}$, does not establish a connection to the transaction and thus does not solve the problem. To solve the problem once and for all, the violation enforcer needs to be able to *autonomously* relate the physical identification (e.g. a photo) to some information about the transaction without relying on the PoS to assist with this mapping honestly.

In practice, the solution is quite easy. An improved prove-participation tag would encode the actual whereabouts of the transaction including a location, which is already given by the PoS' identity and position, and a timestamp. This timestamp would also be included in the photo and thus could be matched. A timestamp is an example of a "publicly verifiable information" (cp. Section 2.4). Each party has its own time source which it trusts. Depending on the scenario and the frequency in which a user participates in a transaction with the same PoS the timestamps only need to match approximately. A practical solution would be as follows: The user commits to its public key $pk_{\mathcal{U}}$ as before and sends $c_{pk_{\mathcal{U}}}$ to the PoS together with its own timestamp $ts_{\mathcal{U}}$. If $ts_{\mathcal{U}}$ is sufficiently accurate, i.e. within a specified distance from $ts_{\mathcal{P}}$, the PoS signs the tuple $(c_{pk_{\mathcal{U}}}, ts_{\mathcal{U}})$ and sends σ_{pp} back to the user. If anything fails, the PoS triggers the violation enforcer (as before) which takes a photo and equips it with its own timestamp ts_{VE}. Later, the physically identified user is challenged on $(pid_{\mathcal{P}}, ts_{VE})$. If the user can present a prove-participation tag which is signed by the correct PoS, has a timestamp $ts_{\mathcal{U}}$ close to ts_{VE} and can be unveiled to the user's own public key $pk_{\mathcal{U}}$, then the user is discharged. Note, that this way the violation enforcer does not need any input from the PoS.

Unfortunately, this apparent solution cannot easily be modeled in the UC framework, although the basic idea of $\mathcal{F}_{\mathrm{ts}}$ seems easy. The hybrid $\pi_{\mathrm{P5C}}^{\mathcal{F}_{\mathrm{CRS}},\mathcal{F}_{\mathrm{bb}},\mathcal{F}_{\mathrm{msg}}}$ is augmented by an ideal timestamping functionality $\mathcal{F}_{ts}$. $\mathcal{F}_{ts}$ is a n-ary functionality (for arbitrary n) that upon request outputs the same timestamp to all n parties. Within the scope of the (abstract) model a simple integer that is increased for each request suffices as a timestamp. As each of the n parties per request gets the identical timestamp, we do not need to deal with (real-world) inaccuracies neither. The main problem is the formalization of $\mathcal{F}_{ts}$ and is more involved than it may seem. UC is inherently asynchronous and message driven, i.e. to be accurate $\mathcal{F}_{ts}$ cannot output to n parties at once, but looses its activation after each output to a single party. Moreover, the adversary is not obliged to re-schedule $\mathcal{F}_{ts}$ right away, but may let other parties run first. This also accounts to the problem that $\mathcal{F}_{ts}$ cannot know if the n first parties which request $\mathcal{F}_{ts}$ for a timestamp actually belong to the same transaction and thus should receive the same timestamp or if these n parties belong to different transactions and therefore some of them should receive a different timestamp. These problems can be overcome ([Kat+13]), but the formalization is surprisingly intricate.

As already said in the previous section, the improved prove-participation tags and the improved recalculation tags suggest themselves to be combined into on sort of tag, as they share a lot of identical information after the extension.

10.2 Towards Full-Fledged Corruption

In Chapter 8 π_{P5C} is proven to be secure UC-realization of $\mathcal{F}_{apc}$ for restricted sets of corruption. We observe, that full-fledged indistinguishability is possible, if an extractable commitment scheme is used.

Let's temporarily ignore the commitment scheme C4 for the serial number s in IssueWallet and the Blum cointoss as well as the the commitment scheme C2 used by the prove-participation tags to hide the user's public key. We fist concentrate on the commitment scheme C1, which is used to create the fixed and updatable commitment c_{fix}, c_{upd} of a wallet, and the NIZK proofs P1, P2 and P3 in IssueWallet, Deposit and Disburse, resp.

A close look at the simulators for operator and user security, especially how they setup the CRS (cp. Figs. 8.2 and 8.19), shows that

(1) The NIZK proof schemes P1, P2 and P3 are used in extraction mode (for operator security) and in simulation mode (for user security).

(2) The commitment scheme C1 is setup honestly (in both cases).

(3) All (secret) witnesses which are extracted from the NIZK proofs π (in case of operator security) are also contained in the commitments c_{fix}, c_{upd}, resp.

(4) A user only creates the commitments c_{fix} and c_{upd}, but never unveils them.

With respect to the second item, we note that C1 allows to be setup for equivocation, but this property is not needed in the proof. With respect to the last item, we stress that c_{fix} and c_{upd} are neither unveiled in IssueWallet nor in Deposit, but only homomorphically modified. Although the balance b is unveiled in Deposit, the commitment c_{upd} itself is not opened but only unveiled indirectly by means of a NIZK proof that shows that the user knows a consistent opening information. These both observation in combination with the third item from the list allow the following solution under the assumption that C1 is replaced by an extractable scheme.

For a full-fledged corruption model, the simulator setups the NIZK schemes P1, P2 and P3 for simulation and the commitment scheme C1 for extraction. When the simulator needs to simulate a message of an honest user towards a corrupted PoS/operator, it commits to some random value (which never needs to be opened) and simulates a proof exactly the same way as currently done in the case for user security. If the simulator plays an honest PoS (or operator) in an interaction with a corrupted user, the simulator extracts the user's secrets from the commitments (instead from the proof as it is done now in case of operator security) and inputs the extracted values into $\mathcal{F}_{\text{apc}}$.

We stress that this modified proof strategy does not need any modifications on the protocol level. But it rules out shrinking commitments, because these go along with an information-theoretic loss and thus cannot be extractable. Hence, full UC security could be traded against a little less efficiency.

We now consider the commitment scheme C2 for the prove-participation tags. Here, the same trick of an indirect opening can be applied. To this end, only the realization of the task ProveParticipation needs to be modified. The user does not unveil $c_{pk_{\mathcal{U}}}$ directly and thereby shows that it contains $pk_{\mathcal{U}}$, but instead the user sends a NIZK proof to the violation enforcer and thereby demonstrates that $c_{pk_{\mathcal{U}}}$ could correctly be unveiled. Note that this already happens in the context of Deposit when the (anonymous) user proves to the PoS that $c_{pk_{\mathcal{U}}}$ contains the correct value. The modification of ProveParticipation is cheap, as the proof is small and ProveParticipation is not time critical. Then C2 can be put into extraction mode for the security proof. For corrupted users the used $pk_{\mathcal{U}}$ is extracted from $c_{pk_{\mathcal{U}}}$ in the scope of Deposit, while for honest users the NIZK proof is simulated in the scope of ProveParticipation.

Lastly, we need to deal with the commitment scheme C4 which is used in IssueWallet and Deposit to jointly draw a random serial number s by means of a Blum cointoss. At the moment, C4 is either setup for equivocation (in case of operator security) or for extraction (in case of user security) to consistently simulate the cointoss for either side. Surely, the same trick could be applied again: Instead of opening the commitment c''_{ser} to the share s'', the operator could send a NIZK proof and show an indirect opening. However, opposed to ProveParticipation this is computationally prohibitive as Deposit is a time critical task. But a much easier solution is possible. If the interface of $\mathcal{F}_{\text{apc}}$ is changed as outlined in Section 10.1.1 such that the serial number s is removed from the input/output, then the necessity to simulate a consistent Blum cointoss is remedied. Instead, a random commitment could be used to simulate the cointoss blindly.

In summary, full simulatability under arbitrary corruption is possible in exchange for a different (less efficient, non-shrinking, extractable) instantiation of C1 and a minor modification of ProveParticipation.

An Open Problem The unmodified poof as presented in Chapter 8 and especially in Section 8.4 uses the NIZK scheme to assert that corrupted users indeed know their committed secrets, i.e. the NIZK proofs are proofs of knowledge. The proposed modification moves this attestation from the NIZK proofs to the commitments and thus allows to prove full-fledged security using a different proof strategy. However, the modification does not affect the NIZK scheme at all. Especially an adversary does not gain any further capabilities how to create NIZK proofs and cannot (and must not) know whether the NIZK scheme is running in extraction mode or not. Hence, from the adversary's perspective it does not make any difference, if the true value is extracted from the NIZK proof (given the prerequisite that it the CRS is setup this way) or if the true value is extracted from the commitment scheme.

Let's express the idea differently: In theory, a non-extractable (and shrinking) commitment scheme might quash security, because the adversary might be able to find a way to send commitments whose message is not known by the adversary itself at the time when the commitment is sent, e.g. the adversary could try to blindly forward a commitment from another message and get away with it. However, this kind of attack is ruled out by the zero-knowledge proof of knowledge. Hence, as long as the NIZK scheme has the knowledge property, switching the commitment scheme between a non-extractable (and shrinking) or an extractable commitment scheme does not open up room for attacks. However, the adversary does not know, if the CRS of the NIZK is setup for extraction.

This leads to the conjecture that the inability to prove the unmodified protocol π_{P5C} secure under arbitrary corruption is not a real insecurity of the scheme, but a formal problem of the proof strategy. Hence, it is tempting to assume that π_{P5C} is also secure under arbitrary corruption using shrinking (non-extractable) commitments. Finding an adequate proof strategy seems interesting.

10.3 Summary and Future Work

In this thesis we have formalized the concept of anonymous point collection as an abstract building block. The proposed definition does not only heavily extend the functional requirements of such a building block over previous approaches and thereby widens the practical applicability, but also is—to the best of our knowledge—the first one that provides a comprehensive definition as an ideal functionality in the UC framework and thereby treats correctness, security and privacy in an integrated way. A realization has been constructed (in pseudo-code) and formally been proven secure. Again, to the best of our knowledge, the rigorous and thorough security analysis of our building block is the first one in its area, i.e. among comparable proposed building block which target similar scenarios. Along that way a lot of technical subtleties had to be considered to eventually find a definition of security that is not overly idealized and thus cannot be realized on the one hand, but still captures a meaningful notion of security and is not too weak on the other hand, while allowing for a practically efficient realization at the same time. The resulting building block is the first one that

(1) allows for anonymous two-way transactions,

(2) has (periodic) offline capabilities,

(3) requires only constant storage size (with respect to the balance), and

(4) is provably secure.

Moreover, the proposed construction has been actually implemented on real-world hardware to document its efficiency for practical deployment. Here, a challenging task has been to select the right set of instantiations of the building blocks which could be fine-tuned to nicely interplay with each other. The last two points have to be entirely credited to the author's co-workers.

However, this thesis' contribution should not only be perceived as an improved definition and construction of an abstract building block for a specific purpose, but this thesis also demonstrates that the UC framework is the "right" method to formalize the security and privacy of complex systems. This thesis' genesis is a perfect evidence: In [Nag+17] operator security as well as user security and privacy are treated as different problems. Operator security is formalized under the game-based paradigm using a list of desired properties and an individual game per property. User security is already formalized under the simulation-based paradigm, but rather in an ad-hoc model than a rigorously defined model such as the UC framework. Especially, this ad-hoc model is not very precise on how the simulator knows which user needs to be simulated, the simulator simply "does the right thing". In [Nag+20] the system is modeled in the UC framework, but ignores the synchronization of the distributed state. Instead Nagel et al. [Nag+20] vaguely states that the tags "somehow" roam from one party to the other. Both transitions from [Nag+17] to [Nag+20] and from [Nag+20] to this thesis have unveiled flaws in the previous attempt which have turned out to be oversights and would have allowed for real-world attacks.

This thesis also has shown how the classical game-based approach that uses a list of individual objectives can be combined with the simulation-based paradigm. Surely, a list of individual security properties (as in the game-based approach) tends to be more appealing as each of the security games is usually connected to a desired objective while an ideal functionality (for a complex system) tends to deprive itself from an immediate interpretation.[1] But, the game-based approach has the inherent problem that it remains unclear when the list of properties is complete. In other words, each of the security games rules out a certain attack (e.g. claiming a wrong balance), but there is no guarantee what else may go wrong beyond that list. En contraire, the simulation-based approach is very good at making explicit what cannot be achieved. Starting with an overly ideal functionality more and more "backdoors" for the simulator are incorporated until it becomes realizable. For each backdoor there must either be a justification why it is inherent to the problem and thus cannot be avoided or a better realization must be contrived. This thesis gives an example how both methodologies can be combined for a complex system: At first a list of desired objectives is compiled, but then an ideal functionality needs to be defined. Instead of showing that a particular realization fulfills each objective by means of an individual security game, one shows that the ideal functionality fulfills the objective as done in this thesis in Sections 5.1 and 5.2.

The same approach also lends itself for a privacy analysis of a complex system as shown in Section 5.3. Instead of analyzing the privacy for a concrete (cryptographic) realization and a concrete dataset (for a particular deployment), the privacy should be analyzed using the ideal model. The ideal functionality abstracts away the cryptographic complexity and "pulls it out of the equation".

Although this thesis has (hopefully) contributed to the question how the security of complex systems can be captured, it has unveiled two problems which we deem interesting for further (long-term) research. Anonymous point collection might be a complex system from the usual cryptographic perspective compared to much simpler primitives like encryption, signatures, commitments and so on, but is by far not a complex system from the perspective of IT security (or even general software engineering) which deal with much larger systems. Nonetheless, already for this middle-size systems UC proofs become cumbersome and tedious, which might also explain why rigorous formal treatment at the same level of granularity is less common in the IT security domain. In the author's personal opinion, two problems need to be overcome to remedy this issue: (1) The UC framework needs to be relaxed (or extended) such that modular proofs are not only a theoretical promise, but actually possible in a way that reflects

[1] Indeed, one of the (anonymous) reviewer of [Nag+20] declared to feel more confident about the security of the scheme, if there were individual security games instead of a single ideal functionality, because the functionality were a complex protocol on its own and it was hard to tell what security it provides.

the way how existing building blocks are combined in practice (cp. Section 5.4.3). (2) We require tools that allow computer-aided, automatic proofs of indistinguishability between ideal functionalities and their realization. Automated reasoning about security properties has gained much attention in the IT security field. However, existing tools (e.g. ProVerif, CryptoVerif, etc.) are usually very good at showing that given a certain set of pre-conditions the execution of some code fulfills some post-conditions and thus are very close to the game-based approach [Bla+18].

Notation

Identifier		Definition	Description
$a_{\mathcal{O}}$	$\in$	$\mathcal{A}_{\mathcal{P}}$	Operator attributes
$a_{\mathcal{P}}$	$\in$	$\mathcal{A}_{\mathcal{P}}$	PoS attributes
$\mathcal{A}_{\mathcal{P}}$	$=$	G_1^y	Set of operator/PoS attributes
$a_{\mathcal{U}}$	$\in$	$\mathcal{A}_{\mathcal{U}}$	User attributes
$\mathcal{A}_{\mathcal{U}}$	$=$	G_2^j	Set of user attributes
b	$\in$	$\mathbb{Z}_p$	Balance of the wallet
B	$\in$	$\mathbb{Z}_p$	Base or "width" for the chunks of the wallet ID; fixed system parameter
bl_{Φ}	$\ni$	φ	Blacklist of fraud-detection IDs; used by PoSes
c_{fix}	$\in$	G_2	Commitment on fixed part of the wallet
$c_{pk_{\mathcal{U}}}$	$\in$	G_2	Hidden user ID; part of ω_{pp}
c''_{ser}	$\in$	G_1^2	Commitment on the PoS' share of the serial number
c_{upd}	$\in$	G_2	Commitment on the updatable part of the wallet
c'_{wid}	$\in$	G_2	Commitment on the user's share of the wallet ID
$cert_{\mathcal{O}}$	$=$	$(pk_{\mathcal{O}}^{\text{upd}}, a_{\mathcal{O}}, \sigma_{\mathcal{O}}^{\text{cert}})$	Operator self-signed certificate
$cert_{\mathcal{P}}$	$=$	$(pk_{\mathcal{P}}, a_{\mathcal{P}}, \sigma_{\mathcal{P}}^{\text{cert}})$	PoS certificate
d_{fix}	$\in$	G_1	Opening for c_{fix}
$d_{pk_{\mathcal{U}}}$	$\in$	G_1	Opening for $c_{pk_{\mathcal{U}}}$; part of ψ_{pp}
d''_{ser}	$\in$	$\mathbb{Z}_p^2$	Opening for c''_{ser}
d_{upd}	$\in$	G_1	Opening for c_{upd}
d'_{wid}	$\in$	G_1	Opening for c'_{wid}
$f_{\mathcal{A}_{\mathcal{P}}}$	:	$\mathcal{PID}_{\mathcal{P}} \to \mathcal{A}_{\mathcal{P}}$	(Partial) mapping assigning a PoS attribute $a_{\mathcal{P}}$ to a PoS PID $pid_{\mathcal{P}}$
$f_{\mathcal{A}_{\mathcal{U}}}$	:	$\mathcal{L} \to \mathcal{A}_{\mathcal{U}}$	(Partial) mapping assigning a user attribute $a_{\mathcal{U}}$ to a wallet ID λ
f_{π}	:	$\mathcal{PID}_{\mathcal{U}} \times \Pi \to \{\mathsf{OK}, \mathsf{NOK}\}$	(Partial) mapping assigning a validity bit to a pair of user PID $pid_{\mathcal{U}}$ and proof of guilt π

Identifier		Definition	Description
j	$\in$	$\mathbb{N}$	Dimension of the user attribute vector; fixed system parameter
ℓ	$\in$	$\mathbb{N}$	Number of chunks the wallet ID is split into; fixed system parameter
n	$\in$	$\mathbb{N}$	Security parameter
p	$\in$	$\mathbb{Z}_{\mathfrak{p}}$	Price to pay at an PoS
$\mathfrak{p}$	$\in$	$\mathbb{P}$	Prime-order of the underlying groups; fixed system parameter
$\mathcal{PID}_{\text{corr}}$	$\subseteq$	$\{0,1\}^*$	Set of identifiers of corrupted parties
pid_{DR}	$\in$	$\{0,1\}^*$	Party identifier of the dispute resolver
$pid_{\mathcal{O}}$	$\in$	$\{0,1\}^*$	Party identifier of the operator
$pid_{\mathcal{P}}$	$\in$	$\{0,1\}^*$	Party identifier of a PoS
$\mathcal{PID}_{\mathcal{P}}$	$\ni$	$pid_{\mathcal{P}}$	Set of party identifiers of the PoSes
$pid_{\mathcal{U}}$	$\in$	$\{0,1\}^*$	Party identifier of a user
$\mathcal{PID}_{\mathcal{U}}$	$\ni$	$pid_{\mathcal{U}}$	Set of party identifiers of the users
pk_{DR}	$\in$	$G_1^3 \times G_2^3 \times (G_1^2)^{\ell+2} \times (G_2^2)^4 \times (G_2^2)^{\ell+2}$	Public key of the dispute resolver
$pk_{\mathcal{O}}$	$=$	$(pk_{\mathcal{O}}^{\text{fix}}, pk_{\mathcal{O}}^{\text{cert}}, pk_{\mathcal{O}}^{\text{upd}}, pk_{\mathcal{O}}^{\text{rc,sig}}, pk_{\mathcal{O}}^{\text{rc,enc}})$	Public key of the operator
$pk_{\mathcal{O}}^{\text{cert}}$	$\in$	$G_1^6 \times G_2^{y+5}$	Public key of the operator for verifying a PoS-certificate; part of $pk_{\mathcal{O}}$
$pk_{\mathcal{O}}^{\text{fix}}$	$\in$	$G_1^3 \times G_2^j$	Public key of the operator for verifying the fixed part of the wallet; part of $pk_{\mathcal{O}}$
$pk_{\mathcal{O}}^{\text{upd}}$	$\in$	$G_1^3 \times G_2$	Public key of the operator for verifying the updatable part of the wallet; part of $pk_{\mathcal{O}}$
$pk_{\mathcal{O}}^{\text{rc,sig}}$	$\in$	$G_1^2 \times G_2^3$	Public key of the operator for verifying the recalculation tag; part of $pk_{\mathcal{O}}$
$pk_{\mathcal{O}}^{\text{rc,enc}}$	$\in$	$G_1^2 \times G_2^2$	Public key of the operator for encrypting the recalculation tag; part of $pk_{\mathcal{O}}$
$pk_{\mathcal{P}}$	$\in$	$(pk_{\mathcal{P}}^{\text{upd}}, pk_{\mathcal{P}}^{\text{rc}}, pk_{\mathcal{P}}^{\text{pp}})$	Public key of the PoS
$pk_{\mathcal{P}}^{\text{upd}}$	$\in$	$G_1^3 \times G_2$	Public key of the PoS for verifying the updatable part of the wallet; part of $pk_{\mathcal{P}}$
$pk_{\mathcal{P}}^{\text{pp}}$	$\in$	G_1^3	Public key of the PoS for verifying the prove-participation tag; part of $pk_{\mathcal{P}}$

Identifier		Definition	Description
$pk_{\mathcal{P}}^{\mathrm{rc}}$	$\in$	$G_1^2 \times G_2^3$	Public key of the PoS for verifying the recalculation tag; part of $pk_{\mathcal{P}}$
$pk_{\mathcal{U}}$	$\in$	G_1	Public key of the user
s	$\in$	S	Serial number
S	$=$	G_1	Space of serial numbers
sk_{DR}	$\in$	$\mathbb{Z}_p^{2\ell+8}$	Secret key of the dispute resolver
sk_{O}	$=$	$(sk_{O}^{\mathrm{fix}}, sk_{O}^{\mathrm{cert}}, sk_{O}^{\mathrm{upd}}, sk_{O}^{\mathrm{rc,sig}}, sk_{O}^{\mathrm{rc,enc}})$	Secret key of the operator
sk_{O}^{cert}	$\in$	$\mathbb{Z}_p^{y+11}$	Secret key of the operator for certifying a PoS; part of sk_{O}
sk_{O}^{fix}	$\in$	$\mathbb{Z}_p^{j+3}$	Secret key of the operator for signing the fixed part of the wallet; part of sk_{O}
sk_{O}^{upd}	$\in$	$\mathbb{Z}_p^{4}$	Secret key of the operator for signing the updatable part of the wallet; part of sk_{O}
$sk_{O}^{\mathrm{rc,sig}}$	$\in$	$\mathbb{Z}_p^{5}$	Secret key of the operator for signing the recalculation tag; part of sk_{O}
$sk_{O}^{\mathrm{rc,enc}}$	$\in$	$\mathbb{Z}_p^{4}$	Secret key of the operator for decrypting the recalculation tag; part of sk_{O}
$sk_{\mathcal{P}}$	$=$	$(sk_{O}^{\mathrm{upd}}, sk_{\mathcal{P}}^{\mathrm{rc}}, sk_{\mathcal{P}}^{\mathrm{pp}})$	Secret key of the PoS
$sk_{\mathcal{P}}^{\mathrm{upd}}$	$\in$	$\mathbb{Z}_p^{4}$	Secret key of the PoS for signing the updatable part of the wallet; part of $sk_{\mathcal{P}}$
$sk_{\mathcal{P}}^{\mathrm{pp}}$	$\in$	$\mathbb{Z}_p^{3}$	Secret key of the PoS for signing the prove-participation tag; part of $sk_{\mathcal{P}}$
$sk_{\mathcal{P}}^{\mathrm{rc}}$	$\in$	$\mathbb{Z}_p^{5}$	Secret key of the PoS for signing the recalculation tag; part of $sk_{\mathcal{P}}$
$sk_{\mathcal{U}}$	$\in$	$\mathbb{Z}_p$	Secret key of the user
t	$\in$	$\mathbb{Z}_p$	Double-spending response
u_1	$\in$	$\mathbb{Z}_p$	Double-spending mask
u_2	$\in$	$\mathbb{Z}_p$	Double-spending challenge
x	$\in$	$\{0, \dots, x_{\mathrm{bound}}\}$	(PRF) counter
x_{bound}	$\in$	$\mathbb{N}$	Upper bound on the number of transactions per wallet and upper bound on the number of fraud-detection IDs in bl_{Φ} per wallet; fixed system parameter

Identifier		Definition	Description
y	$\in$	$\mathbb{N}_0$	Dimension of the operator/PoS attribute vector; fixed system parameter
λ	$\in$	$\mathbb{Z}_p$	Wallet ID; used as PRF seed
$\mathcal{L}$	$\ni$	λ	Set of wallet IDs
λ'	$\in$	$\mathbb{Z}_p$	User's share of the wallet ID
λ'_i	$\in$	$\{0, \dots, B-1\}$	A chunk of the user's share of the wallet ID
λ''	$\in$	$\mathbb{Z}_p$	Operator's share of the wallet ID
π			Depending on context an arbitrary ZK-proof or a proof of guilt
Π	$\ni$	π	Set of π's
φ	$\in$	G_1	Fraud-detection ID
Φ	$\ni$	φ	Set of fraud-detection IDs
$\sigma_{\mathcal{O}}^{\text{cert}}$	$\in$	$G_2^2 \times G_1$	Signature on $(pk_{\mathcal{O}}^{\text{upd}}, a_{\mathcal{O}})$ under $pk_{\mathcal{O}}^{\text{cert}}$; part of $cert_{\mathcal{O}}$
$\sigma_{\mathcal{P}}^{\text{cert}}$	$\in$	$G_2^2 \times G_1$	Signature on $(pk_{\mathcal{P}}, a_{\mathcal{P}})$ under $pk_{\mathcal{O}}^{\text{cert}}$; part of $cert_{\mathcal{P}}$
σ_{fix}	$\in$	$G_2^2 \times G_1$	Signature on $(c_{\text{fix}}, a_{\mathcal{U}})$ under $pk_{\mathcal{O}}^{\text{fix}}$; the fixed part of the wallet
σ_{pp}	$\in$	$G_2^2 \times G_1$	Signature on $c_{pk_{\mathcal{U}}}$ under $pk_{\mathcal{P}}^{\text{pp}}$; part of ψ_{pp}
σ_{rc}	$\in$	$G_2^2 \times G_1$	Signature on (s, φ, g_1^p) under $pk_{\mathcal{O}}^{\text{rc,sig}}/pk_{\mathcal{P}}^{\text{rc}}$; part of the recalculation tag ω_{rc}
σ_{upd}	$\in$	$G_2^2 \times G_1$	Signature on (c_{upd}, s) under $pk_{\mathcal{O}}^{\text{upd}}$ or $pk_{\mathcal{P}}$; the updatable part of the wallet
ψ_{bl}	$\in$	$(G_1^3 \times G_2^3) \times G_1^{\ell+2} \times G_T$	Encryption of $(\Lambda'_0, \dots, \Lambda'_{\ell-1}, \Lambda'', pk_{\mathcal{U}})$ under pk_{DR}; part of the blacklisting tag
ψ_{pp}	$=$	$(pk_{\mathcal{P}}^{\text{pp}}, \sigma_{\text{pp}}, d_{pk_{\mathcal{U}}})$	Secret part of prove-participation tag
ψ_{rc}	$=$	$(s, \varphi, p, pk_{\mathcal{P}}^{\text{rc}}, \sigma_{\text{rc}})$	Secret part of recalculation tag
ω_{bl}	$=$	$(\lambda'', \psi_{\text{bl}})$	Blacklisting tag
Ω_{bl}	$\ni$	ω_{bl}	Set of blacklisting tags
ω_{ds}	$=$	(φ, t, u_2)	Double-spending tag
Ω_{ds}	$\ni$	ω_{ds}	Set of double-spending tags
ω_{pp}	$=$	$c_{pk_{\mathcal{U}}}$	Prove-participation tag
Ω_{pp}	$\ni$	ω_{pp}	Set of prove-participation tags
ω_{rc}	$\in$	$\{0,1\}^*$	Recalculation tag; encryption of ψ_{rc} under $pk_{\mathcal{O}}^{\text{rc,enc}}$
Ω_{rc}	$\ni$	ω_{rc}	Set of recalculation tags

Bibliography

[Abe+11] Masayuki Abe et al. "Optimal Structure-Preserving Signatures in Asymmetric Bilinear Groups." In: *Advances in Cryptology – CRYPTO 2011* (Santa Barbara, CA, USA, Aug. 14–18, 2011). Ed. by Phillip Rogaway. Vol. 6841. Lecture Notes in Computer Science. Heidelberg, Germany: Springer, 2011, pp. 649–666.

[Abe+14] Masayuki Abe et al. "Converting Cryptographic Schemes from Symmetric to Asymmetric Bilinear Groups." In: *Advances in Cryptology – CRYPTO 2014, Part I* (Santa Barbara, CA, USA, Aug. 17–21, 2014). Ed. by Juan A. Garay and Rosario Gennaro. Vol. 8616. Lecture Notes in Computer Science. Heidelberg, Germany: Springer, 2014, pp. 241–260.

[Abe+15] Masayuki Abe et al. "Fully Structure-Preserving Signatures and Shrinking Commitments." In: *Advances in Cryptology – EUROCRYPT 2015, Part II* (Sofia, Bulgaria, Apr. 26–30, 2015). Ed. by Elisabeth Oswald and Marc Fischlin. Vol. 9057. Lecture Notes in Computer Science. Heidelberg, Germany: Springer, 2015, pp. 35–65.

[AG16] D. F. Aranha and C. P. L. Gouvêa. *RELIC is an Efficient Library for Cryptography.* 2016. URL: `https://github.com/relic-toolkit/relic`.

[Aim16] Aimia Coalition Loyalty UK Ltd. *The Nectar loyalty program.* 2016. URL: `https://www.nectar.com/`.

[AIR01] William Aiello, Yuval Ishai, and Omer Reingold. "Priced Oblivious Transfer: How to Sell Digital Goods." In: *Advances in Cryptology – EUROCRYPT 2001* (Innsbruck, Austria). Ed. by Birgit Pfitzmann. Vol. 2045. Lecture Notes in Computer Science. Heidelberg, Germany: Springer, 2001, pp. 119–135.

[AK12] Man Ho Au and Apu Kapadia. "PERM: practical reputation-based blacklisting without TTPS." In: *ACM CCS 2012: 19th Conference on Computer and Communications Security* (Raleigh, NC, USA, Oct. 16–18, 2012). Ed. by Ting Yu, George Danezis, and Virgil D. Gligor. New York, NY, USA: ACM Press, 2012, pp. 929–940.

[AKS12] Man Ho Au, Apu Kapadia, and Willy Susilo. "BLACR: TTP-Free Blacklistable Anonymous Credentials with Reputation." In: *ISOC Network and Distributed System Security Symposium – NDSS 2012* (San Diego, CA, USA, Feb. 5–8, 2012). Ed. by Radu Sion and Andrew White. Reston, VA, USA: The Internet Society, 2012.

[Alb+18] Carolin Albrecht et al. "Knapsack Problems: A Parameterized Point of View." In: *Theoretical Computer Science* (2018).

[And+08] Elli Androulaki et al. "Reputation Systems for Anonymous Networks." In: *PETS 2008: 8th International Symposium on Privacy Enhancing Technologies* (Leuven, Belgium, July 23–25, 2008). Ed. by Nikita Borisov and Ian Goldberg. Vol. 5134. Lecture Notes in Computer Science. Heidelberg, Germany: Springer, 2008, pp. 202–218.

[ASM06] Man Ho Au, Willy Susilo, and Yi Mu. "Constant-Size Dynamic k-TAA." In: *SCN 06: 5th International Conference on Security in Communication Networks* (Maiori, Italy, Sept. 6–8, 2006). Ed. by Roberto De Prisco and Moti Yung. Vol. 4116. Lecture Notes in Computer Science. Heidelberg, Germany: Springer, 2006, pp. 111–125.

[Bal+10] Josep Balasch et al. "PrETP: Privacy-Preserving Electronic Toll Pricing." In: *USENIX Security 2010: 19th USENIX Security Symposium* (Washington, DC, USA, Aug. 11–13, 2010). Ed. by Ian Goldberg. Berkeley, CA, USA: USENIX Association, 2010, pp. 63–78.

[Bal+15] Foteini Baldimtsi et al. "Anonymous Transferable E-Cash." In: *PKC 2015: 18th International Conference on Theory and Practice of Public Key Cryptography* (Gaithersburg, MD, USA, Mar. 30–Apr. 1, 2015). Ed. by Jonathan Katz. Vol. 9020. Lecture Notes in Computer Science. Heidelberg, Germany: Springer, 2015, pp. 101–124.

[Bar+04] Boaz Barak et al. "Universally Composable Protocols with Relaxed Set-Up Assumptions." In: *45th Annual Symposium on Foundations of Computer Science* (Rome, Italy, Oct. 17–19, 2004). Ed. by Irene Finocchi and Andrea Vitaletti. IEEE Computer Society Press, 2004, pp. 186–195.

[Bar+16] Amira Barki et al. "Private eCash in Practice (Short Paper)." In: *FC 2016: 20th International Conference on Financial Cryptography and Data Security* (Christ Church, Barbados, Feb. 22–June 26, 2016). Ed. by Jens Grossklags and Bart Preneel. Vol. 9603. Lecture Notes in Computer Science. Heidelberg, Germany: Springer, 2016, pp. 99–109.

[BB04] Dan Boneh and Xavier Boyen. “Short Signatures Without Random Oracles.” In: *Advances in Cryptology – EUROCRYPT 2004* (Interlaken, Switzerland, May 2–6, 2004). Ed. by Christian Cachin and Jan Camenisch. Vol. 3027. Lecture Notes in Computer Science. Heidelberg, Germany: Springer, 2004, pp. 56–73.

[BD15] Alberto Blanco-Justicia and Josep Domingo-Ferrer. “Privacy-Preserving Loyalty Programs.” In: *Data Privacy Management, Autonomous Spontaneous Security, and Security Assurance. 9th International Workshop, DPM 2014, 7th International Workshop, SETOP 2014, and 3rd International Workshop, QASA 2014.* Revised Selected Papers (Wroclaw, Poland, Sept. 10–11, 2014). Ed. by Joaquín García-Alfaro et al. Vol. 8872. Lecture Notes in Computer Science. Heidelberg, Germany: Springer, 2015, pp. 133–146.

[BD17] Razvan Barbulescu and Sylvain Duquesne. *Updating key size estimations for pairings.* 2017. Cryptology ePrint Archive (IACR): Report 2017/334.

[Bea92] Donald Beaver. “Foundations of Secure Interactive Computing.” In: *Advances in Cryptology – CRYPTO’91* (Santa Barbara, CA, USA, Aug. 11–15, 1991). Ed. by Joan Feigenbaum. Vol. 576. Lecture Notes in Computer Science. Heidelberg, Germany: Springer, 1992, pp. 377–391.

[Bel+08] Mira Belenkiy et al. “P-signatures and Noninteractive Anonymous Credentials.” In: *TCC 2008: 5th Theory of Cryptography Conference* (San Francisco, CA, USA, Mar. 19–21, 2008). Ed. by Ran Canetti. Vol. 4948. Lecture Notes in Computer Science. Heidelberg, Germany: Springer, 2008, pp. 356–374.

[Bel+98] Mihir Bellare et al. “Relations Among Notions of Security for Public-Key Encryption Schemes.” In: *Advances in Cryptology – CRYPTO’98* (Santa Barbara, CA, USA, Aug. 23–27, 1998). Ed. by Hugo Krawczyk. Vol. 1462. Lecture Notes in Computer Science. Heidelberg, Germany: Springer, 1998, pp. 26–45.

[Bel15] Mihir Bellare. “New Proofs for NMAC and HMAC: Security without Collision Resistance.” In: *Journal of Cryptology* 28.4 (Oct. 2015), pp. 844–878.

[BL12] Daniel J. Bernstein and Tanja Lange. *Computing small discrete logarithms faster.* 2012. Cryptology ePrint Archive (IACR): Report 2012/458.

[Bla+18] Bruno Blanchet et al. *ProVerif 2.00. Automatic Cryptographic Protocol Verifier, User Manual and Tutorial.* May 16, 2018. URL: `https://prosecco.gforge.inria.fr/personal/bblanche/proverif/manual.pdf` (visited on 10/13/2019).

[BN06] Paulo S. L. M. Barreto and Michael Naehrig. "Pairing-Friendly Elliptic Curves of Prime Order." In: *SAC 2005: 12th Annual International Workshop on Selected Areas in Cryptography* (Kingston, Ontario, Canada, Aug. 11–12, 2005). Ed. by Bart Preneel and Stafford Tavares. Vol. 3897. Lecture Notes in Computer Science. Heidelberg, Germany: Springer, 2006, pp. 319–331.

[BNR18] Jürgen Beyerer, Matthias Nagel, and Matthias Richer. *Pattern Recognition. Introduction, Features, Classifiers and Principles.* Oldenbourg: De Gruyter, 2018.

[BPW04] Michael Backes, Birgit Pfitzmann, and Michael Waidner. "A General Composition Theorem for Secure Reactive Systems." In: *TCC 2004: 1st Theory of Cryptography Conference* (Cambridge, MA, USA, Feb. 19–21, 2004). Ed. by Moni Naor. Vol. 2951. Lecture Notes in Computer Science. Heidelberg, Germany: Springer, 2004, pp. 336–354.

[Bro+17] Brandon Broadnax et al. "Concurrently Composable Security with Shielded Super-Polynomial Simulators." In: *Advances in Cryptology – EUROCRYPT 2017, Part I* (Paris, France, Apr. 30–May 4, 2017). Ed. by Jean-Sébastien Coron and Jesper Buus Nielsen. Vol. 10210. Lecture Notes in Computer Science. Heidelberg, Germany: Springer, 2017, pp. 351–381.

[BS05] Boaz Barak and Amit Sahai. "How To Play Almost Any Mental Game Over The Net - Concurrent Composition via Super-Polynomial Simulation." In: *46th Annual Symposium on Foundations of Computer Science* (Pittsburgh, PA, USA, Oct. 23–25, 2005). Ed. by Eva Tardos. Los Alamitos, CA, USA: IEEE Computer Society Press, 2005, pp. 543–552.

[Cam+11] Jan Camenisch et al. "Structure Preserving CCA Secure Encryption and Applications." In: *Advances in Cryptology – ASIACRYPT 2011* (Seoul, South Korea, Dec. 4–8, 2011). Ed. by Dong Hoon Lee and Xiaoyun Wang. Vol. 7073. Lecture Notes in Computer Science. Heidelberg, Germany: Springer, 2011, pp. 89–106.

[Cam+15] Jan Camenisch et al. "Composable and Modular Anonymous Credentials: Definitions and Practical Constructions." In: *Advances in Cryptology – ASIACRYPT 2015, Part II* (Auckland, New Zealand, Nov. 30–Dec. 3, 2015). Ed. by Tetsu Iwata and Jung Hee Cheon. Vol. 9453. Lecture Notes in Computer Science. Heidelberg, Germany: Springer, 2015, pp. 262–288.

[Can+02] Ran Canetti et al. "Universally composable two-party and multi-party secure computation." In: *34th Annual ACM Symposium on Theory of Computing* (May 19–21, 2002). Ed. by John H. Reif. New York, NY, USA: ACM Press, 2002, pp. 494–503.

[Can+07] Ran Canetti et al. "Universally Composable Security with Global Setup." In: *TCC 2007: 4th Theory of Cryptography Conference* (Amsterdam, The Netherlands, Feb. 21–24, 2007). Ed. by Salil P. Vadhan. Vol. 4392. Lecture Notes in Computer Science. Heidelberg, Germany: Springer, 2007, pp. 61–85.

[Can00] Ran Canetti. *Universally Composable Security: A New Paradigm for Cryptographic Protocols.* Version Original revision. 2000. Cryptology ePrint Archive (IACR): Report 2000/067.

[Can01] Ran Canetti. "Universally Composable Security: A New Paradigm for Cryptographic Protocols." In: *42nd Annual Symposium on Foundations of Computer Science* (Las Vegas, NV, USA, Oct. 14–17, 2001). Ed. by Moni Naor. Los Alamitos, CA, USA: IEEE Computer Society Press, 2001, pp. 136–145.

[Can03] Ran Canetti. *Universally Composable Signatures, Certification and Authentication.* 2003. Cryptology ePrint Archive (IACR): Report 2003/239.

[Can05] Ran Canetti. *Universally Composable Security: A New Paradigm for Cryptographic Protocols.* Version 2nd major revision. 2005. Cryptology ePrint Archive (IACR): Report 2000/067.

[Can07] Ran Canetti. *Obtaining Universally Composable Security: Towards the Bare Bones of Trust.* 2007. Cryptology ePrint Archive (IACR): Report 2007/475.

[Can13] Ran Canetti. *Universally Composable Security: A New Paradigm for Cryptographic Protocols.* Version 3rd major revision. 2013. Cryptology ePrint Archive (IACR): Report 2000/067.

[Can18] Ran Canetti. *Universally Composable Security: A New Paradigm for Cryptographic Protocols.* Version 4th major revision. 2018. Cryptology ePrint Archive (IACR): Report 2000/067.

[CCs08] Jan Camenisch, Rafik Chaabouni, and abhi shelat. "Efficient Protocols for Set Membership and Range Proofs." In: *Advances in Cryptology – ASIACRYPT 2008* (Melbourne, Australia, Dec. 7–11, 2008). Ed. by Josef Pieprzyk. Vol. 5350. Lecture Notes in Computer Science. Heidelberg, Germany: Springer, 2008, pp. 234–252.

[CDN10] Jan Camenisch, Maria Dubovitskaya, and Gregory Neven. "Unlinkable Priced Oblivious Transfer with Rechargeable Wallets." In: *FC 2010: 14th International Conference on Financial Cryptography and Data Security* (Tenerife, Spain, Jan. 25–28, 2010). Ed. by Radu Sion. Vol. 6052. Lecture Notes in Computer Science. Heidelberg, Germany: Springer, 2010, pp. 66–81.

[CDT19] Jan Camenisch, Manu Drijvers, and Björn Tackmann. *Multi-Protocol UC and its Use for Building Modular and Efficient Protocols.* 2019. Cryptology ePrint Archive (IACR): Report 2019/065.

[CF01] Ran Canetti and Marc Fischlin. "Universally Composable Commitments." In: *Advances in Cryptology – CRYPTO 2001* (Santa Barbara, CA, USA, Aug. 19–23, 2001). Ed. by Joe Kilian. Vol. 2139. Lecture Notes in Computer Science. Heidelberg, Germany: Springer, 2001, pp. 19–40.

[CG08] Sébastien Canard and Aline Gouget. "Anonymity in Transferable E-Cash." In: *ACNS 08: 6th International Conference on Applied Cryptography and Network Security* (New York, NY, USA, June 3–6, 2008). Ed. by Steven M. Bellovin et al. Vol. 5037. Lecture Notes in Computer Science. Heidelberg, Germany: Springer, 2008, pp. 207–223.

[Che+13] Xihui Chen et al. "Design and Formal Analysis of A Group Signature Based Electronic Toll Pricing System." In: *JoWUA* 4.1 (2013), pp. 55–75. URL: `http://isyou.info/jowua/papers/jowua-v4n1-3.pdf`.

[CHL05] Jan Camenisch, Susan Hohenberger, and Anna Lysyanskaya. "Compact E-Cash." In: *Advances in Cryptology – EUROCRYPT 2005* (Aarhus, Denmark, May 22–26, 2005). Ed. by Ronald Cramer. Vol. 3494. Lecture Notes in Computer Science. Heidelberg, Germany: Springer, 2005, pp. 302–321.

[Chr+11] Delphine Christin et al. "A survey on privacy in mobile participatory sensing applications." In: *Journal of Systems and Software* 84.11 (2011), pp. 1928–1946.

[CK02] Ran Canetti and Hugo Krawczyk. "Universally Composable Notions of Key Exchange and Secure Channels." In: *Advances in Cryptology – EUROCRYPT 2002* (Amsterdam, The Netherlands, Apr. 28–May 2, 2002). Ed. by Lars R. Knudsen. Vol. 2332. Lecture Notes in Computer Science. Heidelberg, Germany: Springer, 2002, pp. 337–351.

[CKS08] David Cash, Eike Kiltz, and Victor Shoup. "The Twin Diffie-Hellman Problem and Applications." In: *Advances in Cryptology – EUROCRYPT 2008* (Istanbul, Turkey, Apr. 13–17, 2008). Ed. by Nigel P. Smart. Vol. 4965. Lecture Notes in Computer Science. Heidelberg, Germany: Springer, 2008, pp. 127–145.

[CLP10] Ran Canetti, Huijia Lin, and Rafael Pass. "Adaptive Hardness and Composable Security in the Plain Model from Standard Assumptions." In: *51st Annual Symposium on Foundations of Computer Science* (Las Vegas, NV, USA, Oct. 23–26, 2010). Ed. by Luca Trevisan. Los Alamitos, CA, USA: IEEE Computer Society Press, 2010, pp. 541–550.

[CLZ12] Rafik Chaabouni, Helger Lipmaa, and Bingsheng Zhang. "A Non-interactive Range Proof with Constant Communication." In: *FC 2012: 16th International Conference on Financial Cryptography and Data Security* (Kralendijk, Bonaire, Feb. 27–Mar. 2, 2012). Ed. by Angelos D. Keromytis. Vol. 7397. Lecture Notes in Computer Science. Heidelberg, Germany: Springer, 2012, pp. 179–199.

[Cou19] Counter Solutions Ltd. *Counter Solutions*. 2019. URL: `https://countersolutions.co.uk/`.

[CR03] Ran Canetti and Tal Rabin. "Universal Composition with Joint State." In: *Advances in Cryptology – CRYPTO 2003* (Santa Barbara, CA, USA, Aug. 17–21, 2003). Ed. by Dan Boneh. Vol. 2729. Lecture Notes in Computer Science. Heidelberg, Germany: Springer, 2003, pp. 265–281.

[CSV16] Ran Canetti, Daniel Shahaf, and Margarita Vald. "Universally Composable Authentication and Key-Exchange with Global PKI." In: *PKC 2016: 19th International Conference on Theory and Practice of Public Key Cryptography, Part II* (Taipei, Taiwan, Mar. 6–9, 2016). Ed. by Chen-Mou Cheng et al. Vol. 9615. Lecture Notes in Computer Science. Heidelberg, Germany: Springer, 2016, pp. 265–296.

[CV12] Ran Canetti and Margarita Vald. "Universally Composable Security with Local Adversaries." In: *SCN 12: 8th International Conference on Security in Communication Networks* (Amalfi, Italy, Sept. 5–7, 2012). Ed. by Ivan Visconti and Roberto De Prisco. Vol. 7485. Lecture Notes in Computer Science. Heidelberg, Germany: Springer, 2012, pp. 281–301.

[Day+11] Jeremy Day et al. "SPEcTRe: Spot-checked Private Ecash Tolling at Roadside." In: *WPES '11: Proceedings of the 10th Annual ACM Workshop on Privacy in the Electronic Society* (Chicago, IL, USA, Oct. 17, 2011). Ed. by Yan Chen and Jaideep Vaidya. New York, NY, USA: ACM Press, 2011, pp. 61–68.

[DDS12] Morten Dahl, Stéphanie Delaune, and Graham Steel. "Formal Analysis of Privacy for Anonymous Location Based Services." In: *Theory of Security and Applications* (2012), pp. 98–112.

[Dow+17] Rafael Dowsley et al. "A survey on design and implementation of protected searchable data in the cloud." In: *Computer Science Review* 26 (2017). Ed. by Josep Díaz and Jaroslav Nešetril, pp. 17–30.

[Dwo06] Cynthia Dwork. "Differential Privacy (Invited Paper)." In: *ICALP 2006: 33rd International Colloquium on Automata, Languages and Programming, Part II* (Venice, Italy, July 10–14, 2006). Ed. by Michele Bugliesi et al. Vol. 4052. Lecture Notes in Computer Science. Heidelberg, Germany: Springer, 2006, pp. 1–12.

[Dwo09] Cynthia Dwork. "The Differential Privacy Frontier (Extended Abstract)." In: *TCC 2009: 6th Theory of Cryptography Conference* (San Francisco, CA, USA, May 15–17, 2009). Ed. by Omer Reingold. Vol. 5444. Lecture Notes in Computer Science. Heidelberg, Germany: Springer, 2009, pp. 496–502.

[Dwo10] Cynthia Dwork. "Differential Privacy in New Settings." In: *21st Annual ACM-SIAM Symposium on Discrete Algorithms* (Austin, TX, USA, Jan. 17–19, 2010). Ed. by Moses Charika. Philadelphia, PA, USA: ACM Society for Industrial and Applied Mathematics, 2010, pp. 174–183.

[DY04] Yevgeniy Dodis and Aleksandr Yampolskiy. *A Verifiable Random Function With Short Proofs and Keys.* 2004. Cryptology ePrint Archive (IACR): Report 2004/310.

[EC17] European Commission. *Proposal for a Directive of the European Parliament and of the Council on the Interoperability of Electronic Road Toll Systems and Facilitating Crossborder Exchange of Information on the Failure to Pay Road Fees in the Union (recast).* 2017. URL: https://ec.europa.eu/transport/sites/transport/files/com20170280-eets-directive.pdf (visited on 04/19/2019).

[EC18] European Commission. *The EU General Data Protection Regulation (GDPR).* 2018. URL: https://www.eugdpr.org/ (visited on 04/19/2019).

[ECO18] ECONOLITE Group. *Connected Vehicle CoProcessor Module.* 2018. URL: http://www.econolitegroup.com/wp-content/uploads/2017/05/controllers-connectedvehicle-datasheet.pdf (visited on 04/07/2018).

[EFS04] Matthias Enzmann, Marc Fischlin, and Markus Schneider II. "A Privacy-Friendly Loyalty System Based on Discrete Logarithms over Elliptic Curves." In: *FC 2004: 8th International Conference on Financial Cryptography* (Key West, FL, USA, Feb. 9–12, 2004). Ed. by Ari Juels. Vol. 3110. Lecture Notes in Computer Science. Heidelberg, Germany: Springer, 2004, pp. 24–38.

[EG14] Alex Escala and Jens Groth. "Fine-Tuning Groth-Sahai Proofs." In: *PKC 2014: 17th International Conference on Theory and Practice of Public Key Cryptography* (Buenos Aires, Argentina, Mar. 26–28, 2014). Ed. by Hugo Krawczyk. Vol. 8383. Lecture Notes in Computer Science. Heidelberg, Germany: Springer, 2014, pp. 630–649.

[Gar+08] Flavio D. Garcia et al. "Dismantling MIFARE Classic." In: *ESORICS 2008: 13th European Symposium on Research in Computer Security* (Málaga, Spain, Oct. 6–8, 2008). Ed. by Sushil Jajodia and Javier López. Vol. 5283. Lecture Notes in Computer Science. Heidelberg, Germany: Springer, 2008, pp. 97–114.

[Gar+09] Flavio D. Garcia et al. "Wirelessly Pickpocketing a Mifare Classic Card." In: *2009 IEEE Symposium on Security and Privacy* (Oakland, CA, USA, May 17–20, 2009). Ed. by Andrew Myers and David Evans. Los Alamitos, CA, USA: IEEE Computer Society Press, 2009, pp. 3–15.

[GMR88] Shafi Goldwasser, Silvio Micali, and Ronald L. Rivest. "A Digital Signature Scheme Secure Against Adaptive Chosen-message Attacks." In: *SIAM Journal on Computing* 17.2 (Apr. 1988), pp. 281–308.

[GMW86] Oded Goldreich, Silvio Micali, and Avi Wigderson. "Proofs that Yield Nothing But their Validity and a Methodology of Cryptographic Protocol Design. Extended Abstract." In: *27th Annual Symposium on Foundations of Computer Science* (Toronto, Ontario, Canada, Oct. 27–29, 1986). Ed. by John Edward Hopcroft. Los Alamitos, CA, USA: IEEE Computer Society Press, 1986, pp. 174–187.

[Gon+15] Yanmin Gong et al. "A Privacy-Preserving Scheme for Incentive-Based Demand Response in the Smart Grid." In: *IEEE Transactions on Smart Grid* 7.3 (May 2015), pp. 1304–1313.

[GS08] Jens Groth and Amit Sahai. "Efficient Non-interactive Proof Systems for Bilinear Groups." In: *Advances in Cryptology – EUROCRYPT 2008* (Istanbul, Turkey, Apr. 13–17, 2008). Ed. by Nigel P. Smart. Vol. 4965. Lecture Notes in Computer Science. Heidelberg, Germany: Springer, 2008, pp. 415–432.

[Han+11] Uwe Hanebeck et al. "Nonlinear information filtering for distributed multisensor data fusion." In: *Proceedings of the 2011 American Control Conference* (San Francisco, CA, USA, June 29–July 1, 2011). Ed. by Rahmat A. Shoureshi. Los Alamitos, CA, USA: IEEE Computer Society Press, July 2011, pp. 4846–4852.

[Her+17] Gottfried Herold et al. "New Techniques for Structural Batch Verification in Bilinear Groups with Applications to Groth-Sahai Proofs." In: *ACM CCS 2017: 24th Conference on Computer and Communications Security* (Dallas, TX, USA, Oct. 31–Nov. 2, 2017). Ed. by Bhavani M. Thuraisingham et al. New York, NY, USA: ACM Press, 2017, pp. 1547–1564.

[HS15] Dennis Hofheinz and Victor Shoup. "GNUC: A New Universal Composability Framework." In: *Journal of Cryptology* 28.3 (July 2015), pp. 423–508.

[ILV11] Malika Izabachène, Benoît Libert, and Damien Vergnaud. "Block-Wise P-Signatures and Non-interactive Anonymous Credentials with Efficient Attributes." In: *13th IMA International Conference on Cryptography and Coding* (Oxford, UK, Dec. 12–15, 2011). Ed. by Liqun Chen. Vol. 7089. Lecture Notes in Computer Science. Heidelberg, Germany: Springer, 2011, pp. 431–450.

[IPS08] Yuval Ishai, Manoj Prabhakaran, and Amit Sahai. "Founding Cryptography on Oblivious Transfer - Efficiently." In: *Advances in Cryptology – CRYPTO 2008* (Santa Barbara, CA, USA, Aug. 17–21, 2008). Ed. by David Wagner. Vol. 5157. Lecture Notes in Computer Science. Heidelberg, Germany: Springer, 2008, pp. 572–591.

[Jar+14] Roger Jardí-Cedó et al. "Electronic Road Pricing System for Low Emission Zones to Preserve Driver Privacy." In: *Modeling Decisions for Artificial Intelligence – MDAI 2014* (Tokyo, Japan, Oct. 29–31, 2014). Vol. 8825. Lecure Notes in Artificial Intelligence. Heidelberg, Germany: Springer, 2014, pp. 1–13.

[Jar+16] Roger Jardí-Cedó et al. "Privacy-preserving Electronic Road Pricing System for Multifare Low Emission Zones." In: *SIN '16: Proceedings of the 9th International Conference on Security of Information and Networks* (Newark, NJ, USA, July 20–22, 2016). New York, NY, USA: ACM Press, 2016, pp. 158–165.

[JCV15] Roger Jardí-Cedó, Jordi Castellà-Roca, and Alexandre Viejo. "Privacy-Preserving Electronic Toll System with Dynamic Pricing for Low Emission Zones." In: *Data Privacy Management, Autonomous Spontaneous Security, and Security Assurance. 9th International Workshop, DPM 2014, 7th International Workshop, SETOP 2014, and 3rd International Workshop, QASA 2014.* Revised Selected Papers (Wroclaw, Poland, Sept. 10–11, 2014). Ed. by Joaquín García-Alfaro et al. Vol. 8872. Lecture Notes in Computer Science. Heidelberg, Germany: Springer, 2015, pp. 327–334.

[JR16] Tibor Jager and Andy Rupp. "Black-Box Accumulation: Collecting Incentives in a Privacy-Preserving Way." In: *Proceedings on Privacy Enhancing Technologies* 2016.3 (July 2016), pp. 62–82.

[Kap18] Kapsch. Personal Communication. 2018.

[Kat+13] Jonathan Katz et al. "Universally Composable Synchronous Computation." In: *TCC 2013: 10th Theory of Cryptography Conference* (Tokyo, Japan, Mar. 3–6, 2013). Ed. by Amit Sahai. Vol. 7785. Lecture Notes in Computer Science. Heidelberg, Germany: Springer, 2013, pp. 477–498.

[Kat07] Jonathan Katz. "Universally Composable Multi-party Computation Using Tamper-Proof Hardware." In: *Advances in Cryptology – EUROCRYPT 2007* (Barcelona, Spain, May 20–24, 2007). Ed. by Moni Naor. Vol. 4515. Lecture Notes in Computer Science. Heidelberg, Germany: Springer, 2007, pp. 115–128.

[Kaw+16] Yuto Kawahara et al. *Barreto-Naehrig Curves.* Internet Draft. Work in Progress. Internet Engineering Task Force, Mar. 2016.

[KHG08] Gerhard de Koning Gans, Jaap-Henk Hoepman, and Flavio D. Garcia. "A Practical Attack on the MIFARE Classic." In: *Smart Card Research and Advanced Applications. 8th IFIP WG 8.8/11.2 International Conference.* Proceedings (London, UK, Sept. 2008). Ed. by Gilles Grimaud and François-Xavier Standaert. Vol. 5189. Lecture Notes in Computer Science. Heidelberg, Germany: Springer, 2008, pp. 267–282.

[KPW15] Eike Kiltz, Jiaxin Pan, and Hoeteck Wee. "Structure-Preserving Signatures from Standard Assumptions, Revisited." In: *Advances in Cryptology – CRYPTO 2015, Part II* (Santa Barbara, CA, USA, Aug. 16–20, 2015). Ed. by Rosario Gennaro and Matthew J. B. Robshaw. Vol. 9216. Lecture Notes in Computer Science. Heidelberg, Germany: Springer, 2015, pp. 275–295.

[KT05] Willett Kempton and Jasna Tomic. "Vehicle-to-grid power fundamentals: Calculating capacity and net revenue." In: *Elsevier Journal of Power Sources* 144.1 (2005), pp. 268–279.

[Küs06] Ralf Küsters. "Simulation-based security with inexhaustible interactive Turing machines." In: *CSFW 2006 – 19th IEEE Security Foundations Workshop* (Venice, Italy, July 5–7, 2006). Los Alamitos, CA, USA: IEEE Computer Society Press, 2006, pp. 309–320.

[Lin03] Yehuda Lindell. *Composition of Secure Multi-Party Protocols. A Comprehensive Study.* Vol. 2815. Lecture Notes in Computer Science. Springer, 2003.

[Mar17] Markets and Markets. *Electronic Toll Collection Market Study.* 2017. URL: `https://www.marketsandmarkets.com/Market-Reports/electronic-toll-collection-system-market-224492059.html` (visited on 04/19/2018).

[Mau11] Ueli Maurer. "Constructive Cryptography – A New Paradigm for Security Definitions and Proofs." In: *Theory of Security and Applications – TOSCA 2011. Revised Selected Papers* (Saarbrücken, Germany, Mar. 31–Apr. 1, 2011). 2011, pp. 33–56.

[Mei+11] Sarah Meiklejohn et al. "The Phantom Tollbooth: Privacy-Preserving Electronic Toll Collection in the Presence of Driver Collusion." In: *USENIX Security 2011: 20th USENIX Security Symposium* (San Francisco, CA, USA, Aug. 8–12, 2011). Ed. by David Wagner. Berkeley, CA, USA: USENIX Association, 2011.

[Mil+15] Milica Milutinovic et al. "uCentive: An efficient, anonymous and unlinkable incentives scheme." In: *14th IEEE International Conference on Trust, Security and Privacy in Computing and Communications* (Helsinki, Finland, Aug. 20–22, 2015). Vol. 1. Los Alamitos, CA, USA: IEEE Computer Society Press, Aug. 2015, pp. 588–595.

[Moo+15] Dustin Moody et al. "Report on Pairing-based Cryptography." In: *Journal of Research of the National Institute of Standards and Technology*. Vol. 120. Gaithersburg, MD, USA: National Insititute of Standards and Technology, Feb. 2015, pp. 11–27.

[MR11] Ueli Maurer and Renato Renner. "Abstract Cryptography." In: *Innovations in Computer Science – ICS 2010. Proceedings* (Beijing, China, Jan. 7–9, 2011). 2011, pp. 1–21.

[MR92] Silvio Micali and Phillip Rogaway. "Secure Computation (Abstract)." In: *Advances in Cryptology – CRYPTO'91* (Santa Barbara, CA, USA, Aug. 11–15, 1991). Ed. by Joan Feigenbaum. Vol. 576. Lecture Notes in Computer Science. Heidelberg, Germany: Springer, 1992, pp. 392–404.

[Nag+17] Matthias Nagel et al. "BBA+: Improving the Security and Applicability of Privacy-Preserving Point Collection." In: *ACM CCS 2017: 24th Conference on Computer and Communications Security* (Dallas, TX, USA, Oct. 31–Nov. 2, 2017). Ed. by Bhavani M. Thuraisingham et al. New York, NY, USA: ACM Press, 2017, pp. 1925–1942.

[Nag+20] Matthias Nagel et al. "P4TC—Provably-Secure yet Practical Privacy-Preserving Toll Collection." In: *Proceedings on Privacy Enhancing Technologies* 2020.3 (July 2020), pp. 62–152.

[NMO05] Waka Nagao, Yoshifumi Manabe, and Tatsuaki Okamoto. "A Universally Composable Secure Channel Based on the KEM-DEM Framework." In: *TCC 2005: 2nd Theory of Cryptography Conference* (Cambridge, MA, USA, Feb. 10–12, 2005). Ed. by Joe Kilian. Vol. 3378. Lecture Notes in Computer Science. Heidelberg, Germany: Springer, 2005, pp. 426–444.

[NXP14] *MIFARE Classic EV1 4K Product Data Sheet Revision 3.1.* NXP Semiconductors Netherlands B.V. Sept. 2014.

[NXP16] *MIFARE DESFire EV2 contactless multi-application IC Data Sheet Rev. 2.0.* NXP Semiconductors Netherlands B.V. Feb. 2016.

[OP11] David Oswald and Christof Paar. "Breaking Mifare DESFire MF3ICD40: Power Analysis and Templates in the Real World." In: *Cryptographic Hardware and Embedded Systems – CHES 2011* (Nara, Japan, Sept. 28–Oct. 1, 2011). Ed. by Bart Preneel and Tsuyoshi Takagi. Vol. 6917. Lecture Notes in Computer Science. Heidelberg, Germany: Springer, 2011, pp. 207–222.

[Pas03] Rafael Pass. "Simulation in Quasi-Polynomial Time, and Its Application to Protocol Composition." In: *Advances in Cryptology – EUROCRYPT 2003* (Warsaw, Poland, May 4–8, 2003). Ed. by Eli Biham. Vol. 2656. Lecture Notes in Computer Science. Heidelberg, Germany: Springer, 2003, pp. 160–176.

[PAY16] PAYBACK GmbH. *The Payback loyalty program.* 2016. URL: https://www.payback.net/.

[PBB09] Raluca A. Popa, Hari Balakrishnan, and Andrew J. Blumberg. "VPriv: Protecting Privacy in Location-Based Vehicular Services." In: *USENIX Security 2009: 18th USENIX Security Symposium* (Montreal, Québec, Canada, Aug. 10–14, 2009). Ed. by Fabian Monrose. Berkeley, CA, USA: USENIX Association, 2009, pp. 335–350.

[PS04] Manoj Prabhakaran and Amit Sahai. "New notions of security: Achieving universal composability without trusted setup." In: *36th Annual ACM Symposium on Theory of Computing* (Chicago, IL, USA, June 13–16, 2004). Ed. by László Babai. New York, NY, USA: ACM Press, 2004, pp. 242–251.

[PW01] Birgit Pfitzmann and Michael Waidner. "A Model for Asynchronous Reactive Systems and its Application to Secure Message Transmission." In: *2001 IEEE Symposium on Security and Privacy* (Oakland, CA, USA, May 13–16, 2001). Ed. by Li Gong. Los Alamitos, CA, USA: IEEE Computer Society Press, 2001, pp. 184–200.

[RP10] Alfredo Rial and Bart Preneel. "Optimistic Fair Priced Oblivious Transfer." In: *AFRICACRYPT 10: 3rd International Conference on Cryptology in Africa* (Stellenbosch, South Africa, May 3–6, 2010). Ed. by Daniel J. Bernstein and Tanja Lange. Vol. 6055. Lecture Notes in Computer Science. Heidelberg, Germany: Springer, 2010, pp. 131–147.

[Rup+15] Andy Rupp et al. "Cryptographic Theory Meets Practice: Efficient and Privacy-Preserving Payments for Public Transport." In: *ACM Transactions on Information and System Security* 17.3 (2015), 10:1–10:31.

[Sav17] Savari.net. *MobiWAVE On-Board-Unit (OBU).* 2017. URL: http://savari.net/wp-content/uploads/2017/05/MW-1000_April2017.pdf (visited on 02/05/2018).

[Swe02] Latanya Sweeney. "k-Anonymity: A Model for Protecting Privacy." In: *International Journal of Uncertainty, Fuzziness and Knowledge-Based Systems* 10.5 (2002), pp. 557–570.

[Tra19] Transport for London. *Oyster Cards.* 2019. URL: https://oyster.tfl.gov.uk/oyster/entry.do.

[Tsa+07] Patrick P. Tsang et al. "Blacklistable anonymous credentials: blocking misbehaving users without ttps." In: *ACM CCS 2007: 14th Conference on Computer and Communications Security* (Alexandria, Virginia, USA, Oct. 28–31, 2007). Ed. by Peng Ning, Sabrina De Capitani di Vimercati, and Paul F. Syverson. New York, NY, USA: ACM Press, 2007, pp. 72–81.

[ven19] ventopay GmbH. *ventopay Customized Payment Systems.* 2019. URL: https://ventopay.com/.

List of Tables

List of Figures

List of Theorems

Own Publications

[BNR18] Jürgen Beyerer, Matthias Nagel, and Matthias Richer. *Pattern Recognition. Introduction, Features, Classifiers and Principles.* Oldenbourg: De Gruyter, 2018.

[Bro+17] Brandon Broadnax et al. "Concurrently Composable Security with Shielded Super-Polynomial Simulators." In: *Advances in Cryptology – EUROCRYPT 2017, Part I* (Paris, France, Apr. 30–May 4, 2017). Ed. by Jean-Sébastien Coron and Jesper Buus Nielsen. Vol. 10210. Lecture Notes in Computer Science. Heidelberg, Germany: Springer, 2017, pp. 351–381.

[Dow+17] Rafael Dowsley et al. "A survey on design and implementation of protected searchable data in the cloud." In: *Computer Science Review* 26 (2017). Ed. by Josep Díaz and Jaroslav Nešetril, pp. 17–30.

[Han+11] Uwe Hanebeck et al. "Nonlinear information filtering for distributed multisensor data fusion." In: *Proceedings of the 2011 American Control Conference* (San Francisco, CA, USA, June 29–July 1, 2011). Ed. by Rahmat A. Shoureshi. Los Alamitos, CA, USA: IEEE Computer Society Press, July 2011, pp. 4846–4852.

[Nag+17] Matthias Nagel et al. "BBA+: Improving the Security and Applicability of Privacy-Preserving Point Collection." In: *ACM CCS 2017: 24th Conference on Computer and Communications Security* (Dallas, TX, USA, Oct. 31–Nov. 2, 2017). Ed. by Bhavani M. Thuraisingham et al. New York, NY, USA: ACM Press, 2017, pp. 1925–1942.

[Nag+20] Matthias Nagel et al. "P4TC—Provably-Secure yet Practical Privacy-Preserving Toll Collection." In: *Proceedings on Privacy Enhancing Technologies* 2020.3 (July 2020), pp. 62–152.